THE ETHICAL
JOURNALIST

GENE FOREMAN

THE ETHICAL JOURNALIST

MAKING RESPONSIBLE DECISIONS IN THE PURSUIT OF NEWS

WILEY-BLACKWELL

A John Wiley & Sons, Ltd., Publication

This edition first published 2010
© 2010 Gene Foreman

Blackwell Publishing was acquired by John Wiley & Sons in February 2007. Blackwell's publishing program has been merged with Wiley's global Scientific, Technical, and Medical business to form Wiley-Blackwell.

Registered Office
John Wiley & Sons Ltd, The Atrium, Southern Gate, Chichester, West Sussex, PO19 8SQ, United Kingdom

Editorial Offices
350 Main Street, Malden, MA 02148-5020, USA
9600 Garsington Road, Oxford, OX4 2DQ, UK
The Atrium, Southern Gate, Chichester, West Sussex, PO19 8SQ, UK

For details of our global editorial offices, for customer services, and for information about how to apply for permission to reuse the copyright material in this book please see our website at www.wiley.com/wiley-blackwell.

The right of Gene Foreman to be identified as the author of this work has been asserted in accordance with the Copyright, Designs and Patents Act 1988.

Library of Congress Cataloging-in-Publication Data

Foreman, Gene.
    The ethical journalist : making responsible decisions in the pursuit of news / Gene Foreman.
        p. cm.
    Includes bibliographical references and index.
    ISBN 978-1-4051-8445-8 (hardcover : alk. paper—ISBN 978-1-4051-8394-9 (pbk. : alk. paper)
1. Journalistic ethics.   2. Reporters and reporting.   3. Journalistic ethics–Case studies.   4. Reporters and reporting–Case studies.   I. Title.
    PN4756.F67 2009
    174′.907—dc22

2009021973

A catalogue record for this book is available from the British Library.

Set in 10.5 on 13 pt Bembo by SNP Best-set Typesetter Ltd., Hong Kong
Printed in Singapore by Ho Printing Singapore Pte Ltd

01   2010

For JoAnn
and our children and grandchildren

Contents

Detailed Contents

Part I: A Foundation for Making Ethical Decisions   1

1 Why Ethics Matters in Journalism   3
Our society needs news professionals who do the right thing

- Two reasons, one moral and one practical, argue that journalists should be ethical.
- In a profession that cannot legally be regulated, responsible practitioners adhere voluntarily to high standards of conduct.
- The goal of this book and course is to teach how to make ethically sound decisions.
- Discussing case studies in class is crucial to learning the decision-making process.
- Traditional ethics standards of the profession apply to journalism on the Internet.
- Ethical journalism and vigorous journalism are compatible.

Point of View: A "Tribal Ferocity" Enforces the Code [*John Carroll*]

2 Ethics: The Bedrock of a Society   16
An introduction to terms and concepts in an applied-ethics course

- Ethics is about discerning the difference between right and wrong – and then doing what is right.
- Ancient societies developed systems of ethics that still influence human behavior.
- Ethics and law may be related, but they are not the same; law prescribes minimum standards of conduct, while ethics prescribes exemplary conduct.
- A member of a society absorbs its ethical precepts through a process of socialization.
- A person's values shape the choices he or she makes.

- Ethical dilemmas represent a clash of ethical values.
- The ethical person learns how to make decisions when facing ethical dilemmas.

- Ethical journalists have reached a consensus on journalism's purpose and guiding principles.
- Journalism, like other professions and institutions, owes society a moral duty called social responsibility.
- In the 1940s, the Hutchins Commission defined social responsibility for journalism – providing reliable information for the community.
- An ethical awakening occurred in journalism during a decade beginning in the mid-1970s.
- During this period of reform, many news organizations codified their principles.
- Today's technological and business environment presents new ethical challenges for journalism.

Point of View: A Manifesto for Change in Journalism [*Geneva Overholser*]

- In the abstract, journalists should avoid becoming involved with the events and the people they cover.
- However, certain situations require journalists to decide whether they should step out of their observer role and become participants.
- In those situations, guidelines can help journalists reach sound decisions.

Case Study No. 1: The Journalist as a Witness to Suffering

- Even as the news media mature and accept their social responsibility, the public is increasingly hostile.
- Journalists need to be aware of this hostility and the possible reasons for it.
- You should treat the audience with respect and take complaints seriously.
- Stripping away the rancor, you can find useful lessons in the public's criticism.

- The public's hostility has to be put in perspective; it may not be as bad as it seems.

Point of View: Journalism, Seen From the Other Side [*Jane Shoemaker*]
Case Study No. 2: Roughed Up at Recess

Ancient philosophy can help you make sound decisions

- Introducing four classic theories of ethics.
- Strengths and weaknesses of rule-based thinking.
- Strengths and weaknesses of ends-based thinking.
- Strengths and weaknesses of the Golden Rule.
- Strengths and weaknesses of Aristotle's Golden Mean.
- The value of blending rule-based thinking and ends-based thinking in the practice of journalism.

Professional standards are valuable in resolving dilemmas

- Ethics codes in journalism trace their origins to the early twentieth century.
- Codes adopted by professional associations are voluntary and advisory; codes adopted by news outlets for the direction of their staffs are enforceable.
- The profession continues to disagree about the value of codes.
- Codes can be useful as a part of the decision process, not as a substitute for that process.
- The Society of Professional Journalists' 1996 code, a model for the profession, contains four guiding principles: seek truth and report it; minimize harm; act independently; and be accountable.

Point of View: Reporting a Fact, Causing Harm [*William F. Woo*]
Point of View: Being Accountable Through a Digital Dialogue [*Mark Bowden*]
Case Study No. 3: The Death of a Boy

The key ingredients are critical thinking and a decision template

- You can polish your decision-making skills by drawing on the practical skills of journalism: gathering facts, analyzing them, and making judgments.
- Critical thinking, or thoughtful analysis, is an essential component of the decision process.
- A step-by-step template can guide you to a better decision.
- You must test your decision to see if it can be defended.

- In this course, approach the case studies as a laboratory for decision-making.

Point of View: Rationalizations in Decision-Making [*Michael Josephson*]
Case Study No. 4: Deciding Whether to Identify a CIA Agent

9   Stolen Words, Invented Facts ... Or Worse   123
Plagiarism, fabrication, and other mistakes that can kill a career

- Plagiarism and fabrication are morally wrong. *Plagiarism* is stealing the creative work of another. *Fabrication* is making things up and presenting them as fact.
- The offenses of plagiarism and fabrication destroy journalism's credibility and cost offenders their jobs and their careers.
- Committing illegal acts is unacceptable in the pursuit of news.
- Following sound work practices can help you avoid any hint of impropriety.
- Newsroom leaders have a duty to establish clear rules about journalistic misconduct and to enforce them.

10   Conflicts of Interest: Divided Loyalties   137
Journalists owe their first allegiance to the audience

- Because it gives the audience reason to doubt the journalist's loyalty, a conflict of interest undermines credibility.
- An appearance of a conflict of interest can damage credibility even if the journalist's reporting is fair.
- By following reasonable guidelines, you can avoid most conflicts, real or apparent.
- This chapter discusses situations that commonly lead to conflicts.

Case Study No. 5: Covering Police, Wearing Their Uniform
Case Study No. 6: Carrying the Torch, Stirring Controversy
Case Study No. 7: On Lunch Break, Defending Reagan
Case Study No. 8: A Love Triangle on the Evening News

11   The Business of Producing Journalism   159
News outlets' dual role: serving the public and earning money

- Technological and economic transition has caused tensions in today's news media.
- These tensions arise from a media company's dual role as a business and as a civic institution.
- Although advertisers finance journalism, they cannot be allowed to influence journalism.

- Media companies' efforts to increase revenue have led to some ethically questionable practices.
- The business and news executives of media companies frequently have a strained relationship, mainly because their cultures are so different.

Point of View: Tangoing Without a Partner [*Gene Roberts*]
Case Study No. 9: Sharing Ad Profits, Creating a Crisis

- Accuracy and fairness are ethical values fundamental to journalism.
- You need to keep an open mind as reporting progresses; your duty is not to a certain hypothesis but to the search for truth.
- If you can't prove the facts in your story, you can't use them.
- This chapter discusses other reporting situations that could lead to inaccuracy, unfairness, or both.

Point of View: The Importance of a Second Look [*William F. Woo*]
Case Study No. 10: Duke Lacrosse: One Newspaper's Journey
Case Study No. 11: On TV, a 4-Year-Old's Visit to Death Row

- Ethical issues arise in the reporter's efforts to cultivate sources while maintaining an independence from those sources.
- The ethical challenges are acute in beat reporting, in which a journalist works with the same sources over a long period.
- If you agree to protect a source who provides information on condition of anonymity, honoring that agreement is a solemn ethical duty.
- This chapter examines recurring situations in which ethical issues arise in source relationships.

Point of View: Sometimes, Different Rules Apply [*Jeffrey Fleishman*]
Case Study No. 12: *Newsweek* and the Flushing of the Koran
Case Study No. 13: Swimming in a Newsmaker's Backyard Pool

- Journalists often have to decide between the public's legitimate need to have certain information and the desire for privacy by the individuals involved.

- Although there are certain legal restraints on publicizing private information, most decisions are made on the basis of ethics rather than law.
- A three-step template can help you make decisions in privacy cases.
- This chapter examines reporting situations in which privacy is central to decision-making.

Case Study No. 14: Revealing Arthur Ashe's Secret
Case Study No. 15: Identifying a 13-Year-Old Rape Victim

15 Making News Decisions About Taste   252
The conflict between reflecting reality and respecting the audience

- Journalists often have to decide whether to publish, broadcast, or post content that could offend a significant element of the audience.
- Offensive content falls into three categories: perceived insensitivity, offensive words, and offensive images.
- A two-step process will help you make decisions, weighing the news value against the offensiveness.
- Legal limits on offensive content pertain mainly to the broadcast media.

Case Study No. 16: Reporting on a Vulgar List in the News
Case Study No. 17: Covering a Public Official's Public Suicide

16 Deception, a Controversial Reporting Tool   268
A collision in values: Lying while seeking the truth

- To decide whether to use a deceptive reporting practice, you first must acknowledge the deceit and not rationalize about it.
- Before engaging in undercover reporting – pretending to be someone else – you must meet exacting standards.
- This chapter discusses other situations, short of undercover, in which journalists could deceive or could be perceived as deceiving.
- Even if you think it may rarely be acceptable to deceive sources, you should never deceive the audience or your colleagues.

Case Study No. 18: Rumsfeld's Q&A With the Troops
Case Study No. 19: Spying on the Mayor in a Chat Room

17 Covering a Diverse, Multicultural Society   288
An ethical duty to be sensitive in reporting on minority groups

- Covering society's diversity is an ethical responsibility; news organizations have a duty to cover the entire community.
- Careful, sensitive reporting is required to analyze the complex issues of racial and ethnic conflicts.

- You should study techniques that can help you do a better job of covering cultures other than your own.
- Reporters who cover new immigrants can find that the assignment presents specific ethical issues.
- Sensitivity is needed in covering gays and lesbians in the news.

Point of View: Gaining Respect By Showing Respect [*Joann Byrd*]
Point of View: In Writing About Race, Be Precise [*Keith Woods*]
Case Study No. 20: When a Story Gets Its Subject Arrested

- Traditional ethics standards apply to all platforms for reporting the news, including the Internet.
- Verification is vital even in a medium that emphasizes speed.
- Blogging by journalists can provide benefits, but it also can undermine their credibility as impartial observers.
- An Internet "conversation" with the audience is valuable, but unmonitored comments can cause problems.
- Journalists and citizen bloggers share the Internet, but their standards diverge.

Point of View: It's the Ideas, Not the Names, That Count [*Carole Tarrant*]
Case Study No. 21: For a Reporter-Blogger, Two Personalities

- The public must be able to trust the truthfulness of the news media's photographs and video.
- Because an image can be distorted either by stage-managing the scene or by manipulating the image, responsible photojournalists have adopted standards to assure the integrity of their images.
- Recognizing that some images can offend, journalists weigh these images' news values against the likely offense.
- The presence of photojournalists and their cameras can cause psychological harm, even if the images are not disseminated.

Case Study No. 22: Would You Run This Photograph?
Case Study No. 23: Just How Fast Do Ice Boats Go?

- "Infotainment" – focusing on the sensational – remains a problem because it siphons news organizations' resources from important stories that the public needs.

- The future of journalism may depend on devising a business plan that makes Internet sites profitable enough to support larger staffs of journalists.
- Although aspiring journalists should learn multimedia skills, the industry should realize that performance standards could be lowered if everyone is expected to report every story in all media.
- News websites, the dominant news platform of the future, face lingering ethics issues.
- The traditional definition of journalism takes on new importance in an environment in which the audience has access to many sources of information and needs to find a source it can trust.
- Journalists, though no longer the gatekeepers, still have the responsibility of helping their audience make sense of the news.

Point of View: Decision-Making in the Digital Age [*James M. Naughton*]
Point of View: A Difference in How Rumors Are Reported [*Kelly McBride*]
Case Study No. 24: NBC's Controversial "To Catch a Predator"

Foreword
Journalism Genes

When Gene Roberts left *The New York Times* in 1972 to begin elevating one of America's worst newspapers, *The Philadelphia Inquirer*, he quickly realized he needed help. "I was looking," he recalls, "for someone who was everything I was not." Roy Reed, then a national reporter for *The Times*, and others who knew Roberts well told him they had just the right person to be his managing editor: Gene Clemons Foreman. And so the two editors became Gene and Gene, or as the staff in Philadelphia dubbed them, The Chromosomes. They were indeed an odd couple – Roberts an unmade bed of an intuitive strategist and Foreman a con- scientious pillar of reasoned exactitude – and they were a perfect match. Roberts always has been given, rightly, credit for the development of a literate *Inquirer* staff that may well have been, pound for pound, the most enterprising in American newspapering. In his 18 years in Philly, the staff was awarded 17 Pulitzer Prizes. Yet Roberts would be the first to say, and others of us who had the privilege of helping improve *The Inquirer* would echo, that it was Gene Foreman whose stan- dards were at the center of the remarkable transformation.

It was Foreman who commissioned, edited and published newspapering's most thorough and high-minded policy manual. It was Foreman who established and conducted standards and procedures training sessions for every staff member. It was Foreman who encountered Michael Josephson, a lawyer who was creating an ethics institute in Los Angeles, and tutored him in news issues so that Josephson could train journalists anywhere – including *The Inquirer* – in news ethics. It was Foreman who defined what the paper should look like and made sure it did. It was Foreman who built an exceptional core of copy editors, in part by creating a pre-employment editing test that became a model for the industry. It was Foreman who relentlessly examined each issue of the newspaper and delivered detailed guidance about where there was room for improvement.

My favorite Foreman tale involves his exacting standards and his focus on even the most minute aspects of accuracy, standards, and style. In September 1979, *The Inquirer* had a talented foreign correspondent named Richard Ben Cramer based in London. When the British Lord Mountbatten was killed by IRA terrorists in an explosion of his yacht, Cramer wrote and *The Inquirer* published this lede on the funeral:

LONDON – Louis Francis Albert Victor Nicholas Mountbatten, born prince of the house of Battenberg, nephew of Czar Nicholas II, great-grandson of Queen Victoria, created Earl Mountbatten of Burma, Knight of the Garter, privy-councillor, holder of the Order of Merit, Knight Grand Cross of the Bath, Knight Grand Commander of the Star of India, Knight Grand Cross of Royal Victorian Order, Knight Grand Commander of the Indian Empire, Companion of the Distinguished Service Order and Baron Romsey of Southampton, got a funeral yesterday that became his lineage and life.

That lede provoked a debate in the newsroom. Some focused on its 87-word length, saying that if you read it aloud you'd run out of breath before reaching the period. There were those who said it caricatured a great man, making light of the British peerage. There were those, myself included, who thought it brilliantly captured the bygone British era of which Mountbatten was the last heroic figure. As the debate raged, Gene Foreman emerged from his office and strode to the bulletin board nearest the copy desk in the middle of the newsroom. On it he thumbtacked a typed note admonishing all of us that the word "yesterday" had been misplaced in the lede of the Mountbatten story.

Never has there been a newspaper editor more focused on fact, honesty, reality, ethics, truth, accuracy, style.

Without either of the Genes, the remaking of *The Inquirer* likely would have collapsed. With the two as a team, yin and yang, it prospered as we performed a little more enterprisingly and a little more carefully each day. Many of us came to regard working for the Genes as the golden era of our careers. Plus it was great fun. They fostered the kind of newsroom in which on one of Gene Foreman's birthdays his fanatical devotion to the Philadelphia Phillies could be celebrated by creating a huge sheet cake on which there was a deliberate typo in the icing spelling Foreman's name. Just as Gene was about to cut the "cake," it popped open and up came Larry Bowa, the Phillies' shortstop. I've often thought Foreman identified with Bowa because both did their utmost to perform at a high level without error. Gene certainly deserved a gold glove for editing. When Gene Foreman retired in 1998 after a quarter-century at *The Inquirer*, the staff threw a huge family picnic in his honor. One of the mementoes was a "baseball" card celebrating how much he loved both journalism and his baseball team.

As Gene's editing career wound down, Penn State arranged for him to continue to advocate best practices by joining the journalism faculty. Every week, Foreman made the rigorous round-trip from his home outside Philadelphia to the main campus in State College. Four noteworthy things happened:

1   Students aspiring to careers in journalism came to revere him for his meticulous teaching and his energetic mentoring. Here's how Leann Frola, class of '06 and now a copy editor at the *Dallas Morning News*, put it:

   Professor Foreman was my most influential teacher at Penn State. Not only did he give me a solid foundation for copy editing and ethical journalism, he went above and beyond to help me with my career. Inside the classroom, he was impeccably organized and made each grading point count. He taught in a way that challenged us to intimately learn the material. And he was sure to explain why what we learned mattered. Professor Foreman was also a great resource outside the classroom. He made me aware of editing opportunities and encouraged me to work hard and apply for them. At his urging, I applied for a program that led me to the job I have today.

2   Foreman's peers on the faculty honored him for his skill as a teacher.
3   His car died on a long uphill climb in the Alleghenies.
4   Professor Foreman once more set about standardizing how journalism ought to be practiced.

In preparing to teach ethics, Gene concluded that there were people in the craft and the academy who advocated high-minded practices, but no single text that explained to his satisfaction why and how journalism should be done right. Over nearly a decade he kept pulling together material from everywhere he could find it – accounts of best practices, case studies of news coverage gone awry, quotations from exemplars of the craft, and breaking news about how news was being broken in print, on the air and online.

Now he has put all of it, and more, into this book. *The Ethical Journalist: Making Responsible Decisions in the Pursuit of News* is like GPS for sound decision-making. It will not tell you what path to take but rather where you are on the journey to an ethical decision. It is invaluable for anyone who practices or cares about the craft. It is up-to-the-minute in relevance. It will serve not merely to teach but to exemplify Gene Foreman's conviction that while there are immutable principles to guide the honest and careful delivery of news, ethical values are not static but alive. Standards cannot merely be proclaimed, they must be experienced, for every day, every broadcast, every edition, every deadline brings some unforeseen wrinkle in the who, what, when, where, why and how of the world.

James M. Naughton

(James M. Naughton headed the Poynter Institute of Media Studies at St. Petersburg, Florida, from 1996 to 2003 and is its president emeritus. He joined *The Philadelphia Inquirer* in 1977 and was the paper's executive editor when he left for Poynter. Before joining *The Inquirer*, he was *The New York Times'* White House correspondent during the Nixon and Ford administrations.)

Preface

This book is intended to inform your professional life, and perhaps save your career from egregious behavior.

Technically, it is published as a textbook for college courses in journalism ethics and communications ethics, and as the ethics textbook in a course combining journalism ethics and law. I hope that practicing journalists – especially young journalists who did not take journalism courses in college – also will find it useful for its comprehensive discussion of the standards of the profession.

If you fit those categories of student journalist and practicing journalist, you will find yourself addressed directly in this book. I want to reach out to you in two ways: first, to help you learn to make ethically defensible decisions in the practice of journalism; and second, to give you the benefit of the thinking of generations of professionals and scholars that resulted in today's consensus guidelines for ethical conduct.

With these goals in mind, I have divided the book into two parts. Part I examines ethics in a general way, shows the relevance of ethics to journalism, and outlines a decision-making strategy. Part II discusses specific subject areas in which journalists frequently confront ethical problems.

Throughout the book, the consensus guidelines are explained, not to dictate your decision-making but to offer a starting point for thinking through the issues. The idea is that you don't have to start from a zero base; you can build on the best thinking of your predecessors. Where there is disagreement in the profession, I have noted that, too. All this is fodder for classroom discussion.

The book is largely the product of my half-century in journalism – more than 41 years in the newsroom and more than eight as a college professor. Although my approach is an entirely practical one of trying to improve decision-making in the profession, I have been influenced by ethics scholars as well as newsroom colleagues. One theme of the book is the value of ethical theory as a resource in the decision process. In my role as a longtime newspaper managing editor, I acknowledge that the newsroom has benefited from the scholars' thoughtful analysis of issues whose nuances we sometimes overlooked as we focused on the next deadline.

To learn journalistic techniques like writing headlines for a website, I presume that you will take other courses and read other textbooks. In contrast, the purpose of this book is to encourage you to ponder the ethical ramifications of what journalists do, whether the consumer gets the news from a newspaper or a TV set or a computer screen or a hand-held device.

The case studies and other actual experiences of journalists recounted in this book illustrate the ethical choices you may have to make. Those experiences have occurred in all types of news media – print, broadcast, and, though it is a far newer platform, online. As the delivery of news increasingly migrates to the web, more and more of these challenges will be evident there. Knowing how journalists have dealt with them in any medium will be useful to you.

The timeless values of journalism apply to online journalists no less than they do to their counterparts in print and broadcast. These values are explained in the book's first 17 chapters. And, because online journalism presents additional ethics issues that are specific to the medium, Chapter 18 of the book is devoted exclusively to discussing those issues. Similarly, the specific issues of visual journalism are covered in Chapter 19. Since journalists may be called on to deliver the news in multiple media, these chapters – along with Chapter 20, Ethics in the Changing Media Environment – are essential to gaining an understanding of the role that ethics should play in the new environment.

On the book's accompanying website, you will find a trove of additional resources: more readings in print and online, more case studies, and related videos and still photographs. The texts of reports and articles cited in the chapters can be accessed by clicking on the hyperlinks. You can expand the book's content to an almost infinite degree by following the links – much in the way that online journalists offer their audience the ability to read the documents underpinning their reporting.

The journalists' decisions in the book's examples are open to debate, which is precisely why you should study them. If you decide that the journalist involved in a case study made a mistake, bear in mind that in nearly every instance those were mistakes of the head and not of the heart. In teaching the journalism ethics course 16 semesters, I frequently told my students of my own decisions that I regretted. In many ways, learning journalism ethics is about learning from our mistakes.

Gene Foreman
St. Davids, Pennsylvania, April 2009

Acknowledgments

As I conducted the research for this textbook, I shamelessly exploited the friendships I forged in my rewarding careers in the newsroom and the academy. In each career, I had the privilege of working alongside people who are among the best in their chosen line of work. The readers of *The Ethical Journalist* will benefit from the wisdom they shared with me.

My research was supported by a generous grant from the Arthur W. Page Center for Integrity in Public Communications, housed in the College of Communications at Pennsylvania State University. The Page Center grant made it possible for Shannon Miller Kahle, a doctoral student in media studies at Penn State, to assist me throughout calendar 2008. It's hard for me to imagine completing this project without Shannon's capable research. For the grant, I especially thank associate dean John Nichols and curriculum and research director Cinda Kostyak.

Doug Anderson, Dean of the College and himself the coauthor of a popular newswriting textbook, was an enthusiastic supporter of the project from the beginning. Debora Cheney, the Foster Librarian at Penn State, contributed valuable research and advice throughout.

The manuscript was immeasurably improved by the careful reading of my editors: former *Philadelphia Inquirer* colleagues Steve Seplow and Jim Naughton, and Wiley-Blackwell's Elsa Peterson. Steve and Jim approached the task as seasoned practitioners of journalism and Elsa as an experienced editor of textbooks. Theirs was an indispensable combination. Not only did my editors gently repair mistakes and point out things I had overlooked, they also were sources of encouragement throughout the writing phase. Others who graciously read and commented on specific chapters or case studies were Fred Blevens, Bill Dedman, Rick Edmonds, Ron Farrar, Lucinda Hahn, Dennis Hetzel, Tom Kennedy, Devon Lash, Fred Mann, Arlene Notoro Morgan, Bob Richards, Ford Risley, Bob Steele, and Ted Vaden.

This text reflects the research and writing of many ethics scholars. Their work is cited in the chapter endnotes, but I would like to make special mention of three who are my longtime mentors: Louis W. Hodges, the inaugural Knight Professor of Ethics in Journalism at Washington and Lee University; Bob Steele, Nelson Poynter Scholar for Journalism Values at the Poynter Institute and Eugene S. Pulliam Distinguished Visiting Professor of Journalism at DePauw University; and Michael Josephson, who switched in mid-career from law professor to ethicist, a role in which he champions character-building for children and advises people in many occupations, including journalism.

This text owes much to Bill Kovach and Tom Rosenstiel's *The Elements of Journalism: What Newspeople Should Know and the Public Should Expect*, which defines the principles that contemporary journalists stand for. Four other books were especially useful. Bob Haiman and Av Westin wrote wonderfully detailed "best practices" books – Haiman for newspapers and Westin for television – as part of The Freedom Forum's Free Press/Fair Press Study directed by Bob Giles. *The Authentic Voice* by Arlene Notoro Morgan, Alice Irene Pifer, and Keith Woods is an essential guide for writing about a diverse, multicultural society. For a clear discussion of news values on the World Wide Web, I benefited from *Online Journalism Ethics: Traditions and Transitions* by Cecilia Friend and Jane B. Singer.

The Poynter Institute at St. Petersburg, Florida, provides an immense service to journalism with its training and research programs. Jim Naughton, who headed Poynter for a decade after leaving *The Inquirer*, was my resource on many topics in addition to serving as an editor of the manuscript. In addition to Naughton and Bob Steele, Poynter folks who assisted me in this project were Bob Haiman, who like Naughton is a president emeritus of Poynter; Roy Peter Clark, Rick Edmonds, Don Fry, Kenny Irby, Bill Mitchell, David Shedden, Al Tompkins, Butch Ward, and Keith Woods. The essays of others at Poynter are quoted in the text, and many of the vignettes and case studies originated in Jim Romenesko's news-media blog on *poynteronline*.

American Journalism Review, *Columbia Journalism Review*, and *Nieman Reports* are powerful forces in journalism ethics, and they too influenced this text. Rem Rieder, editor of *AJR*, was particularly helpful in arranging for my manuscript to include condensations of articles from his magazine.

For help at various points in the research, I tapped the journalism organizations: Scott Bosley and Craig Branson of the American Society of News Editors; Mark Mittelstadt of the Associated Press Managing Editors; Barbara Cochran, Kathleen Graham, and Carol Knopes of the Radio-Television News Directors Foundation; and Kinsey Wilson and Ken Sands of the Online News Association.

I pestered other old and new friends for their thoughts about ethics in the profession we love. I thank them all: Vin Alabiso, Mike Arrieta-Walden, Tony Barbieri, Don Barlett, John Beale, Jim Bettinger, Mark Bowden, Joann Byrd, Barney Calame, John Carroll, Kathleen Carroll, Andrew Cassel, Jerry Ceppos, Curt Chandler, Alex Cruden, John Curley, Bill Dedman, Jere Downs, Ernie Dumas, Deni Elliott, Russ Eshleman, David Folkenflik, Russell Frank, Tommy Gibbons, Bob Giles, Amy Goldstein, Howard Goodman, Joe Grimm, Kevin Hagopian, Marie Hardin, Aimée Harris, Katherine Hatton, Gary Haynes, Eric Hegedus, Clark Hoyt, Anne Hull, Tony Insolia, Gerald Jordan, Max King, Hank Klibanoff, Tom Kunkel, Ann Kuskowski, Paul Martin Lester, Norman Lewis, Emilie Lounsberry, Dianne Lynch, Reid MacCluggage, Fred Mann, Bill Marimow, John McMeel, Eric Mencher, Gwenn Miller, Bob Mong, Malcolm Moran, Arlene Notoro Morgan, Ron Ostrow, Geneva Overholser, Patrick Parsons, Chris Peck, Deborah Potter, Jeff Price, Mike Pride, Roy Reed, Bob Richards, Rem Rieder, Chris Ritchie, Gene Roberts, Sandra Rowe, Nila Saliba, John Sanchez, Mark

Schaver, Jeff Schogol, Jane Shoemaker, Steve Stecklow, Jim Steele, David Sullivan, Lil Swanson, Mike Vitez, Thor Wasbotten, Sherman Williams, David Zeeck, Wendy Zomparelli, and David Zucchino. I also thank the journalists who gave permission for their writing to be repackaged as Point of View essays in the book or on the accompanying website, and the former Penn State students who allowed me to incorporate their research into several of the case studies. All are credited where their work appears. I thank Martha Shirk for allowing me to reprint the writing of her late husband, William F. Woo.

Two former *Inquirer* colleagues spent hours helping me with the book's illustrations: Bill Marsh produced the graphics, and Clem Murray collected and processed the photographs. Gary Haynes, Hal Buell, and Simon Li also helped in locating photographs. Tony Auth created an editorial cartoon especially for this book; it is in Chapter 18.

Finally, I thank my new friends at Wiley-Blackwell for guiding my work into print. Elizabeth Swayze, who made the decision to publish *The Ethical Journalist*, will always have my gratitude for the confidence she showed in this rookie author. Mervyn Thomas meticulously reviewed the manuscript and the research notes, spotting typos and suggesting deft improvements in phrasing. Margot Morse, Desirée Zicko, and Jana Pollack were unfailingly helpful and cheerful as we journeyed through the process of creating a book.

Gene Foreman
St. Davids, Pennsylvania, April 2009

Part I   A Foundation for Making Ethical Decisions

This part of the book will prepare you to make ethical decisions in journalism.

Chapter 1 explains why journalists should understand ethics and apply ethical principles in their decision-making.

Chapter 2 explores the history of ethics and the way that members of society develop their ethical values.

Chapters 3, 4, and 5 discuss journalism's role in society, the shared values of the profession, and the often tenuous relationship of journalism and the public.

Chapters 6, 7, and 8 lay the foundation for moral decision-making in journalism, which is the goal of this course in applied ethics. Chapter 6 discusses classic ethical theories; Chapter 7, codes of ethics; and Chapter 8, the decision process.

1 Why Ethics Matters in Journalism

Our society needs news professionals who do the right thing

Learning Goals

This chapter will help you understand:

- the importance of ethics in a journalist's everyday work;
- two reasons that journalists should be ethical – one moral, one practical;
- why journalists should adhere voluntarily to high standards of conduct;
- how the journalism profession has matured in recent decades;
- that the purpose of this book, and your college course, is to help you make ethically sound decisions;
- that discussing the case studies in class is crucial to learning the decision-making process;
- that the historical ethics standards of the journalism profession apply across all media platforms; and
- that ethical journalism and vigorous journalism are compatible.

Lovelle Svart, a 62-year-old woman with short, sandy hair, faced the video camera and calmly talked about dying. "This is my medication," she said, holding an orange bottle of clear liquid. "Everyone has told me … I look better than I did ten years ago, but inside, I hurt like nobody's business." On that afternoon of September 28, 2007, after she had danced the polka one last time and said her goodbyes to family and close friends, the contents of the orange bottle quietly killed her.[1]

Svart's death came three months after her doctor informed her she would die of lung cancer within six months. The former research librarian disclosed the grim

Figure 1.1
Lovelle Svart faces
the camera during
one of her "Living
to the End" video
diaries on *The
Oregonian's*
website
PHOTO BY ROB FINCH.
REPRINTED BY
PERMISSION OF *THE
OREGONIAN*

prognosis to a reporter friend at *The Oregonian* in Portland, the newspaper where she had worked. She said she had decided to avail herself of Oregon's assisted-suicide law. Svart also said she wanted to talk to people frankly about death and dying, hoping she could help them come to grips with the subject them-selves. Out of that conversation grew an extraordinary mutual decision: On its website and in print, *The Oregonian* would chronicle Lovelle Svart's final months on earth.

In her series of tasteful "video diaries" (see Figure 1.1), she talked about living with a fatal disease and about her dwindling reservoir of time. In response, hundreds of people messaged her on the website, addressing her as if they were old friends.

But before Svart taped her diaries, journalists at *The Oregonian* talked earnestly about what they were considering. Most of all, they asked themselves questions about ethics.

The threshold question was whether their actions might influence what Svart did. Would she feel free to change her mind? After all the attention, would she feel obligated to go ahead and take the lethal dose? On this topic, they were comforted by their relationship to this story subject. Familiarity was reassuring, although in the abstract they would prefer to be reporting on someone who had never been involved with the paper. In 20 years of working with her, they knew Svart was strong-willed; nobody would tell her what to do. Even so, the journalists constantly reminded her that whatever she decided would be fine with them. Michael Arrieta-Walden, a project leader, personally sat down with her and made that clear. The story would be about death and dying, not about Svart's assisted suicide.

Would the video diaries make a statement in favor of the controversial state law? No, they decided. The debate was over; the law had been enacted and it had passed court tests. Irrespective of how they and members of the audience felt about assisted suicide, they would just be showing how the law actually worked – a journalistic purpose. They posted links to stories that they had done earlier reflect-ing different points of view about the law itself. Other links guided readers to organizations that supported people in time of grief.

In debates among themselves and in teleconferences with an ethicist, they raised countless other questions and tried to arrive at answers that met the test of their collective conscience. For example, a question that caused much soul-searching was what to do if Svart collapsed while they were alone with her. It was a fact that she had posted "do not resuscitate" signs in her bedroom and always carried a document stating her wishes. Still, this possibility made them very uncomfortable – they were journalists, not doctors. Finally they resolved that if they were alone with her in her bedroom and she lost consciousness, they would pull the emer-gency cord and let medical personnel handle the situation. As Svart's health declined, they made another decision: They would not go alone with her outside the assisted-living center where she lived. From then on, if they accompanied her outside, there would also be another person along, someone who clearly had the duty of looking out for Svart's interests.[2]

The self-questioning in the *Oregonian* newsroom illustrates ethics awareness in contemporary journalism. "Twenty years ago, an ethical question might come up when someone walked into the editor's office at the last minute," said Sandra Rowe, editor of *The Oregonian*. "We've gone through a culture change. Now an ethical question comes up once or twice a week at our daily news meeting, where everyone can join the discussion. We are confident we can reach a sound decision if everyone has a say."[3]

Although lapses surely occur – and this book will detail numerous examples, as well as some disturbing trends – journalism has matured ethically in recent decades. Most journalists see theirs as a noble profession serving the public interest. They *want* to behave ethically.

Two Powerful Incentives for Ethical Behavior

Why should journalists practice sound ethics? If you ask that question in a crowd of journalists, you would probably get as many answers as there are people in the room. But while the answers may vary, their essence can be distilled into two broad categories. One, logically enough, is moral; the other could be called practical.

- *The moral incentive*: Journalists should be ethical because they, like most other human beings, want to see themselves as decent and honest. It is natural to crave self-esteem, not to mention the respect of others. There is a psychic reward in knowing that you have tried to do the right thing. As much as they like getting a good story, journalists don't want to be known for having exploited someone in the process.
- *The practical incentive*: In the long term, ethical journalism promotes the news organization's credibility and thus its acceptance by the public. This translates into commercial success. What journalists have to sell is the news – and if the public does not believe their reporting, they have nothing to sell. Consumers of the news are more likely to believe journalists' reporting if they see the journalists as ethical in the way they treat the public and the subjects of news coverage. Just as a wise consumer would choose a product with a trusted brand name over a no-name alternative when seeking quality, journalists hope that consumers will choose their news organization because it behaves responsibly. Thus ethical journalism can also be a profitable journalism that provides a livelihood for the journalists and their families, along with a financial return

for the investors in the newspaper, broadcast station, or online news organization.

The Case for Voluntary Ethics Standards

There are also practical arguments for ethical behavior that flow from journalism's special role in American life.

The First Amendment guarantee of a free press means that unlike other professionals, such as those in medicine and the law, journalists are not regulated by the state and are not subject to an enforceable ethics code. And that is a good thing, of course. The First Amendment insulates journalists from retribution from office holders who want to control the flow of information to the public and who often resent the way they are covered in the media. If a state board licensed journalists, it is a safe bet that some members of the board would abuse their power to rid themselves of journalists who offend them. The public would be the loser if journalists could be expelled from the profession by adversaries in government.

But there is a downside to press freedom: Anybody, no matter how unqualified or unscrupulous, can become a journalist. It is a tolerable downside, given the immense benefit of an independent news media, but bad journalists taint the reputation of everyone in the profession. Because they are not subject to an enforceable code, honest journalists have an individual obligation to be responsible and to adhere voluntarily to high standards of professional conduct. Ethical journalists do not use the Constitution's protection to be socially destructive.

Yet another argument for sound ethics is the dual nature of a news organization. Journalism serves the public by providing reliable information that people need to make governing decisions about their community, state and nation. This is a news organization's *quasi-civic* function. But the news organization has another responsibility, too – and that is to make a profit. Like any other business, the newspaper, broadcast station, or online news site must survive in the marketplace.

The seeming conflict of those two functions – serving the public, yet making money – is often regarded cynically by the public. Decisions about news coverage tend to be portrayed by critics as calculated to sell newspapers or raise broadcast ratings rather than to give the citizens the information they need. The truth is that good journalism is expensive, and the best news organizations invest significant sums in deeply reported projects that could never be justified in an accountant's profit-and-loss ledger. If there is a pragmatic return in such projects, it is in the hope that they build the organization's reputation as a source of reliable information.

Journalists cannot expect their work to be universally acclaimed. But they have an obligation to themselves and their colleagues to never deliberately conduct themselves in a way that would justify the criticism. They have an obligation to practice sound ethics.

A Half-Century of Rising Professionalism

loe lodt

Journalism in the mid-twentieth century had its tawdry aspects. Accepting gifts from newsmakers was condoned; at Christmas, it was typical to see cases of liquor being carted into the newsroom. A reporter might earn money on the side by writing news releases and speeches for a politician he covered. Or, if he needed to buy a car, the automobile manufacturer would be pleased to provide a discount. Journalists would brush aside questions about these practices by insisting that they could still be objective – and, besides, it was just compensation because newsroom salaries were so low.

For reasons that are explored in Chapter 3, journalism matured in the second half of the century. The following are some examples of that trend.

Ethics standards have been articulated in comprehensive codes

Not only professional organizations of journalists, but individual newspapers, broadcast stations and online news sites typically have comprehensive ethics codes. Professional organizations' codes date to the first half of the twentieth century. The American Society of Newspaper Editors (ASNE) established its Canons of Journalism, outlining commonly accepted ethical principles, in 1923. However, it was not until the late 1970s that the practice of adopting ethics codes by individual newspapers became common. There is a distinct difference in the effect of these two different kinds of ethics codes. Although the codes of professional organizations like ASNE fulfill an important purpose of establishing profession-wide standards, they are voluntary and without enforcement provisions. But when a newsroom adopts a code, violations can be enforced by suspension or dismissal of the violators. Of course, codes are valuable only to the extent that they are practiced, and newsroom leaders have a responsibility both to enforce their codes and to set the example of propriety.

Journalists new to the profession may be surprised to find that the rank-and-file reporters, editors, and photojournalists often are more effective than their bosses in enforcing the code. John Carroll, former editor of the *Los Angeles Times*, says that among journalists "certain beliefs are very deeply held," and that the core of these beliefs is a newspaper's duty to the reader. "Those who transgress against the reader will pay dearly," Carroll says, adding that this intensity usually is masked by a laid-back newsroom demeanor. "There's informality and humor, but beneath the surface lies something deadly serious. It is a code. Sometimes the code is not even written down, but it is deeply believed in. And, when violated, it is enforced with tribal ferocity."[4] See John Carroll's Point of View "A 'Tribal Ferocity' Enforces the Code" for more of his thoughts on the subject.

Today's journalists are better educated

A journalist without a college degree is a rarity in newsrooms today. Although possessing a diploma does not automatically make someone a better journalist, the rising education level signifies better preparation for the challenges of a complex profession. Journalism schools have become more professional in their curricula and in the qualifications of their instructors. Specifically, more journalism schools either are offering free-standing courses in applied ethics, or they are integrating this discipline into skills courses like news reporting and news editing. The best schools do both.

Newsrooms are more diverse

Just as important, the diversity in the composition of news staffs is reflected in news coverage that is more likely to examine the whole community. The journalists of the mid-twentieth century, nearly all white men, tended to write for people like themselves. The profession has been profoundly changed by the influx of women and people of color into the workforce in the second half of the century. This is a work in progress, but in that period editors and news directors moved from a policy of exclusion to one in which they universally recognized the need to diversify.

Journalists and the companies they work for are more accountable to the public

They recognize that, like any other business, they owe a social responsibility (that is, a responsibility to society, to make the community better). A news organization's social responsibility is to provide honest, impartial, reliable information about current events that their fellow citizens need to make their democratic institutions work. This responsibility also entails being responsive to questions and complaints from the audience – the readers, viewers, listeners, and online users. In years past, journalists were reluctant to correct their mistakes because they reasoned that this would lower credibility by confirming that they were fallible. Today, the opposite view prevails; journalists realize that mistakes are going to happen and that the public is served if mistakes are speedily acknowledged and the record set straight. In another change of mind, journalists are more likely today to explain their controversial decisions rather than arrogantly asserting that their decisions speak for themselves. The Internet makes accountability more important than ever, for two reasons: first, citizen bloggers form an army of fact-checkers calling attention to journalists' mistakes, and second, the web's interactivity fosters a conversation between journalists and their audience.

Today's journalists are more compassionate

Where many journalists of the mid-century liked to project an image of toughness toward the people they covered, today's journalists generally show empathy. To use a common expression, they acknowledge that they are in the chip-falling business as well as the wood-cutting business. They are concerned not just with reporting the news but also with how their reporting will affect the people involved. The columnist and author Anna Quindlen has written that journalists' most important obligation might well be owed to the subjects of their stories. She wonders if journalism schools "should teach not just accuracy, but empathy" by training journalists to imagine themselves in the place of the people they write about.[5] In fact, "minimizing harm" is one of the four cornerstone principles of the Society of Professional Journalists' code of ethics and is, as well, a key component of a course in journalism ethics.

There is more "watchdog" journalism

Journalists, especially through investigative reporting, have increasingly functioned as what a scholarly book has called "Custodians of Conscience."[6] They have used their platform to expose wrongdoing and to illuminate solutions to public ills. When the government's democratic system of checks and balances breaks down, journalists have stepped in to investigate and report to the public on the system failure. In February 2007, for example, reporters Dana Priest and Anne Hull of *The Washington Post* reported neglect by Walter Reed Army Medical Center in caring for outpatients – soldiers and Marines who had been physically and psychologically damaged in the wars in Iraq and Afghanistan. Congress and the White House immediately responded by promising sweeping reforms and by firing the officials who they thought should have prevented the failure. Although officials and the citizens do not always respond so forcefully when the news media alert them to dysfunction, that does not deter responsible journalists from continuing to try to raise the public conscience.

However, in spite of the exponential improvement in journalism's standards, there continue to be lapses. In times of intense competition, journalists too often discard their ethical principles. And mainstream news media – newspapers, broadcast networks and stations, and their online news sites – have sometimes succumbed to the pressure to match the sensational disclosures of media with lower standards of factual accuracy, such as citizen blogs, talk shows, and supermarket tabloids. There is a danger that in the competitive 24/7 news arena, the lowest common denominator may prevail.

The Goal: Make Ethically Sound Decisions

In this text and in the ethics course you are studying, you will continue your preparation for a journalism career by examining how good journalists make professional decisions. The text will identify and discuss the principles of applied ethics that are a foundation for sound decision-making. As the course progresses, you will practice your decision-making skill in case studies. The goal is to encourage you to think critically and in concrete terms about the situation confronting you – to employ logic rather than responding reflexively.

You should know that there are capable, intelligent journalists who reject the idea that journalism ethics can be taught in a college course. They argue that journalists, and journalism students, are either honorable or they are not. If they are honorable, this hypothesis continues, they will automatically make the right decision and so do not need this course. If they are not honorable, no college course is going to straighten them out. As an esteemed editor remarked to a college audience, "If your mom didn't teach you right from wrong, your college teacher is not going to be able to."

Although there is truth to that statement, it misses the point. The author of this textbook assumes that you *did* learn honesty and propriety in your early life. In fact, this course is intended to build on your own sense of right and wrong and to show how to apply that sense to solving ethical problems in the profession.

Journalism prizes essentially the same values as the rest of society – values like honesty and compassion – but sometimes journalists have conflicts in values that their fellow citizens do not. For example, your mom would instruct you to *always* intervene to help someone in need. However, journalists might have to weigh intervention to help one person against their duty to inform the public about thousands of other people in the same sort of adversity. If they intervene, they destroy the story's authenticity. And they fail to inform the public.

Another flaw in the critics' argument is the presumption that honorable journalists will reflexively do the right thing. Your mom may not have taught you a decision-making procedure. As you will discover, "the right thing" is not always obvious. You will see that sound decision-making goes beyond instinct and carefully considers – in a process called critical thinking – the pros and cons of various courses of action.

Honing Decision Skills Through Case Studies

The case-study method gives you a chance to work through difficult decisions in the classroom without consequences and without deadline pressure. The experience will prepare you for making on-the-spot ethical decisions in the real world. Each of the case studies selected for class discussion is intended to teach an important nuance about news media ethics.

In addition to explaining the principles of journalism ethics and teaching a decision-making process, this course in journalism ethics gives you two valuable opportunities:

1   You can study the thinking of academics and experienced practitioners on recurring problems that journalists face. While you should always do your own critical thinking, you don't have to start with a blank slate. You can draw on the trial-and-error efforts of people who have gone before you in the profession. Their experiences can help you think clearly about the issues.
2   You can practice your decision-making technique in a classroom setting where no one is hurt if a decision proves to be flawed. Just as a musician, an actor, or an athlete improves through practice, you benefit by thinking through the courses of action you might take in the case studies. You should emerge from the course with a deeper understanding of the challenges of the profession and infinitely more confidence about your own decision-making.

An applied-ethics course prepares you for a career in which you will be dealing with people who want to influence the way you report the news. Because journalists work for the public, it would be a betrayal of the public's trust to allow themselves to be diverted from the truth. Bob Steele of the Poynter Institute describes the manipulators:

> You will be stonewalled by powerful people who will deter you from getting to the truth. You will be manipulated by savvy sources who do their best to unduly influence your stories. You will be used by those with ulterior motives who demand the cover of confidentiality in exchange for their information. You will be swayed by seemingly well-intentioned people who want to show you some favor in hopes that you, in return, will show them favoritism in the way you tell their story.[7]

Ethics and the Internet

The ethics standards discussed in this text apply no matter how the news is delivered. If a journalist fails to seek truth, or exploits the news subject, or is swayed by a conflict of interest, that breach of ethics deprives the citizen of an honest news account. It is irrelevant whether the breach occurred in print, in broadcast, or on a website.

The news industry is in a tumultuous period of transition as audiences sort out where they want to go for news. Eight out of ten Americans get the news every day, but the sources of that news are changing, the Pew Center for the People & the Press reported in 2008. A Pew Center survey showed that on a typical day, 57 percent of those seeking news watched television, 35 percent listened on the radio,

34 percent read newspapers, and 29 percent went online (the percentages exceed 100 because many people use more than one source of news). According to Pew, television news is remaining stable (although cable has surpassed the broadcast networks); radio and newspapers are declining rapidly; and the Internet is gaining rapidly. Among adults 35 years of age and younger who check the news daily, more than half turn to the Internet. Younger adults also dominate the audience of the cable shows that parody the news – *The Colbert Report* with Stephen Colbert and *The Daily Show* with Jon Stewart.[8]

The survey results underscore the likelihood that online journalism, which burst on the scene in the 1990s, will be the news medium of the future. The web matches radio and television's speed; it can far exceed newspapers' depth of content; and it adds the unique dimension of an instantaneous conversation with the audience.

With its convergence of prose, video, still images, and audio, the web offers exciting opportunities. It also presents significant ethical challenges. The standards of online journalism are being forged right now, in the web's adolescence, sometimes without the players' recognizing that they are creating a template for the future of the profession. Compromises are being made:

- Tempted by the new medium's emphasis on speed, some online sites skimp on verification in order to be first to report a news development.
- Seduced by the ease with which news accounts can be corrected on the web, some online sites post the news first and correct it later.
- Struggling with restrictive financial budgets, some online sites skip editing on web logs ("blogs") created by their staff members, and even when they are edited, some blogs do not adhere to established principles of the profession.

In 1999, Michael Oreskes, who later became Associated Press senior managing editor, observed that "pressures are great at times of change, and so it follows that times of change are when standards matter most."[9] Having a website, Oreskes wrote, "doesn't change a simple editing rule: You shouldn't run something before you know it's true."[10]

Getting the Story – Honorably

A cautionary note is in order here. You should be wary of viewing this course or a companion course in media law as a brake on aggressive journalism. Being aggressive and being ethical are not mutually exclusive. Keep in mind that your job is to inform your audience, and that means being a good, resourceful reporter who gets the story into the paper, on the air, or on the web.

RED LIGHT ETHICS:	GREEN LIGHT ETHICS:
Focuses on journalists' misbehavior	Focuses on journalistic opportunities
Prescribes what journalists "ought not" to do	Considers "how to" rather than "ought not"
Emphasizes caution and restraint	Emphasizes journalism's power and duties
Keeps things out of print and off the air	Uses ingenuity and craft to get things in the paper and on the air
Sees journalists as too aggressive	Sees journalists as too timid

Figure 1.2 Two approaches to journalism ethics
GRAPHIC COURTESY OF BILL MARSH

Source: Roy Peter Clark, "Red Light, Green Light: A Plea for Balance in Media Ethics," *poynteronline*, May 17, 2005.

Given the real-life problems you will study in this course, it may be easy to conclude that the ethical choice is simple: Decide *against* publishing, broadcasting, or posting any news story that is the least bit questionable. But such a choice would itself be unethical. It would signify a failure to fulfill the journalist's mission of informing the public.

Roy Peter Clark of the Poynter Institute argues eloquently for balance in media ethics. He asserts that Red Light Ethics – instructing journalists about what they must *not* do – is "an absolutely necessary but destructively insufficient method for achieving responsible journalism."

What is needed, Clark writes in an essay for *poynteronline*, is Green Light Ethics to help journalists report honorably, even in delicate situations. "Red Light says: Let's back off. Green Light says: Let's pin it down." Clark's distinctions between the two approaches are depicted in Figure 1.2.

Clark writes: "These distinctions go beyond semantics although we should not underestimate the effect on students and professionals when we shift from Red Light imperatives to Green Light ones, from negative words to positive ones. Red Light language says: Don't invade privacy; don't sensationalize; don't exploit; don't lie; don't re-victimize. Green Light language says: Tell the truth; inform the public; reveal social ills; preserve human dignity; be brave."[11]

You can get the story and still be a decent human being.

Point of View

A "Tribal Ferocity" Enforces the Code

John Carroll

One reason I was drawn to my chosen career is its informality, in contrast to the real professions. Unlike doctors, lawyers or even jockeys, journalists have no entrance exams, no licenses, no governing board to pass solemn judgment when they transgress. Indeed, it is the constitutional right of every citizen, no matter how ignorant or how depraved, to be a journalist. This wild liberty, this official laxity, is one of journalism's appeals.

I was always taken, too, by the kinds of people who practiced journalism. My father, Wallace Carroll, was editor and publisher of a regional newspaper, in Winston-Salem, North Carolina. The people he worked with seemed more vital and engaged than your normal run of adults. They talked animatedly about things they were learning – things that were important, things that were absurd. They told hilarious jokes. I understood little about the work they did, except that it entailed typing, but I felt I'd like to hang around with such people when I grew up. Much later, after I'd been a journalist for years, I became aware of an utterance by Walter Lippmann that captured something I especially liked about life in the newsroom. "Journalism," he declared, "is the last refuge of the vaguely talented."

Here is something else I've come to realize: The looseness of the journalistic life, the seeming laxity of the newsroom, is an illusion. Yes, there's informality and humor, but beneath the surface lies something deadly serious. It is a code. Sometimes the code is not even written down, but it is deeply believed in. And, when violated, it is enforced with tribal ferocity.

Consider, for example, the recent events at *The New York Times*.

Before it was discovered that the young reporter Jayson Blair had fabricated several dozen stories, the news staff of *The Times* was already unhappy. Many members felt aggrieved at what they considered a high-handed style of editing. I know this because some were applying to me for jobs at the *Los Angeles Times*. But until Jayson Blair came along, the rumble of discontent remained just that, a low rumble.

When the staff learned that the paper had repeatedly misled its readers, the rumble became something more formidable: an insurrection. The aggrieved party was no longer merely the staff. It was the reader, and that meant the difference between a misdemeanor and a felony. Because the reader had been betrayed, the discontent acquired a moral force so great that it could only be answered by the dismissal of the ranking editors. The Blair scandal was a terrible event, but it also said something very positive about *The Times*, for it demonstrated beyond question the staff's commitment to the reader.

Several years ago, at the *Los Angeles Times*, we too had an insurrection. To outsiders the

Continued

issue seemed arcane, but to the staff it was starkly obvious. The paper had published a fat edition of its Sunday magazine devoted to the opening of the city's new sports and entertainment arena, called the Staples Center. Unknown to its readers – and to the newsroom staff – the paper had formed a secret partnership with Staples. The agreement was as follows: The newspaper would publish a special edition of the Sunday magazine; the developer would help the newspaper sell ads in it; and the two would split the proceeds. Thus was the independence of the newspaper compromised – and the reader betrayed.

I was not working at the newspaper at the time, but I've heard many accounts of a confrontation in the cafeteria between the staff and the publisher. It was not a civil discussion among respectful colleagues. Several people who told me about it invoked the image of a lynch mob. The Staples episode, too, led to the departure of the newspaper's top brass.

What does all this say about newspaper ethics? It says that certain beliefs are very deeply held. It says that a newspaper's duty to the reader is at the core of those beliefs. And it says that those who transgress against the reader will pay dearly.

Excerpted from the Ruhl Lecture on Ethics delivered at the University of Oregon, May 6, 2004. John Carroll was then the editor of the *Los Angeles Times*.

Notes

1 Svart video diary at http://next.oregonianextra.com/lovelle/, Sept. 28, 2007.
2 Author's telephone interviews with Michael Arrieta-Walden, Nov. 15, 2007, and Dec. 7, 2007.
3 Author's telephone interview with Sandra Rowe, Sept. 21, 2007.
4 John Carroll: Ruhl Lecture on ethics at the University of Oregon, May 6, 2004.
5 Anna Quindlen: "The great obligation," column in *Newsweek*, April 19, 2004.
6 James S. Ettema and Theodore L. Glasser, *Custodians of Conscience: Investigative Journalism and Public Virtue* (New York: Columbia University Press, 1998).
7 Bob Steele, "Why ethics matters," http://www.poynter.org/content/content_view.asp?id=9512, Aug. 9, 2002.
8 Pew Center for the People & the Press, "Key news audiences now blend online and traditional sources," http://people-press.org/report/444/news-media, Aug. 17, 2008. The study was based on telephone interviews between April 30 and June 1, 2008, among a nationwide sample of 3,615 adults. Interviews were conducted by both landline and cell phones. The margin of error is plus or minus 2 percentage points.
9 Michael Oreskes, "Navigating a minefield," *American Journalism Review*, November 1999, 23.
10 Ibid.
11 Roy Peter Clark, "Red light, green light: a plea for balance in media ethics," http://www.poynter.org/content/content_view.asp?id=82553, May 17, 2005.

2 Ethics: The Bedrock of a Society

An introduction to terms and concepts
in an applied-ethics course

Learning Goals

This chapter will help you understand:

- the definition of ethics – discern the difference between right and wrong, then act on what is right;
- how ancient societies developed systems of ethics;
- how ethics and the law are similar, and how they differ;
- how a member of a society absorbs its ethical precepts;
- how a person's values shape the choices he or she makes;
- the meaning of the term *ethical dilemma*; and
- how the ethical person makes decisions.

Virginia Gerst knows something about ethics. In May 2003, when she was arts and entertainment editor for the *Pioneer Press* chain of weeklies in the Chicago area, she ran a critical review of a restaurant. (The baby back ribs "tasted more fatty than meaty"; several other dishes were "rather run-of-the-mill.")

That displeased the restaurant owner, who was both a prospective advertiser and county president of the restaurant owners' association. Once the *Pioneer Press* publisher became aware of the restaurateur's displeasure, he had an advertising executive write a new, favorable review of the restaurant, and Gerst was ordered to run it. Instead, she quit.

"I understand that these are tough times for newspapers," she wrote in her letter of resignation. "But economic concerns are not sufficient to make me sacrifice the integrity of a section I have worked for, cared about and worried over for two decades."[1]

John Cruickshank understands ethics, too. In the midst of a management upheaval in November 2003, this career journalist was thrust into the job of publisher of the *Chicago Sun-Times* (owned by the same company as the *Pioneer Press* weeklies).

Months later, he discovered a breach of trust that astonished and angered him. Using accounting ruses that fooled even the agency responsible for auditing newspaper circulations, departed executives had been overstating the paper's circulation by up to 50,000 copies a day, or 11 percent.

Cruickshank did not hesitate to go public with his discovery. This was not just a commendable display of candor; it was costly to a paper already a distant second to the *Chicago Tribune*. The paper was acknowledging that its advertisers had not been getting the exposure they had paid for, and it eventually had to repay those advertisers millions of dollars.[2]

Defining Ethics: Action Is Required

Ethics is a set of moral principles, a code – often unwritten – that guides a person's conduct. But more than that, as Gerst and Cruickshank demonstrated, ethics requires action.

"There are two aspects to ethics," the ethicist Michael Josephson says. "The first involves the ability to discern right from wrong, good from evil, and propriety from impropriety. The second involves the commitment to do what is right, good, and proper." As a practical matter, Josephson says, "ethics is about how we meet the challenge of doing the right thing when that will cost more than we want to pay."[3] Or, in the words of Keith Woods, dean of faculty of the Poynter Institute, "ethics is the pursuit of right when wrong is a strong possibility."[4]

Gerst and Cruickshank were practicing *applied ethics*, the branch of moral philosophy that deals with making decisions about concrete cases in a profession or occupation.[5] That is what this text is about. Your study of applied ethics in journalism is intended to help you solve the challenges you may face in your career. To do so, you need to draw on your own sense of right and wrong, enhanced by an understanding of ethical theory and a systematic way of making decisions. The idea is to put ethics into action.

Although some scholars see a fine distinction between *ethics* and *morals*, the terms are used interchangeably in this text. *The Cambridge Dictionary of Philosophy*[6] defines *ethics* as "the philosophical study of morality" and says *ethics* "is commonly used interchangeably with *morality*" to mean the subject matter of such a philosophical study.

The Origins of Ethical Theory

Tracing the origins of ethical thinking underscores the importance of ethics as a society's bedrock foundation. Ethical theory evolved in ancient societies as a basis for justice and the orderly functioning of the group, a purpose it still serves today.

The most familiar example is the Ten Commandments from the Judeo-Christian heritage setting forth the rules that would govern the Hebrews freed from Egyptian captivity in about 1500 BCE. Among other things, they were admonished not to kill, steal, or lie.

An earlier example is Babylonia's Code of Hammurabi. The laws promulgated by the ruler Hammurabi (1728–1646 BCE) directed that "the strong might not oppress the weak" and outlined a system of justice that meant "the straight thing." Hammurabi's justice centered on rules governing property and contracts. A surgeon who caused the blindness of a man of standing would have his hand cut off, but if he caused the blindness of a slave, he could set things right by paying the owner half the value of the slave.[7]

Ancient Greece gave the English language the word *ethics*, which is derived from the Greek *ethos*, meaning character. The citizens of Athens created the concept that an ethical reasoning system should be based on an individual's virtue and character, rather than rules. Because virtue was to be practiced as a lifelong habit, a Greek citizen would be honest simply because it would be unthinkable to be dishonest. The virtue philosophers of Athens – Socrates (469–399 BCE), Plato (427–347 BCE), and Aristotle (384–322 BCE) – believed that "the individual, in living a virtuous life, would form part of an overall virtuous community."[8]

Socrates, who made the famous declaration that "the unexamined life is not worth living," established a line of questioning intended to provoke thought. Socrates "roamed Greece probing and challenging his brethren's ideas about such abstract concepts as justice and goodness," ethics scholar Louis A. Day writes. "This Socratic method of inquiry, consisting of relentless questions and answers about the nature of moral conduct, has proved to be a durable commodity, continuing to touch off heated discussions about morality in barrooms and classrooms alike."[9]

Ethical thinking evolved in societies around the world. A common thread is found in how various cultures articulated what is best known as the Golden Rule. This rule defines the essence of being an ethical person, which is to consider the needs of others. Today we state it as "Do unto others as you would have them do unto you." The author Rushworth M. Kidder traces the "criterion of reversibility":

This rule, familiar to students of the Bible, is often thought of as a narrowly Christian dictum. To be sure, it appears in the book of Matthew: "All things whatsoever ye would that men should do to you, do ye even so to them: for this is the law and the prophets." But Jews find it in the Talmud, which says, "That which you hold as detestable, do not do to your neighbor. That is the whole law: the rest is but commentary." Or, as it appears in the teachings of Islam, "None of you is a believer if he does not desire for his brother that which he desires for himself." ... The label "golden" was applied by Confucius (551–479 BCE), who wrote: "Here certainly is the golden maxim: Do not do to others which we do not want them to do to us."[10]

The Relationship of Ethics and the Law

Some laws are based on ethical precepts, such as those forbidding murder and stealing, and civil lawsuits can be filed to require someone to live up to contractual promises. However, ethics and law emphatically are not the same. Law sets forth minimal standards of conduct. Law states what a person *is required* to do; ethics suggests what a person *ought* to do. An ethical person, Michael Josephson says, "often chooses to do more than the law requires and less than the law allows." Potter Stewart, a former US Supreme Court justice, put it this way: "There is a big difference between what we have a right to do and what is right to do."

Some laws of the past are universally regarded today as morally wrong. The Supreme Court, in *Dred Scott vs. Sandford* (1857), upheld the principle of slavery, and, in *Plessy vs. Ferguson* (1896), upheld the principle of racial segregation. Courageous leaders like Martin Luther King Jr. defied state segregation laws in the South in the civil rights movement of the 1950s and 1960s. Theirs were acts of *civil disobedience*, in which the person who disobeys is convinced of the laws' immorality, is nonviolent, and is willing to pay the price for disobedience.[11]

In the late-1940s trials of Germans accused of war crimes, the Nuremberg tribunals representing the victorious allied powers established the principle that the crimes cannot be excused because they are committed under orders of the state. An individual has the moral duty to reject blatantly criminal orders.

Transmitting a Society's Ethical Precepts

Through the centuries, societies have passed down ethical precepts from one generation to the next. Over time, through a process called *socialization*, the new generation absorbs the values of the community. Louis A. Day identifies four main conduits for transmitting values, in this chronological sequence: family, peer groups, role models, and societal institutions.

Think about how each group influenced you as you grew up. You should be aware, too, that the process continues endlessly through adulthood.

Consider the influence of family. When parents urge toddlers to share with their siblings or friends, they get their first exposure to the idea of considering the needs of others. Not all lessons learned in the home are positive, of course. Day points out that a parent who writes a phony excuse to a teacher saying that "Johnny was sick yesterday" signals to the child that lying is permissible, even though the parent would never state such a thing.

Next are peer groups. As children grow older, the values instilled in the home are exposed, for good or ill, to the influence of friends in the neighborhood and in school. There is a powerful urge to "go with the crowd."

Then there are role models. They could be famous people, living or dead, such as athletes or musicians. Or they could be people one knows personally, such as teachers or ministers, or drug dealers. What these disparate individuals have in common is the fact that they occupy a prominent place in the minds of impressionable young people who want to emulate them.

The fourth source of influence is societal institutions. Through drama, television and the cinema transmit ethical standards – as well as standards that some would say are *not* ethical. When you graduate and go into the workforce, you will find that companies also are influential societal institutions. "Within each organization there is a moral culture, reflected both in written policies and the examples set by top management, that inspires the ethical behavior of the members," Day writes.[12]

In the process of socialization, members of the new generation learn that benefits flow from living in a society in which people *generally* behave morally – they treat each other civilly, they keep promises, they help a person in distress, and so on. These are moral duties that young learn to embrace. They also become aware that there are consequences for violating the group culture. These consequences, depending on the seriousness of the violation, range from being snubbed to being criminally prosecuted.

Though they still have moral duties that other humans have, people in certain occupations are permitted to function by different standards in some respects. The rights of the individual prevail over the needs of the community in conversations between lawyer and client, doctor and patient, minister and parishioner. In making the exceptions, society recognizes that those conversations need to be extremely candid. Indeed, through "shield laws" adopted in nearly every state, journalists are given similar protection to keep secret their conversations with confidential sources. This protection, however, is far from absolute, and it does not exist in federal law.

How Values Determine a Person's Choices

A person's *values* shape how he or she will react when confronted with a choice. Josephson defines values as "deeply held convictions and beliefs about what is effective, desirable, or morally right." He notes that the values we consistently rank higher than the others "are our core values, defining character and personality." Values, then, are "what we prize, and our values system is the order in which we prize them." These values may or may not be ethical values.

Ethical values directly relate to beliefs about what is right and proper: honesty, promise-keeping, fairness, compassion, respect for the privacy of others. *Nonethical values* relate not to moral duty but to desire: wealth, status, happiness. Josephson labels them *non*ethical (not *un*ethical) because they are ethically neutral. Pursuing nonethical values is not morally wrong so long as ethical values are not violated in the process.[13] Nonethical values that a journalist might hold include selling more newspapers, raising broadcast ratings, or increasing a website's traffic count – values achieved mainly by getting interesting stories ahead of the competition. Those are worthy values, but the crucial question is how they are achieved.

The controversy over abortion, the most divisive domestic issue in the United States, is illustrative here because it reflects the core values of people on both sides. To the abortion opponent, the core value is the sanctity of life, and that person believes life begins at conception. To the abortion-rights advocate, the core value is the autonomy of the individual, and that person believes the state has no right to tell a woman what she must do with her body.

The Ethical Dilemma: A Conflict in Ethical Values

Inevitably, a person faces a situation in which his or her ethical values conflict. The result is an *ethical dilemma*. The person confronted with the dilemma has to weigh the conflicting ethical values and choose one over the other.

A classic hypothetical story devised by the ethics scholar Lawrence Kohlberg illustrates the ethical dilemma: Heinz's wife is dying from cancer. A druggist has a life-saving drug but wants $2,000 for it. Heinz, who has only $1,000, pleads with the druggist to sell it for that amount. When the druggist refuses, Heinz has to decide between ethical values – honesty (not stealing the drug) or compassion (not letting his wife die). Choosing one ethical value means that he must violate the other. In Kohlberg's story, Heinz breaks into the store and steals the drug. Kohlberg asks: "Should the husband have done that? Was it right or wrong? … If you think it is morally right to steal the drug, you must face the fact that it is legally wrong."[14]

The ethical dilemma, pitting one ethical value against another, is distinguished from what Josephson calls a *false ethical dilemma*. In such equations only one side has an ethical value. On the other side is a nonethical value. The clear choice for the ethical person is to reject the nonethical value and act on the ethical value, to "choose ethics over expediency."[15]

This is not to say that such choices are easy. To the contrary, these choices often result in self-sacrifice. In journalism, for example, a reporter might have to give up doing a story that will raise broadcast ratings (a nonethical value) if it requires invading someone's privacy (an ethical value). This underscores the point made at the beginning of this chapter – that doing the right thing requires action, and it often entails a heavy cost.

When Virginia Gerst quit her job over a principle and John Cruickshank acknowledged to advertisers that they had been short-changed, they were making sacrifices in order to the right thing. To do nothing, to go along, might have been an easier choice for either – but it would have been wrong. Gerst and Cruickshank were confronted not with an ethical dilemma (which Rushworth Kidder labels a right-versus-right choice) but a false ethical dilemma (right-versus-wrong). This observation takes nothing away from the courage of either Gerst or Cruickshank.

How the Ethical Person Makes Decisions

The person who makes a decision in a given situation is called the *moral agent*. To be an effective moral agent, you can't decide on a whim. Clear thinking is needed. Ultimately, your decision must be one that you can defend as having been rationally chosen by a caring individual.

Josephson describes the complexity of the process:

> Most decisions have to be made in the context of economic, professional and social pressures which can sometimes challenge our ethical goals and conceal or confuse the moral issues. In addition, making ethical choices is complex because in many situations there are a multitude of competing interests and values. Other times, crucial facts are unknown or ambiguous. Since many actions are likely to benefit some people at the expense of others, the decision maker must prioritize competing moral claims and must be proficient at predicting the likely consequences of various choices.[16]

With practice you will be more confident and consistent in your decision-making. This does not mean that you will not make mistakes. Everyone does.

"We need to acknowledge the mistakes, figure out how and why mistakes are made, and then try to do better," ethics scholars Deni Elliott and Paul Martin Lester have written. In the view of Elliott and Lester, professionals who take ethics seriously will "stay conscious of the power that they have and the responsibility that they have to use that power judiciously." They will treat people fairly, with respect and compassion; they will keep an open mind to alternatives.[17]

Elliott and Lester suggest a final check. If you think you have made your decision in a rational way, would you be willing to allow your decision process to be published on the front page or run in the first news segment on television?[18] If you wince at that prospect, you ought to think again.

Notes

1 Michael Miner, "Pioneer Press aims at foot, fires," Sept. 5, 2003, and "Yes, Virginia, some people still care about ethics," *Chicago Reader*, May 7, 2004.

2 Eric Herman, "Paper sales inflated up to 50,000 a day," *Chicago Sun-Times*, Oct. 6, 2004, and Jacques Steinberg, "Sun-Times managers said to defraud advertisers," *The New York Times*, Oct. 6, 2004.

3 Michael Josephson, paper on definitions in ethics (Los Angeles: The Josephson Institute, 2001).

4 Keith Woods, Oweida Lecture in Journalism Ethics, Pennsylvania State University, April 11, 2006.

5 Louis A. Day, *Ethics in Media Communications: Cases and Controversies*, 5th edn (Belmont, CA: Thomson Wadsworth, 2006), 5.

6 Robert Audi (ed.), *The Cambridge Dictionary of Philosophy* (Cambridge: Cambridge University Press, 1999).

7 Gerald A. LaRue, "Ancient ethics," in Peter Singer (ed.), *A Companion to Ethics* (Oxford: Blackwell Publishers, 1991), 32.

8   Elaine E. Englehardt and Ralph D. Barney, *Media and Ethics: Principles for Moral Decisions* (Belmont, CA: Thomson Wadsworth, 2002), 25.

9   Day, *Ethics in Media Communications*, 3.

10 Rushworth M. Kidder, *How Good People Make Tough Choices: Resolving the Dilemmas of Ethical Living* (New York: HarperCollins, 1995), 159.

11 This definition of civil disobedience appears in Day, *Ethics in Media Communications*, 34.

12 Ibid, 15–16.

13 Michael Josephson, *Becoming an Exemplary Police Officer* (Los Angeles: Josephson Institute, 2007), 21. Although the book was written for police officers, it offers Josephson's thinking on ethics in a general sense.

14 Lawrence Kohlberg, *Essays in Moral Development: Vol. I, The Philosophy of Moral Development: Moral Stages and the Idea of Justice* (New York: Harper & Row, 1981), 12.

15 Michael Josephson, *Ethical Issues and Opportunities in Journalism* (Marina del Rey, CA: The Josephson Institute, 1991), 26.

16 Michael Josephson, paper on ethical decision-making (Los Angeles: The Josephson Institute, 2001).

17 Deni Elliott and Paul Martin Lester, *News Photographer* magazine, May 2004.

18 Ibid.

3 The News Media's Role in Society

How the profession has matured and accepted social responsibility

---

Learning Goals

This chapter will help you understand:

- journalism's purpose and its guiding principles;
- the meaning of the term *social responsibility*, and how it applies to journalism;
- how the Hutchins Commission defined social responsibility for journalism;
- the ethical awakening that occurred in the decade beginning in the mid-1970s;
- the thrust of the ethics codes adopted by many news organizations;
- the reasons for this period of reform; and
- how today's technological and business environment presents new ethical challenges for journalism.

In the horror of September 11, 2001, many journalists risked their lives to do their jobs.

Through the day, television, radio and Internet news sites reassured Americans by providing reliable information about the stunning events at the World Trade Center, the Pentagon, and a field in Shanksville, Pennsylvania. Wire services sent bulletin after bulletin around the world. The next day, newspapers added context and analysis. Newsmagazines published special editions.

"In those early defining moments of mid-September, the nation's news media conducted themselves with the courage, honesty, grace, and dedication a free society deserves," Gloria Cooper wrote in *Columbia Journalism Review*.[1]

There were casualties. A photojournalist and six television transmission engineers were killed at the World Trade Center.

"On this day of unimaginable fear and terror, journalists acted on instinct," Cathy Trost and Alicia C. Shepard wrote in a 2002 oral history that documents the heroism. "They commandeered taxis, hitched rides with strangers, rode bikes, walked miles, even sprinted to crash sites." Appropriately, the book's title is *Running Toward Danger*.

It wasn't competition that motivated these men and women – cable and broadcast networks, for example, shared video that day. It wasn't profit – the networks aired no commercials for 93 hours, and all news organizations broke their budgets to cover the story. As Trost and Shepard concluded, it could only be instinct that drove these journalists, an ingrained conviction that their profession is a high calling to public service.[2]

In their 2001 book *The Elements of Journalism*, Bill Kovach and Tom Rosenstiel compared today's journalists to the messengers picked by ancient tribes to "run swiftly over the next hill, accurately gather information, and engagingly retell it." What those brave, capable messengers brought back fulfilled the tribes' need to know what they couldn't see with their own eyes.[3] Contemporary society needs the same kind of information, and it was especially in demand on September 11.

Journalism's Purpose and Guiding Principles

In 1997, Kovach and Rosenstiel began three years of interviews, forums, and surveys intended to define journalism's purpose. There were clues in the ethics codes adopted by national journalism organizations. Those codes asserted that journalists serve the public and that they are dedicated to truth and fairness.

Beyond writing the codes, journalists had not spent much time analyzing what their guiding principles were. For one thing, journalists thought it was evident that they worked in the public interest and that the news they published or broadcast defined their standards. For another, their lawyers had cautioned against putting these standards in writing, lest they be used against them in court. And finally, meeting the deadlines for today's newscast or tomorrow's newspaper always seemed to take priority over the intellectual exercise of writing down their professional beliefs.

However, as Kovach and Rosenstiel's research proceeded, it became clear that certain beliefs were widely and strongly held. These beliefs guided the authors to a definition of journalism's primary purpose: "to provide citizens with the information they need to be free and self-governing." They elaborated in *The Elements of Journalism*: "The news media help us define our communities, and help us create a common language and common knowledge rooted in reality. Journalism also helps identify a community's goals, heroes and villains."[4]

An affirming statement of journalism's purpose was crafted by Leonard Downie Jr., editor of *The Washington Post*, and Robert G. Kaiser, *The Post*'s managing editor, in their 2002 book *The News About the News*. Downie and Kaiser wrote:

> Citizens cannot function together as a community unless they share a common body of information about their surroundings, their neighbors, their governing bodies, their sports teams, even their weather. Those are all the stuff of news. The best journalism digs into it, makes sense of it, and makes it accessible to everyone.[5]

Kovach and Rosenstiel identified the key principles – which they called the "elements" – of journalism. Six of those are listed here:

1 *Journalism's first obligation is to the truth.* Although *truth* is difficult to define, there was unanimity among journalists that the first step is "getting the facts right." Kovach and Rosenstiel concluded that "the disinterested pursuit of truth" is what distinguishes journalism from other forms of communication, like advertising and entertainment.[6]

2 *Journalism's first loyalty is to citizens.* The authors described "an implied covenant with the public, which tells the audience that the movie reviews are straight, that the restaurant reviews are not influenced by who buys an ad, that the coverage is not self-interested or slanted for friends." This first allegiance to the readers, viewers, and listeners is the basis for journalistic independence. Journalists are most valuable to their employers if they put their duty to the audience ahead of the employer's short-term financial interests.[7]

3 *Journalism's essence is a discipline of verification.* This principle is about techniques that reporters and editors rely on to get the facts right, such as "seeking multiple witnesses to an event, disclosing as much as possible about sources, and asking many sides for comment."[8]

4 *Journalists must maintain an independence from those they cover.* Journalists are observers, not players. For their reporting to be trusted, reporters have to be detached from the people and events they cover. They also have to be sure there is not an *appearance* of a relationship that would conflict with their journalistic duties.[9]

5 *Journalists must serve as an independent monitor of power.* News media have a watchdog role, "watching over the powerful few in society on behalf of the many to guard against tyranny." Essentially, journalism is a court of last resort when the systems of government and business break down. The authors also note that the media should report when powerful institutions are working effectively, as well as when they are not.[10]

6 *Journalists must provide a forum for public criticism and compromise.* The news media have an obligation to amplify the community conversation, allowing citizens a voice in letters to the editor, op-ed essays, radio and television talk shows, and comments on news websites. The authors caution that the journalist has to be

"an honest broker and referee" who deciphers "the spin and lies of commercialized argument, lobbying, and political propaganda."[11]

Defining the Term "Social Responsibility"

For more than a century before *The Elements of Journalism* articulated them, journalism standards had been steadily improving. Underlying this trend was the news media's growing acceptance of "social responsibility" – a concept that, in its application to commerce, imposes on business enterprises a moral duty to make their communities better. This is a duty that goes beyond merely obeying laws. Although social responsibility is not discussed here as a religious matter, a principle in Judaism known as *tikkun olam* seems to define it. *Tikkun olam* (pronounced tee-KOON oh-LUHM) is Hebrew for "repairing the world" – an obligation to fix the problems of society, including violence, disease, poverty, and injustice.[12]

In the world of commerce, a company's acts of social responsibility might involve contributing money and executive time to charities, or hiring the handicapped, or going beyond legal requirements to prevent pollution. A classic business example is the straightforward way that Johnson & Johnson responded to the Tylenol tragedy of 1982. Someone tampered with containers of Tylenol on store shelves in Chicago, inserting cyanide that caused the deaths of seven people. Through the news media, the company immediately warned the public not to buy or use Tylenol until the source of the contamination had been found. Next, Johnson & Johnson recalled every container of the pain reliever. The company did not put the product back on the market until its containers had been made tamper-proof. A lesser corporate response might have doomed the popular pain reliever, but Tylenol's sales quickly rebounded.[13]

In journalism, Adolph Ochs embraced the idea of social responsibility when he bought *The New York Times* in 1896 and immediately published a pledge "to give the news impartially, without fear or favor, regardless of party, sect or interests involved."[14] Eugene Meyer, who bought *The Washington Post* in 1933, similarly adopted a business plan based on journalistic independence: "In pursuit of the truth, the newspaper shall be prepared to make sacrifices of its material fortunes, if such a course be necessary for public good."[15] In the twenty-first century, under the leadership of descendants of Ochs and Meyer, both newspapers continue striving to live up to those promises.

One impetus for social responsibility in the news media was commerce. America's first newspapers were political organs, but in the 1830s that was changing, "stimulated by industrial growth, the development of larger cities, and technological innovations including steam-driven printing presses." Publishers and editors began aiming at a mass market, one in which it made economic sense to report the news neutrally instead of from a party perspective.[16] By the 1880s, the concept of objective reporting was well established.

By the first half of the twentieth century, journalists' aspirations for professionalism were growing. Better-educated people were joining the workforce, and the world's first journalism school was launched in 1908 at the University of Missouri.[17] National organizations of journalists were founded and quickly adopted codes expressing their responsibility to report the truth and to be fair. The first of these codes was the Canons of Journalism ratified by the new American Society of Newspaper Editors in 1923.[18]

In spite of these signs of growing awareness of press responsibility, the historical record shows examples of journalism practiced through the mid-twentieth century that would horrify today's practitioners and news consumers alike.

Fabrication was not uncommon. In an article in *Columbia Journalism Review* in 1984, Cassandra Tate described one telling episode. *The New York World* established a Bureau of Accuracy and Fair Play in 1913, and the bureau's director noticed a peculiar pattern in the newspaper's reporting on shipwrecks: Each story mentioned a cat that had survived. When the director asked the reporter, he was told:

> One of those wrecked ships had a cat, and the crew went back to save it. I made the cat a feature of my story, while the other reporters failed to mention the cat, and were called down by their city editors for being beaten. The next time there was a shipwreck, there was no cat, but the other ship news reporters did not wish to take a chance, and put the cat in. I wrote the report, leaving out the cat, and then I was severely chided for being beaten. Now when there is a shipwreck all of us always put in the cat.[19]

Some news photography similarly was suspicious. In his final column for *The Wall Street Journal*, which he had served as managing editor, Paul E. Steiger reminisced about a photographer colleague at a California paper who carried "a well-preserved but very dead bird" in his car trunk. "The bird, he explained, was for feature shots on holidays like Memorial Day. He'd perch it on a gravestone or tree limb in a veterans' cemetery to get the right mood. Nowadays such a trick would get him fired, but in the 1950s, this guy said, there was no time to wait for a live bird to flutter into the frame."[20]

Impersonation was an accepted reporting technique in some places. As an 18-year-old rookie police reporter in Chicago, Jack Fuller followed the lead of his elders and told a crime victim on the phone that he was a police officer. His ruse was exposed when the victim called back with a few additional details – on the police desk sergeant's line. A few years later, when Fuller returned to Chicago journalism after school and military service, he stopped misrepresenting himself. Fuller explains in his book *News Values*: "Times simply had changed, and so had I." The reformed impersonator went on to win a Pulitzer Prize and become editor of the *Chicago Tribune*.[21]

Racism permeated the news and editorial columns of newspapers. In 1921 in Tulsa, Oklahoma, a black teenager was accused of assaulting a white female elevator operator. *The Tulsa Tribune* published a news story headlined "Nab Negro for attacking girl in elevator," and an editorial headlined "To lynch a Negro tonight." The inflammatory notices set off a chain of events that led to a week of terror and violence in which up to three hundred people were killed. More than 10,000 residents were left homeless when a mob of whites burned nearly the entire black residential district of 35 square blocks.[22]

Reporters did not always distance themselves from the people and agencies they covered. An extraordinary conflict of interest was described by Robert J. Lifton and Greg Mitchell in their 1995 book *Hiroshima in America: Fifty Years of Denial*. The authors wrote that William L. Laurence of *The New York Times* was on the payroll of the Pentagon in 1945, having been hired at a secret meeting at *The Times'* offices. Laurence wrote many of the government press releases that followed the August 6, 1945, bombing of Hiroshima. For *The Times,* Laurence wrote a news story casting doubt on Japanese descriptions of radiation poisoning. However, the authors said, he had witnessed the July 16, 1945, atomic test in New Mexico and was aware of radioactive fallout that poisoned residents and livestock in the desert.[23] Laurence was awarded the Pulitzer Prize in 1946 "for his eye-witness account of the atom-bombing of Nagasaki and his subsequent ten articles on the development, production, and significance of the atomic bomb."[24]

The Hutchins Commission Defines Journalistic Duty

Social responsibility in journalism was defined most persuasively not by journalists but by a panel of intellectuals. Robert Maynard Hutchins, chancellor of the University of Chicago, was asked in 1942 by Henry Luce, publisher of *Time* magazine, to "find out about freedom of the press and what my obligations are." Luce put up $200,000 (about $2,500,000 in 2009 currency). Hutchins assembled a dozen men from universities, government and finance to join him on what was formally titled the Commission on Freedom of the Press but was to become better known as the Hutchins Commission.

In 1947, the commission issued its conclusions. The report was an indictment of journalism as it was practiced in that era. As the commission saw it, the press was neglecting its social responsibility – reporting accurately on news important to society – and choosing instead to focus on sensational stories designed to attract readers rather than inform them. The report warned that if the press did not reform, it could face government intervention.[25]

In the passage that was to have its most enduring influence on journalism, the commission declared that the press has the responsibility of providing "the current intelligence needed by a free society." It then identified five things that American society needed from the press:

1   *A truthful, comprehensive, and intelligent account of the day's events in a context that gives them meaning.* In essence, the commission was saying that being accurate is essential but not enough. The commission then made a statement that journalists and the public recognize today as an important duty of the news media, and that is to distinguish between fact and opinion: "There is not fact without a context and no factual report which is uncolored by the opinions of the reporter."

2   *A forum for the exchange of comment and criticism.* "The great agencies of mass communication," the commission said, "should regard themselves as common carriers of public discussion." They should publish "significant ideas contrary to their own," using such devices as letters to the editor (or columnists offering a wide range of commentary, which would become a standard practice). The commission, which lamented that some ideas could be stifled because their authors had no access to newspaper printing presses, presumably would be gratified today by the ease with which ideas are spread on the Internet.

3   *The projection of a representative picture of the constituent groups in society.* The commission denounced stereotypes and "hate words." It observed that "when the images [the media] portray fail to present the social group truly, they tend to subvert judgment." The commission thus prodded the era's news media, composed almost entirely of white males, to cover the entire community. The admonition was not taken seriously until the 1950s and 1960s, when the civil rights movement awakened the media to the need to broaden their news coverage.

4   *The presentation and clarification of the goals and values of society.* The media "must assume a responsibility like that of educators in stating and clarifying the ideals toward which the community should strive." Sketching an agenda for the community has become a function that editorial pages and television panel discussions typically perform.

5   *Full access to the day's intelligence.* The commission urged "the wide distribution of news and opinion" so that citizens could choose what they wanted to use.[26] In the decades that followed, news outlets broadened the definition of "full access." As surrogates for the citizens, they campaigned for legislation and court orders to compel governments to open meetings and records. They took the position that citizens should know how their business was being transacted.

The press didn't like the Hutchins Commission's report. Critics pointed to the fact that not a single journalist was on the commission. Columnist George Sokolsky said that having this commission critique the press was like having "a jury of saloonkeepers" assess the quality of education. Luce himself was unimpressed, saying the report suffered from a "most appalling lack of even high school logic."

Journalists also recoiled at the commission's suggestion that citizen panels should be set up to monitor their performance. They didn't like the idea of outsiders judging their work, and they warned that voluntary commissions could lead to regulatory agencies with legal powers. It was not until 1973 that a National News Council was established to investigate complaints against the news media. It died a decade later, having failed to gain the support of either the public or the industry.[27]

An Ethical Awakening of the Profession

Press criticism did not begin or end with the Hutchins Commission, as George Seldes, I.F. Stone, and others were publishing press critiques in the decades before and after the commission made its study. Over the years, however, the Hutchins report was debated in journalism schools. The commission's findings were elaborated on by scholars, notably in the 1956 book *Four Theories of the Press* by Frederick S. Siebert, Theodore Peterson, and Wilbur Schramm.[28]

In time, the commission's definition of journalism's social responsibility made an impression on journalists, even though they rarely acknowledge the source. This was borne out at the end of the century when Kovach and Rosenstiel grilled journalists on what they stood for. Reading the purpose of journalism and the principles of journalism defined in *The Elements of Journalism*, one cannot miss the influence of the Hutchins Commission.

Somehow, journalists absorbed the ideas of Hutchins' intellectuals and made them their own. These ideas found their way into the codes of ethics adopted by organizations of journalists. New, stronger codes were adopted in 1966 by the Radio Television News Directors Association, in 1973 by the Society of Professional Journalists, in 1974 by the Associated Press Managing Editors, and in 1975 by the American Society of Newspaper Editors. The Hutchins influence also can be seen in the revised code adopted in 1996 by the Society of Professional Journalists and discussed in detail in Chapter 7.

In an activist decade between the mid-1970s and the mid-1980s, many newspapers and broadcast stations formulated their own codes. The growth of newsroom codes during this period is documented by two surveys. An inquiry in 1974 by the Associated Press Managing Editors found that fewer than one in ten newspapers had ethics codes. Nine years later, journalism professor Ralph Izard of Ohio University found that three out of four newspapers and broadcast stations had written policies on newsroom standards and practices.[29]

These newsroom codes aimed at improving credibility by eliminating conflicts of interest. Broadly defined, a conflict of interest is anything that could divert a journalist – or a news outlet – from performing the mission of providing reliable, unbiased information to the public. Journalists can be conflicted by accepting gifts from the people being covered, by their personal political or civic interests, or by part-time jobs that create divided loyalties. News outlets are conflicted if they allow their commercial interests to interfere with gathering the news, such as killing a story under pressure from an advertiser. To their credit, many have resisted this pressure and done their journalistic duty even at a cost of millions of dollars in withheld advertising.

Initially, ethics reform centered on the practice of accepting gifts. As the 1970s began, a press pass entitled the bearer and his or her family to so-called freebies – free admittance to ball games, circuses, and amusement parks, and gifts of all kinds from business executives and politicians. Although accepting those gratuities could be seen as selling out to the people being covered, only a minority of journalists abstained.

Typically, the journalist protested that he wouldn't slant news coverage to get a bottle of free liquor. This rationalization "underestimates the subtle ways in which gratitude, friendship, and the anticipation of future favors affect judgment," the ethicist Michael Josephson writes in his book *Making Ethical Decisions*: "Does the person providing you with the benefit believe that it will in no way affect your judgment? Would the person still provide the benefit if you were in no position to help?"[30]

At the time, an argument for accepting freebies was that it was a way of supplementing salaries, which were notoriously low in most places. In fact, when the *Madison* (Wisconsin) *Capital Times* in 1974 promulgated an ethics code forbidding staff members from accepting gifts and discounts, the journalists' union complained that the paper had committed an unfair labor practice. After hearing testimony in the case, a National Labor Relations Board judge ruled in 1975 in favor of the union. The judge said the paper could not unilaterally impose an ethics code on its employees but must instead bargain with the union. Fifteen months later, the hearing judge was overruled by the NLRB. The board held that newspapers do not have to bargain with unions over whether employees may accept gifts from news sources, but any discipline for violating an ethics code would have to be bargained.[31]

Initially, many ranking editors and news directors were unconvinced that freebies were a problem. A 1972 study by APME found that two out of three managing editors themselves would accept an expenses-paid overseas trip if offered. Almost half of the editors permitted their sports writers to serve in jobs as official scorers or announcers at professional sports events, jobs in which they were paid by the teams they covered.[32] The late Paul Poorman, managing editor of *The Detroit News*, ordered his staff in 1973 to stop accepting gifts, but he was not encouraged that reform would occur. He lamented, "The whole issue is greeted with tightly controlled apathy on the part of many newspapermen."[33]

A decade later, newsroom attitudes had changed drastically, and any journalist who valued the respect of colleagues would always turn down freebies.

The conflict-of-interest standards were not just about freebies. The codes also warned journalists not to take secondary jobs with competitors or businesses they might cover; not to engage in political activity other than voting; and not to state publicly their opinions on controversial issues in the news.

Some of those standards met resistance. In 1985, two Detroit journalists acknowledged in a *Columbia Journalism Review* article that a ban on gifts was "non-controversial" but argued that the codes went too far when they kept staff members from exercising "their rights as citizens." They wrote that a journalist should be allowed to participate in civic activities, including being a candidate for an office the journalist is not assigned to cover. They warned: "The danger is that news organizations, in their zeal to demonstrate their purity, will reach too far into the personal lives of their employees by regulating outside activities that pose no real conflict."[34]

Today, journalists are more accepting of the premise that the public always sees them in their professional role, whether they are on or off duty. This text discusses conflicts of interest for individual journalists in Chapter 10 and for news outlets in Chapter 11.

In many newsrooms, there was a second wave of code-writing in the 1980s. Spelling out rules on conflicts of interest had addressed the most glaring ethical abuses. Now, journalists decided that it was even more important to define best practices for covering the news.

The process of staff committees used in formulating the conflict-of-interest guidelines was put to work on news policies. This made media lawyers uncomfortable. They feared that if the policies were subpoenaed by the attorney for someone suing for libel, they could be used to show that a news organization was negligent by its own standard. Ultimately, many lawyers worked with newsrooms to forge a compromise. Mainly, this was achieved by hedging the codes' language: "shall" became "should," and "always" became "usually." Also, the codes made clear that their provisions were guidelines, not absolute rules, and that sometimes the circumstances would dictate a course of action different from that stated in the guidelines.

In Part II of this book, you can consider some of the thinking of journalism practitioners and scholars that evolved over the decades to deal with recurring ethical issues in news coverage. These topics include:

- Achieving fairness and accuracy in gathering the news (Chapter 12).
- Striking the right balance in how reporters deal with their sources (Chapter 13).
- Deciding between an individual's entitlement to privacy and the public's entitlement to information it needs (Chapter 14).
- Deciding when it is appropriate to print or broadcast content that is likely to offend the audience (Chapter 15).
- Deciding when, if ever, deception in reporting is justified (Chapter 16).

What Prompted the Growth in Ethical Awareness?

The code-writing in the 1970s and 1980s was a manifestation of greater ethical awareness in the newsroom, a maturing of the profession. Why did the phenomenon occur when it did? These are some likely reasons:

- *Embarrassment.* Scandals were rocking the industry, the most noteworthy being the Janet Cooke case at *The Washington Post. The Post* had to give back a Pulitzer Prize in 1981 after Cooke, under intense questioning, admitted that she had made up her prize-winning story of an 8-year-old heroin addict named in the paper only as Jimmy. Roy Peter Clark of the Poynter Institute calls this episode "the alpha event in the history of media ethics." The Cooke scandal, Clark has written, "did not invent the field of media ethics, but it certainly fertilized it. Articles, seminars, programs, journals sprang up everywhere."[35]
- *A new generation of journalists.* As older journalists retired, the traditions of their era faded. The new generation, better educated and more idealistic, had come into the profession in the decades after the Hutchins Commission defined social responsibility. The drive for professionalism came not just from newsroom leaders but also from the rank-and-file newsroom staff.
- *The nature of the news.* Journalists were covering government and society's institutions more critically than ever, and they were reporting on officials who lied to the public. The Vietnam War and Watergate were prime examples. If you are going to point out transgressions by people in public life, it follows that you need to get your own house in order.
- *More scrutiny.* The media watchdogs were themselves being increasingly watched. Back then, the scrutiny came from *Columbia Journalism Review, Washington Journalism Review* (later renamed *American Journalism Review*), alternative weeklies, and a handful of mainstream media critics. In more recent times, this function has also become the province of all manner of critics who have the capacity through the Internet to call the media to account.
- *Chain ownership.* The shift from local ownership of newspapers and broadcast stations was not without its negative effects, but many papers and stations improved under chain ownership. The new corporate owners tended to be attuned to industry trends, including ethics awareness, unlike some local owners who had often been isolated and arbitrary. Under a local owner, the *Lexington* (Kentucky) *Herald* and its sister *Lexington Leader* ignored the 1960s civil rights demonstrations that were changing the city's social fabric.[36] In 1985, under the ownership of Knight Ridder, the merged *Herald Leader* courageously reported cash payoffs to University of Kentucky basketball players in violation of NCAA regulations, enduring a storm of criticism from the state's basketball fans.
- *Fear of libel lawsuits.* The news industry was reeling from big libel judgments. Gil Cranberg of the University of Iowa, after surveying 164 libel plaintiffs for

a study published in 1987, concluded that if journalists are seen as ethical, they are less likely to be sued. Most of the plaintiffs in the survey told Cranberg that they would not have sued if the newspaper or station had taken their complaints seriously and run a correction.[37]

Whatever its origins, the emphasis on written professional standards produced yet more awareness of ethics. It became common in the newsroom to talk about ethics and to raise questions – the process that Sandra Rowe, editor of *The Oregonian*, described in Chapter 1. These discussions often were facilitated by outside ethicists like those at the Poynter Institute in St Petersburg, Florida, which was established in 1975 and has become journalism's leading in-service training center and think tank. Over time, newsrooms placed the stress on having a process for discussing and deciding ethics issues rather than on trying to envision a comprehensive set of commandments.

For all that, there is still mild debate about whether journalism is a profession. This text takes the position that it is, while conceding that it lacks a few of the distinguishing characteristics of a profession. The most significant of these differences is that journalists are not governed by a formal organization with authority to set educational requirements for entering the profession and performance standards for continuing in it.[38] The First Amendment prohibits such regulation. To distinguish themselves from the pretenders, responsible journalists subscribe voluntarily to standards of accuracy, fairness, and independence.

The Challenges of Contemporary Journalism

In the early twenty-first century, journalism is undergoing an economic and technological transition that raises profound ethical challenges. Those contemporary issues – such as a trend toward infotainment, questions of how journalism will be paid for as news consumers move online, and the unresolved issues of Internet journalism – are discussed in detail elsewhere in this text and are reviewed in Chapter 20.

In her Point of View "A Manifesto for Change in Journalism," educator and former editor Geneva Overholser challenges journalists to be receptive to change that can lead to "a reinvention of journalism that is richer and better than the old, with its essential values intact."

As formidable as they are, the profession's contemporary challenges can be solved by the next generation of journalists – including those of you reading this text. Remember that journalism remains a high calling. Whether they are covering 9/11 or the city council meeting, ethical journalists provide the kind of information that society cannot do without.

Point of View
A Manifesto for Change in Journalism
Geneva Overholser

To embrace opportunity, one must believe in the future and be open to the unknown. These are not common attitudes among journalists today.

No wonder journalists find comfort in the way things were. The scrappy little Colorado newsroom that made a reporter out of me in the early 1970s hummed with opportunity. In a competitive race with a larger newspaper, our readers passionately cheered us on. They relied on us – and frequently told us so – to tell them what they needed to know, to give them what they wanted to read. For most of us working in the craft in that era, to be a journalist was very heaven. Even the criticisms thrown our way (many of which were valid) reflected the lofty status of journalism: It was arrogant, monolithic, exclusive, a fortress unassailable. Who was watching the watchdogs, people asked, fearful of the evident power of the Watergate-era press. And they cautioned: Never argue with those who buy ink by the barrel.

What about today? A mighty chorus is more than happy to argue with those who deal with ink – or airtime – wholesale. A thousand bloggers train keen, unloving eyes on the watchdogs. There are fewer newspapers, fewer local owners, fewer (but larger) newspaper-owning companies. Pressure on broadcast operations to produce 40 percent profits has hollowed out news staffs all across the country. Commercial radio news has all but been extinguished. As eyeballs and advertisers stage a mass migration onto new digital territories, the addictive grip of the profits that the old media have trained Wall Street to expect has kept newsrooms from anything but grudging and belated forays to the new frontier.

The near-paralysis of unhappy nostalgia has given way to an urge to do something about the looming questions: Who will keep journalism alive? Who will pay for this unique and expensive commodity – original reporting – that is so essential to self-governance and democracy? How will we ensure that the old values are translated into the new digital view?

There are hopeful prospects on the horizon. To pursue them, though, requires even more receptivity to change. Given the self-important, tradition-bound craft we're dealing with, questioning dogma does not come easily. Journalists have good reason to think they are keepers of a sacred flame. But we're bad at identifying which bits of dogma are truly essential. Inverted pyramid and ink on paper? No. A commitment to public service and the fair representation of differing points of view: Yes.

But what about ads on the front page: Are they a breach of that hallowed wall separating business and editorial? Are journalists well-advised to run from anything smelling faintly of lobbying? Is it naïve (not to mention inaccurate) to hold that government has no role in guaranteeing a free and responsible press?

Continued

Can we put on the table for discussion the merits of credentialing journalists?

It is just such apparently heretical notions that we must open to light and air if we are to move forward. With the ground under foot unknown and fast-shifting, journalists must be bold enough to scrutinize our many inviolate principles – or be willing to abandon the lead role in the information revolution that a thriving democracy depends upon us to play.

The efforts to distinguish between what must be carried forward and what must be jettisoned, and to embrace new and hopeful steps into the future, can lead to a reinvention of journalism that is richer and better than the old, with its essential values intact.

The story of American journalism is undergoing a dramatic rewrite. The pace of change makes many anxious, and denunciations are lobbed from all sides – and from within. It's easy to overlook the promise of the many possibilities that lie before us.

Excerpted from a report that Geneva Overholser wrote in 2006 for a project of the Annenberg Foundation Trust at Sunnylands, in partnership with the Annenberg Public Policy Center of the University of Pennsylvania. The complete report can be found at http://www.annenbergpublicpolicycenter.org/Overholser/20061011_JournStudy.pdf. The writer has posted updates to the manifesto at http://genevaoverholser.com/. Overholser now is director of the School of Journalism at the University of Southern California's Annenberg School for Communication.

Notes

1 Gloria Cooper, "Laurel," *Columbia Journalism Review*, November/December 2001.

2 Cathy Trost and Alicia C. Shepard for the Newseum, *Running Toward Danger: Stories Behind the Breaking News of 9/11* (Lanham, MD: Rowman & Littlefield, 2002), ix–xiii.

3 Bill Kovach and Tom Rosenstiel, *The Elements of Journalism: What Newspeople Should Know and the Public Should Expect* (New York: Crown Publishers, 2001), 9.

4 Ibid., 17–18.

5 Leonard Downie Jr and Robert G. Kaiser, *The News About the News: American Journalism in Peril* (New York: Alfred A. Knopf, 2002), 6.

6 Kovach and Rosenstiel, *The Elements of Journalism*, 37, 42.

7 Ibid, 51–2.

8 Ibid, 71.

9 Ibid, 97, 103.

10 Ibid, 112, 114, 115.

11 Ibid, 135–6.

12 David Shatz, Chaim I. Waxman, and Nathan J. Diament (eds), *Tikkun Olam: Social Responsibility in Jewish Thought and Law* (Northvale, NJ: Jason Aronson, 1997).

13 Conrad C. Fink, *Media Ethics: In the Newsroom and Beyond* (New York: McGraw-Hill, 1998), 246–7.

14 Susan E. Tifft and Alex S. Jones, *The Trust: The Private and Powerful Family Behind The New York Times* (London: Little, Brown, 1999), xix.

15 Downie and Kaiser, *The News About the News*, 13.

16 W. David Sloan and L. M. Parcell (eds), *American Journalism: History, Principles and Practices* (Jefferson, NC: McFarland, 2002), 46.

17 The University of Missouri, http://www.missouri.edu/about/history/journalism.php

18 The American Society of News Editors, http//asne.org

19 Cassandra Tate, "What *do* ombudsmen do?", *Columbia Journalism Review*, May–June 1984. Tate's article cited "a 1916 issue of *American*

Magazine." The reporter's response was quoted by Kovach and Rosenstiel in *The Elements of Journalism,* 39.

20 Paul E. Steiger, "Read all about it," *The Wall Street Journal,* Dec. 29, 2007.

21 Jack Fuller, *News Values* (Chicago: University of Chicago Press, 1996), 45–6.

22 Neil Henry, *American Carnival: Journalism under Siege in an Age of New Media* (Berkeley: University of California Press, 2007), 76.

23 Robert J. Lifton and Greg Mitchell, *Hiroshima in America: Fifty Years of Denial* (New York: Putnam, 1995), 10–22; 51–2.

24 The Pulitzer Prizes, http://www.pulitzer.org

25 Steven K. Knowlton and Patrick Parsons, *The Journalist's Moral Compass* (Westport, CT: Praeger, 1995), 207–8.

26 Commission on Freedom of the Press, *A Free and Responsible Press: A General Report on Mass Communication: Newspapers, Radio, Motion Pictures, Magazines, and Books* (Chicago: University of Chicago Press, 1947), 20–30.

27 A. David Gordon and John Michael Kittross, *Controversies in Media Ethics,* 2nd edn (New York: Longman, 1999), 97.

28 Frederick S. Siebert, Theodore Peterson, and Wilbur Schramm, *Four Theories of the Press* (Urbana: University of Illinois Press, 1956).

29 Karen Schneider and Marc Gunther, "Those newsroom ethics codes," *Columbia Journalism Review,* July/August 1985. Through his work with the Associated Press Managing Editors, the author also observed the exponential growth of newsroom codes in the 1970s and 1980s.

30 Michael Josephson, *Making Ethical Decisions* (Los Angeles: Josephson Institute of Ethics, 2002), 29.

31 Mark A. Nelson, "Newspaper ethics code and the NLRB," *Freedom of Information Center Report No. 353,* Columbia, MO.

32 George N. Gill, "It's your move, publishers," *The Quill,* August 1973.

33 Poorman was quoted in "Junketing journalists," *Time,* Jan. 28, 1974.

34 Schneider and Gunther, "Those newsroom ethics codes."

35 Roy Peter Clark, "Red light, green light: a plea for balance in media ethics," http://www.poynter.org/content/content_view.asp?id=82553, May 17, 2005.

36 The author is indebted to the following for their insights into the reasons for increased ethical awareness during this period: John Carroll, Bob Giles, Bill Marimow, Jim Naughton, Mike Pride, Steve Seplow, and Bob Steele.

37 Alicia C. Shepard, "To err is human, to correct divine," *American Journalism Review,* June 1998.

38 Wilbert E. Moore, *The Professions: Roles and Rules* (New York: Russell Sage, 1970), pp. 4–22.

4 For Journalists, a Clash of Moral Duties

Responsibilities as professionals and as human beings can conflict

Learning Goals

This chapter will help you understand:

- how journalists sometimes find that their journalistic duties are in conflict with their moral obligations as citizens and human beings;
- why journalists should, in the abstract, avoid being involved with the events and the people they cover;
- the kinds of situations in which journalists have to decide whether they are going to stop being observers and become participants; and
- guidelines that can help journalists make those decisions.

When hurricane Katrina struck New Orleans and the Gulf Coast in late August 2005, journalists arriving to report the disaster often felt morally obliged to assume the role of relief workers.

Assessing their experience a few months later in *American Journalism Review*, Rachel Smolkin found:

> countless acts of kindness by journalists who handed out food and water to victims, pulled them aboard rescue boats or out of flooded cars, offered them rides to safer ground, lent them cell phones to reassure frantic family members, and flagged down doctors and emergency workers to treat them.[1]

At first glance the decision to stop reporting and help may seem obvious – journalists, after all, are human beings. However, their professional responsibility makes the decision more complex. To be blunt, the reason these journalists were sent to the scene was to report the news, not to give aid. If they had chosen to do so, the journalists could have spent all their time helping victims, but then they could not have done their reporting. The public, including the victims of the hurricane, desperately needed reliable information that only journalists could provide.

Generally speaking, journalists should be detached observers who do not intervene in the events they are covering. There are two good reasons for this:

1   Intervention changes the nature of the event, rendering it no longer authentic.
2   Intervention can lead the audience to perceive bias on the journalist's part.

However, to say that the journalists' choices in Katrina were complex rather than obvious does not mean that their decisions to give aid were wrong. They were temporarily subordinating the moral obligations of their profession to their moral obligations as human beings. If they hadn't given aid, suffering or death might have resulted.

The ethicist Michael Josephson told Smolkin flatly that the journalist's primary obligation is to act as a human being. "We shouldn't be too finicky about the notion that rendering some simple assistance would compromise objectivity." He said that when people are in dire straits, "the more obligated someone is, regardless of who they are, to render assistance. The other factor is whether there are others there who can render assistance." Sometimes, he said, journalists could fulfill their moral duty by summoning help.[2]

In contrast, Paul McMasters of the Freedom Forum's First Amendment Center was equivocal. He said factors to consider before getting involved were "how natural or instinctive the journalist's impulse is and whether or not there is a potential for immediate harm or injury without the journalist's involvement." McMasters cautioned that when a journalist acts as a relief worker, "you're not observing, you're not taking notes; you're not seeing the larger picture." It is very important, he said, that the journalist return to his or her professional role "as soon as the moment passes."[3]

In most situations in Katrina, the journalists were not reporting on the people they helped, or their plight was tangential to the larger stories the journalists were writing. But for Anne Hull of *The Washington Post*, intervention would have kept her from reporting the story. That made her decision heartbreaking.

Hull wrote about Adrienne Picou and her six-year-old grandson in a poignant *Post* article headlined "Hitchhiking from Squalor to Anywhere Else." She found the pair near an interstate exit ramp and told how they had twice become homeless, once from the flood and then from "the dire conditions of the city Convention Center." On the boy's red Spiderman shirt her grandmother had written, "Eddie Picou, DOB 10/9/98," just in case they became separated or his body was found.

After the interview, Adrienne Picou asked the reporter for a ride to Baton Rouge. Although Hull did not have a car, she knew a colleague did. But Hull explained to Picou that she had to sit down to start writing. As Hull sat under an interstate overpass typing the story on her laptop, a medic in a rescue truck asked her for directions. Hull pointed to the Picous. "See that woman and child over there? She will know, and she needs your help."

The medic initially declined, but Hull pleaded, and the Picous were given the first ride on their journey out of New Orleans. That journey led to a shelter in northern Louisiana to a cattle ranch in Texas to a new job in Smyrna, Georgia.

Hull, who had handed out water and Power Bars to hurricane victims, felt torn over refusing to give the Picous a ride. "How you can you explain to somebody you can't take them to a shelter?" But she also told Smolkin, "I believe journalists should have an ethical framework to guide them, and in the case of covering catastrophe or hardship, we must try to remember that we are journalists trying to cover a story. That is our role in the world, and if we perform it well, it is an absolutely unique service: helping the world understand something as it happens."[4]

When journalists do intervene, they also have to decide whether to reveal their actions to their audience. That is another conundrum: Will this disclosure be accepted by the audience as a well-intentioned effort to be transparent? Or will it come across as self-aggrandizement? (One television producer who helped a driver escape from a flooded car in New Orleans was videotaped by colleagues as he did so, and the dramatic rescue was aired repeatedly.)[5]

On the question of disclosing the intervention, Smolkin's ethicists disagreed. Jeffrey Dvorkin, then the ombudsman for National Public Radio, said broadcasting the journalist's involvement "ends up looking, sounding self-serving and manipulative," and should not be part of the story unless it changes the outcome. Josephson would report the involvement and let the readers decide whether it's grandstanding. "If you take the hit, well, that's unfortunate, but the alternative is you let somebody suffer."[6]

Front-Line Decisions: Observer or Participant?

In the episodes described below, journalists had to decide instantly whether they would step out of their roles as detached observers. They illustrate the importance of ethical preparation by journalists: thinking through the situations they might face and deciding – often in consultation with other journalists – how they will respond. This is the kind of preparation that editor Sandra Rowe of *The Oregonian* mentioned in Chapter 1.

"Fly-on-the-wall" reporting

Sonia Nazario envisioned worst-case scenarios she might encounter in doing the arduous field work for "Enrique's Journey," a 2002 *Los Angeles Times* series that told the story of young Latinos who traveled from Central America to join parents working in the United States. Nazario is the *Times* reporter who wrote the "Orphans of Addiction" series discussed in Case Study No. 1 "The Journalist as a Witness to Suffering." In preparing for "Enrique's Journey," Nazario drew on lessons learned in the earlier series. "Enrique's Journey" won Pulitzer Prizes for both Nazario and photographer Don Bartletti.

To report realistically on the 48,000 Latino children who have made the lonely journey, the *Times* journalists followed a boy from Honduras who was trying to reach his mother. Enrique was five years old when his mother left; he was seventeen when they were reunited in North Carolina.

Nazario and Bartletti followed Enrique and other children, observing them through the majority of the trip, most notably as they rode on the tops of freight trains in Mexico. Nazario followed in Enrique's footsteps to conduct interviews and make observations that would enable her to reconstruct parts of the journey that she did not witness.

In an article in *Nieman Reports* magazine, Nazario defined her journalistic purpose: "to try to give an unflinching look at what this journey is like for these children and what these separations are like through one thread, through one child. I wanted to take the audience into this world, which I assume most readers would never see otherwise. I tried to bring it to them as vividly as possible so they could smell what it's like to be on top of the train. They could feel it. They could see it. They literally would feel like they were alongside him."[7]

Nazario knew that she would be confronted with difficult decisions about whether to continue to observe or to intervene to make the journey easier for Enrique and the other children. "You have to think these things out ahead of time," Nazario wrote, "because things can happen so quickly that it's too late to react in an appropriate way if you're not prepared." As part of the preparation, Nazario spent time at Immigration and Naturalization Service shelters and jails along the border, and she interviewed children who had made the entire journey.

She realized that if she did intervene on Enrique's behalf, she could not use him in the story, because her intervention would destroy the authenticity of the account of his journey.

She wrote that reporters have to accept that they are going to see a lot of misery in such an assignment. This is an emotional struggle, especially when children are involved. For example, Enrique realized that he did not have a telephone number of his mother in North Carolina, so he had to work for two weeks to raise enough money to make a telephone call to Honduras to get the number. All the while, Nazario had a cell phone, which she kept out of sight. "Sometimes you need to watch that play out to be able to write a really powerful story. Those aren't often things the public understands very well. I got some e-mails that basically said, 'Aren't you a human being? How could you do this?'"

Nazario devised a test for an intervention decision: "The dividing line was whether or not I felt the child was in imminent danger. Not discomfort, not 'things are going really badly,' not 'I haven't eaten in twenty-four hours.' … The bottom line on all this is that I try not to do anything I can't live with."

Riding on top of a freight train, the *Times* journalists shared danger with the children they were observing. Of course, they had resources that their subjects did not – resources they did not flaunt. Nazario wrote: "When I was on top of the train I would refrain from calling my husband until I could go to a part of the train that was empty. I would never eat in front of the kids. I would never drink water in front of the kids."

Ultimately the reporter did not accompany Enrique on the Rio Grande crossing. Here, ethical questions were intertwined with legal ones. "If I was with a child and was viewed as helping him across, then that would be aiding and abetting, which is a felony," Nazario wrote. But she did think in advance of what she might do if she were in the water with Enrique:

> Crossing the Rio Grande is a very dangerous challenge. Hundreds of people drown there, sucked under by whirlpools. ... I was going to have an inner tube, even though I'm a former lifeguard. ... If the kid's in trouble in the water I was obviously going to help him, but short of that I was not going to help him. He would not use my inner tube because that would be altering reality, and I didn't want to do that, if at all possible.

Helping the police catch a suspect

When photographer Russ Dillingham of the Lewiston (Maine) *Sun Journal* heard on the police radio that officers had cornered a fugitive in an apartment building, he rushed to the scene. He watched from the ground while police searched the third floor. "I've been doing this a long time," the 25-year veteran said later. "I kind of figured he'd be where the cops weren't."

His calculation was correct. He started taking pictures as the fugitive, Norman Thompson, leaped from the building's balcony onto a garage roof next door (Figure 4.1). From there, Thompson jumped to the ground – "like a cat," Dillingham remembered later.

"Tackle him, Russ! Tackle him!" Detective Sergeant Adam Higgins called down.

Dropping his camera, Dillingham chased Thompson, tackled him, and held him down until the officers could catch up. Then he retrieved his camera and photographed Thompson as he was handcuffed and taken to jail on multiple charges of automobile theft and fleeing police in high-speed car chases. Thompson was not armed, but Dillingham hadn't known that when he made his tackle.

Police praised Dillingham, saying they could not have made the arrest without the photographer's help. *The Sun Journal's* executive editor, Rex Rhoades, also was effusive: "We're all very proud of Russ. He's a stud."[8]

However, in a column in *News Photographer* magazine, ethics scholar Paul Martin Lester raised questions about the 2007 incident, including: What if

Figure 4.1   After taking this picture of a fugitive fleeing police, newspaper photographer Russ Dillingham tackled him at the officers' request PHOTO BY RUSS DILLINGHAM. REPRINTED BY PERMISSION OF *LEWISTON SUN JOURNAL*

Dillingham had been severely injured? What if the suspect had been injured and sued Dillingham? What if the suspect was innocent? What happens the next time Dillingham is asked by police for help? What if a more dangerous suspect mistakes him for a cop?

Lester noted that the ethics code of the National Press Photographers Association says photographers should not "intentionally contribute to, alter, or seek to alter or influence events." He recommended that Dillingham and his colleagues meet with the police to make clear that tackling suspects is not something journalists will do in the future, and that officers should not take it personally when they refuse.[9]

Dillingham's decision was instinctive. "In a split second, I made a decision to be a citizen, a community member, an American," he said. "I did what I thought was right and would do it again in a heartbeat."[10] "You don't even think about it," Dillingham said. "You just react." In his column Lester made it clear he wasn't criticizing Lester but urging that journalists think in advance about how to respond to situations they might face, much as a baseball fielder anticipates what he will do if the ball is hit in his direction.[11]

Dillingham was not confronted with saving someone from death, injury, or suffering. Instead, the photographer was asked to help the police do their jobs. Lester argues convincingly for saying no.

Yet, refusing to tackle the suspect would have almost certainly subjected Dillingham and the journalism profession to scorn not only of the police but of the public as well. What kind of citizen would not stop someone fleeing from police officers, especially when the officers were asking him to do so?

Both the police and the journalists who cover them have important missions in the community, and sometimes those missions are in conflict. Such a conflict occurs when, after a riot, the police ask the news media to turn over photographs and videos that have not been published or broadcast. They want to use the images to identify and prosecute wrongdoers.

Philip Seib and Kathy Fitzpatrick framed this journalist's dilemma in their book *Journalism Ethics*:

> The "good citizen" response might be: "Sure; use our tapes. We're not pro-looter here. If we can help you lock up criminals, we'll be glad to do so." That reply sounds noble, but it contains a significant problem. Journalists were able to do their reporting after police had left the riot area because the rioters were angry with the police but not with the news media. If, however, the news gatherers turn out to have been evidence gatherers, the next time a similar event occurs the public may not treat police and reporters differently. The journalists might not be able to cover the event from the vantage points they previously enjoyed, and they may even find themselves in danger.[12]

In his book *Don't Shoot the Messenger*, media lawyer Bruce W. Sanford writes:

> The media have long opposed these attempts to press them into service as a sort of litigation resource or video library for the prosecution or defense. Reporters fear that they seem to take sides when their testimony or work product becomes the subject of a trial. And when confidential sources are involved, compelling reporters to testify or to surrender their notes, video- or audiotapes may reveal identities and dry up important sources of information.[13]

Giving criminals access to the news media

Even so, when law enforcement asks for help, the choice can be difficult. Journalists at KKTV in Colorado Springs, Colorado, helped authorities in January 2001 because they thought their cooperation could defuse a threat of lethal violence.

Two heavily armed Texas prison escapees were holed up in a Colorado Springs hotel room. They told negotiators they would surrender if they could be interviewed on live television and allowed to vent their complaints about the Texas prison system. The negotiators agreed to ask the station to give them five minutes each.

The station went along, and the interviews were carried live with the video showing anchor Eric Singer at a desk talking with the men on a telephone. Singer allowed them to make opening statements and then asked questions. An FBI agent sat off-camera and kept time.[14]

Singer said that before the interviews began, he briefed officers on the questions he planned to ask. He said he agreed to "stay away from hot-button words," so he did not ask the fugitives what happened when they allegedly shot a police officer in Texas.

The limitations on his interview did not disturb Singer. In his experience, he said, it is not uncommon for people being interviewed to "dictate how they want it done." He said interview subjects frequently specify "what questions will be on or off limits."

Singer said the viewers were told what was happening before the interviews were aired. Afterward, he said, the station made sure that the viewers "were clear about the questions that I came up with and the ones that weren't asked. … There was nothing hidden."[15]

After the interviews, at about 3:45 a.m., the fugitives surrendered.[16]

Singer expressed satisfaction with the station's role in the event. "We are in the business to know things and report on them," he said. "These two men were the hottest stories of the day. We got to interview them and also helped keep the community safe."[17]

The episode ended well, but ethical questions remain – questions that other broadcasters should consider *before* they face similar requests.

The situation faced by the Colorado Springs station replicated the issues that the publishers of *The New York Times* and *The Washington Post* faced in 1995. A person known only as the Unabomber had been mailing bombs that in the previous 17 years had killed three people and injured 23. Now he demanded that the two newspapers publish his 35,000-word manifesto denouncing "the industrial system" and advocating a revolution to wreck that system. If the publishers refused, he wrote, he would resume bombing.

The newspapers complied, even though some in journalism warned that they were setting a precedent and leaving the media open to further blackmail. "You print and he doesn't kill anybody else, that's a pretty good deal," *Times* publisher Arthur O. Sulzberger Jr said in a message to his staff. "You print it, and he continues to kill people, what have you lost? The cost of newsprint?"

The publication of the manifesto led to the arrest and conviction of Theodore Kaczynski, the Unabomber. His brother David recognized the writing style and informed authorities, who tracked down Theodore Kaczynski in a mountain cabin in Montana.[18]

Intervention at Central High

September 4, 1957, was to have been the day that 15-year-old Elizabeth Eckford would be among the first African American students admitted to the previously all-white Central High School in Little Rock. But when Eckford arrived by bus at Central High that morning, she found herself the only African American in a sea of angry white people. Her path to the school was quickly blocked by the raised rifles of National Guardsmen, who had been sent by Governor Orval E. Faubus ostensibly to prevent disorder.

Eckford and the eight other African American students turned away later that morning would earn a place in history as the Little Rock Nine. Because her family did not have a telephone, she had failed to receive instructions to go to Central with the others. So she was terrified and alone as she sat on a bench awaiting a bus to take her away from a jeering crowd that appeared to be on the verge of a riot.

In different ways and for very different reasons, two journalists intervened in the event they were covering.

Robert Schakne, a *CBS News* television and radio reporter, discovered that his network's cameras had not captured the yelling and Confederate flag-waving as Eckford walked the distance of a city block to the bus stop. What Schakne did next is described by Gene Roberts and Hank Klibanoff in *The Race Beat*, the Pulitzer Prize-winning history of the news media's coverage of the civil rights movement:

> He did something that revealed the raw immaturity of this relatively new medium of newsgathering: he ordered up an artificial retake. He urged the crowd, which had fallen quieter, to demonstrate its anger again, this time for the cameras. "Yell again," Schakne implored as his cameraman started filming.
>
> The television reporter had carried journalism across a sacrosanct line. ... [H]ere in Little Rock, where a domestic confrontation of unsurpassable importance was unfolding, where journalistic propriety and lack of it were being put on public display, reporters who were inches from the drama found themselves making up the rules as they went along and doing it in front of everyone in a volatile situation with a hot, erratic new technology.[19]

The second journalist to intervene was reporter Benjamin Fine of *The New York Times*. Roberts and Klibanoff write that as Fine observed tears stream down Eckford's cheeks behind her sunglasses, he "began thinking about his own fifteen-year-old daughter. His emotions carried him beyond the traditional journalistic role of detached observer. He moved toward Eckford and sat beside her. He put his arm around her, gently lifted her chin, and said, 'Don't let them see you cry.'"

Soon afterward, a white woman named Grace Lorch, whose husband was a teacher at a local college for African Americans, joined Fine and Eckford. When the girl boarded a bus a few minutes later, Lorch went with her.

Fine's effort to comfort Eckford, the authors of *The Race Beat* write, "was seen by many around him as humane but completely inappropriate and probably provocative. [Fine] had inserted himself into a live story – only to remove himself from it when he wrote about the day's events a few hours later for *The Times*."[20]

Other reporters at the scene felt compassion for Eckford, too. Jerry Dhonau and Ray Moseley of the *Arkansas Gazette* and Paul Welch of *Life* magazine arranged themselves in an informal protective cordon around her as she sat at the bus stop. "It was all that they, as professionals, felt they could do," David Margolick wrote a half-century later on *vanityfair.com*.[21]

Lessons from the battlefield

The experience of journalists who cover wars also is instructive, because the violence and danger define the intervention question in stark terms. Reporters and photographers who covered the combat in Iraq in 2003 were "embedded" with American military units. They bonded with the soldiers and, more important, depended on them for protection when the shooting began.

When soldiers in his unit sneaked off and got drunk, Jules Crittenden of the *Boston Herald* reassured their sergeant: "Don't sweat it. That didn't happen." Later he reconsidered, and so he went back to the sergeant to let him know of his change of heart and get his agreement to let the story be told.[22]

Crittenden explained afterward why he had initially told the sergeant he would not write about the incident: "I didn't intend to ruin my relationship with the unit and its leadership on the first night … by humiliating them in the international press over a disciplinary issue." As for why he changed his mind, Crittenden said:

> I witnessed the discipline being meted out – a remarkably open handling of sensitive personnel matters that would have never happened in the civilian world. … My story in the *Herald* was not about a soldier getting drunk, but about the platoon sergeant's leadership in a period immediately prior to hostilities. I took the unusual step of seeking [the sergeant's] permission and gave him the courtesy of a veto because I had made a commitment to him, and it was important for him to understand in our ongoing relationship under difficult circumstances that I could be expected to do what I said I was going to do.[23]

On another occasion, Crittenden gave the unit the location of Iraqi military positions he had spotted. In the resulting firefight, three enemy soldiers were killed. Shortly afterward, he wrote: "I'm sure there are some people who will question my ethics, my objectivity, and so forth. I'll keep the argument short. Screw them, they weren't there."[24]

Meg Laughlin, a Knight Ridder reporter, took a different view of her role as a noncombatant. When she was offered an M-16 rifle and asked to take a place in her unit's perimeter defense, she declined. "Are you crazy?" she asked. "We're all in trouble if you're depending on me to guard you."[25]

Crittenden said he did pick up a rifle once when the enemy ambushed the unit he was accompanying, but he intended to use it only for self-defense and put it down without firing.

Crittenden disputes any assumption that embedded reporters are "automatically influenced" by the security provided by the soldiers. "Reporters in war zones typically operate on goodwill and good sense," he said, and they "share whatever security is enjoyed by whichever group they happen to be with." He acknowledged that "eating, sleeping, and enduring hardship with generally likeable and well-behaved young men day in and day out creates personal relationships."[26]

For Crittenden, the context of the war itself is relevant in a discussion of American journalists' conduct. He said:

> We were riding with the United States Army as it was engaged in removing a dangerous, murderous despot and his forces. Any question of objectivity and balance has to be objectively balanced against those facts. Applying any kind of moral equivalence to the United States Army and the Iraqi Republican Guard or the Saddam Fedayeen in that situation would be immoral.[27]

In his gripping account of the US Army's capture of Baghdad, author David Zucchino tells how reporter Ron Martz of the *Atlanta Journal-Constitution* helped a medic administer aid to two soldiers gravely wounded in an armored personnel carrier as they drove into the capital. His was a humane intervention, even though the soldiers were actors in the drama he was covering.[28] "Once we crawl inside the Abrams tank and trundle our way to Baghdad with the boys, we should not kid ourselves about 'objectivity,'" Julie McCarthy of National Public Radio said.[29]

Covering the fighting in Afghanistan in 2002, *Wall Street Journal* reporter Alan Cullison went shopping in Kabul for spare parts for his damaged laptop. He bought a hard drive that turned out to have been used by an al Qaeda agent. *The Journal* turned the hard drive over to the American military, which downloaded its contents, including information about the agent's target-scouting mission. *The Journal* also reported the find to its readers.

Paul E. Steiger, then *The Journal's* managing editor, said the decision to turn over the hard drive was an easy one. "In moral terms, we would have been devastated if we had withheld information that could have saved the lives of our servicemen or of civilians."[30]

The Search for Intervention Guidelines

So when do you stop reporting and get involved in the story? The answer to this question – and many other ethical questions presented in this book – is: "It depends." Every situation is different. There are no absolute answers.

Even so, you will benefit from the framework of guidelines to help you make your decision in a rational way. Note the word "guidelines." Not rules. Over the years, journalism practitioners and scholars have reached a consensus guideline:

A journalist should act to save a life or prevent injury if he or she is the best person or the only person in a position to intervene.

Amplifying that guideline, Bob Steele of Poynter outlines a four-question process:

1 Is the danger imminent?
2 Is the danger profound?
3 Is there anyone else present who can help?
4 Do you, the journalist, possess special skills needed in the situation?

To illustrate, Steele offers a hypothetical: You arrive after a car has gone off a bridge and into the river. It is about to sink. Thus the answers to questions 1 and 2 are yes – there is imminent danger, and it is profound.

If paramedics and divers are already in action, you can do your journalist job in good conscience, shooting pictures and gathering facts. The answer to question 3 is yes – others on the scene are in a better position to help.

But the situation changes if the answer to question 3 is no. If you're the only one at the scene or there are only a few others, you might go into the river to attempt a rescue. But only if you're an expert swimmer. In that case the answer to question 4 is yes; you possess the special skill desperately needed in this situation.

If you are not a skilled swimmer, to try to make a rescue would likely be futile and perhaps suicidal. You still have a duty to intervene, and you do so by summoning help.[31]

As useful as the guideline and Steele's questions are in framing the decision-making, the journalist still may need to make a dire judgment call. This can be especially painful if the judgment involves a medical decision that the journalist is technically unqualified to make. In Case Study No. 1 "The Journalist as a Witness to Suffering," for example, the reporter had to decide whether the girl's fever from the spider bite was serious enough to warrant stepping out of her journalist role to drive her to the hospital.

Rachel Smolkin, who wrote about journalists who intervened in Katrina's aftermath, offers this guidance:

• Follow your conscience. Your humanity – your ability to empathize with pain and suffering, and your desire to prevent it – does not conflict with your professional standards. Those impulses make you a better journalist, more attuned to the stories you are tasked with telling.
• If you change an outcome through responsible and necessary intervention because there's no one else around to help, so be it. Tell your bosses, and when it's essential to a story, tell your readers and viewers, too.
• Remember, though, that your primary – and unique – role as a journalist is to bear witness. If you decide to act, do so quickly, then get out of the way.[32]

Case Study No. 1
The Journalist as a Witness to Suffering

When writer Sonia Nazario and photographer Clarence Williams set out in 1997 to document the lives of children in homes where the adults were drug and alcohol addicts, they wanted to show the suffering of these children with what Nazario called "grab-you-by-the-throat" reality.

Only by being detached, "fly-on-the-wall" observers, the *Los Angeles Times* journalists reasoned, could they report with power what life is like, day in and day out, for the millions of American children who grow up in these dire circumstances. And only powerful journalism could motivate citizens and their elected representatives to alleviate their suffering.

For three months Nazario and Williams spent long days with two Long Beach families, one with a three-year-old girl named Tamika and the other with siblings, eight-year-old Kevin and ten-year-old Ashley. In a two-part series in November 1997, "Orphans of Addiction," Nazario described some of the scenes the journalists watched:

- Tamika going 24 hours without eating, while her mother focuses on her own hunger for drugs.
- With her mother out looking for drugs, Tamika passing the time alone in the kitchen, "where she steps on shards from a broken jar. The toddler hobbles to the sofa, sits down, and digs two pieces of glass from her bleeding feet. Not a tear is shed."
- The mother so "intent on smoking the last crumbs of crack, she gently lowers her girl onto a mattress moist with urine and semen. As Mom inhales, Tamika sleeps, her pink and white sundress absorbing the fluids of unknown grownups."
- Kevin and Ashley missing school for four months because their father worries that enrolling them "might bring too much attention to them – and to him – from campus officials." Sometimes, Nazario wrote, Ashley "walks to a nearby elementary school so she can watch the children spill out onto the playground."
- Kevin's father disparaging his emotionally troubled, rebellious son as a "retard" and disciplining him by letting his hand fly. He "beats me all the time," Kevin said. "I don't want to be like him. He's nasty. He'd be nice if he didn't use drugs."
- Kevin and Ashley going weeks without bathing, in part because the bathtub "brims with dirty clothes alive with fleas." At one point Kevin rummages through a dumpster looking for clothes for his sister, finding a pair of canvas shoes. When the shoes turn out to be too small, "a familiar look of disappointment crosses her face."

In the spring of 1997, looking for subjects for their story, Nazario approached about 50

Continued

parents in the social services office of a university before settling on the mother of Tamika and the father of Kevin and Ashley.

The directing editor of the *Times* investigation, Joel Sappell, told Susan Paterno of *American Journalism Review* in 1998: "My only instruction was: Don't tamper with reality. ... We're making a documentary here ... Don't intrude into it. Because that changes it."

Reflecting on the assignment a decade later, Nazario wrote: "I believe that witnessing some suffering, even by children, was acceptable *if those children were not in imminent danger* and if I thought the telling of their story in the most powerful way possible might lead to a greater good." The italics are Nazario's.

She said: "I was clear in my mind about one thing. If I felt these children were in imminent danger, I would immediately report them to child welfare authorities. Yes, they were clearly being neglected. Yet I never felt the three children I spent time with were *in imminent danger.*"

One factor that gave Nazario confidence was that at least two individuals, a neighbor and a nearby pastor, were keeping "a careful eye" on the children. "When the children got hungry, or needed help, they would often go a few blocks away to Pastor Bill Thomas in Long Beach and ask for food or assistance or advice." She said Pastor Thomas agreed with her that the children were not in imminent danger.

Nazario pointed out that if she and Williams had immediately told authorities about the neglect of the children they observed, there would have been no story. Not only would they have been ejected from the homes they were observing, but word would have quickly spread in the neighborhood, and it would have been "very difficult or impossible for me to gain the trust of another family." Sometimes, she said, "it is necessary to witness some harm to be able to tell a story in the most powerful way. Your goal is to move people to act in a way that might bring about positive change."

But the *Times* did not make clear the surveillance of the neighbor or pastor, nor did it explain to readers any ground rules that the reporter and photographer had set for themselves. When the story came out, readers blistered the *Times* for callously allowing children to suffer so the paper could have a good story.

Nazario recounted the criticism: "I had watched a girl go hungry for 24 hours and done nothing. I had allowed these children to be neglected. Someone who claimed to be a child abuse investigator called three times to let me know he had urged police to arrest me. ... [One reader said], 'Was winning an award so important to you that you would risk the life of a three-year-old child to do so?'"

One of Williams' photographs and its caption especially outraged readers. It showed Tamika's teeth being brushed by her mother's boyfriend. The caption read: "Johnny brushes Tamika's teeth with a toothbrush she is sharing this day with Theodora [the mother], who is HIV-positive. After noticing that her own gums were bleeding, Theodora asked him to clean Tamika's teeth first."

Photographer Williams said he took only a couple of frames of the toothbrushing scene. "It all happened so quickly. After it was over, I was, like, whoa, that's screwed up."

On at least two occasions, the journalists did intervene, but those actions were not reported to readers.

Continued

Williams told Susan Paterno for the *American Journalism Review* article that he saw a baby, left alone in a room, was about to bite down on an electrical cord. "I made one frame, but at that point, it's crazy. I just ended up holding the baby that afternoon." When a life is in danger, he said in a 2008 interview, "you help."

Nazario told Paterno that she arrived one morning to find Tamika screaming in pain from infected spider bites. She "didn't think twice" when the mother asked her for a ride to the hospital. "I got into the car and drove her."

Both journalists spoke of the anguish they felt during the assignment. "I never cried so much doing a piece," Williams said in 2008. "I would come home at night and just stare in the mirror and cry." Nazario told Paterno in 1998: "I think you would not be a human being if you didn't go into these situations, seeking some of these things, and not coming home with a knot in your stomach."

At a seminar at the Poynter Institute in 2000, Nazario said she had to "buffer" herself in the manner that police officers and social workers detach themselves emotionally from the suffering they see. Otherwise, she said, "you couldn't function day to day doing these kinds of stories. ... It is a real balancing act."

Describing how she watched Tamika go 24 hours without eating, Nazario told the Poynter seminar:

> There were times when I purposefully allowed hunger to play out. I knew that this girl often went 24 hours without eating and I wanted to see that. I was willing to watch that happen. ... I was reporting the neglect that occurred to these kids in the most powerful way I could, by putting it on the front page of a major newspaper.

After the *Times* series was published, the county's child-abuse hotline registered a 45 percent increase in reports from the public of children being abused or neglected. More important, the series led to systemic reforms. One of those was a revamping of Los Angeles County's child-abuse hotline after reports surfaced that four people, including a doctor, had reported Tamika's situation to the hotline without anything being done. More money was put into federal and state programs to provide treatment for addicted women with children. A task force representing 20 agencies was set up to identify and help endangered children through the schools and police. Schools in the county changed policies to identify children like Kevin and Ashley who had dropped out of one school but never enrolled in another.

Even though use of email in 1997 was a fraction of today's traffic, Nazario received more than 1,000 phone calls and emails. The majority of reader comments were words of praise. One man thanked Nazario on behalf of the three children she had written about: "You may have saved not just their lives, but the lives of millions of other innocent children throughout the country."

Tamika was picked up and put in foster care the day the story was published. Her mother, Theodora, got free drug-rehabilitation treatment at a residential facility whose director had read the story. She lived, clean and sober, at the facility for 18 months only to go back to drugs a few weeks before she was to have regained custody of Tamika. Ultimately, Tamika was adopted by a foster-care family.

Continued

Kevin and Ashley had moved with their father to central California before the *Times* published its report. They came under scrutiny of the social-welfare system as a result of the publicity, but authorities decided not to remove the children from their father's custody.

Nazario wrote in 2008 that although she would have reported and written the story in much the same way, there are some things she would do differently.

First, she would write the story in less than the two months she took in 1997, after the three months of observation. "I should have taken greater care to drop in on the children and monitor their situation much more closely during the writing phase."

Second, the *Times* should have run a note explaining to readers the rationale for why the journalists chose not to intervene. The *Times* did consider such a note but decided against it because of an aversion to writing about itself and concerns that a note would detract from the story's power. For her 2002 series, "Enrique's Journey" [a Honduran boy's odyssey described in this chapter], Nazario wrote 7,000 words of footnotes "in an effort to provide greater transparency."

Third, she would be much more methodical in thinking through potential ethical dilemmas and deciding in advance how she would react. What are the worst things that could happen? How would I react in an instant?

After Nazario's seminar at the Poynter Institute in 2000, Poynter faculty member Bob Steele said the *Times* journalists had faced a dilemma in which there were competing principles. "There clearly is an obligation for the newspaper to reveal the truth about this issue to readers," Steele told reporter Tran Ha of *poynteronline.*

> There also is the journalistic principle that journalists do not become overly involved with their sources or subjects in ways that change the story or that will make the newspaper seem as if it is an arm of law enforcement or the government. The third principle is one of minimizing harm and what obligation the journalist has in preventing further harm or profound harm to vulnerable people.

Questions for Class Discussion

- How did the project editor, Joel Sappell, explain the decision to have the reporter and photographer avoid involvement in the story? How do you react to the decision?
- Should the journalists have agreed in advance on the kinds of situations that would compel them to intervene? Should they have informed readers of those ground rules?
- On at least two occasions the journalists did intervene to protect the children. Did their actions violate their instructions to avoid involvement? Did they damage the story's authenticity? Should these interventions have been disclosed to the readers?
- Do you agree with the three things Nazario said she would do differently if she were doing the story over? Are there any other things you would change?

Notes

1   Rachel Smolkin, "Off the sidelines," *American Journalism Review*, December/January 2006.

2   Ibid.

3   Ibid.

4   Ibid.

5   Ibid.

6   Ibid.

7   This section of the chapter is based on: Sonia Nazario, "Ethical dilemmas in telling Enrique's story," *Nieman Reports*, Fall 2006, 27–9.

8   Mark LaFlamme, "Fugitive caught in flash," Lewiston (Maine) *Sun Journal*, Oct. 4, 2007.

9   Paul Martin Lester, "Think fast," *News Photographer*, November 2007.

10   Russ Dillingham, email to Shannon Kahle, April 30, 2008.

11   Lester, "Think fast."

12   Philip Seib and Kathy Fitzpatrick, *Journalism Ethics* (Fort Worth, TX: Harcourt Brace, 1997), 122.

13   Bruce W. Sanford, *Don't Shoot the Messenger: How Our Growing Hatred of the Media Threatens Free Speech for All of Us* (New York: The Free Press, 1999), 128.

14   The Associated Press, "TV interview helps end Texas escape standoff," Jan. 24, 2001.

15   Eric Singer, email to Shannon Kahle, July 8, 2008.

16   The Associated Press, "TV interview helps end Texas escape standoff."

17   Singer, email to Kahle.

18   Clifford G. Christians, Kim B. Rotzoll, Mark Fackler, Kathy Brittain McKee, and Robert H. Woods Jr, *Media Ethics: Cases and Moral Reasoning*, 7th edn (Boston: Allyn and Bacon, 2005), 61.

19   Gene Roberts and Hank Klibanoff, *The Race Beat: The Press, the Civil Rights Struggle, and the Awakening of a Nation* (New York: Alfred A. Knopf, 2006), 159–60.

20   Ibid., 161.

21   David Margolick, "Through a lens, darkly," *vanityfair.com*, Sept. 24, 2007.

22   Jim Bettinger of the Knight Fellowships Program at Stanford University, "Detail provided by embedding was invaluable, and haunting," a report for the American Society of Newspaper Editors, 2003.

23   Jules Crittenden, email to Shannon Kahle, April 6, 2008.

24   Ibid.

25   Bettinger, "Detail provided by embedding was invaluable, and haunting."

26   Crittenden, email to Kahle.

27   Crittenden, emails to the author, July 16 and Oct. 2, 2008.

28   David Zucchino, *Thunder Run: The Armored Strike to Capture Baghdad* (New York: Atlantic Monthly Press, 2004), 57–8.

29   Bettinger, "Detail provided by embedding was invaluable, and haunting."

30   Felicity Barringer, "Why reporter's discovery was shared with officials," *The New York Times*, Jan. 21, 2002.

31   Author's telephone interview with Bob Steele, Jan. 15, 2008.

32   Smolkin, "Off the sidelines."

5 The Public and the Media: Love and Hate

The goal for the journalist should be respect, not popularity

Learning Goals

This chapter will help you understand:

- the widespread public hostility to the news media, which has been documented repeatedly in surveys;
- the possible reasons for the hostility;
- how journalists should respond to criticism;
- the types of complaints that the public most often makes about the news media, and the lessons that can be learned from these complaints; and
- how to apply perspective to the complaints.

When the Red River overflowed in the spring of 1997 and flooded Grand Forks and East Grand Forks, North Dakota, the *Grand Forks Herald* surmounted one obstacle after another to keep the community informed. *The Herald*'s printing plant was flooded and then destroyed by fire, inspiring the newspaper's grim headline: "Hell and High Water."

Still the papers kept coming. The newsroom was moved to an elementary school, where the news was transmitted to the St. Paul (Minnesota) *Pioneer Press*. The papers were printed there and flown to Grand Forks for free distribution to the beleaguered North Dakotans.[1]

That was public service in journalism's finest tradition.

But the goodwill soon dissipated in a torrent of criticism. What angered many of the *Herald*'s readers was its decision to disclose the identity of the donor who had given the towns $15 million and requested anonymity. From that gift, $2,000 was distributed to each of the 7,500 households hardest hit by the flood.

The disclosure was a result of a visit by Joan Kroc, widow of McDonald's founder Ray Kroc. When *Herald* reporters learned that the donor was being given a tour of the flood area, they drove to the airport and established her identity from the tail markings on her private jet, from fuel receipts, and from interviews with airport employees.[2] The lede of their story ran: "Angel was in town Saturday night. So was Joan Kroc's jet. This appears to be no coincidence."[3]

"You owe the community and state an apology, as well as Mrs. Kroc," one reader wrote in a letter to the editor. Another wrote, "If she was nice enough to give that much money, her wishes should have been respected." A man who called in to a radio station's talk show lamented: "The *Herald* has been wonderful through this whole thing, keeping the paper printed and distributing it for free. … This has ruined it all."[4] The newspaper's own poll showed that 85 percent of respondents thought Kroc's name should not have been published.[5]

The *Herald's* decision to name the Angel is addressed here to illustrate the mercurial nature of the public's attitudes toward the news media. Whether the *Herald* was right or wrong can be – and has been – debated in journalism circles. It should be noted, however, that the paper did not pursue the matter until the Angel toured the flood area. At that point, her identity became widely known in the community – knowledge shared by political and civic leaders but shielded from the average citizen.

The *Herald* explained in a front-page statement: "[W]e believe printing the news is part of the bargain we have made with the community. We'd be breaking the bargain if we didn't print the news."[6] Reflecting on that statement later, *Herald* editor Mike Jacobs told an audience of journalists: "News, we said, is timely information of general interest. The Angel's identity was clearly news. Besides, we said, if she really wanted to remain anonymous she should have driven into Grand Forks in a pickup truck. With a gun rack."[7]

The controversy in Grand Forks did, in Jacobs' words, "blow over." But the newspaper's precipitous fall from community hero to community villain demonstrates a paradox in American society: People *do* rely on the information that independent news media provide – and even praise it in times of crisis like September 11 and the flood in Grand Forks. Yet the people who value the information also like to complain – and they are apt to react in anger when they think the media's agenda differs from their own.

The public's relationship with the news media is, indeed, one of love and hate.

Documented Evidence of the Hostility

It is an irony that, even as the news media mature and strive to fulfill an obligation of social responsibility, the public has grown hostile. Anyone answering the telephone or reviewing incoming email at news outlets is painfully aware of this hostility. There also is empirical proof. With occasional upticks, the public's declining trust has been documented in surveys since the 1980s.

The Project for Excellence in Journalism (PEJ), a research organization and think tank, addressed the public's perception in one of its annual reports on *The State of the News Media*: "Americans think journalists are sloppier, less professional, less moral, less caring, more biased, less honest about their mistakes, and generally more harmful to democracy than they did in the 1980s."[8]

The PEJ saw a disconnect between the public and the news media over motive. *The State of the News Media* observed that while journalists think they are working in the public interest and trying to be fair and independent, the public thinks otherwise. In the public's eyes, news organizations are operating largely to make money and their journalists are primarily motivated by professional ambition and self-interest.

The Gallup Poll reported in 2007 that more than half of Americans had some degree of distrust in the news media – 35 percent said they had "not very much" trust and 17 percent said they had "none at all." By comparison, in a Gallup survey 30 years earlier, a quarter of the population expressed a lack of trust.[9]

Similar results were produced by a survey also conducted in 2007 by the Pew Research Center for the People & the Press: "In 1985, most Americans (55 percent) said news organizations get the facts straight. Since the 1990s, consistent majorities – including 53 percent in the current survey – have expressed the belief that news stories are often inaccurate."

The Pew Center also noted a growing partisan divide in the way the public perceives the media, with Democrats generally much more trusting in the media than Republicans and independents. And a growing number of people, predominantly Republicans, think the news media are "too critical of America." When the Pew Center asked that question in 1985, 30 percent of those questioned said yes. In 2007, the percentage was 43.[10]

All that research is important to journalists because it underscores a threat to credibility – whether their reporting is believed. "The bottom line ... is believability. Trust is the lifeblood of the media's relationship with the people," the Pew Center wrote in an analysis of its surveys in 2005.[11]

The public is skeptical of journalists' ethics. When a Gallup Poll ranked the "honesty and ethical standards" of various occupations in 2007, reporters placed in the bottom half (Figure 5.1). Only 23 percent of respondents thought television reporters had "very high" or "high" ethical standards, and only 22 percent thought that highly of newspaper reporters. The ratings have declined in recent decades. In Gallup's survey in 1981, 36 percent of respondents thought television journalists had "high" or "very high" ethical standards, and 30 percent rated newspaper journalists that highly.[12]

Possible Explanations for the Hostility

Although public hostility to the news media has been well documented, the reasons for the hostility have not been. Thus the question is open to speculation.

Roy Peter Clark of the Poynter Institute sees a correlation between the plummeting credibility ratings and relentless attacks on the news media. Clark says the

Results of a 2007 Gallup poll that asked:
How would you rate the honest and ethical standards of people
in these different fields — very high, high, average, low or very
low?

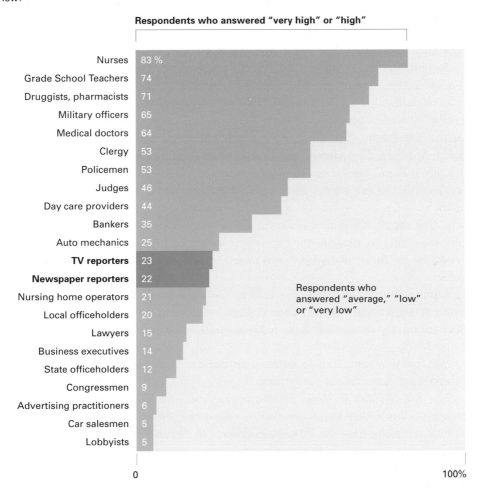

Respondents who answered "very high" or "high"

Nurses	83 %
Grade School Teachers	74
Druggists, pharmacists	71
Military officers	65
Medical doctors	64
Clergy	53
Policemen	53
Judges	46
Day care providers	44
Bankers	35
Auto mechanics	25
TV reporters	23
Newspaper reporters	22
Nursing home operators	21
Local officeholders	20
Lawyers	15
Business executives	14
State officeholders	12
Congressmen	9
Advertising practitioners	6
Car salesmen	5
Lobbyists	5

Respondents who
answered "average," "low"
or "very low"

0   100%

Figure 5.1
Honesty and
ethics in
professions
REPRINTED BY
PERMISSION OF THE
GALLUP
ORGANIZATION

attacks are coming from many directions, with a persuasive cumulative effect on
"a public that has been conditioned to hate us."

In a column in January 2008, Clark gave these examples:

- "Politicians under pressure – from every political party – try to kill the media
  messenger."
- "On radio talk show after talk show, in best-seller after best-seller, an industry
  has grown up with many agendas. Among the greatest of the agendas is to
  destroy the credibility of the mainstream press."
- The "geek news revolution" on the Internet has undermined public confidence
  in the press, not only by endorsing the attacks of partisan bloggers, but also by
  routinely dismissing the value of the mainstream news media.

- Journalists are portrayed negatively in films and television dramas, as exemplified by the long-running "Law and Order" TV show in which reporters and photographers typically appear as "slimeballs or part of the wolf pack."

Clark concluded, "The public bias against the press is a more serious problem for American democracy than the bias (real or perceived) of the press itself."

As one antidote to the assaults, Clark suggested that the news media find ways to explain their best practices to the public. Essentially, he was proposing a public-relations campaign. "Let's remind them of the journalists who have risked their lives as war correspondents, or who have worked hard to create an environment on the home front (I'm thinking of *The Washington Post*'s investigation of Walter Reed Army Medical Center) where returning military men and women can get the physical and mental health care they might need."[13]

Over the longer term, suspicion of the news media has been fueled by the media's dual nature – stations and newspapers have to make a profit at the same time that they fulfill their quasi-civic functions of informing the community. It is easy for cynics to ask: Are they reporting this story because it is news the public needs, or are they just trying to sell papers, raise broadcast ratings, or attract web traffic?

Another chronic problem, discussed by the authors of *Doing Ethics in Journalism,* is the way journalists explain their newsgathering decisions to the public. Rather than reflexively citing their legal right to publish the information, they should be emphasizing their moral obligation to report the news, the authors write. "There is a tendency by journalists to wrongly assume the public understands the rationale behind First Amendment protections."[14]

The late William F. Woo, a newspaper editor and later a Stanford University professor, wrote that journalists had to take some of the blame for the public's lack of sympathy with the First Amendment. In *Letters From the Editor*, he wrote: "Many of us seem to think that the amendment was written for the press, rather than for the people, and that it confers upon us special privileges or rights that are not given to others. ... There is almost no phrase used by journalists that I dislike more than 'the public's right to know,' for it so often justifies not courage and independence but excess, intrusion and abuse."[15]

Another cause of tension, for newspapers at least, is that the editorial pages express opinions about the people and events covered on the news pages. Readers often conclude that a paper's editorial position influences its news coverage. Unquestionably, this perception is a downside, but journalists tolerate it because they think it is important to offer informed opinion on current issues.

The public sometimes misunderstands journalism's mission, which quite likely was a factor in the reaction to the *Grand Forks Herald*'s outing of Joan Kroc as the Angel. In another common misunderstanding of journalism's purpose, people watching televised interviews and news conferences perceive that journalists are being discourteous when they ask tough but appropriate questions of public officials.

How Journalists Should Respond to Criticism

The incessant criticism in the surveys might tempt journalists to conclude that since there is no way to please the public, why even try?

That would be a mistake. Journalists have to take their credibility very seriously. Whether they think readers, viewers and listeners are right or wrong, they ignore the audience's opinions at their peril.

People who make complaints about the news ultimately may not get satisfaction. The owners of some department stores tell their employees that "the customer is always right" – a policy that may be smart in retailing but not in news. The final resolution of a complaint is determined by the facts, not what would make the customer happy.

Of course, the customer isn't always wrong, either. A reasonable customer – not one who calls for the sole purpose of mindless screaming – is entitled to serious consideration of a complaint of inaccuracy. The news organization's proper response is: "We'll check it out."

If the complaint proves valid, the news organization should speedily correct the record. In addition, the journalists ought to analyze how the error occurred. That could lead them to improve their procedures of gathering and presenting the news.

If, however, the investigation shows the original report was correct, the news organization should explain its decision-making. The explanation could be delivered in a telephone conversation, an email message, or a private letter. Citizen critics often are astonished, and pleased, that the news organization would take the time to address their complaints in a thoughtful way. If the critic's point of view is widely shared, a way could be found – a letter to the editor or a comment posted online – to accommodate a customer who wants to explain his or her perspective.

No matter how their motives are misunderstood, journalists must not consciously do anything that would validate the criticism and justify the lack of trust.

Nor should journalists pander to the public – shaping the news to fit the perceived desires of the audience. In the first place, the public is far from monolithic, and no one can precisely determine what it wants to be told about a news event. Far more important, journalists would be betraying their audience's trust by making popularity their goal instead of an honest search for truth.

In short, journalists:

- have to accept that they are not going to be loved by their audience, but ...
- can't stop trying to improve their credibility in the eyes of the public.

Nobody said this job was going to be easy!

Learning Lessons from the Complaints

The rational way to deal with citizen complaints to the news media is to look beyond the vitriol to find the constructive criticism. This requires keeping an open mind. "We're too thin-skinned," said Kathleen Carroll, executive editor of The Associated Press, speaking of the industry as a whole. "We should not take questioning by the public as an assault."[16]

So it is useful to compile a list of what – according to the surveys – irritates the public the most. Like market research in the business world, the complaints can identify patterns that need attention.

In some cases, this exercise might suggest that instead of changing their newsgathering techniques, journalists should do a better job of explaining themselves. "We have not been good at explaining our methodology – the reasons why we do the things we do," said James M. Naughton, president emeritus of the Poynter Institute. "There is less fear of conspiracy if the newsgathering process is open."[17]

What follows is a discussion of the recurring themes found in the surveys.[18]

Complaint: Too many mistakes

Although journalists are far better educated today, the public thinks they still don't know enough. When The Freedom Forum invited members of the public to a series of forums to discuss media credibility in the late 1990s, the guests expressed concern that journalists "don't have an authoritative understanding of the complicated world they have to explain to the public."[19]

The results were similar when the American Society of Newspaper Editors conducted a survey in 1998 to discern the reasons for public distrust of newspapers. The biggest reason turned out to be mistakes – not just factual errors but sloppiness in grammar and punctuation as well. The public was saying that if journalists can't get the little things right, how can they be trusted on the larger issues?[20]

The twenty-first-century surveys by Gallup, Pew and others confirm that those suspicions continue to be strongly held. The findings should challenge journalists to work harder than ever to report accurately, fairly, and in context.

The surveys show that it helps credibility if news organizations run corrections, but the public thinks news organizations, especially television, are reluctant to acknowledge their mistakes. They also think newspaper corrections should be published more prominently.

Accuracy in the news is discussed in more detail in Chapter 12.

Complaint: Bias

This complaint is undoubtedly overstated in the surveys. Most often, bias is perceived in political coverage, and what a news consumer ascribes to media bias might well be a report that is factual but at odds with the citizen's own biases. However, it is one thing to discount the degree of bias the public perceives in news reporting, and quite another to deny that bias exists at all.

Bias exists in part because journalism is a subjective art. Its practitioners continually make decisions about the news – what stories to cover, what facts to use, what facts to highlight in the stories, and what stories to present most prominently. Each decision is an opportunity for opinions to seep in. Conscientious journalists adopt an attitude of professional detachment, blocking out their opinions and following where the facts lead them.

The Editorial Eye, an editing text, describes the process:

> "The facts speak for themselves," the heroes of detective novels like to say. Honest journalists, however, acknowledge that the facts alone say little. What delivers the message is the writer's selection and arrangement of those facts. By using one fact and omitting another, by juxtaposing facts in a certain way, the writer illuminates the news ... Editors help ensure that the choosing hasn't resulted in inaccuracy and unfairness.[21]

Much of the bias in supposedly neutral news accounts results from an unconscious failure of the journalist to block out opinions. These opinions sometimes are manifest in word selection.

A more egregious ethical transgression is to decide what the story is going to say before the facts are reported. In her Point of View, "Journalism, Seen From the Other Side," Jane Shoemaker, a veteran journalist who became a business executive, writes about reporters she has seen doing this: "They had already drawn a conclusion and were simply collecting facts to dress it up."

The vocabulary of the news should be neutral – no pejoratives, no stereotypes, no code words. "Ethical journalists use language ethically, considering the truthfulness, the precision, the impact, and the long-term consequences of the words used. Unethical journalists, on the other hand, are careless with the language," ethics scholar John C. Merrill writes in *Journalism Ethics*.[22]

Keith Woods of the Poynter Institute identifies some of the errant language:

> Inference substitutes for fact. Language is loaded. Euphemisms reign. A man "admits" that he is gay. A pregnant woman "peddles" her story to the press. Richard Jewell "bounces" from job to job. "Inner-city" replaces black or Hispanic. "Conservative," "suburban," or "blue-collar" replace white.[23]

Gerald Jordan, a former *Philadelphia Inquirer* reporter and editor who teaches journalism at the University of Arkansas, sees a problem not just in word choice, but also in how reporters frame, or establish the context of, their stories. The framing, too, can reflect journalist bias. "The command to 'make sense' and 'write with authority' is an invitation to surmise and analyze," Jordan said.[24]

Story framing can be flawed if the reporter, perhaps without realizing it, adopts the position of one side in a conflict. An example: To reduce chronic delays for travelers at a metropolitan airport, the Federal Aviation Administration orders new takeoff patterns that will cause aircraft noise over certain neighborhoods near the airport. The news coverage emphasizes the neighbors' protests and barely mentions the benefits of the new takeoff patterns. The fair approach is to offer thoughtful, detailed treatment of both the protests and the benefits, allowing the audience to judge the wisdom of the tradeoffs the FAA made. Framing is discussed in more detail in Chapter 12.

A recurring complaint from the public is the media's focus on bad news. The public thinks "the press is biased – not with a liberal bias, but with a negative one," Robert H. Giles wrote after The Freedom Forum's study of news consumers' attitudes. "There is too much focus on what is wrong and what is in conflict, and not enough on reporting and explaining what is working and succeeding."[25]

Negativity, of course, is part of the nature of news because one of its definitions is an event that deviates from the norm. Although the hundred planes that land safely at the airport today are not news, the one that crashes becomes the lede story on the evening newscast. Yet the traditional definition of news also validates the point Giles was making. If a dozen towns in the region have an identical problem and one of them discovers an innovative solution, the success story deserves media attention.

Stephen Seplow, retired reporter and editor for *The Philadelphia Inquirer*, suggests yet another bias – a bias toward the front page or the lede story on the newscast:

> Reporters and editors understandably want the best possible play for the stories they write and edit. I think we are all sometimes guilty of hyping stories by moving less important – but more sexy – details higher in the story than they deserve. There is nothing inaccurate in the reporting, but it distorts reality a little by emphasizing the wrong thing.[26]

Complaint: Insensitivity

News consumers may be interested in how victims of tragedy are coping with their ordeals, but they are disgusted when reporters, especially those on television, appear to trample on the victims' feelings. Unlike public officials and business executives who are accustomed to media questioning, these ordinary citizens are thrust involuntarily into the news. They are vulnerable to exploitation and have a right to be left alone. Approaching traumatized people for interviews, reporters should be aware of their vulnerability.

In *Best Practices for Newspaper Journalists*, Robert J. Haiman quotes an editor as telling his staff:

> The mayor, the police chief, the people who run the big companies in town … they deal with us all of the time and they are all big boys and girls who can take care of

themselves. But let's not treat somebody's old Uncle Harry or Aunt Millie the same way we treat the pols and the pros.[27]

These are among the guidelines developed by Michigan State University's Victims and the Media Program:

- Switch out of investigative reporter mode. Don't be afraid to open the conversation with "I'm sorry for your loss" or "I'm sorry for what happened to you."
- In cases of death, celebrate the life. Inform the family that an interview will allow your article to go beyond the facts on the official record provided by police or hospitals.
- Tell their side of the story. There are times when victims want to put their version on the record (the warning light wasn't flashing, the attacker threatened to kill her if she called police, etc.). Many victims complain that initial articles contained glaring errors that they were not given the opportunity to correct.
- Discuss the ground rules. Make sure that victims know you are there as a reporter, not their friend, but that your goal is to help them tell their stories.[28]

In Case Study No. 2, "Roughed Up at Recess," a lesson was learned by the television station whose stunning video made the public aware of playground assaults at local schools. The video crews often tried to stop the fighting, but they did not realize the importance of telling the audience how they intervened. As a result, much of the public's anger was directed at the messenger instead of at the school employees who were responsible for patrolling the playgrounds.

Complaint: Unnamed sources

When journalists use anonymous sources, they are asking their audience – proved in the surveys to be skeptical – to trust their judgment that the sources know what they are talking about. Without the source's name and position, the public has no way to assess the validity of the information or its possible bias.

Thus the use of an anonymous source places a special burden on the reporter, because the news organization effectively is vouching for the accuracy of what is attributed to the source.

News accounts are more authoritative when sources are identified. Journalists in the abstract tend to agree that they should get their sources to go on the record by name. In practice, it is a different matter, as reporters are tempted to trade anonymity for information that is not vital but merely interesting.

Anonymity should be granted to protect a whistleblower – someone with inside knowledge of wrongdoing who is willing to come forward but would be in jeopardy if identified. Protecting such a source enables journalists to give the public information that it otherwise would not receive.

This topic is discussed in more detail in Chapter 13.

Complaint: Sensationalism

The public thinks journalists chase stories about sex, scandal, and celebrities not because they are important but because they think they will sell newspapers, build broadcast ratings, or attract web traffic. This is "infotainment," a frothy blend of information and entertainment.

The infotainment story gets saturation coverage, as if it is the only thing happening that matters. But as soon as the genre's next story appears, the earlier story is quickly forgotten.

A perennial form of sensationalism is the way local television news stations overcover crime and accident news, living up to the "if it bleeds, it leads" cliché. Another example is hyping forecasts of snow or other bad weather.

Sensationalism is indeed a problem in the news media. Chapter 20 addresses infotainment and other forms of sensationalism in more detail.

Complaint: Journalists' ethics

Although many of the complaints that the public makes about journalists are exaggerated, this one is outrageously so.

As president of the Poynter Institute, James M. Naughton would occasionally be asked by a nonjournalist what the institute does. "I explain that it is a mid-career training center for professional journalists that teaches craft skills and values, especially ethics," Naughton said. "Invariably, mentioning ethics evokes a smirk or a nudge or a sarcastic comment, as if to suggest there are none in journalism."[29]

Based on a career's worth of observation, the author of this book is convinced that journalists take ethical standards seriously. Most get into the profession because they want to make a difference; they see a noble calling in journalism's mission of public service.

Ethics might be yet another area in which journalists should do a better job of explaining themselves. One way news organizations might do this is to post their ethics codes online and invite their audience to hold them to those standards.

In contrast to the Gallup Poll that shows little public respect for journalists' ethics, a study of moral development by two professors shows that journalists are skilled at working through the ethical dimensions of problems in their profession.

The professors, Lee Wilkins of the University of Missouri and Renita Coleman of Louisiana State University, reported that their study of 249 journalists placed them fourth among 20 groups that have taken the Defined Issues Test, designed to assess moral development.[30]

"Thinking like a journalist requires moral reflection, both done dynamically and at a level that in most instances equals or exceeds that of members of the other learned professions," Wilkins and Coleman wrote.[31]

Complaint: Advertisers' influence

As mentioned above, the dual nature of newspapers and broadcast stations creates an unavoidable appearance of a conflict of interest. The media perform a quasi-civic function of providing information to the public, but they cannot survive in the marketplace if they don't make a profit. Nearly all their income is derived from selling advertisements to businesses that want their messages to reach the news organization's audience.

Given that reality, it is easy for a skeptical consumer to assume that the news organization will slant the news to cater to the wishes of an advertiser. This has happened, but journalists are zealous about guarding against such occurrences or blowing the whistle on them if they do occur. Time and again, news organizations have rebuffed advertisers' pressure at great financial sacrifice.

The commercial aspect of news organizations, along with its implications for journalism ethics, is explored in Chapter 11.

Applying Perspective to the Complaints

It is well to conclude this chapter by trying to put the public criticism in perspective.

Despite the complaints, people do say good things about the news media in the surveys. They like local television news, network news, cable television news, and the newspapers they know best[32] – notwithstanding the *Grand Forks Herald*'s experience in the Angel controversy.

Media scholar Lawrence T. McGill, in a 1997 analysis of surveys about press fairness, made the same point:

> Questions referring to specific news organizations ask people something they know about firsthand. For example, when people are asked about CNN, they can describe what they think of CNN because they've watched it themselves. If people are asked about their local newspaper, they can describe what they think about it because they've read it themselves. But questions about "news organizations in general" ask people about something they know about only secondhand, either through conversations with others about "the media," or, ironically, through news reports about "the media."[33]

For that matter, "the media" is a nebulous, inaccurate term that contributes to public misunderstanding about journalism. *The New York Times* and *The New York Post* have little in common. Likewise, Rush Limbaugh differs from National Public Radio. Likewise, partisan blogs differ from the websites of the mainstream newspapers and broadcast networks.

Significantly, the public continues to support journalism's watchdog role. The Pew Center for the People & the Press reported in 2007:

> In every Pew survey conducted since 1985, a majority has said that press criticism of political leaders does more good than harm. Currently, fifty-eight percent say press criticism of political leaders is worth it because it keeps leaders from doing things that should not be done.[34]

Although it is true that credibility has fallen sharply since the 1980s, you should bear in mind that complaints about journalists are nothing new.

Consider these complaints: "News is distorted. Some newspapers invade privacy. Scandal and 'sex' stories are printed solely to sell papers. Innocent persons are made to suffer needlessly by publicity. The real interest of the press is money-grubbing."

Those appeared in Leon Nelson Flynt's book, *The Conscience of the Newspaper.*[35] It came out in 1925.

Point of View
Journalism, Seen From the Other Side
Jane Shoemaker

After a quarter-century as a reporter and editor, I became head of communications for a regional brokerage and investment-banking firm. When I switched to the other side, it was an eye-opener to see the wide variance in standards and ethics from one reporter to the next.

To my distress, I found that far too many journalists are lazy. The lazy ones did not come to an interview prepared, and their shallow questions reflected that. Lazy reporters accepted whatever we told them, not questioning anything. Trade publications and smaller newspapers were alarmingly willing to take my writing and publish it as fact. My news releases often were printed word for word as news stories by publications short of help and eager to fill space. I could have written self-serving drivel, and readers would not have had any way to know it.

And it was a great surprise to learn how many reporters, particularly those who consider themselves specialists, came to interviews with an obvious bias. They had already drawn a conclusion and were simply collecting facts to dress it up. A telltale sign was questioning

Continued

intended to back the interviewee into a corner: "Don't you agree that … ?" "Isn't it true that … ?"

Even worse were those who tried to push their own words onto the unwitting subject. I warned executives to be wary of any reporter who said, "So what you're saying is …" or "In other words …" That was a red flag that the reporter was choosing the words he or she wanted to attribute to the subject.

We found that many reporters want stories to be black or white. Good guys or bad guys. Right or wrong. The truth is that most events are in shades of gray and need to be presented in perspective. That was particularly difficult when working with television reporters, who hate anything gray because it takes too much time on the air to explain.

The most challenging situation for us was to continue to work with reporters we knew to be lazy or to have a strong point of view. The best was the opportunity to work with reporters who were prepared, ready to listen, willing to learn, and balanced and fair in their stories. Fortunately, there were plenty of them.

Jane Shoemaker was a reporter for United Press International; a reporter, foreign correspondent and departmental editor for *The Philadelphia Inquirer*; and managing editor of *The Charlotte Observer*.

Case Study No. 2
Roughed Up at Recess

The investigative team at WITI-TV in Milwaukee received multiple phone calls from viewers who reported their children had been bullied and "beaten up" by classmates on school playgrounds.

Bob Clinkingbeard, WITI's vice president and news director, was impressed by the volume of calls the station had received on the topic. Soon after the school year began in fall 2003, reporter Bob Segall began investi-gating the issue by conducting surveillance at area elementary schools. Segall went alone, carrying a home video camera, to sit in his car and watch children play on randomly selected schoolyard playgrounds.

At the first stop, Segall videotaped children taunting, hitting and kicking each other. In one case, a 7-year-old boy was repeatedly hit, kicked, and dragged by a group of older students on the playground. The boy tried

Continued

to escape his elementary-aged assailants by climbing a tall chain-link fence, but when the boy climbed down, he was hit and kicked some more.

Segall found the same kind of physical violence on schoolyard after schoolyard across the Milwaukee area. In 37 of 52 schools the station visited over a few weeks, WITI recorded kids hitting and/or kicking other kids during recess on what were supposed to be supervised school playgrounds.

The station aired its findings in a special sweeps story, "Roughed Up at Recess." Clinkingbeard said:

> I thought viewers would be shocked and angry that this was going on in schools. We thought we knew how people would react. The reporter who did the story has children. An editor with children put the story together, and the photographers who shot the story have children. Other people in the newsroom who have children saw the story and while they were amazed – and maybe it is because they were journalists – nobody said to Segall, "Why didn't you do something to stop the attacks?"

Because the story was a lengthy one – 13 minutes – the station divided it into two segments within the same newscast, separated by a commercial break. Before the first segment ended, the assignment desk began getting phone calls from viewers who were angry because they thought the journalists had not intervened. These calls intensified during the commercial break.

Segall said, "We decided the best way to handle the dilemma was for a news anchor to address the issue by asking me a question"

during the live "tag" that followed the second segment. The anchor asked, "Bob, what would you say to parents who are calling our newsroom now saying, 'Why didn't you step in and alert a teacher or break up the fight yourself?'" Segall responded by explaining what he did – and did not do – at the time he witnessed the incidents.

"In retrospect," Segall said, "this fell far short of the thorough explanation and broader context viewers needed to better understand the ethical issues we faced while reporting the story."

Segall said he and his colleagues underestimated the importance of informing viewers about what he had done to intervene. About the first little boy Segall witnessed being attacked, Segall said: "I put down my video camera to intervene three times. The first time the boys ran off before I got ten steps from my car. The second time I got as far as the street before the fighting broke up, and the kids ran off. On occasion number three, I didn't even have a chance to get out of the car before they ran away."

Segall said he called the school district's safety director, whose cell phone number he had programmed into his phone, and the director in turn called the principal. "I thought the school would act more quickly getting a call from him, than by getting a call from a stranger. The safety director did respond right away, so I think it was a good decision." In suburban districts, school districts were also notified – some as soon as 15 minutes after an altercation, and all of them within a week.

As Clinkingbeard pointed out, the powerful video overwhelmed the problem the

Continued

station had exposed. Segall agreed: "Everything that followed – the additional detail, insight and resolution – did not matter to some of our viewers. They did not hear any of it because they were just too angry."

Segall said the actions of the journalists were not a part of the original report because the focus was intended to be on the behavior of the children, and there was concern that a lengthy explanation would detract from the pacing of the report and shift the focus onto the journalists instead of the students. "What we failed to realize was without providing at least some of that context to accompany the video, *my* action and perceived inaction became the focus for some viewers," he said.

Clinkingbeard said that in retrospect he wished he and Segall had given more thought to what their protocol would be if the station witnessed abuse on the playground. "I had no idea that we would catch something that awful on camera," he said.

Such up-front conversations, Segall later said, might have included instructions to "look at each child on the playground as if it were your own child. Make sure the decisions you make about when to intervene would be the same decisions you would make if that child were your own."

The video was edited to obscure the identities of children involved in the fights, both the assailants and the victims. The finished report showed how WITI-TV crews videotaped the fighting.

The investigation and an ensuing community-service project resulted in extensive reforms. The Wisconsin Department of Health conducted a statewide bullying education program. The state's largest school districts carried out comprehensive bullying prevention programs, and another program trained school police officers statewide. The Milwaukee Public Library set up a Bully Project resource center with books, videos, and other resources for teachers, students, and parents.

This case is adapted from *Newsroom Ethics: Decision-Making for Quality Coverage*, 4th edn (Washington, DC: Radio Television News Directors Foundation, 2006), 20–1.

Questions for Class Discussion

- Was it appropriate for the WITI-TV crews to intervene in the playground fighting?
- What kind of "front-end" instructions should have been given to crews in advance of reporting this story?

- What should WITI-TV have told its viewers about what its crew members did to stop the fighting and to notify school officials?
- Why do you think the news staff underestimated the viewers' reaction to the video?

Notes

1 Mike Jacobs, editor of the *Grand Forks Herald*, in remarks at the 2003 convention of the American Society of Newspaper Editors; posted at: http://www.poynter.org/content/content_view.asp?id=38399

2 Jay Black, Bob Steele, and Ralph Barney, *Doing Ethics in Journalism: A Handbook With Case Studies*, 3rd edn (Boston: Allyn & Bacon, 1999), 245–6.

3   "Angel appears in GF, EGF; Angel's wings registered to Kroc," *Grand Forks Herald*, May 19, 1997.

4   "Flood of complaints follows newspaper's disclosure of donor" and "On the radio waves," *Grand Forks Herald*, May 20, 1997.

5   Black, Steele, and Barney, *Doing Ethics in Journalism*, 246.

6   "The Herald's first commandment: Never hold the news," *Grand Forks Herald*, May 20, 1997.

7   Jacobs, remarks to the American Society of Newspaper Editors, 2003.

8   Project for Excellence in Journalism, *The State of the News Media 2004*, http://www.stateofthemedia.org/2004/

9   "Media use and evaluation," Copyright © 2007 Gallup Inc. All rights reserved. The survey of 1,010 adults was conducted Sept.14–16, 2007, with a sampling error of plus or minus three percentage points.

10   Pew Research Center for the People & the Press, August 9, 2007, "Views of press values and performance: 1985–2007." The survey of 1,503 adults was conducted July 25–29, 2007, with a sampling error of plus or minus three percentage points.

11   "Media: More voices, less credibility," Pew Research Center for People & the Press, 2005, 49.

12   "Honesty/ethics in professions," Copyright © 2007 Gallup Inc. All rights reserved. The survey of 1,006 adults was conducted Nov. 30–Dec. 2, 2007, with a sampling error of plus or minus three percentage points.

13   Roy Peter Clark, "The public bias against the press," http://www.poynter.org/content/content_view.asp?id=136625, Jan. 30, 2008.

14   Black, Steele, and Barney, *Doing Ethics in Journalism*, 17–18.

15   William F. Woo, *Letters From the Editor: Lessons on Journalism and Life* (Columbia, MO: University of Missouri Press, 2007), 24.

16   Author's telephone interview with Kathleen Carroll, Nov. 2, 2007.

17   Author's telephone interview with James M. Naughton, Sept. 14, 2007.

18   This list is derived from one created in November 1997 by Lawrence T. McGill, then director of research for the Freedom Forum Media Studies Center.

19   Robert H. Giles, Introduction to Robert J. Haiman, *Best Practices for Newspaper Journalists* (Arlington, VA: The Freedom Forum's Free Press/Fair Press Project, 2000), 2.

20   "Examining our credibility: Perspectives of the public and the press," a report by Urban & Associates for the American Society of Newspaper Editors, 1999. The telephone survey of 3,000 people was conducted during April and May 1998.

21   Jane T. Harrigan and Karen Brown Dunlap, *The Editorial Eye*, 2nd edn (Boston: Bedford/St. Martin's, 2004), 118.

22   John C. Merrill, *Journalism Ethics: Philosophical Foundations for News Media* (New York: St. Martin's Press, 1997), 167.

23   Keith Woods, "Transmitting values: A guide to fairer journalism," included in Michele McLellan, *The Newspaper Credibility Handbook* (American Society of Newspaper Editors, 2001), 107.

24   Author's telephone interview with Gerald Jordan, Sept. 17, 2007.

25   Robert H. Giles, Introduction to Haiman, *Best Practices for Newspaper Journalists*, 2.

26   Stephen Seplow, email to the author, Feb. 4, 2008.

27   Haiman, *Best Practices for Newspaper Journalists*, 32.

28   Bonnie Bucqueroux and Sue Carter, of Michigan State University's Victims and the Media Program, "Interviewing victims," *Quill*, December 1999.

29   James M. Naughton, email to the author, Jan. 30, 2008.

30   Renita Coleman and Lee Wilkins, *The Moral Media: How Journalists Reason About Ethics* (Mahwah, NJ: Lawrence Erlbaum Associates, 2005), 39.

31   Ibid., 136.

32   Pew Research Center, "Views of Press Values and Performance: 1985–2007."

33   Lawrence T. McGill, "The history of public perception that the press is unfair," contained

in Haiman, *Best Practices for Newspaper Journalists*, 68.

34 Pew Research Center, "Views of press values and performance: 1985–2007."

35 Leon Nelson Flynt, *The Conscience of the Newspaper: A Case Book in the Principles and Problems of Journalism*, (New York: D. Appleton and Company, 1925) 7–11.

6 Applying Four Classic Theories of Ethics

Ancient philosophy can help you make sound decisions

Learning Goals

This chapter will help you understand:

- four classic theories that can be tools in making decisions;
- rule-based thinking and its strengths and weaknesses;
- ends-based thinking and its strengths and weaknesses;
- the Golden Rule and its strengths and weaknesses;
- Aristotle's Golden Mean and its strengths and weaknesses; and
- the value of blending rule-based thinking and ends-based thinking in the practice of journalism.

In the spring of 1971, a fierce debate was being waged in the executive conference rooms of *The New York Times*. The paper had its hands on a historic exclusive: a 7,000-page Pentagon document revealing that over three decades the government had lied to American citizens about how their country got increasingly involved in the fighting in Vietnam.

There were two problems with what was to become known as the Pentagon Papers. First, the document had been stolen from the government by one of its authors, Daniel Ellsberg, a military analyst working for the Rand Corporation think tank. Ellsberg had handed it over to *Times* reporters. Second, it was classified "top secret."

Publishing the Pentagon Papers would be a crime.

The paper's editors argued unanimously that the citizens were entitled to the information in the Pentagon history of the war, stolen or not, classified or not. Their lawyers, nearly unanimously, pointed to the law violations and warned that publishing could lead to criminal prosecution that could ruin *The Times*.

Finally, the debate was decided by the one person whose vote counted. Arthur Ochs Sulzberger, the publisher, wanted to leave no doubt about his decision, so he put it in a formal memorandum: "I have reviewed once again the Vietnam story and documents that will appear on Sunday, and I am prepared to authorize their publication …"

That Sunday, June 13, 1971, *The Times* published the first of a series of articles under the purposely understated headline "Vietnam Archive: Pentagon Study Traces 3 Decades of Growing U.S. Involvement." On Tuesday, after three installments, the government got a court order to halt *The Times*' series. With *The Times* silenced, *The Washington Post, The Boston Globe* and the *St. Louis Post-Dispatch* obtained copies of the Pentagon Papers from Ellsberg and defiantly began publishing their own reports.[1]

On June 30, the United States Supreme Court handed down a decision that has stood as a landmark affirmation of press freedom. The court, by a vote of six-to-three, held that the government was unjustified in exercising "prior restraint" to prevent *The Times* from continuing its series.[2] Siding with the majority, Justice Hugo Black referred to the nation's founding principles: "The press was protected so that it could bare the secrets of government and inform the people. Only a free and unrestrained press can effectively expose deception in government."[3]

Max Frankel, in 1971 the chief of *The Times*' Washington bureau and later the paper's top editor, reflected after a quarter of a century: "As the prosecutors of the case confessed decades later, no damage was done. No military battles were lost. The national security bureaucracy had fought not to protect information from aliens but to enlarge its authority to deny information to Americans."[4]

In the weeks-long debate at *The Times* that spring, ends-based thinking triumphed over rule-based thinking.

Most of the lawyers argued in favor of following *the rule*. Embodied in the law, the rule says that citizens don't use stolen property. And they certainly don't publicize information that the government has legally declared to be "top secret."

The editors argued for looking beyond the rule and focusing on *the ends*. The citizens of the United States have sacrificed blood and treasure in the Vietnam War, they were saying, and now we have a document that shows their government has repeatedly lied to them about that war. The people deserve to know what is in the document. *The Times* has a moral obligation to tell them.

The publisher ultimately decided that the editors were right. Less than three weeks later, so did the Supreme Court majority. "In revealing the workings of government that led to the Vietnam War," Justice Black wrote, "the newspapers nobly did precisely that which the founders hoped and trusted they would do."[5]

How Ethical Theories Influence Decisions

Although there is no evidence that either the editors or the lawyers cited those classic theories of ethics in *The Times*' debate, the case has significance in terms of news media ethics as it does in news media law. It illustrates the role that the classic theories of ethics, consciously or not, play in journalists' decision-making.

This chapter discusses four classic theories as tools in the decision process: rule-based thinking, ends-based thinking, the Golden Rule, and Aristotle's Golden Mean. The descriptions that follow are summarized from ethics scholars' analysis of the four theories.

Rule-Based Thinking
(also known as deontology, duty-based thinking)

Rule-based thinking is absolutist. A person has a duty to do the right thing – no excuses, no exceptions, and no worrying about the consequences. Ethical obligations must be obeyed regardless of the situation and, as ethicist Michael Josephson writes, "in spite of social conventions and natural inclinations to the contrary."[6]

The champion of rule-based thinking was Immanuel Kant (1724–1804), a German philosopher whose concept of "the categorical imperative" is central to the theory.

The categorical imperative, as Kant articulated it, is: "I ought never to act except in such a way that I can also will that my maxim should become universal law." Kant was saying that a person should act as if he or she were setting a standard for other people to follow, and that if everyone followed that standard, the world would be a better place.[7]

Kant believed that people should live up to standards of conduct "because they are good, not because of the consequences that might result," Louis A. Day writes in *Ethics in Media Communications: Cases and Controversies*. Although people are free to make their own choices – a fundamental requirement of ethics – "they have a responsibility to live up to moral principles." Truthfulness is a universal good, so everyone should always tell the truth. It doesn't matter that sometimes the truth can cause harm.[8]

Kant also urged respect for all. Everyone is intrinsically important as a human being. People should treat others with dignity and grant others the same autonomy they enjoy.

Rule-based thinking is sometimes called duty-based thinking because of its emphasis on an individual's moral duty. Philosophers label it deontology, derived from the Greek word *deon* (duty). A person who adheres to rule-based thinking is a deontologist.

The strength of rule-based thinking lies in its simplicity. "If we follow the rules, we are ethical; if we break them, we are unethical," John C. Merrill writes in *Journalism Ethics: Philosophical Foundations for News Media*.[9] Using rule-based thinking, a decision-maker (called "a moral agent" by the philosophers) does not have to calculate the consequences of the decision.

The weakness of rule-based thinking is that it is rigid. A person confronted with two or more competing ethical values – by definition, an ethical dilemma

– has no way to make a choice. Think of the Heinz Dilemma in Chapter 2: Heinz has to decide whether to steal the drug or allow his wife to die; choosing one value would mean rejecting the other. If Heinz is a deontologist, he would be paralyzed by indecision.

A journalist who is a strict deontologist would never quote a source anonymously because the source's identity is a truth that the journalist feels morally obligated to report, John C. Merrill writes. Similarly, a deontologist would always identify a rape victim. Such a journalist:

> feels a loyalty to the integrity of the story and not to any person connected to the story. This journalist is not concerned with all the possible consequences that might result from the story; these are considered irrelevant to good journalism. Just tell the truth and let the chips fall where they will.[10]

In the Pentagon Papers case, deontology would have guided *The Times* to a decision not to publish. The law embodies a universal rule that people should refuse to accept property that they know is stolen; otherwise, they aid and abet thievery. Also, in the abstract, it is essential to national security that the government be allowed to protect secrets.

Ends-Based Thinking
(also known as consequentialism, utilitarianism, teleology)

Ends-based thinking is flexible. It allows the decision-maker to weigh competing values according to the consequences that might occur. "In essence," Michael Josephson writes, "the ends can justify the means."[11]

Ends-based thinking directs a choice in favor of the course of action that brings the most good to the most people. It is a calculation of the preponderance of good over evil, or benefits over harm – a sort of "cost-benefit analysis," as the author Rushworth M. Kidder phrased it in *How Good People Make Tough Choices*.[12]

Jeremy Bentham (1748–1832) and John Stuart Mill (1806–1873), British philosophers, were the champions of this theory. Mill held that people should choose the greatest happiness for the greatest number of people – the greatest balance of pleasure over pain. Later adherents of this theory argued that happiness is not the only desirable value, so it is more commonly known today as the greatest good for the greatest number, Clifford G. Christians and his co-authors explain in *Media Ethics: Cases and Moral Reasoning*.[13]

Ends-based thinking requires thoughtful consideration of who will be helped and who will be harmed by a decision, and to what degree. These people are commonly called stakeholders, because they have a stake in the decision.

Not to be overlooked in examining ends-based thinking is its principle that the rights of a minority are to be respected. "In a society of ten people, nine sadists cannot justly persecute the tenth person even though it yields the greatest happiness," Christians and his associates write.[14] In the United States, the constitutional guarantee of a fair trial cannot be disregarded because most of the people in a town have already concluded the guilt of the accused.

Since Bentham and Mill called their ethical system "the theory of utility," it is known in philosophy as utilitarianism. Another name is consequentialism, derived from the theory's focus on the consequences of a decision. In contrast to deontology, ends-based thinking is called teleology, from the Greek word *telos* (end).

The strength of ends-based thinking is that its flexibility permits a person to make a choice between competing ethical principles. Heinz could decide, for example, that the principle of compassion for his wife's well-being is more important than the moral rule (and law) prohibiting stealing.

Ends-based thinking directs the decision maker to consider all the possible courses of action and to weigh the benefits and harms likely to result from each alternative.[15] If the process is carried out thoughtfully, this can contribute to a sound decision.

The flexibility of ends-based thinking also is its main weakness. In Michael Josephson's view, the theory can be "manipulated by self-serving rationalizations to produce … an end-justifies-the-means credo that elevates expediency over principle."[16] Another problem with ends-based thinking is that sometimes it is difficult or impossible to predict the consequences of a decision.

The journalist who is a teleologist might deceive a source if the journalist judges that the deception will elicit important information. In such a case the journalist would contend that the harm of deception is outweighed by the good of informing the public – that the ends justify the means. A deontologist, on the other hand, would reject all forms of deception.

Teleology permits compassion to influence decisions. Unconcerned about the consequences, a deontologist would not omit any verified fact from a news story that is embarrassing to a private individual. In contrast, a teleologist would likely discard harmful facts if they are irrelevant to the story's point. The teleologist thus would "inflict only the harm required to put the story in perspective," Louis A. Day writes. "To do more would be merely an appeal to the morbid curiosity of the public."[17]

In deciding to publish the Pentagon Papers, *The Times* concluded that the document's value to the public outweighed the principles of refusing stolen property and respecting the top-secret classification. The decision was model of teleology in action.

The Golden Rule

"Do unto others as you would have them do unto you." This rule of reversibility, found in the teachings of the world's great religions, is the best single rule of ethical decision-making. Imagine yourself in the place of the person affected by your decision and, from that perspective, assess the fairness of the decision. No wonder that it is the only rule of ethics many people profess to know.[18]

Consider how instructive the Golden Rule is. As Michael Josephson writes, "If you don't want to be lied to or deceived, don't lie to or deceive others. If you want others to keep their commitments to you, keep your commitments to them."[19] Applying the Golden Rule tells you which of your contemplated actions are ethical and which are not. The Golden Rule counsels people to use restraint and self-discipline to avoid inflicting harm. It stresses love, not self-interest, as the moral base of conduct.[20] People are to be treated with dignity as ends in themselves, not as the means to an end.

The Golden Rule has broad application to journalism. A reporter following the Golden Rule would not write a story subjecting people to ridicule and voyeurism, because the reporter would not want to be exploited if the tables were turned. Such a reporter would not secretly record a source, because the reporter would not want to be secretly recorded.

However, if a journalist is reporting on a situation in which two or more stake-holders have competing interests, the Golden Rule alone is not a sufficient guide. The Golden Rule cannot tell the journalist how to decide among the competing stakeholders. That is the Golden Rule's singular weakness.

There were a multitude of stakeholders in the decision facing publisher Arthur Ochs Sulzberger in the Pentagon Papers case. His fellow owners depended on his judgment to shield the paper from financial harm, which could have been a consequence of prosecution. The thousands of employees likewise looked to his stewardship of a business that provided a livelihood for them and their families. Among those employees, however, were newsroom staff members who likely would have agreed with their editors that the paper would be failing its journalistic duty if it did not publish. And finally there were the millions of American citizens who, depending on Sulzberger's decision, would either be informed or kept in the dark about what their government had done in Vietnam. As good as it is, the Golden Rule could not have guided Sulzberger's decision.

Aristotle's Golden Mean

The ancient Greek philosophers emphasized a virtuous character. Aristotle (384–322 BCE) saw virtue in moderation – finding the mean, or intermediate, between an excess and a deficiency. He saw *courage* as the mean between *recklessness* and *cowardice*, and *proper pride* as the mean between *empty vanity* and *undue humility*.[21]

From Aristotle's virtue ethics, contemporary moral agents can draw on his theory of the Golden Mean (not to be confused with the Golden Rule). He believed that the virtuous person learns to avoid the extremes in a given situation. Thus, "the Golden Mean provides a moderate solution in those cases where there are identifiable extreme positions, neither of which is likely to produce satisfactory results," Louis A. Day writes.[22]

"Aristotle was not advocating a bland, weak-minded consensus or the proverbial middle-of-the road compromise," Clifford G. Christians and co-authors write. "Although the word *mean* has a mathematical flavor and a sense of average, a precise equal distance from two extremes is not intended."[23]

Aristotle's Golden Mean is at work in the decisions of the Federal Trade Commission on tobacco sales and advertising. The FTC could have chosen one extreme of allowing tobacco, as a legal product, to be sold and advertised without regulation. Or, in the face of medical evidence of tobacco's hazards, the FTC could have gone to the opposite extreme and prohibited tobacco sales. Instead, the FTC has taken moderate steps like prohibiting sales to minors, banning cigarette ads on television, and requiring health warnings on cigarette packages.[24]

Journalists can often find a Golden Mean to guide their decisions. As an example, consider a highly newsworthy video or still photograph whose graphic nature is certain to offend a segment of the audience. For television, the Golden Mean might lead to a decision to warn the audience before showing the video, and not to show it in the daytime or early evening when children likely will be in the audience. For a newspaper or magazine, the Golden Mean might result in publishing the photo in black and white rather than in color, on an inside page rather than the front, or in a smaller size rather than a larger one. An online news site could offer a cautionary description of the photo and require users to click on a link in order to see it.

Not every situation offers a Golden Mean. For example, there was no compromise available for publisher Sulzberger in the Pentagon Papers case. Either *The Times* would publish the document or it would not.

Blending Rule- and Ends-Based Thinking

Taken as a whole, the classic ethical theories give you a solid foundation for decision-making in journalism. You should not feel compelled to align yourself with a single theory. In particular, you do not have to choose between being a strict deontologist or a strict teleologist. You can benefit from the wisdom of an ethics code laid out in advance (rule-based thinking), but you also need to sense when the circumstances call for a different solution (ends-based thinking).

The Golden Rule deserves consideration in every situation. This overarching ethical guideline is a revealing test of the fairness of your proposed course of action. It may not be the ultimate solution of an ethical problem you face, but it is a useful step in that direction.

Rule-based thinking provides structure in the decision-making process. Your newsroom may have a policy that applies to a particular situation you are facing in gathering the news. In the absence of a newsroom policy, consider the accepted standards of the profession, such as those in the ethics code of the Society of Professional Journalists.

Policies and standards are useful because they are the product of thoughtful, off-deadline discussions and reflect the wisdom of experience. They are what the news organization has decided is "best practice" in given situations. They help a news organization be consistent and fair.

But no policy can anticipate every situation that might arise. Departing from the teaching of Kant, journalists should view policies as guidelines, not rules. In developing your skills as a moral agent, learn to analyze the circumstances. There may be reasons *not* to follow the policy in a given situation.

That does not mean that you set aside a policy on a whim, nor on your own authority. To the contrary, you conduct a careful analysis that prepares you to articulate the reasons for choosing a different course of action. Except in rare cases, there is time for you to discuss your reasoning with a newsroom supervisor. You will need to argue convincingly that departing from the policy is the best choice.

The process illustrates the constructive tension between rule-based thinking and ends-based thinking. Start with the policy, consider the circumstances, consult with experienced colleagues, and decide with them which should govern.

Aristotle's Golden Mean comes into play when other courses of action would likely result in unacceptable consequences. When that happens, search for an ethical compromise.

In your analysis of the case studies in the rest of this book – and in the decisions you will make in your journalism career – you should find the four classic ethical theories can be important tools in your decision-making process.

Rushworth M. Kidder sees these principles as useful not because they are "part of a magic answer kit that produces infallible solutions," but because they help us reason.

The principles, Kidder writes, "give us a way to exercise our moral rationality. They provide different lenses through which to see our dilemmas, different screens to use in assessing them."[25]

Notes

1   Susan E. Tifft and Alex S. Jones, *The Trust: The Private and Powerful Family Behind The New York Times* (London: Little, Brown, 1999), 480–93.

2   "Supreme Court, 6–3, upholds newspapers on publication of Pentagon report," *The New York Times,* July 1, 1971.

3   Bill Kovach and Tom Rosenstiel, *The Elements of Journalism: What Newspeople Should Know and the Public Should Expect* (New York: Crown Publishers, 2001), 113.

4   Max Frankel, "Top secret," *The New York Times,* June 16, 1996.

5   *The New York Times*, July 1, 1971.

6   Michael Josephson, *Ethical Issues and Opportunities in Journalism* (Marina del Rey, CA: The Josephson Institute, 1991), 21.

7   Rushworth M. Kidder, *How Good People Make Tough Choices: Resolving the Dilemmas of Ethical Living* (New York: HarperCollins, 1995), 24.

8   Louis A. Day, *Ethics in Media Communications: Cases and Controversies*, 5th edn (Belmont, CA: Thomson Wadsworth, 2006), 58.

9   John C. Merrill, *Journalism Ethics: Philosophical Foundations for News Media* (New York: St. Martin's Press, 1997), 62.

10   Ibid.

11   Josephson, *Making Ethical Decisions* (Los Angeles: The Josephson Institute, 1999).

12   Kidder, *How Good People Make Tough Choices*, 24.

13   Clifford G. Christians, Kim B. Rotzoll, Mark Fackler, Kathy Brittain McKee, and Robert H. Woods Jr, *Media Ethics: Cases and Moral Reasoning*, 7th edn (Boston: Allyn & Bacon, 2005), 16–17.

14   Ibid., 17.

15   Day, *Ethics in Media Communications,* 63.

16   Josephson, *Ethical Issues and Opportunities in Journalism*, 22.

17   Day, *Ethics in Media Communications*, 63.

18   Kidder, *How Good People Make Tough Choices*, 25.

19   Josephson, *Making Ethical Decisions* (Los Angeles: The Josephson Institute, 2002), 22. (The 2002 edition is a revision of the booklet that was first published in 1999.)

20   Josephson, *Making Ethical Decisions* (1999).

21   Kidder, *How Good People Make Tough Choices*, 70.

22   Day, *Ethics in Media Communications*, 64.

23   Christians et al., *Media Ethics*, 13–14.

24   Ibid., 13.

25   Kidder, *How Good People Make Tough Choices*, 26.

7 Using a Code of Ethics as a Decision Tool

Professional standards are valuable in resolving dilemmas

Learning Goals

This chapter will help you understand:

- the history of codes of ethics for journalists;
- the arguments for and against ethics codes;
- how an ethics code can be a useful tool in decision-making;
- the four guiding principles of the code adopted in 1996 by the Society of Professional Journalists:
  1 Seek truth and report it.
  2 Minimize harm.
  3 Act independently.
  4 Be accountable.

When magazine writer Will Irwin surveyed the state of American newspapers in 1911, he concluded that the best reporters followed unwritten rules. These rules commanded them to be honest with their sources and empathetic toward the people they wrote about.

Irwin wrote that these reporters would "never, without special permission, print information which you learn at your friend's house, or in your club"; that sources would always be advised what newspaper the reporter represented; and that, unless the source was a criminal, nothing would be printed without prior consent.

In addition, he wrote, good reporters "remember that when the suicide lies dead in the chamber there are wretched hearts in the hall, that when the son is newly in jail intrusion is torment to the mother."

The word-of-mouth standards Irwin described in his critique of the press for *Collier's Weekly* formed a sort of code of ethics. As journalism embraced professionalism in those early decades of the twentieth century, ethical guidelines would soon be put in writing.[1]

When the American Society of Newspaper Editors (ASNE) organized, one of its first actions, in 1923, was to adopt its Canons of Journalism. Sigma Delta Chi, the forerunner of today's Society of Professional Journalists, adopted ASNE's canons in 1926, then wrote its own code in 1973, and revised it in 1984, 1987 and 1996. ASNE's canons were revised in 1975 and renamed Statement of Principles.

The 1923 canons commanded newspapers to be independent of "all obligations except that of fidelity to the public interest," to be accurate and truthful, to distinguish between news reports and expressions of opinion, to give subjects of news coverage a chance to reply to charges against them, and to avoid "pandering to vicious instincts" by reporting in detail on crime and vice.[2]

In 1946, the new National Association of Radio News Directors adopted a resolution calling for stations to have autonomous news departments staffed by trained journalists. The next year, the radio directors resolved that commercials should be clearly separated from news content, preferably not read by the newscaster. These resolutions evolved into the code of ethics of the Radio Television News Directors Association (RTNDA), last revised in 2000.[3]

The Online News Association (ONA), formed in 1999, pledged to uphold the "traditional high principles in reporting original news" for the Internet and to make clear the distinction between news and "paid promotional information and other non-news."

One crucial aspect shared by all these codes – and the codes adopted by other national associations of journalists – is that compliance is voluntary.

The code adopted by the Society of Professional Journalists (SPJ) in 1973 called for journalists to "actively censure" violators. Fourteen years later, SPJ retreated, in part because of a realization that enforcing the code could invite costly litigation. The 1987 amendment deleted the "censure" clause and substituted an education program to encourage journalists to adhere to the code's ideals. SPJ's current code, which was adopted in 1996 and forms the basis for most of this chapter, skirts the enforcement question and calls instead for journalists to be accountable to their audience.[4]

In contrast to the voluntary codes, the standards adopted by individual newspapers, broadcast stations, and websites can be enforced, to the point of firing violators. To be sure, such discipline is subject to the collective-bargaining agreements in unionized newsrooms. Although the National Labor Relations Board permits newsroom management to promulgate codes without bargaining, these unilateral codes lack the authority of enforceable work rules.

As noted in Chapter 3, the number of newsrooms with written codes increased exponentially in the 1970s and 1980s. The inclination of editors and news directors to provide *a priori* guidance to their staffs overcame the resistance of their lawyers, who feared that written codes would make it easier for plaintiffs' attorneys to prove negligence in libel cases by showing that a journalist had failed to live up to the organization's own standards.

The current versions of ethics statements by national organizations like ASNE, SPJ, RTNDA, and ONA provide journalists with broad guidance for avoiding conflicts of interest and for covering the news accurately, fairly, and compassionately. The codes of individual newsrooms tend to be more specific in identifying unacceptable conflicts of interest. In addition, the newsroom codes may spell out policies for recurring news-coverage situations such as whether to identify rape victims or juveniles accused of crimes.

The Debate over the Value of Codes

Although codes are well established in the profession, journalism scholars and practitioners continue to debate their worth. Critics make these arguments:

- *The codes are too vague.* Since the codes can't cover every conceivable situation, they dwell on lofty ideals that no serious journalist disagrees with. In a nod to the lawyers, the language might be hedged further, leading to a lack of clarity that defeats the purpose of written instructions.
- *The codes discourage thoughtful decision-making.* Some journalists, intimidated by the code, follow its directions slavishly instead of engaging in the kind of critical thinking needed to resolve ethical dilemmas. Edmund B. Lambeth writes in *Committed Journalism*: "[A] strong case can be made that a combination of moral imagination, professional ingenuity, and interpersonal communication skills is more effective in establishing and maintaining ethical standards in the newsroom than codes of ethics."[5]
- *The codes are merely public-relations ploys.* Instead of setting an example of probity, some newsroom leaders may signal through their behavior that the organization's published codes really don't count.
- *The owners don't follow the codes.* Most codes "are aimed entirely wrong, in focusing on journalists rather than on owners, who are the ones with real autonomy and decision-making power," journalism professor Carol Reuss writes.[6] As an example, newsroom staff members scrupulously avoid involvement in outside activities that the organization may have to cover, but company executives routinely take active civic roles. The executives maintain that this kind of involvement is in the spirit of the company's social responsibility to the community.

All of those criticisms have some degree of validity. For some critics, the minuses of ethics codes outweigh the pluses, so they reject codes altogether. As autonomous moral agents, they are entitled to that conclusion.

Another assessment, however, is that the negatives demonstrate only that codes of ethics are not *absolute* solutions to ethical problems.

Ethics Codes as a Decision-Making Tool

This text takes the position that codes are a useful tool in decision-making. Journalists benefit from the guidance found in well-thought-out codes such as the exemplary statement of professional principles adopted in 1996 by the Society of Professional Journalists.

The key is to view the code as part of a step-by-step process in making news-coverage decisions, not as a substitute for the process.

Thanks to the code, a journalist does not have to begin the process with a blank canvas. The code offers conventional wisdom – the best practice as defined by experienced journalists thinking together in a relaxed, off-deadline setting. Defining best practices helps a news organization be fair and consistent in the way it covers the news. James M. Naughton, a member of a staff committee that drafted *The Philadelphia Inquirer*'s code in 1978, remembers the process as a useful exercise because it provided "a baseline for collegial understanding of what the standards are." It is important, Naughton said, that staff members understand the strengths and weaknesses of codes.[7]

Fairness and consistency are essential in dealing with conflicts of interest that the newsroom management considers unacceptable. An important step toward fairness is informing staff members in advance about what those conflicts are. A written code does that.

The authors of *Doing Ethics in Journalism* wrote that ethics codes are "supposed to act as the conscience of the professional, of the organization, of the enterprise. … The strength of an ethics code is a function not only of its various principles and mandates, but of its legitimacy and power in the eyes of those for whom it is written."[8]

Codes can be counterproductive if they focus only on what journalists should *not* do. As mentioned in Chapter 1, Roy Peter Clark of the Poynter Institute views such an approach as Red Light Ethics, which places obstacles in the path of journalists trying to report stories that the public needs. Clark's preference is Green Light Ethics, which helps journalists figure out ways to publish or broadcast those stories while behaving decently.[9]

Newsroom codes vary drastically in degree of detail. At one extreme, *The New York Times* published a 54-page "handbook of values and practices for the news and editorial departments" in September 2004. It is a model of clear, carefully explained guidelines. No one expects a staff member to memorize the book, but it is reasonable to expect that journalists *be familiar* with the guidelines and to consult them when the need arises. Like other newspapers, *The Times* has put its code online for instant access.[10]

Commenting on the detailed *Times* code, public editor Manning Pynn of the *Orlando Sentinel* wrote a column playfully suggesting an alternative – a code that would fit on a wallet card. His succinct code also is a model of good counsel: "Don't accept free stuff. Don't cover friends, families – or enemies. Don't use your position for personal benefit. Don't make stuff up. Explain where you got your information. Don't steal other people's work. Don't alter photographs."[11]

SPJ's Four Guiding Principles

The Society of Professional Journalists' 1996 code contains four fundamental guiding principles: seek truth and report it; minimize harm; act independently; and be accountable.

In the SPJ code, these abstract principles appear in large type. Below them, in smaller type, are standards of practice to guide journalists as they try to live up to the principles.

The standards are as specific as the principles are generalized. For the most part, the standards are framed in language that is affirmative ("thou shalt") rather than negative ("thou shalt not"). "This was a conscious choice on the part of the code writers, believing as they did that more professional, ethical behavior will result from conscientious application of principles than from blind obedience to mini-malistic rules."[12]

Each standard represents a consensus of the profession – as in "[d]iligently seek out subjects of news stories to give them the opportunity to respond to allegations of wrongdoing." To compose the standards, the code writers interviewed hundreds of working journalists. They also consulted with philosophers and media critics, and they reviewed the contents of media ethics codes and policy statements.[13]

The four guiding principles are intended to work in tandem, not in isolation. A journalist might have to balance two or more of the principles in making a decision. Frequently, the journalist's duty to seek and report truth conflicts with the desire to minimize harm.[14]

In Point of View "Reporting a Fact, Causing Harm" by William F. Woo, the late editor and teacher decided that in the case of a benefactor who was found to have a skeleton in his closet, "minimize harm" should have trumped "report truth." Woo questioned whether the information about the man's long-ago prison sentence was valuable enough to overcome the harm caused by disclosing it.

The writers of the SPJ code wanted journalists to start their thinking with the "truth" principle, because it is their job to convey information to the public, not to suppress it. Then, in recognition that telling the truth can hurt, "minimize harm" enters the process. In Case Study No. 3 "The Death of a Boy," the tragic accident needed to be reported, even though reading it could deepen the family's pain. You should explore how useful it was to publish the photograph of the boy's distraught mother or to report certain details in the news story. Did the photograph and details inflict unnecessary pain?

As part of your reading for this chapter, review the SPJ code's small-type standards beneath the four large-type guiding principles. To help you in your decision-making in Part II of the book, you need to be familiar with the standards. For that reason, you will find the 1996 SPJ code reprinted in Box 7.1.

Box 7.1   Society of Professional Journalists' Ethics Code

Preamble

Members of the Society of Professional Journalists believe that public enlightenment is the forerunner of justice and the foundation of democracy. The duty of the journalist is to further those ends by seeking truth and providing a fair and comprehensive account of events and issues. Conscientious journalists from all media and specialties strive to serve the public with thoroughness and honesty. Professional integrity is the cornerstone of a journalist's credibility. Members of the Society share a dedication to ethical behavior and adopt this code to declare the Society's principles and standards of practice.

Seek Truth and Report It

Journalists should be honest, fair and courageous in gathering, reporting and interpreting information. Journalists should:

- Test the accuracy of information from all sources and exercise care to avoid inadvertent error. Deliberate distortion is never permissible.
- Diligently seek out subjects of news stories to give them the opportunity to respond to allegations of wrongdoing.
- Identify sources whenever feasible. The public is entitled to as much information as possible on sources' reliability.
- Always question sources' motives before promising anonymity. Clarify conditions attached to any promise made in exchange for information. Keep promises.
- Make certain that headlines, news teases and promotional material, photos, video, audio, graphics, sound bites and quotations do not misrepresent. They should not oversimplify or highlight incidents out of context.
- Never distort the content of news photos or video. Image enhancement for technical clarity is always permissible. Label montages and photo illustrations.
- Avoid misleading re-enactments or staged news events. If re-enactment is necessary to tell a story, label it.
- Avoid undercover or other surreptitious methods of gathering information except when traditional open methods will not yield information vital to the public. Use of such methods should be explained as part of the story.
- Never plagiarize.
- Tell the story of the diversity and magnitude of the human experience boldly, even when it is unpopular to do so.
- Examine their own cultural values and avoid imposing those values on others.
- Avoid stereotyping by race, gender, age, religion, ethnicity, geography, sexual orientation, disability, physical appearance or social status.
- Support the open exchange of views, even views they find repugnant.
- Give voice to the voiceless; official and unofficial sources of information can be equally valid.
- Distinguish between advocacy and news reporting. Analysis and commentary should be labeled and not misrepresent fact or context.
- Distinguish news from advertising and shun hybrids that blur the lines between the two.

Continued

- Recognize a special obligation to ensure that the public's business is conducted in the open and that government records are open to inspection.

Minimize Harm

Ethical journalists treat sources, subjects and colleagues as human beings deserving of respect. Journalists should:

- Show compassion for those who may be affected adversely by news coverage. Use special sensitivity when dealing with children and inexperienced sources or subjects.
- Be sensitive when seeking or using interviews or photographs of those affected by tragedy or grief.
- Recognize that gathering and reporting information may cause harm or discomfort. Pursuit of the news is not a license for arrogance.
- Recognize that private people have a greater right to control information about themselves than do public officials and others who seek power, influence or attention. Only an overriding public need can justify intrusion into anyone's privacy.
- Show good taste. Avoid pandering to lurid curiosity.
- Be cautious about identifying juvenile suspects or victims of sex crimes.
- Be judicious about naming criminal suspects before the formal filing of charges.
- Balance a criminal suspect's fair trial rights with the public's right to be informed.

Act Independently

Journalists should be free of obligation to any interest other than the public's right to know. Journalists should:

- Avoid conflicts of interest, real or perceived.
- Remain free of associations and activities that may compromise integrity or damage credibility.
- Refuse gifts, favors, fees, free travel and special treatment, and shun secondary employment, political involvement, public office and service in community organizations if they compromise journalistic integrity.
- Disclose unavoidable conflicts.
- Be vigilant and courageous about holding those with power accountable.
- Deny favored treatment to advertisers and special interests and resist their pressure to influence news coverage.
- Be wary of sources offering information for favors or money; avoid bidding for news.

Be Accountable

Journalists are accountable to their readers, listeners, viewers and each other. Journalists should:

- Clarify and explain news coverage and invite dialogue with the public over journalistic conduct.
- Encourage the public to voice grievances against the news media.
- Admit mistakes and correct them promptly.
- Expose unethical practices of journalists and the news media.
- Abide by the same high standards to which they hold others.

Reprinted with the permission of the Society of Professional Journalists.

The four guiding principles chosen by the SPJ code-makers are worthy of class discussion because they articulate the most fundamental beliefs of journalists. The sections below are offered as a way to provoke that discussion.

1. Seek truth and report it

From the SPJ code: "Journalists should be honest, fair and courageous in gathering, reporting and interpreting information." That duty is journalists' professional reason for being: to gather information of importance to the community and disseminate it to their fellow citizens.

As you read the standards beneath the "truth" principle in the SPJ code, notice the emphasis on sound techniques of newsgathering and verification.

Any discussion of truth in journalism leads to the overarching question of how to define truth. Indeed, some would argue that truth is an abstract – an ideal to be strived for but not achievable because the facts can be viewed from so many perspectives.

Each day, journalists struggle to piece together a semblance of truth from fragments of information. *The Washington Post*'s longtime politics writer, David Broder, eloquently expressed the difficulty of their mission in this famous summary:

> [T]he newspaper that drops on your doorstep is a partial, hasty, incomplete, inevitably somewhat flawed and inaccurate rendering of some of the things we have heard about in the past twenty-four hours – distorted, despite our best efforts to eliminate gross bias, by the very process of compression that makes it possible for you to lift it from the doorstep and read it in about an hour.[15]

Journalists today tend to agree that truth cannot be achieved through what has been called *objectivity*. In the first half of the twentieth century, objective reporting was the accepted practice. Supposedly bias-free, it stated the surface facts without interpretation or analysis.

Senator Joseph McCarthy of Wisconsin exposed the flaws of objective reporting in the early 1950s with his reckless accusations of communist influence in government. Though he never documented the charges, he reaped the publicity he sought. To objective reporters, statements made by a United States senator met the definition of news whether they were substantiated or not. Though the reporters sought out McCarthy's targets to record their denials, by the time they were published they had been overshadowed by new accusations by McCarthy.

Amazingly, some reporters were aware, through their private conversations with McCarthy, that the charges lacked documentation. That did not keep those reporters from continuing to be conduits for his character assassination.

The McCarthy debacle led journalists to the sober realization that they fail in their mission if they simply write what they are told. Former reporter and educator Tom Goldstein has written that reporters have "a greater responsibility than to just transcribe what someone in authority has to say.[16] … They must dig beneath the rhetoric to get at the primary sources."[17]

Reporting thus becomes a subjective, not objective, process. It requires judgment and an ability to find sources with firsthand knowledge. As journalists go beyond the surface facts to discover context, they must also practice discipline to filter out their biases.

Bill Kovach and Tom Rosenstiel write in *The Elements of Journalism* about the search for what they call "journalistic truth." This version of truth is "more than mere accuracy," although the essential foundation is built by getting the facts straight. Kovach and Rosenstiel write that journalistic truth emerges from "a sorting-out process that develops between the initial story and the interaction among the public, newsmakers, and journalists over time."[18]

In sorting out the facts, the responsible journalist goes where the facts lead, not where his or her private opinions would take the story. Dick Polman, former *Philadelphia Inquirer* politics analyst, is guided by a song lyric by the rock group Steely Dan: "Let's take it where it goes." The journalist, Polman says:

> is a lot like an emergency-room doctor. There is a patient on the table in front of him. The patient could be a thief or a saint, but it doesn't matter to the doctor, because if the doctor is to perform professionally, he or she will suspend personal feelings and take the case wherever it needs to go.[19]

Balance can be a virtue in framing a story if it leads a reporter to examine all sides of a controversy instead of emphasizing a single perspective or the polar opposites.

But reflexively seeking balance can cause distortion. In his book and film *An Inconvenient Truth*, former presidential candidate Al Gore chastised journalists for giving the public the impression that scientists were divided over whether human behavior was causing global warming. Mentioning two studies, he wrote that peer-reviewed articles by scientists showed zero disagreement on the subject, while half of journalists' accounts managed to find dissenting voices.[20]

2. Minimize harm

From the SPJ code: "Ethical journalists treat sources, subjects and colleagues as human beings deserving of respect." If a story is harmful to some stakeholders, the SPJ code obliges journalists to refrain from doing any more harm than necessary in the course of informing the public.

The authors of *Doing Ethics in Journalism* write that minimizing harm is connected to the values of humaneness – values like fairness, compassion, empathy, kindness, respect. "It is based on our responsibility to treat others with decency and to allow them their dignity even in the worst of circumstances. It is connected to a concern for the consequences of our actions."[21]

In the interest of minimizing harm, journalists should omit a detail from a story if its news value does not justify the harm caused by reporting it. For example, newspaper writers routinely consult the electronic archives to see if the subject of an obituary has been in the news. But if the search reveals a single embarrassing incident, recounting that incident in the obituary of an ordinary citizen could be an injustice. (In contrast, the careers of public officials and public figures should be evaluated critically in obituaries. Imagine an obituary of President Richard M. Nixon without mention of the Watergate scandal.)

The concept of minimizing harm might lead to a decision *not* to publish a news development, though most journalists are troubled by the notion of withholding information from the audience.

If law-enforcement officers ask journalists to withhold a certain fact because it might put a kidnapping victim in jeopardy, the journalists are morally obliged to take the request seriously. The Poynter Institute's Bob Steele recommends that journalists would do well to seek the advice of a "rabbi" – in this case, an authority on police matters – to help them assess such a request. Withholding information ideally should be temporary.

In certain situations, information is withheld routinely. Combat correspondents do not report troop movements because doing so would endanger the soldiers. In covering a police siege, broadcast journalists must assume that the hostage-taker has access to a radio or television and for this reason they do not disclose the location of police assault teams. Journalists routinely shield the identity of sex-crime victims, juvenile defendants, and jurors.

Late in 2007, all major news organizations operating in Britain – including the US-based Associated Press and CNN – agreed not to report that Prince Harry had been deployed to combat in Afghanistan. The news organizations agreed to the blackout to avoid jeopardizing the prince, who is third in line to the throne, and members of his unit. They also were promised "special access" to Harry before, during, and after his deployment, and an opportunity to share pooled interviews, video, and photographs taken while he was in the combat zone. Harry's presence in Afghanistan was reported first in an Australian magazine and then on Feb. 28, 2008, by the Drudge Report website. The day after Drudge posted the news, the British military brought Harry home, four weeks before the scheduled end of his 14-week tour.[22]

The leaders of large news organizations have been pressed – sometimes by the president himself – to withhold information that government officials characterize as a threat to national security. Leonard Downie Jr, as editor of *The Washington Post*, cited as an example Dana Priest's stories in 2005 about the CIA's secret interrogation sites abroad. "In the end," Downie said, "we decided to publish the stories but leave out some of the locations for what we decided were legitimate national security risks."[23]

Critics of the news media object that journalists have that kind of authority, noting bitterly that they can override the judgment of officials the people have elected. But, as mentioned in Chapter 6's account of the Pentagon Papers case, the

First Amendment confers that authority so that journalists can inform citizens about government behavior.

By their very presence, journalists can inflict harm. Compassion should be a priority when interviewing ordinary people who find themselves thrust into the news – as, for example, the kin of someone who has been killed in a tragic accident. Even experienced newsmakers are entitled to common courtesy.

Mirthala Salinas, a television newscaster, was herself the subject of media pursuit in 2007 when her affair with Los Angeles Mayor Antonio Villaraigosa became public knowledge (see Chapter 10, Case Study No. 8 "A Love Triangle on the Evening News"). Shawn Hubler, who interviewed Salinas for *Los Angeles Magazine*, described the experience:

> At her condo complex, reporters trooped past the swimming pool, stood on her doormat, and pounded on her door. The doormat said LEAVE. She had bought it as a novelty, but now the joke wasn't funny. "I'd be in my bedroom watching TV, trying not to know they were knocking," she says. Her dogs grew hoarse from barking. "I couldn't leave my house. They would sit at the front door for hours, one reporter in the front, and the other in the back. I wasn't going to come out and be rude, and I wasn't going to come out and give them what they wanted. … I just let them knock on the door. I thought eventually they would get tired." She pauses for a beat. "It took them a long time to get tired. Months."[24]

In the minds of many people, Princess Diana's death in a Paris car crash in 1997 is blamed on the photographers who pursued Princess Diana's automobile in Paris and took pictures of the wreckage. Indeed, Diana's brother, Lord Spencer, blamed not just the so-called paparazzi – photographers who stalk celebrities – but also the editors who publish or broadcast their images. Lord Spencer said: "It would appear that every proprietor and editor of every publication that has paid for intrusive and exploitative photographs of her, encouraging greedy and ruthless individuals to risk everything in pursuit of Diana's image, has blood on his hands today."[25]

Magazine and newspaper circulation and television ratings spiked in the aftermath of Diana's death. *Time*, *Newsweek*, *People*, and *TV Guide* published special commemorative editions. Nearly twenty-six million households in the United States tuned in to the televised funeral.[26]

In the months after the fatal accident, there was a clamor in the United States for laws to limit the press' access to public figures. The mainstream media generally opposed legislation of that kind, while simultaneously expressing disapproval of the methods of the paparazzi.[27] When the late actor Charlton Heston made a speech at the National Press Club two weeks after Diana's death, he took the occasion to tweak mainstream journalists for trying to distance themselves from the paparazzi. Heston said:

> How quick you have been, to finger the paparazzi with blame and to eye the tabloids with disdain. How eager you've been to draw a line where there is none, to demand

some distinction within the First Amendment that sneers "they are not one of us." How readily you let your lesser brethren take the fall, as if their rights were not as worthy, and their purpose not as pure, and their freedom not as sacred as yours.[28]

3. Act independently

From the SPJ code: "Journalists should be free of obligation to any interest other than the public's right to know." The SPJ standards call for avoiding both real and perceived conflicts and for informing the audience about any conflicts that cannot be avoided. Specifically, journalists are urged to refuse gifts and other favors they might be offered to influence them in performing their professional duties.

Journalists are observers; they are not players. They serve a vital role in society by providing reliable information. If journalists take part in the events they cover, they rightfully lose credibility in the eyes of their audience, and the public no longer benefits from the unique service of the neutral observer.

In the months after the September 11 attacks, some journalists – especially on television – started wearing American-flag pins on their lapels. Other journalists worried that their colleagues were sending an ambiguous message. Did the flags mean that the journalists were demonstrating patriotism, concern for the families who lost loved ones in the attack, and support for the troops? Or did the flags represent unquestioning support for whatever military or domestic response the government might take?

Bob Steele of the Poynter Institute, who had served in Vietnam as an Army officer, wrote presciently on September 20, 2001:

> There is nothing wrong with journalists loving their country. And displays of patrio-tism can be a natural expression of that loyalty, particularly during these trying times. But the true measure of journalism's worth to our democracy will be measured not by our outward displays of patriotism, but by the work we produce. Our contribu-tions to the United States of America – and in many respects the global community beyond our borders – will be gauged not by any ribbons and flags we wear, but by the vigor and rigor we bring to our coverage and our commentary.[29]

Possibly because they feared being seen as unpatriotic, most of the news media failed to deliver a critical examination of President George W. Bush's rationale for invading Iraq in 2003. The rationale was that Saddam Hussein posed a threat to the United States because he possessed weapons of mass destruction and because Hussein was allied with Al Qaeda, the Muslim group responsible for the September 11 attacks. After the combat phase ended, no such weapons were found and no link to Al Qaeda was proven. Ultimately, *The New York Times* and *The Washington Post* acknowledged to their readers that they should have asked tougher questions before the invasion. As the costly war extended into years and an Iraqi insurgency inflicted thousands of American casualties, the public's support for the war dwindled. Would the course of history have been changed if the media had asked more probing questions in 2002 and early 2003?

4. Be accountable

From the SPJ code: "Journalists are accountable to their readers, listeners, viewers and each other." This principle is about treating the audience with respect and responding constructively to criticism from the public. In particular, this means being responsive to allegations of factual error or unfairness in reporting the news.

"The quality-driven news organization," Jack Fuller writes in *News Values*,

> examines each serious complaint of error, open to the possibility that it may have been wrong, and takes the time to be sure before either correcting itself or reaffirming the truth of what it said. … [W]hen it errs, such a newspaper quickly and without defensiveness acknowledges its mistake and corrects it.[30]

In addition to a willingness to correct error, accountability translates into a responsibility to police the profession.

The Hutchins Commission, the panel of intellectuals who defined social responsibility of the press in a 1947 report, proposed that journalists "engage in vigorous mutual criticism." It wrote: "Professional standards are not likely to be achieved as long as the mistakes and errors, the frauds and crimes, committed by units of the press are passed over in silence by other members of the profession." The commission called on journalists to discipline each other "by the only means they have available, namely, public criticism."[31]

In a similar vein, the SPJ code instructs journalists to "encourage the public to voice grievances against the news media" and to "expose unethical practices of journalists and the news media."

Today, *American Journalism Review*, *Columbia Journalism Review*, and *Nieman Reports* analyze issues in the news media. Journalists keep abreast of news and commentary about the profession through a popular blog by Jim Romenesko on *poynteronline* and a daily online briefing on the Project for Excellence in Journalism's website. The PEJ's annual *State of the News Media* offers a penetrating analysis of trends.

However, only a handful of media critics work in the news media, and fewer than 40 news organizations have ombudsmen, or public editors, to assess citizen complaints. Ombudsmen have varying degrees of independence to criticize their news organizations. But at minimum, these positions mean that there is someone at those organizations who is dedicated to listening and responding to the public.

News organizations beset by scandal have sometimes unstintingly reported on their own embarrassments. In 1977, Laura Foreman (no relation to this book's author) was found to have been involved in a romantic relationship with a leading political figure while she was covering politics for *The Philadelphia Inquirer*. The editors assigned their Pulitzer Prize-winning team, Donald L. Barlett and James B. Steele, to investigate. The paper published their 17,000-word report.

William Green, who was *The Washington Post*'s ombudsman in 1981, produced an 18,000-word examination – reported and written in just four days – after the paper determined that Janet Cooke had fabricated her Pulitzer Prize-winning story about an 8-year-old heroin addict. Other exhaustive examples of the genre include: the *Los Angeles Times*' 14-page special section reporting on its Staples Center fiasco in 1999; *The New York Times*' 14,000-word analysis and correction of stories that Jayson Blair had fabricated or plagiarized, which ran in 2003 under the headline "Times Reporter Who Resigned Leaves Long Trail of Deception"; *USA Today*'s multiple-story report in 2004 detailing the "journalistic sins" that its reporter Jack Kelley committed between 1993 and 2003; CNN's analysis of its "Valley of Death" documentary in 1998 concluding that the evidence did not support the program's premise that the US military used nerve gas against American defectors in the Vietnam War; and CBS's study of how its 2004 report on President George W. Bush's wartime National Guard record was based on documents whose authenticity could not be proved.

A monitoring institution favored by the Hutchins Commission was an independent panel to review charges against the news media and to render a report that would be published. The National News Council was formed in 1973 for such a purpose, but it died ten years later without ever gaining significant support from the media. In recent years, there have been tepid stirrings of sentiment for such a body to give an aggrieved person an alternative to libel suits as a way of seeking redress for damaging falsehoods. News councils in Minnesota, Hawaii, and Washington continue to monitor the media in their states.[32]

The Minnesota News Council, founded in 1970, is the oldest organization monitoring the news media. Individuals or groups that file complaints with the council waive their right to sue. The council first tries to mediate the dispute, but if that fails, the council can decide to hold a hearing. The hearings "relax legalistic rules of procedure and encourage getting to the heart of the matter," Professor Louise Williams Hermanson wrote in an oral history of the council in 1993. After the hearing, the council issues a written decision that is summarized in a news release and posted on its website. Publicity is the only sanction the council can impose.[33]

In addition to the ability to report the news instantaneously, the World Wide Web offers journalists new ways to be accountable to their audience.

One of these is email. To offer a comment to a journalist in the pre-Internet days, a citizen usually wrote a letter, addressed the envelope, put a stamp on it, and took the missive to a mailbox. The alternative, hardly more convenient, was to try to navigate the company's telephone system to have a conversation with the journalist. Today, most news organizations post email addresses and telephone numbers of staff members on websites and beneath their bylines in newspapers. Although some people abuse that access by making personal attacks and using inappropriate language, serious inquiries get the attention of conscientious journalists. The resulting "conversation" not only makes journalism more transparent to the citizen, but it could result in an exchange of information that improves the quality of the news coverage. Mark Bowden's Point of View "Being Accountable Through a Digital Dialogue" explains how his first experience with web journalism helped him tell a better story.

Another way that news organizations are trying to be accountable is by inviting questions from the audience that then are answered by staff members online. At some news organizations, virtual conversations are conducted in real time; at others, journalists select questions submitted by the audience and write responses that are posted later.

A blog can help a news organization be accountable to the audience. *The New York Times* posted an explanation in 2008 about how the newspaper was covering the resignation of Governor Elliot Spitzer after his involvement with a prostitute was made public.[34] Four editors at *The Spokesman-Review* in Spokane, Washington, write an "Ask the Editor" blog to answer reader questions and explain news decisions.[35]

And then there are the instant critiques from citizen bloggers. Although those critiques may be needlessly abusive, they often have substance. Journalists should welcome such critiquing from the blogosphere. After all, it is in the spirit of the SPJ standard that journalists should "[e]ncourage the public to voice grievances against the news media."

The concept that the media should be accountable raises questions of definition. What do *responsibility* and *accountability* mean?

As Professor Louis W. Hodges of Washington and Lee University defines them in a 2004 essay, "responsibility has to do with defining proper conduct, accountability with compelling it."

Hodges writes:

The distinction is clearly reflected in our common language. Notice the prepositions: we talk about being *responsible for* but *accountable to*. For example, we may be *responsible for* the accuracy of the information we deliver, for informing the reader about government, for not invading privacy or inflicting further hurt on victims of a tragedy. However, we are *accountable to* a government, an editor, a court, or a reader.

Hodges theorizes that confusion about the two words may have led the news media to reject the Hutchins Commission's theory of social responsibility in 1947. "The commission addressed press *responsibility*, but the working press read *accountability*. Journalists and news organizations did not want to be accountable to a bunch of intellectuals on the commission who would judge their performance."

To whom, then, do journalists owe accountability? Hodges' answer is: "All those whose lives and well-being are significantly affected by the professional's conduct." For journalists, he wrote, that list of stakeholders includes the audience, the sources and subjects of news stories, and the journalism profession at large.

Journalists morally owe accountability to anyone they can harm through their work, Hodges writes. It doesn't make any difference whether those people have the power to demand accountability. They are still entitled to it.[36]

Point of View

Reporting a Fact, Causing Harm

William F. Woo

Let me tell you about a man named Frank Prince. I should say, with some relief, that all of this took place before I had anything to do with editing the *Post-Dispatch*.

Prince was a prominent St. Louis businessman and chief stockholder in the Universal Match Company. He gave $500,000 to Washington University, back in the days when half a million meant something. The grateful university decided to name a building after him, and the *Post-Dispatch* assigned a reporter to write a story about the benefactor.

The reporter found that the 71-year-old Prince had served 10 years in prison when he was a young man on charges of bad checks, forgery, and larceny − white-collar crimes. Very few people in the community knew that, and when the story appeared, with all the awful details about a life long ago, readers were outraged. Speak about no good deed going unpunished.

Readers thought the story was a piece of vandalism − destructive, irrelevant, and certainly not newsworthy. The public did not need to know that Prince had done time to understand his generosity.

The journalistic justification for this trashing was what you might expect. The story was relevant to understanding Frank Prince and why, now many years later, he was giving back to society. Put another way, that argument declares journalists are psychologists and are qualified to assert why people act the way they do.

Another journalistic justification was the newsworthiness of the story. When somebody is in the news, as Prince was, people want to know more about them. If Prince didn't wish to have information about his life made public, he could have made an anonymous donation to the university.

You can decide for yourself which of these responses − the criticism or the justification − seems most reasonable to you. My view, as you can gather, is that the readers had it right.

William F. Woo was editor of the *St. Louis Post-Dispatch* from 1986 to 1996, culminating a 34-year career at the paper. For the next 10 years, until his death in 2006, he was the Lorry I. Lokey Professor of Journalism at Stanford University. This essay was excerpted from *Letters From the Editor: Lessons from Journalism and Life* (Columbia, MO: University of Missouri Press, 2007), 160–1. The book was compiled from the letters he wrote to his Stanford students.

Point of View
Being Accountable Through a Digital Dialogue
Mark Bowden

When I was paring down the first draft of my book *Black Hawk Down* to run as a 29-part *Philadelphia Inquirer* serial in 1997, editor Jennifer Musser introduced herself and asked for help.

Musser said she was going to prepare the series for publication on *philly.com*, *The Inquirer*'s website. I assumed that she planned to simply run each day's installment, and assured her that she would receive each day's copy promptly.

"No," she said. "I'm interested in more than that. What kind of source material do you have?"

That was the first clue that Musser's understanding of Internet journalism was a generation ahead of my own. She turned my newspaper story into an Internet phenomenon, packaging it with graphics, video, audio, maps, documents, and a Q&A with its readers. The unfolding series drew in hundreds of thousands of online readers from all over the world. At its height, the electronic version of the story was getting 46,000 hits every day. Her work opened my eyes to the marvelous potential of the web to merge all forms of journalism, and to add something entirely new.

When we invited readers to participate in a Q&A, I had anticipated maybe a dozen or so notes, which would have been a solid response for most newspaper articles. Instead, they flowed in by the hundreds daily, from men who had fought in the battle, from soldiers at military bases all over the world, from appreciative and critical readers. I sat for hours every morning while the series ran, answering them one by one. The author of this textbook, then *The Inquirer*'s managing editor, concerned that the final parts of the series had not been finished, walked by my desk one morning and announced how pleased he was to see me writing away so furiously.

"Is that the last part?" he asked, hopefully (no doubt with visions of my being hit by a truck and the paper being left with its highly popular story unfinished).

"No, Gene, I'm answering the email. If I don't do this every morning I'll never keep up with it."

For the rest of the month I was completely swept up in this digital dialogue. One critical way it vastly improved the story was by giving readers all over the world a chance to instantly correct my mistakes. Military experts are notoriously finicky about getting the details of weaponry and equipment exactly right, and because the format was digital, mistakes were fixed immediately. Readers who received an apology and thanks from me saw that they had contributed directly to the story's accuracy.

This greatly enhanced the account's credibility. Instead of dealing with the reporter as a distant "expert," and speculating on the reasons for mistakes or omissions, readers saw

Continued

my own eagerness to simply get the story right, something which in my experience is the primary motivation of most reporters. Those who sent email messages offering more information on key points in the story were contacted immediately, by phone or email. Interactivity helped to break down the normal wall of suspicion between soldiers and reporters, and I found myself suddenly offered whole new sources of information.

I struggled to take advantage of them as the series unfolded and later spent months plumbing these new sources for the book version. Instead of leaning back and wondering how the work was being received, I was in an arena with my readers, explaining, defending and correcting the story as it unfolded. I never had so much fun with a story.

Mark Bowden is the author of *Black Hawk Down* and six other books, the most recent of which is *The Best Game Ever: Giants vs. Colts, 1958, and the Birth of the Modern NFL.* He is a national correspondent for *Atlantic Monthly* magazine.

Case Study No. 3
The Death of a Boy

The St. Petersburg Times published a story June 6, 1996, on the front of its metro section about a 4-year-old boy who was crushed when a large piece of furniture fell on him in his family's living room. The story was accompanied by a photo of the boy's distraught mother, Marilyn Sue Puniska, 39, as she waited for a helicopter to meet the ambulance carrying her son (Figure 7.1).

The story quoted sheriff's deputies as speculating that the boy, Brett Puniska, was eager to play a videotape in the family's new entertainment center. As he climbed it, they said, he pulled the 400-pound unit on top of himself. The furniture still had casters that workers were to remove the next day. The unit was delivered Saturday, "but there was a problem with it and the family had not per-

manently placed it, pending repairs," a sheriff's spokesman said.

The Times' story related how Brett's 12-year-old sister, in the dining room talking on the telephone, heard the crash and screamed for her mother, who was taking a bath. Mrs Puniska rushed from the bathroom and attempted CPR while Jessica called 911. *The Times'* story also reported:

> Neighbors said the Puniskas had moved into the corner house just weeks ago. Marilyn and her husband, Gabriel J. Puniska Jr, 49, were married in a civil ceremony in Pasco on Valentine's Day 1991, records show.
>
> "I hadn't ever met them," said Karen Kuebler, 36, who lives next door. "They never came over. They never asked for anything." ...

Continued

Pasco boy, 4, dies after furniture crushes him

■ Sheriff's officials say the child was trying to climb a 400-pound entertainment center when it fell on him.

By JOHN HILL
Times Staff Writer

NEW PORT RICHEY — A 4-year-old boy, possibly eager to play a videotape, tried to climb his family's new entertainment center Wednesday.

Instead, young Brett Puniska pulled the 400-pound, 6- by 4-foot unit on top of himself, sheriff's officials said. Despite attempts to revive him, he was pronounced dead at 6 p.m.

The furniture still had casters that workers were to remove today. The unit was delivered Saturday, "but there was a problem with it and the family had not permanently placed it, pending repairs," sheriff's spokesman Jon Powers said.

Officials would not speculate whether the absence of wheels would have prevented the accident.

The tragedy happened about 4:45 p.m. as the boy was alone in the living room of his family's home at 7705 Bass Lane, sheriff's officials said.

Brett's 12-year-old sister, Jessica, was in the dining room talking on the phone. She heard the crash and screamed for the pair's mother, Marilyn Sue Puniska, 39.

Mrs. Puniska, who records show has been a licensed practical nurse, rushed from the bathroom and attempted CPR. Jessica called 911.

At 5:15 p.m., rescue workers took Brett from the peach single-story house and drove him to a golf driving range across the street.

Please see **BOY** 8B

Times photos — TONI L. SANDYS
Marilyn Sue Puniska, the mother of the boy, waits Wednesday for a helicopter to meet the ambulance carrying her son. He was pronounced dead shortly afterward.

Figure 7.1 A mother's anguish
REPRINTED BY PERMISSION OF THE *ST. PETERSBURG TIMES*

Mrs Puniska was distraught while awaiting the medical helicopter. She asked authorities to remove news reporters from the scene, and at one photographer she screamed: "My son's inside half-dead, and you're taking my picture!"

Sheriff's officials said Brett suffered head injuries, though the exact cause of death will be determined by the medical examiner's office. Officials characterized the event as an accident, though the investigation is continuing.

Continued

"At this point there is nothing to indicate the tragic incident was anything but accidental," said [the sheriff's spokesman]. ...

The next day, *The Times* published a feature story about Brett, an active child who loved sports, and told how his parents and sister were coping with their loss. But some readers were still upset by the photograph the paper used with its news story about the accident, the one of Mrs Puniska waiting for the helicopter.

In a column on June 10, Bill Stevens, editor of the regional edition in which the coverage appeared, defended the use of that photograph and similar photographs of tragedies. Below the headline "Powerful images can also be lifesavers," Stevens wrote that they were dramatic, "the kind that tug at your heart." He continued:

> And, yes, they were taken over the objections of Mrs Puniska. These were frantic, terrible moments, and the last thing she needed was reporters and photographers swarming to the scene.
>
> One caller challenged me to put myself in the Puniskas' position. How would I feel if my child had just been killed, and a photographer was taking my wife's picture? "Have you no heart?"
>
> I understand the reaction completely. I understand that aggressive, deadline reporting of breaking news often puts us in the position of defending our actions. But I also believe a newspaper is expected to cover major events in its community thoroughly and accurately.
>
> Almost 20 years ago, we responded to a similar tragedy in New Port Richey when a young boy suffocated in a backyard dirt cave-in. Our photographer captured the parents from a distance near the dirt pile, and many callers expressed their anger the next day when we published the picture and story.
>
> They didn't know that the editor in charge had himself lost a young son to a similar accident while at play. He didn't tell them. Time passed and we moved on to other stories.
>
> Then last year, a woman called me to complain that somebody had left a large pile of dirt near the New Port Richey Recreation Center. She was worried that a child might be killed there, because she remembered a photo and story that we carried all those years ago.
>
> Powerful images.
>
> I regret that our words and images can cause such anguish. In the case of the Puniskas, I am grateful that they welcomed us into their home the next day for detailed discussion of their child. And I am convinced that their decision to share the details ... will save another child's life.

This case is excerpted from Michele McLellan, *The Newspaper Credibility Handbook* with a discussion guide by Bob Steele (Washington, DC: American Society of Newspaper Editors, 2001), 182–7.

Questions for Class Discussion

• What arguments can be made for and against publishing the photograph of the distraught mother at the ambulance? Do you think the photograph should have been published? Note that the photographer was on a public street and had a legal right to take the picture, and that it was taken over the mother's objections.

Continued

- The story includes details about the victim's family. Do any of these details raise fairness questions?
- Some journalists think that by publishing stories and photographs about tragedy, the news media help others by offering

what might be called a "warning bell." Stevens ends his column by saying: "I am convinced that their decision to share the details ... will save another child's life." How do you respond to that justification? Does it work in this case?

Notes

1 Will Irwin, *The American Newspaper: A Series First Appearing in Colliers January – July, 1911* (Ames, IA: University of Iowa Press, 1969), 47–8.

2 Craig Branson, "A look at the formation of ASNE," http://www.asne.org/index.cfm?ID=3460, April 25, 2002.

3 Vernon Stone, University of Missouri, "RTNDA Codes of Ethics and Standards Across Half a Century," http://web.missouri.edu/

4 Jay Black, Bob Steele, and Ralph Barney, *Doing Ethics in Journalism: A Handbook With Case Studies*, 3rd edn. (Boston: Allyn & Bacon, 1999), 27.

5 Edmund B. Lambeth, *Committed Journalism: An Ethic for the Profession* (Bloomington: University of Indiana Press, 1986), 76.

6 Carol Reuss, "Media codes of ethics are impotent, and too often they are facades that imply ethical behavior," in A. David Gordon and John Michael Kittross (eds.), *Controversies in Media Ethics*, 2nd edn. (Boston: Allyn & Bacon, 1998) 58.

7 Author's telephone interview with James M. Naughton, Sept. 14, 2007.

8 Black, Steele, and Barney, *Doing Ethics in Journalism*, 24–5.

9 Roy Peter Clark, "Red light, green light: a plea for balance in media ethics," http://www.poynter.org/content/content_view.asp?id=82553, May 17, 2005.

10 *The New York Times, Ethical Journalism: A Handbook of Values and Practices for the News and Editorial Departments*, September 2004.

11 Manning Pynn, "Ethical guidelines keep journalists on track," *Orlando Sentinel*, Feb. 3, 2008.

12 Black, Steele, and Barney, *Doing Ethics in Journalism*, 28.

13 Ibid., 28.

14 Ibid., 29.

15 David Broder, *Behind the Front Page* (New York: Simon and Schuster, 1987), 14.

16 Tom Goldstein, *Journalism and Truth: Strange Bedfellows* (Evanston, IL: Northwestern University Press, 2007), 21.

17 Ibid., 70.

18 Bill Kovach and Tom Rosenstiel, *The Elements of Journalism: What Newspeople Should Know and the Public Should Expect* (New York: Crown Publishers, 2001), 42–3.

19 Dick Polman, an unpublished essay on writing the news analysis, 2001.

20 Al Gore, *An Inconvenient Truth* (Emmaus, PA: Rodale, 2006), 262–3. The scientific study mentioned by Gore is: Naomi Oreskes, "The scientific consensus on climate change," *Science*, vol. 306, Dec. 3, 2004, 1686.

21 Black, Steele, and Barney, *Doing Ethics in Journalism*, 40.

22 "Prince Harry fights on frontlines in Afghanistan; 3 month tour," http://www.drudgereport.com/flashph.htm, Feb. 28, 2008; Kevin Sullivan, "Prince Harry's seeing combat and British media kept quiet," *The Washington Post*, Feb. 29, 2008; Bob Satchwell, "Why we agreed to a media blackout on Harry," *The Guardian*, Feb. 29, 2008; Tariq Panja, "Britain's Prince Harry in Afghanistan," The Associated Press, Feb. 28, 2008; CNN, "Prince Harry: My withdrawal is a shame," http://www.cnn.com/2008/WORLD/europe/03/01/prince.afghanistan1/index.html, March 1, 2008.

23 "*Post* newsroom leader to retire," an online chat between readers and Leonard Downie Jr, http://

www.washingtonpost.com/wp-dyn/content/discussion/2008/06/24/DI2008062401047.html, June 24, 2008.

24 Shawn Hubler, "The mayor and his mistress," *Los Angeles Magazine*, May 2008.

25 Jacqueline Sharkey, "The Diana aftermath," *American Journalism Review*, November 1997.

26 Ibid.

27 Ibid.

28 Charlton Heston, "The Second Amendment: America's first freedom," speech at the National Press Club in Washington, DC, Sept. 11, 1997; accessed at: http://www.whyonearth.com/heston/heston.html

29 Bob Steele, "A pledge of allegiance for journalists," http://www.poynter.org/content/content_view.asp?id=5897, Sept. 20, 2001.

30 Jack Fuller, *News Values* (Chicago: University of Chicago Press, 1996), 14.

31 Commission on Freedom of the Press, *A Free and Responsible Press: A General Report on Mass Communication: Newspapers, Radio, Motion Pictures, Magazines, and Books* (Chicago: University of Chicago Press, 1947), 94.

32 Ron F. Smith, *Ethics in Journalism*, 6th edn. (Malden, MA: Blackwell Publishing, 2008), 89.

33 Louise Williams Hermanson, "The Minnesota News Council: The story behind the creation," *Oral History Review*, vol. 21, no. 1 (Spring, 1993), © Oral History Association, 23–47. Also, Minnesota News Council home page, http://news-council.org/about/.

34 http://cityroom.blogs.nytimes.com/2008/03/13/the-times-answers-spitzer-scandal-questions/index.html?ex=1363233600&en=c856a93b921a27ef&ei=5088&partner=rssnyt&emc=rss&scp=1-b&sq=q%26A+Spitzer+coverage&st=nyt

35 http://www.spokesmanreview.com/blogs/editors/

36 Louis W. Hodges, "Accountability in journalism," an essay appearing in "Accountability in the professions: accountability in journalism," by Lisa H. Newton, Louis Hodges, and Susan Keith, *Journal of Mass Media Ethics*, vol. 19, no. 3&4, 173–80.

8 Making Moral Decisions You Can Defend

The key ingredients are critical thinking and a decision template

Learning Goals

This chapter will help you understand:

- how journalists' decision-making can draw on their practical skills in gathering facts, analyzing them, and making judgments;
- how critical thinking, or thoughtful analysis, is better than a reflexive response to an ethical question;
- how a step-by-step decision template can guide you to a better decision;
- how to test your decision to see if it can be defended on rational grounds; and
- how to approach the case studies as a laboratory for decision-making.

Think for a moment about what makes journalists so good at what they do.

The distinctive occupational skill they possess – rare in the population at large – is their ability to size up a complicated situation and swiftly produce a summary that is accurate, clear, and engaging.

For the seasoned journalist, it seems intuitive, but it's actually a logical process that requires three steps: First, collect facts. Second, analyze the facts. Third, make judgments – about what facts to include and what to discard, what facts to highlight and what to subordinate.

As an aspiring journalist, you've performed this process in your courses in reporting and editing. You've also learned that practice makes you better.

Now think about making ethical decisions in journalism.

The same skill that serves journalists so well in reporting the news can also be a valuable asset in resolving the ethical challenges of the profession. It too is a skill that can be developed through practice in the classroom, which is why this course is taught through case studies.

At this point in your study of applied ethics in journalism, you're ready to start making decisions.

In Chapters 6 and 7, you became familiar with the classic ethical theories and professional codes of ethics. The ethical theories give you different perspectives for studying an ethical problem and considering how to respond. The professional codes give you the benefit of the conventional wisdom for dealing with the kind of problem you are facing.

Think of the ethical theories and the professional codes as tools in the process you will use to make your decisions. Now you need to add two last items to your toolbox: critical thinking and a step-by-step template.

Critical thinking is a systematic way of analyzing ethical problems; it involves applying logic to the available information. Critical thinking is the opposite of reflexive response. Stopping to think, the ethicist Michael Josephson has written, "is a powerful tonic against poor choices. ... It prevents rash decisions. It prepares us for more thoughtful discernment. And it can allow us to mobilize our discipline."[1]

Having a step-by-step template helps you stay on task as you progress toward your decision. The value of a template, as editor Joann Byrd describes it, is that "when a dilemma falls out of the sky, which most of them have a habit of doing, your decision-making is faster, more efficient and more reliable."[2]

You need all of the decision-making tools because you will face complex moral challenges in journalism. Making decisions is not just deciding between two choices, right and wrong, the authors of *Doing Ethics in Journalism* write:

> True ethical decision making is ... about developing a range of acceptable actions and choosing from among them. It's about considering the consequences of those actions. And it's about basing decisions on obligation, on the principles of the journalist's duty to the public.[3]

Applying Critical Thinking

A journalist's gut feeling of right and wrong has a place in this process, but it's not the *whole* process. If you're morally repelled by a course of action your news organization is considering, don't ignore your instincts. If something *seems* wrong, it may well *be* wrong. This preliminary test is what the author Rushworth Kidder calls the stench test:

Does this course of action have about it an indefinable odor of corruption that makes you (and perhaps others) recoil and look askance? The stench test really asks whether this action goes against the grain of your moral principles – even though you can't quite put your finger on the problem.[4]

However, you need to be able to state your case with logic rather than emotion. As a journalist, you will be called on again and again to explain why you made a certain choice. Members of the audience may confront you and demand an explanation. So might your boss, a colleague, the subject of your story, or a source – any stakeholder in the decision you made. You owe them a better answer than "It seemed like a good idea at the time."

Thus the goal of ethical decision-making is to produce a decision that can be defended on rational grounds. Such a decision may not be embraced by everyone, but a reasonable critic would be obliged to concede that you have deliberated conscientiously and that your arguments are plausible.

The authors of *The Virtuous Journalist* write that "no system of ethics can provide full, ready-made solutions to all the perplexing moral problems that confront us, in life or in journalism." All that can be asked, they write, is that decision-makers take "a reasoned and systematic approach" to finding solutions.[5] That's critical thinking.

In his *Committed Journalism*, scholar Edmund B. Lambeth writes that journalism requires "a capacity for self-detachment, deliberative thought, and reflective scrutiny of events, people and circumstances."[6]

Author Barry Beyer defines critical thinking as "making reasoned judgments." He further defines "reasoned" as arrived at by logical thinking, and "judgment" as determining the degree to which something meets a standard. The word *critical* is derived from the Greek word *kriterion*, a standard for judging. In his book *Critical Thinking*, Beyer writes:

In the broadest sense, critical thinking is judging the quality of anything. Whenever we evaluate our own cooking, someone else's performance of a task, the accuracy of a newspaper or TV account, a work of art, or a researcher's conclusion, we are applying criteria to make a judgment – we are engaged in critical, or criterial, thinking.[7]

Applying a Step-By-Step Template

To carry out that "reasoned and systematic approach," various scholars have created templates outlining an orderly decision process. These templates all have merit, and they all have a great deal in common. They explicitly or implicitly invoke the classic ethical theories and the accepted standards of journalism stated in the codes. They tell the moral agent (decision-maker) to gather facts and use critical thinking to analyze those facts. They prod the decision-maker to identify and evaluate multiple ways to solve the problem. They require the decision-maker not just to state a solution but to defend it as well.

In short, the templates replicate the three-step process that guides the journalists in reporting the news: gathering facts, analyzing them, and making judgments.[8]

The template that this text will use is the straightforward series of ten questions devised by Bob Steele of the Poynter Institute:

1 "What do I know? What do I need to know?"
2 "What is my journalistic purpose?"
3 "What are my ethical concerns?"
4 "What organizational policies and professional guidelines should I consider?"
5 "How can I include other people, with different perspectives and diverse ideas, in the decision-making process?"
6 "Who are the stakeholders – those affected by my decision? What are their motivations? Which are legitimate?"
7 "What if the roles were reversed? How would I feel if I were in the shoes of one of the stakeholders?"
8 "What are the possible consequences of my actions? Short term? Long term?"
9 "What are my alternatives to maximize my truth-telling responsibility and minimize harm?"
10 "Can I clearly and fully justify my thinking and my decision? To my colleagues? To the stakeholders? To the public?"[9]

Look again at Steele's ten questions. As you do, think about the three-step process of reporting the news and about the contents of your decision-making toolbox. For the purpose of this discussion, your author divides Steele's ten questions among the three steps (Steele himself does not compartmentalize them).

Step 1: Collect the information (Questions 1, 2, and 3)

If you do a half-hearted job of assembling facts to answer Question 1 (yes, it's actually two questions), the rest of the process will be flawed. It will be like playing a card game without a full deck.

In Question 2, you articulate the journalistic purpose you are trying to achieve.

That leads you to Question 3, in which you define the ethical issues presented by your answers to the first two questions.

As you define those issues, it could become clear that you are not facing an ethical dilemma at all. The situation could instead be a false ethical dilemma, a concept of the ethicist Michael Josephson that was described in Chapter 2 of this book. Instead of *ethical* values on both sides of the equation – the definition of a true ethical dilemma – one side might have only a *nonethical* value.

Ethical values in journalism include truth-telling, promise-keeping, respecting confidentiality and the right of privacy, fostering fairness and justice, minimizing harm, avoiding conflicts of interest, and fulfilling the journalist's responsibility to inform the public about relevant information even when it is unpopular to do so.

Nonethical values include beating the competition and getting an interesting story that raises circulation, broadcast ratings, or the number of online hits. There is nothing wrong with achieving nonethical values unless you do so at the expense of fulfilling ethical values.

The false ethical dilemma can also be expressed as a clash between what you *should do* and what you *would like to do*.

If you conclude that you are dealing with a false ethical dilemma, you already know your ethical duty. That, however, may not make your decision any easier, because now you have to decide whether you are willing to sacrifice to do the right thing.

Step 2: Analyze the information (Questions 4 through 9)

Your answers to these questions constitute a step-by-step analysis of the information you gathered in Step 1. Here, the ethical theories and ethics codes come into play. Remember the strengths and weaknesses of each of the ethical theories.

To answer Question 4 about professional standards, you can consult your newsroom's code or the advisory codes like the one written by the Society of Professional Journalists. This process also reminds you of the value of rule-based thinking – how it provides a structure for decision-making. You think about the "best practices" embodied in the codes, and consider whether those "best practices" apply to the case at hand. You keep in mind the SPJ code's guiding principles of seeking and reporting truth, minimizing harm, acting independently, and being accountable.

Question 5 suggests that you involve other people in your decision-making process, taking advantage of their experience, expertise and unique perspectives. Some journalists would argue there just isn't time for this kind of discussion. To the contrary, there usually *is* time – and you would be short-changing yourself by making the decision alone. Although you remain responsible for the decision, why not tap into the best advice available?

Sometimes ethical questions can be anticipated and discussed thoroughly before there is a crisis, as the journalists at *The Oregonian* did in preparing to cover Lovelle Svart's last weeks of life (Chapter 1). Ethics scholar Paul Martin Lester's advice (Chapter 4) also is apt: Think like a defensive player in baseball, who ponders choices *before* the ball is hit to him.

Questions 6 (about stakeholders) and 8 (about consequences) ask you to apply ends-based thinking. Think about who will be helped by your decision and who will be harmed.

Question 7 sharpens that process by introducing the Golden Rule and its telling test of empathy – how you would feel if you were a person affected by your decision.

As you consider the benefits and consequences of your decision, you also need to be sensitive to how rationalizations can tempt you to make a self-serving decision instead of an ethically defensible one. That is a dangerous trap. In Point of View "Rationalizations in Decision-Making," Michael Josephson describes the most common rationalizations.

Question 9 directs you to assess the multiple responses you could make to resolve the ethical question, possibly including an Aristotle's Golden Mean. "If you can think of only one or two choices, you're probably not thinking hard enough," Josephson writes.[10]

Step 3: Make a judgment and defend it (Question 10)

This defense is the essence of applied ethics, because you are obliged to explain your decision to the stakeholders. You sift the alternatives and settle on the one you will adopt as your course of action.

To help you evaluate your own arguments, measure your decision against this checklist from Michael Josephson: All decisions take into account the well-being of others. Ethical values always take precedence over nonethical ones. It is ethically proper to violate one ethical principle only when it is clearly necessary to advance another in the given situation.[11]

Then take these three easy tests:

1   *The front-page test:* "How would you feel if what you are about to do showed up tomorrow morning on the front pages of the nation's newspapers?" If you are rationalizing a decision on the basis that people will never know what you did, this test exposes a moral flaw. What has been a private process now becomes public.[12] Rushworth Kidder says, "The truly consistent individual, the one who generally wins our highest praise as an exemplar of virtue, is one whose actions in public and in private are morally identical."[13]

2   *The Mom test:* What would your mother think about your decision? Kidder explains that "the focus here is not only on your mother, of course, but on any moral exemplar who cares deeply about you and means a lot to you." If this test makes you uneasy, "think again about what you are on the verge of doing."[14]

3   *The God-is-my-witness test:* Imagine you have just sworn, hand on a Bible, to tell the whole truth and nothing but the truth and must explain your decision in open court. Donald L. Barlett, winner of two Pulitzer Prizes, says he has concluded that "whatever you are going to write, you need to be comfortable with the idea of relating your story to twelve strangers. If you're comfortable telling your story to a jury, that's the gut check."[15]

Practicing Decision Skills in Case Studies

In Case Study No. 4 "Deciding Whether to Identify a CIA Agent," you can practice the decision template you have just studied. Then you will be ready to move on to Part II of this book, studying areas of journalism in which ethical issues frequently occur and examining how journalists have sought to resolve those issues.

In this case, the ethical theory of ends-based thinking is prominently involved as the journalists weigh the needs of the stakeholders – the public's need for information and the CIA agent's need for protecting his identity. The journalists could apply the Golden Rule and imagine themselves in the position of the agent, who is concerned about his safety and that of his family, as well as his privacy. Aristotle's Golden Mean comes into play as the journalists decide to omit the agent's given first name (using his nickname and surname), and in cautioning him about potentially dangerous personal information he has posted on the web.

The SPJ code's guiding principles of seeking truth and minimizing harm are in conflict in this case. Naming the agent makes the news account more credible and informative, but at the possible cost of endangering the agent and his family. The SPJ code's principle of acting independently comes into play as the journalists deal with government pressure to omit the agent's name. The fourth SPJ principle, being accountable, is applied as the editors explain their decision in an Editors' Note and later in responses to the public editor's questions for his column.

The case studies in this text will help you prepare for the decisions you will make in your journalism career, particularly since you have a duty to justify your choices to your instructor and classmates. The ethicist Deni Elliott writes that the case-study approach of studying ethics will help you:

- appreciate the complexity of newsroom decision making;
- understand the context within which difficult decisions are made;
- track the consequences of choosing one action over another; and
- learn both how and when to reconcile and how and when to tolerate divergent points of view.[16]

There are traps in a class discussion of case studies, but these traps can be avoided. Elliott identifies two of them[17]:

1 *Every opinion is equally valid.* As you debate the choices proposed in your class, it should become clear that some are more likely than others to result in benefits for the stakeholders. At the other extreme, some choices are quite likely to result in harm without significant benefit to anybody. In addition, some choices might fail the test of logic – they cannot be reasonably justified by the facts. So there is going to be a difference in the validity of the opinions offered on a case.

2   *Since we can't agree on an answer, there is no right answer.* Although it is true that there may be more than one ethically acceptable solution to a case, one will probably emerge from the debate as being more logically defensible than the others. More important, certain solutions can and should be ruled out on moral grounds. These wrong answers should be rejected because they cause unjustified harm to stakeholders, or because they violate the shared values of the journalism profession. These values are outlined in *The Elements of Journalism*, the Society of Professional Journalists ethics code, and other statements of professional standards. Deni Elliott lists three values as essential:

- Giving readers, viewers, and online users the information they need.
- Striving for news accounts that are accurate, balanced, relevant, and complete.
- Avoiding unnecessary harm in the course of reporting the news.[18]

So, while your discussions can be highly subjective, everyone should recognize that certain values are nonnegotiable. These values include not just journalistic values but basic human values as well.

Ethics professor Christina Hoff Sommers has written that a typical course in applied ethics (like this one) concentrates on problems and dilemmas in which there can be well-argued positions on all sides. That creates a problem: "the atmosphere of argument and counterargument" reinforces the idea that "*all* moral questions have at least two sides, i.e., that all of ethics is controversial."

To the contrary, Sommers maintains that some things are clearly right and some are clearly wrong. When a television interviewer challenged Sommers to name some uncontroversial ethical truths, she replied:

> It is wrong to mistreat a child, to humiliate someone, to torment an animal. To think only of yourself, to steal, to lie, to break promises. And on the positive side, it is right to be considerate and respectful of others, to be charitable and generous.[19]

In addition to avoiding the traps discussed above, keep in mind that the case studies in this book tend to focus on journalist decisions that are questionable. While that is what makes the cases useful for aspiring journalists to study, remember that the journalists involved were trying to do the right thing. You should remember, too, that the overwhelming majority of journalists' decisions, day in and day out, conform to the ethical standards you are studying in this course.

Box 8.1 provides a template for making decisions in journalism.

Box 8.1 A template for making decisions in journalism

Step 1: Collecting information

1 What do I know? What do I need to know?
2 What is my journalistic purpose?
3 What are my ethical concerns?

Step 2: Analyzing the information

4 What organizational policies and professional guidelines should I consider? *(Resources: rule-based thinking; codes of ethics.)*
5 How can I include other people, with different perspectives and diverse ideas, in the decision-making process?
6 Who are the stakeholders – those affected by my decision? What are their motivations? Which are legitimate? *(Resource: ends-based thinking.)*

7 What if the roles were reversed? How would I feel if I were in the shoes of one of the stakeholders? *(Resource: the Golden Rule.)*
8 What are the possible consequences of my actions? Short term? Long term? *(Resource: ends-based thinking.)*
9 What are my alternatives to maximize my truth-telling responsibility and minimize harm? *(Resource: Aristotle's Golden Mean.)*

Step 3: Making a judgment and defending it

10 Can I clearly and fully justify my thinking and my decision? To my colleagues? To the stakeholders? To the public? *(Resources: the front-page test, the Mom test, and the as-God-is-my-witness test.)*

Point of View

Rationalizations in Decision-Making

Michael Josephson

1 *If it's necessary, it's ethical.* This rationalization is based on the false assumption that necessity breeds propriety. The approach often leads to ends-justify-the-means reasoning and treating nonethical tasks or goals as moral imperatives.
2 *If it's legal and permissible, it's proper.* This substitutes legal requirements (which establish minimal standards of behavior) for personal moral judgment. This alternative does not embrace the full range of ethical obligations, especially for those involved in upholding the public trust. Ethical people often choose to do less than the maximally allowable but more than the minimally acceptable.

Continued

3   *It's just part of the job.* Conscientious people who want to do their jobs well often fail to adequately consider the morality of their professional behavior. They tend to compartmentalize ethics into two domains: private and occupational. Fundamentally decent people thereby feel justified doing things at work that they know to be wrong in other contexts. They forget that everyone's first job is to be a good person.

4   *I was just doing it for you.* This is a primary justification of committing "little white lies" or withholding important information in personal or professional relationships, such as performance reviews. This rationalization pits the values of honesty and respect against the value of caring. An individual deserves the truth because he has a moral right to make decisions about his own life based on accurate information. This rationalization overestimates other people's desire to be "protected" from the truth, when in fact most people would rather know unpleasant information than believe soothing falsehoods. Consider the perspective of people lied to: If they discovered the lie, would they thank you for being thoughtful or would they feel betrayed, patronized or manipulated?

5   *I'm just fighting fire with fire.* This is based on the false assumption that promise-breaking, lying and deceit are justified if they are routinely engaged in by those with whom you are dealing.

6   *It doesn't hurt anyone.* Used to excuse misconduct, this rationalization is based on the false assumption that one can violate ethical principles so long as there is no clear and immediate harm to others. It treats ethical obligations simply as factors to be considered in decision-making rather than as ground rules. Problem areas: Asking for or giving special favors to family, friends or public officials; disclosing nonpublic information to benefit others; using one's position for personal advantage.

7   *Everyone's doing it.* This is a false, "safety in numbers" rationale fed by the tendency to treat cultural, organizational or occupational behaviors uncritically as if they were ethical norms, just because they are norms.

8   *It's OK if I don't gain personally.* This justifies improper conduct done for others or for institutional purposes on the false assumption that personal gain is the only test of impropriety. A related but narrower view is that only behavior resulting in improper financial gain warrants ethical criticism.

9   *I've got it coming.* People who feel they are overworked or underpaid rationalize that minor "perks" – acceptance of favors, discounts or gratuities – are nothing more than fair compensation for services rendered. This is also used as an excuse to abuse sick time, insurance claims, overtime, personal phone calls and personal use of office supplies.

10 *I can still be objective.* By definition, if you've lost your objectivity, you can't see that you've lost your objectivity! This rationalization also underestimates the subtle ways in which gratitude, friendship, anticipation of future favors and the like affect judgment. Does the person providing you with the benefit believe that it will in no way affect your judgment? Would the person still provide the benefit if you were in no position to help?

Excerpted from *Making Ethical Decisions* by Michael Josephson; Wes Hanson, ed. (Los Angeles: Josephson Institute of Ethics, 2002), 27–9.

Case Study No. 4
Deciding Whether to Identify a CIA Agent

Readers of *The New York Times* learned on June 22, 2008, about the success of an obscure CIA interrogator in prying secrets from a captured Al Qaeda leader who was believed to have masterminded the 9/11 attacks in New York City and Washington.

The interrogator, according to the front-page story in *The Times*, asked his questions of Khalid Shaikh Mohammed only after the captive had been subjected by other CIA operatives to cold, sleeplessness, pain, and fear – tactics intended to force him to talk.

The interrogator "came in after the rough stuff, the ultimate good cop with the classic skills: an unimposing presence, inexhaustible patience and a willingness to listen to the gripes and musings of a pitiless killer in rambling, imperfect English."

In addition to providing fascinating detail about the interrogation, which occurred in a CIA prison in Poland 18 months after the 2001 attacks, reporter Scott Shane's account created controversy. It named the CIA analyst who had persuaded Mohammed to talk: Deuce Martinez.

In an Editors' Note accompanying the story, *The Times* explained its decision to identify Martinez over the objections of the CIA and Martinez's own attorney, who protested that naming the interrogator "would invade his privacy and would put him at risk from terrorists or harassment from critics of the agency."

The Times said the name was "necessary for the credibility and completeness of the article." It noted that Martinez "had never worked under cover and that others involved in the campaign against Al Qaeda have been named in news stories and books." Martinez was a 36-year-old CIA analyst at the time of the 2003 interrogation. By the time the 2008 article was published, he had taken a job with a consulting company and was coaching other CIA analysts in their efforts to track terrorists.

The *Times'* article described how Martinez would bring Mohammed snacks, usually dates, and listen attentively as his adversary complained about his accommodations and described his despair over the likelihood he would never again see his children. To gain rapport, Martinez also exploited their common experiences: They were about the same age, they both had attended public universities in the American South (Mohammed at North Carolina A&T and Martinez at James Madison University in Virginia); they both were religious (Mohammed follows Islam; Martinez, Catholicism); and they both were fathers.

Eventually, Mohammed "grew loquacious" and, in a gesture of respect to Martinez, wrote poems to Martinez's wife. He also divulged information about plots, past and planned. He revealed that he himself had beheaded *Wall Street Journal* reporter Daniel Pearl, a claim that the CIA believed because of the detail

Continued

he provided. On June 5, 2008, at his arraignment at the American military prison at Guantanamo Bay, Cuba, Mohammed demanded that he be granted his wish for execution and martyrdom.

After *The Times* published its story, many readers wrote to object that the use of Martinez's name had needlessly endangered him and his family. In a column about the controversy on July 6, public editor Clark Hoyt quoted one of those letters. Suzanne Dupre of Evanston, Illinois, wrote that Martinez "was loyally serving his country in a dangerous job. *The Times* has made him a marked man."

The ethical decision that *The Times* faced in the Martinez case provides a classic example of the tension that frequently exists between the guiding principles of *seek truth and report it* and *minimize harm*.

Hoyt's column framed the controversy:

The episode involved the clash of two cultures, journalism and government intelligence, with almost diametrically opposed views about openness. It raised the difficult question of how to weigh the public's right to know about one of the most controversial aspects of the war on terror, the interrogation of prisoners, against the potential harm in naming an honorable public servant.

One aspect of reporting truth is to offer details that make a news account credible to the audience, and *The Times* feared that its story would not be seen as authentic if its central character went nameless.

Hoyt's column elaborated on the arguments the paper had made in the Editors' Note that accompanied the original story. Hoyt wrote:

The reporter and his editors said that nobody provided evidence that Martinez would be in any greater danger than the scores of others who have been identified in the news media for their roles in the war against Al Qaeda. These include other former CIA officers, the warden at Guantanamo, military prosecutors, the lawyer who wrote the justice Department memos justifying harsh interrogation techniques, and even a New York Port Authority policeman who helped arrest a terrorist.

Hoyt also disclosed that the paper had decided that, since Martinez was so worried, it would not use his first name, only his nickname. In addition, *The Times* had alerted Martinez to the easy accessibility of a website where he had posted considerable personal information, which was removed before *The Times* published its story.

Hoyt interviewed Martinez's lawyer, Robert Bennett, who told him Martinez had been threatened repeatedly by Mohammed and others he interrogated. Until the *Times* story, they did not know his identity, Hoyt wrote, but "[n]ow their friends do, at least to some degree."

"*The Times* and other news organizations have been asked over the years to withhold stories for fear of harm," Hoyt wrote. "And they have done so when a persuasive case has been made that the danger – whether to national security or an individual – is real and imminent. In this case, there is no history of Al Qaeda hunting down individuals in the United States for retribution. It prefers dramatic attacks that kill indiscriminately. And *The Times* took reasonable precautions to prevent Martinez from being easily found."

Continued

As *The Times'* independent public editor, Hoyt sometimes is at odds with the paper's news-coverage decisions. This time he found himself in agreement. He concluded his column:

> I can understand how readers can think that if there is any risk at all, a person like Martinez should never be identified. But going in that direction, especially in this age of increasing government secrecy, would leave news organizations hobbled when trying to tell the public about some of the government's most important and controversial actions.

In preparing his column, Hoyt consulted Bob Steele of the Poynter Institute, who posted his own analysis of the case on *poynteronline*. Steele wrote that the case "powerfully exemplifies the essence of ethics and ethical decision-making process." As he saw it, *The Times'* journalists were wrestling with these competing principles:

- "A duty to report accurate, precise and substantive information about a significant issue or event."
- "An obligation to seriously consider and weigh the consequences to a key stakeholder (Martinez) who is described as very vulnerable to harm."
- "A responsibility to protect journalist independence in the face of pressure to withhold a key element (Martinez's name) from the story."

Steele assigned considerable weight to the importance of the story. He said *The Times* made a compelling argument of that importance in the seventh paragraph of the story itself. There, Shane wrote that the description of Martinez's role "provides the closest look to date beneath the blanket of secrecy that hides the program from terrorists and from critics who accuse the agency of torture."

Using Martinez's name, Steele wrote, "gives readers a clear focal point. Using his name – rather than a pseudonym or just referring to him by title – also heightens the reliability and validity in the reporting process. The story is more believable."

Steele saw little merit in the arguments made by the CIA and Martinez's lawyer that the *Times'* story invaded his privacy or damaged his career. If there are any negative consequences in those areas, he wrote, they "don't appear to me to outweigh a duty to publish the story with Martinez's name included."

A far more serious concern, in Steele's opinion, was the potential safety risk to Martinez and his family. To make that assessment, Steele outlined a process:

> Gather all the facts possible. Verify and scrutinize and make sense of those facts. Consider any missing pieces of the puzzle and how they could change things if known. Hear as many opinions as possible from diverse sources. Identify and recognize various motives of the stakeholders, including the journalists. Examine and challenge any assumptions.

Steele wondered whether *The Times*, in addition to considering the pleas of the CIA and Martinez's attorney, could have consulted with independent experts who might have independently assessed the danger to Martinez and his family.

"In the end," Steele wrote, "this case comes down to a judgment call."

Continued

"*Times* executive editor Bill Keller and his colleagues had to make an ethical decision based on which principle deserved the greatest weight. They chose publishing an accurate, precise and substantive account of an important issue that included Deuce Martinez's name. Additionally, they honored the principle of independence through their process of including various key stakeholders in the deliberations. They were transparent and accountable in giving readers information on why and how they made their decisions.

"Ethics is about principles and process. Well-intentioned, thoughtful people can and will disagree."

Questions for Class Discussion

- Visualize how Scott Shane's story would have read if its central character had gone nameless or had been given a pseudonym. Do you agree that the story would have been less credible to readers? Do you agree that this particular story's importance gives added significance to the issue of credibility?
- Analyze the arguments that the CIA and Martinez's attorney made for keeping his name out of the story. Do you agree that the story invades Martinez's privacy or damages his career? That it placed him and his family in danger?
- Now, considering the arguments you have analyzed in the first two questions, put yourself in the place of *Times* executive editor Bill Keller. Would you have included Martinez's name in the story?

Notes

1 Michael Josephson, *Making Ethical Decisions* (Los Angeles: Josephson Institute of Ethics, 2002), 21.
2 Joann Byrd, comments at an American Society of Newspaper Editors conference in 2003, posted on www.asne.org, March 31, 2005.
3 Jay Black, Bob Steele, and Ralph Barney, *Doing Ethics in Journalism: A Handbook With Case Studies*, 3rd edn. (Boston: Allyn & Bacon, 1999), 51.
4 Rushworth M. Kidder, *How Good People Make Tough Choices: Resolving the Dilemmas of Ethical Living* (New York: HarperCollins, 1995), 159.
5 Stephen Klaidman and Tom L. Beauchamp, *The Virtuous Journalist* (New York: Oxford University Press, 1987), 20.
6 Edmund B. Lambeth, *Committed Journalism: An Ethic for the Profession* (Bloomington: University of Indiana Press, 1986), 152.
7 Barry Beyer, *Critical Thinking* (Bloomington, IN: Phi Delta Kappa Educational Foundation, 1995), 8–9.
8 In *Ethics in Media Communications: Cases and Controversies*, 5th edn., Louis A. Day also divides the decision process into three steps, which he labels SAD: (S)ituation Definition, (A)nalysis, and (D)ecision.
9 Bob Steele, "Ask these 10 questions to make good ethical decisions," http://www.poynter.org/content/content_view.asp?id=4346, Feb. 29, 2000.
10 Josephson, *Making Ethical Decisions* (2002), 23.
11 Michael Josephson, *Ethical Issues and Opportunities in Journalism* (Marina del Rey, CA: The Josephson Institute, 1991), 23–4.
12 Kidder, *How Good People Make Tough Choices*, 184.
13 Ibid., 193.
14 Ibid., 184.

15   Author's telephone interview with Donald L. Barlett, Oct. 10, 2007.

16   Deni Elliott, "Cases and moral systems," in Philip Patterson and Lee Wilkins, *Media Ethics: Issues and Cases*, 6th edn. (New York: McGraw-Hill, 2008), 18.

17   Ibid.

18   Deni Elliott, "All is not relative: Essential shared values of the press," *Journal of Mass Media Ethics*, vol. 3, no. 1 (1988), 28–32.

19   Christina Hoff Sommers, "Teaching the virtues," *Public Interest*, vol. 111 (1993, Spring), 3–13.

Part II Exploring Themes of Ethics Issues in Journalism

This part of the book challenges you to practice the decision-making skills you learned in Part I.

Each of the chapters 9 through 17 discusses a topic in which all journalists – print, broadcast, online – frequently confront ethics issues:

Chapters 18 and 19 discuss ethics issues that are specific to the following specialized areas:

Chapter 20 assesses the unresolved ethics issues of a profession in transition:

9 Stolen Words, Invented Facts ... Or Worse

Plagiarism, fabrication, and other mistakes that can kill a career

---

Learning Goals

This chapter will help you understand that:

- plagiarism and fabrication are morally wrong – *plagiarism* is stealing the creative work of another, *fabrication* is making things up and presenting them as fact;
- the offenses of plagiarism and fabrication destroy journalism's credibility and can cost offenders their jobs and their careers;
- illegal acts are unacceptable in the pursuit of news;
- journalists should follow sound work practices to avoid any hint of impropriety; and
- newsroom leaders have a duty to establish clear rules about journalistic malpractice and to enforce them.

Leonard Pitts Jr of *The Miami Herald* devoted his nationally syndicated column on March 11, 2005, to lending support to the outspoken comedian Bill Cosby, who was then embattled over an allegation of sexual misconduct.

"*I like hypocrites,*" Pitts began his column. "*You would, too, if you had this job. A hypocrite is the next best thing to a day off. Some pious moralizer contradicts his words with his deeds and the column all but writes itself. It's different with Bill Cosby.*"

On May 12, *The Daily Tribune News* in Carterville, Georgia, published a column under the byline of its associate managing editor, Chris Cecil. "*I like hypocrites,*" it began. "*You would, too, if you had this job. A hypocrite is the next best thing to a day off. Some pious moralizer contradicts his words with his deeds and the column all but writes itself. It's different with Bill Cosby.*"

Alerted by one of his readers, Pitts checked *The Daily Tribune News'* website and found eight of Cecil's columns in the preceding three months that replicated Pitts' prose. The Pulitzer Prize winner's next column was an indignant open letter to Cecil. Pitts called the Cosby column "a wholesale heist" in which "you essentially took my name off and slapped yours on." The dictionary, Pitts wrote, "is a big book. Get your own damn words. Leave mine alone." When *The Daily Tribune News'* publisher learned of the plagiarism, he immediately fired Cecil.[1]

Compared with high-profile miscreants like Jayson Blair and Jack Kelley, Chris Cecil is an obscure entry in the annals of journalistic malpractice. But Cecil nevertheless finds himself in rare company: His is one of only four known cases of "appropriation plagiarism" committed by full-time journalists in American daily newspapers in an entire decade, from 1997 through 2006.

The statistic and the term are from Norman P. Lewis' 2007 doctoral dissertation at the University of Maryland. Appropriation plagiarism, Lewis wrote, is "blatantly taking another's work without any pretense or uncertainty of what the rules are." He further described appropriation plagiarism as either "serial" or "brazen" or both.[2]

Altogether, Lewis identified 76 cases of plagiarism during the 10 years. He limited his study to full-time employees because "newspapers are most heavily invested in those workers, and an evaluation of full-timers would more accurately reflect how newspapers respond to plagiarism cases." His study thus excluded weekly newspapers, college newspapers, and cases at daily newspapers involving part-timers, nonstaff correspondents, freelancers, or college interns.[3]

Of Lewis' cases, 67 were "research plagiarism" – "blending someone else's words with original reporting or failing to sufficiently paraphrase to disguise the copying."[4]

Lewis also identified three cases of "idea plagiarism," involving the borrowing of the ideas for editorial cartoons or editorials.[5] The remaining two cases were "self-plagiarism," in which writers recycled material they had written for previous employers, without crediting the original publisher; Lewis acknowledged that self-plagiarism is "an imprecise concept."[6]

Defining Plagiarism and Fabrication

Plagiarism is one of two offenses that journalists regard as egregious sins worthy of dismissal. The other is *fabrication*, which is making things up and passing them off as genuine.

Plagiarism and fabrication both transgress against the audience. They destroy the credibility of the journalist and the news organization.

Plagiarists take credit for phrases, sentences, paragraphs, or even an entire story that someone else created. In "The Unoriginal Sin," his seminal essay on the subject in 1983, Roy Peter Clark of the Poynter Institute wrote that plagiarism is "a form of deception ... a violation of language ... a substitute for reporting."[7]

To fabricate, print reporters can invent scenes, characters (including composites of real characters), and quotations to embellish stories. Print photographers can manipulate images or present posed photographs as "found moments." Broadcast journalists can distort what happened by indiscriminately adding sound effects and music, staging misleading reenactments, or abusing special visual effects. Given the wide range of techniques at their disposal, online journalists can deceive in any of those ways.

When they occur, plagiarism and fabrication tend to be committed by journalists who find themselves under pressure to meet high expectations, either their bosses' or their own. Deadlines exacerbate the stress of relentless competition with other media outlets or with their own colleagues. Plagiarists and fabricators give in to delusions: that the pressure is so great that they have no choice; that no one will ever know of their moral shortcut; or even that fictional technique can express a greater truth.

Like many journalism professors, Cynthia Gorney thought the rules were so fundamental that she did not need to spell them out for her students in the Graduate School of Journalism at the University of California at Berkeley. After reading about a spate of plagiarism and fabrication incidents, she changed her mind.

"In the interest of clarity, and with a heavy heart," she wrote in an open letter to her students, "I articulate them now:

"Don't steal.
"Don't lie.
"Don't make things up and pretend that's reporting."[8]

Some perspective is in order. To read the journals and blogs that discuss journalism issues, one could assume that malpractice is common in the profession. The Internet and its search engines assure that any offense, irrespective of degree, becomes common knowledge everywhere. "In the Internet age, there's no rug under which to sweep these problems," *Washington Post* media critic Howard Kurtz wrote in 2005.[9]

Thomas Kunkel, then dean of the University of Maryland's Philip Merrill College of Journalism, told Kurtz that "because we are self-policing so much better, it makes it seem like there's a tremendous cascade of ethical violations. There used to be a lot more in the way of shenanigans and monkey business that we either didn't know about or, if it was caught, it was winked at. There was a boys-will-be-boys quality about it – they were mostly boys – and they would get a slap on the wrist at best."[10]

Jim Romenesko's blog on *poynteronline*, begun in 1999, is so widely read in the profession that his influence has been labeled by *Slate* media critic Jack Shafer as "the Romenesko effect." Shafer praises Romenesko for improving journalism by casting light on its misdeeds. "The site functions brilliantly as an ad hoc, post-publication, peer-review mechanism for the journalistic profession."[11]

The instant peer reviews, as well as the tendency of news organizations to make a public disclosure of ethical breaches by their staffs, carry out one of the "be accountable" standards of the Society of Professional Journalists' code. That standard says, "Expose unethical practices of journalists and the news media."

A side-effect of the disclosures – or perhaps it is just another manifestation of the cynicism discussed in Chapter 5 – is that what journalists see as departures from the norm, the public sees as the norm. In The Freedom Forum's Free Press/ Fair Press surveys in 1998, 76 percent of the respondents said journalists often or sometimes plagiarize, and 66 percent said journalists often or sometimes make up stories and pass them off as real.[12]

More subtly, the public expresses its mistrust by *not* calling news organizations to account when scenes and quotations have been blatantly invented. After Jayson Blair's fabrication and plagiarism in *The New York Times* were exposed in 2003 (see below), Harvard media analyst Alex Jones told *USA Today*'s Peter Johnson that he was troubled because people who were quoted by Blair didn't contact *The Times* to say they had never talked with the reporter. "They didn't say, 'Holy cow, this is somebody who is clearly unscrupulous.' Instead, their response was to shrug their shoulders and say, 'Hey, what do you expect?' "[13]

After the Blair episode, the Associated Press Managing Editors assigned 15 newspapers to contact readers through mass emails to ask why people would fail to tell the papers about obvious errors. One reader wrote back, "What's the point? Do they really care?" The most common explanations readers gave for not contacting the paper were that surely someone in the newsroom would correct obvious errors; that it would take too much time to navigate the newspaper's corrections system; and that the readers thought inaccuracies were intentional in a journalism "that glosses over the fine points and hypes storytelling."[14]

It is worth noting, in contrast to the public's perceptions of widespread malpractice, that the 76 instances of plagiarism identified in Norman Lewis' study took place over an entire decade in a total workforce of 55,000 journalists in America's daily newspapers. Even allowing for incidents not detected or reported, that is relatively small. (A comparable statistical study of fabrication has not been performed.)

To be sure: Although both plagiarism and fabrication vary in degree of seriousness and of intent to deceive, they are *always* morally wrong. And they always give the audience a reason to doubt the work of journalists. Roy Peter Clark, referring to cases of plagiarism, wrote: "Like defensive pass interference in football, they may be blatant or accidental, but they always deserve the yellow flag."[15]

Six Cautionary Examples of Plagiarism and Fabrication

When journalists talk about plagiarism and fabrication, these are the cases they usually bring up.

Janet Cooke, *The Washington Post* (fabrication, 1980)

"Jimmy is 8 years old and a third-generation heroin addict," Cooke wrote in *The Post* on September 28, 1980. Every day, someone "fires up Jimmy, plunging a needle into his bony arm, sending the fourth grader into a hypnotic nod."[16] When Washington authorities asked *The Post* to identify Jimmy so that they could help him, *The Post* refused, saying it would protect its sources.

On April 13, 1981, Cooke's story won the Pulitzer Prize for feature writing. The Associated Press story about the prize reported that she was a Phi Beta Kappa graduate of Vassar and had attended the Sorbonne in Paris, academic achievements she had listed on her Pulitzer entry form. When the AP story was read by staff members at *The Blade* in Toledo, Ohio, where she had formerly worked, they told *The Post* that the statements about her education were untrue.

In lengthy questioning, Cooke broke down and confessed. The next day, she submitted her resignation and a statement in longhand that included the admission, "I never encountered or interviewed an 8-year-old heroin addict." *The Post* returned the Pulitzer Prize.[17]

Stephen Glass, *The New Republic* (fabrication, 1998)

In his two-and-a-half-year career, Glass was a prolific magazine writer who wrote fantastic stories. Having worked as a fact checker at *The New Republic*, he knew how to fool the people assigned to contact his sources and authenticate his reporting. He escaped detection when he made up stories like the ones about "The First Church of George Herbert Walker Christ" and a "get-naked" room at a conservative political conference.

On May 18, 1998, *The New Republic* published Glass' "Hack Heaven," a story about a 15-year-old hacker who had extorted a high-paying job with Jukt Micronics in exchange for not penetrating its databases. *Forbes Digital Tool*, a website covering the industry, thought that was an interesting story and assigned a reporter to check it out. The Forbes reporter could find no evidence that Jukt Micronics existed. His editor called *The New Republic*'s new editor, Charles Lane, who demanded verification from his writer. Glass offered a phone number – that of his brother, who then posed as a Jukt executive in his conversation with Lane – and a Jukt website Glass had created himself. Lane discovered the ruse and fired Glass.

Later, the magazine acknowledged fabrications in 27 of the 41 articles Glass had written.[18]

Patricia Smith, *The Boston Globe* (fabrication, 1998)

In four years as a metro columnist, Smith turned out beautifully written essays about characters who said amazing things. Like the woman named Claire who learns that a drug has cured cancer in mice and wants it to cure her own cancer: "Hell, if I could get my hands on it, I'd swallow the whole … mouse." Superbly talented in both prose and poetry, she was in demand as a speaker at writing workshops.

Doubts about the veracity of her columns had been raised in the *Globe* newsroom for at least 3 years. After the Claire column, and after others in which the paper could not locate people she described, an editor confronted her about six suspicious characters. She admitted that four of the six were made up. With that, Smith resigned.

In a farewell column on June 19, 1998, Smith wrote: "From time to time in my metro column, to create the desired impact or slam home a salient point, I attributed quotes to people who didn't exist. I could give them names, even occupations, but I couldn't give them what they needed most – a heartbeat."[19]

Smith has since written two widely acclaimed books of poetry: *Teahouse of the Almighty*, a collection of narratives, and *Blood Dazzler*, an account of Hurricane Katrina.

Mike Barnicle, *The Boston Globe* (plagiarism and fabrication, 1998)

In a 25-year run as a columnist, Barnicle was a favorite of the paper's working-class readers. He frequently came under suspicion that he was fabricating. It was plagiarism, however, that set in motion the events that led to his departure from the paper. His August 2, 1998, column contained jokes similar to those in comedian George Carlin's 1997 book *Brain Droppings*. The columnist said he hadn't read Carlin's book, but then a Boston television station showed a video clip of Barnicle promoting the book. When Barnicle refused to resign, *Globe* editor Matthew V. Storin suspended him for two months.

In the midst of that controversy, *The Globe* heard from the retired editor in chief of *Reader's Digest*, Kenneth Tomlinson. Three years earlier, the *Digest* had wanted to reprint a Barnicle column about two young cancer patients who formed a friendship in the hospital, but the *Digest*'s fact-checkers had been unable to confirm the story. Tomlinson now told *The Globe* that he had rejected Barnicle's article as a fabrication. When Barnicle could not authenticate the cancer victims' story, Storin again demanded Barnicle's resignation. This time he got it.[20]

The cases of Barnicle, a white man, and Patricia Smith, an African American woman, are linked because some critics, including the famous lawyer Alan Dershowitz, accused *The Globe* of a double standard in the handling of their cases.[21] Afterward, Storin acknowledged concern about giving that impression. He said editors had held off confronting Smith "because of unproved allegations over the years that Barnicle had engaged in some fictions."[22]

Since leaving *The Globe*, Barnicle has been successful on the national scene. He is a political analyst for MSNBC and appears regularly on the network's "Hardball with Chris Matthews" and "Morning Joe" as well as NBC's "Today."[23]

Jayson Blair, *The New York Times* (plagiarism and fabrication, 2003)

Blair, hired as a reporter at *The Times* at age 23, resigned under pressure 4 years later as the paper investigated the stories he had written. The triggering incident was a purported interview in Los Fresnos, Texas, with the mother of a soldier who died in Iraq.

On April 18, reporter Macarena Hernandez had written for *The San Antonio Express-News*: "So the single mother, a teacher's aide, points to the ceiling fan he installed in her small living room. She points to the pinstriped couches, the tennis bracelet still in its red velvet case and the Martha Stewart patio furniture, all gifts from her first born and only son."

Blair's story for *The Times* on April 26 began: "Juanita Anguiano points proudly to the pinstriped couches, the tennis bracelet in its red case and the Martha Stewart furniture out on the patio. She proudly points up to the ceiling fan, the lamp for Mother's Day, the entertainment center that arrived last Christmas and all the other gifts from her only son, Edward."

In addition to the similarities in the two stories, there was a problem with the Martha Stewart furniture: Still in boxes, it had never been placed on the patio. After Hernandez's editor notified *The Times*, Blair's story and ultimately his reporting career unraveled. Mrs Anguiano said Blair had never visited her.[24]

On May 11, *The Times* issued a report on its investigation that started on the front page and covered four full pages inside. The report said Blair:

> misled readers and *Times* colleagues with dispatches that purported to be from Maryland, Texas and other states, when often he was far away, in New York. He fabricated comments. He concocted scenes. He lifted material from other newspapers and wire services. He selected details from photographs to create the impression he had been somewhere or seen someone, when he had not.

He was found to have plagiarized or fabricated in at least 36 articles.[25]

Journalists on the *Times'* staff and elsewhere demanded to know how Blair's deceptions could have gone undetected for so long. The internal investigation showed that the paper had frequently run corrections of Blair's stories and that several supervisors had raised questions about his performance, including metropolitan editor Jonathan Landman, who in 2002 sent an email to newsroom administrators: "We have to stop Jayson from writing for *The Times*. Now."[26] The scandal eventually led to the resignation of the newsroom's top two leaders, executive editor Howell Raines and managing editor Gerald Boyd.

Jack Kelley, *USA Today* (plagiarism and fabrication, 2004)

Kelley, who joined *USA Today* during its founding year of 1982 as an editorial assistant, rose quickly to become the paper's star reporter. For years he roamed the world, sending back eyewitness accounts of stunning sights. In his report on the 2001 bombing of a pizzeria in Jerusalem, he wrote: "Three men, who had been eating pizza inside, were catapulted out of the chairs they had been sitting on. When they hit the ground, their heads separated from their bodies and rolled down the street." A *USA Today* investigation would later show that Kelley was 90 feet from the pizzeria, he had his back turned when the bomb went off, and none of the adult victims were decapitated.[27]

Eventually the paper decided to check the veracity of his stories. Kelley was forced to resign in January 2004 after *USA Today* investigators confronted him over a deception. The investigators had discovered that Kelley, trying to persuade them of the truth of a story from the Balkans, had arranged for a Russian translator to impersonate a Serbian translator. In a telephone call to *USA Today*, the impersonator said she had witnessed Kelley's interview with a Yugoslav human-rights activist.[28]

The newspaper reported on March 21, 2004, that Kelley's "most egregious misdeed occurred in 2000, when he used a snapshot he took of a Cuban hotel worker to authenticate a story he made up about a woman who died fleeing Cuba by boat. The woman in the photo neither fled by boat nor died, and a *USA Today* reporter located her this month." *USA Today* also said evidence contradicted numerous other accounts of intrepid reporting by Kelley, including going on a high-speed hunt for Osama bin Laden in 2003.[29]

USA Today said Kelley had on dozens of occasions used "material from other news organizations or wire services without crediting them."[30]

Besides its detailed report on the results of the investigation, *USA Today* made public an internal report by a team of three distinguished retired editors who had been asked to determine how Kelley's deceptions could have gone undetected. The team said that Kelley's editors had failed to be vigilant and diligent and that some staff members had reported being "scolded and insulted" when they voiced suspicions about his stories.[31] In the wake of the Kelley disclosures, *USA Today* editor Karen Jurgensen retired from the job she had held in the last 5 years of Kelley's time at the paper. Manager editor Hal Ritter resigned.

Two Cases in Which Journalists Broke the Law

In rare cases journalists have broken the law in the course of their work. The following are two noteworthy episodes.

R. Foster Winans, *The Wall Street Journal*

A writer of the "Heard on the Street" column in *The Journal* in the early 1980s, Winans realized that mentioning a company favorably or unfavorably in the column could cause the company's stock to rise or fall. Winans got involved in an illegal conspiracy using his – and *The Journal*'s – ability to move markets. He would tip off a broker about what he was going to write, the broker would invest before publication, and then the broker would share the profits with Winans and his roommate. Federal regulators became aware of the scheme, which they said netted a total of $675,000, only $31,000 of which went to Winans and his roommate. Winans and the others were convicted in 1985 of mail and wire fraud and securities fraud. Winans served eight months in prison.[32]

Mike Gallagher, *The Cincinnati Enquirer*

Under the headline "Chiquita Secrets Revealed," *The Enquirer* published an 18-page investigation report on May 3, 1998, charging that the Cincinnati-based fruit conglomerate had bribed foreign officials and had mistreated its Central American workers. On June 28, *The Enquirer* published another huge headline, "An Apology to Chiquita," at the top of its front page, and beneath it the newspaper expressed regret for "creating a false and misleading impression of Chiquita's business practices."

What happened in the interim was that Chiquita convinced executives of *The Enquirer* and its owner, Gannett, that reporter Mike Gallagher had illegally tapped into the voicemail of Chiquita executives. Gannett also paid $14 million to Chiquita and fired Gallagher. On September 24, 1998, Gallagher pleaded guilty to unlawful interception of communications and unauthorized access to computer systems. Gallagher avoided jail – he was sentenced to five years probation and 200 hours of community service – by cooperating in the prosecution of a Chiquita lawyer who had given him the voicemail passwords. On June 30, 1999, the lawyer, George Ventura, pleaded "no contest" to misdemeanor counts of attempted unauthorized access to computer systems. He received two years of unsupervised probation and 40 hours of community service.[33]

The legal resolution of the case left a lingering question: Was the original reporting about Chiquita true? The Gannett apology did not specifically retract "the factual underpinnings" in the 18-page investigative report, First Amendment lawyer Bruce W. Sanford wrote later. "At the heart of the mystery lay one immutable truth," Sanford wrote. "The editorial integrity of a newspaper (and its financial integrity) depends upon the journalistic integrity of its reporters. Theft is not a protected First Amendment activity."[34]

Work Practices That Avoid Plagiarism

The SPJ code of ethics addresses plagiarism in one of the standards listed under the guiding principle of "seek truth and report it." The code says simply, "Never plagiarize."

In his doctoral dissertation, Norman Lewis wrote that the brief treatment of plagiarism in the SPJ code demonstrates how the profession views the subject as an uncomplicated issue. He sees it differently. "Plagiarism generally is regarded as copying words, but there is no standard for how much copying is unacceptable." His review of newspaper ethics codes found these characterizations of unacceptable copying: "words," "phrases," "distinctive language," and "wholesale lifting."[35]

Lewis also differs with those who contend that inadvertent copying does not constitute plagiarism, although he thinks absence of intent is a mitigating factor to be considered in determining punishment of someone who has plagiarized. He recommends that the industry develop a detailed definition as a step toward consistency in defining offenses and determining punishment.[36]

In an article in *Journalism and Mass Communication Quarterly*, Lewis urged that the industry reevaluate plagiarism as a "one of the worst offenses." He maintains that "other credibility-detracting infractions … rarely result in dismissal, such as when a reporter is caught in a compromising relationship with a source or produces a story so inaccurate a front-page correction is required."

As Lewis sees it, news outlets contradict themselves: They refuse to acknowledge that a competitor had a story first, yet they inflict severe penalties on reporters who insufficiently paraphrase the competitor's story. "Journalists treat plagiarism more seriously because it unmasks *the pretense of originality*" (italics in the original).[37]

"In the absence of any industry-wide guidelines, editors are pretty much on their own to judge the offense and punish it as they wish," Trudy Lieberman wrote in *Columbia Journalism Review*. "Some may use it to get rid of a reporter they don't like, or others may bend over backwards to retain a valued staff member." When editors try to tailor the punishment to fit the seriousness of the offense, Lieberman wrote, there sometimes is uneven treatment at the same publication.[38]

Although Lewis favors the principle of tailoring punishment, his research produced an example of the kind of unevenness Lieberman mentioned. There were plagiarism incidents at the *Columbus* (Ohio) *Dispatch* in 2002 and 2005. In the first case a *Dispatch* journalist copied 111 words from *The Washington Post*, and there was no punishment; three years later, another staff member copied 123 words from *Columbus Business First*, and the reporter was fired.[39]

Lewis, now a professor at the University of Florida, advises his students: Attribution is the opposite of plagiarism, so attribute everything you don't see or hear yourself. "If your editors think there's too much attribution in your story, let them take it out."[40]

Plagiarism often is blamed on bad note-taking. Using the copy-and-paste function, reporters can move chunks of text from the Internet into their computers. Lewis says the process is so easy that journalists have to remind themselves to be meticulous about identifying sources. They have "an affirmative obligation" to prevent errors.[41]

Reporters must tell the audience where they found quotations that they did not hear. Using other reporters' quotations without acknowledgment is called "lifting quotes." Decades ago, this was an acceptable practice in most places. Now it is not.

Professor Edward Wasserman of Washington and Lee University addressed the topic in a 2005 column:

> I write a news story and include comments from somebody I didn't talk to. I don't tell you I got them from another paper. Why is that bad?
>
> Two reasons.
>
> First, if the comments haven't been reported so widely that they're basically public domain – like the president's remarks in a news conference – you will figure I'm vouching for the accuracy of the quotes. And I can't. By concealing my source I've misled you about the authenticity of the report. That matters.
>
> The second problem may matter less: I've helped myself to someone else's work. The reporter who tracked down and spoke to the source got no recognition.[42]

As more consumers turn to the Internet for their news, the trend could have the effect of increasing the amount of attribution and decreasing incidents of plagiarism. That would happen if crediting original sources through hyperlinks becomes a routine practice in writing news stories.[43]

Work Practices That Avoid Fabrication

[handwritten annotation: fabrication is something made up, like a lie]

In contrast to the cursory treatment of plagiarism, some national ethics codes provide more substantive guidance for avoiding fabrication.

SPJ's standards rule out "deliberate distortion" and direct journalists to:

- "Never distort the content of news photos or video. Image enhancement for technical clarity is always permissible. Label montages and photo illustrations."
- "Avoid misleading reenactments or staged news events. If reenactment is necessary to tell a story, label it."

The National Press Photographers Association's code says, "Editing should maintain the integrity of the photographic images' content and context. Do not manipulate images or add or alter sound in any way that can mislead viewers or misrepresent facts."

The Radio Television News Directors Association's code says, "Professional electronic journalists should not manipulate images or sounds in any way that is misleading," and journalists should not "present images or sounds that are reenacted without informing the public."

Photo illustrations present a fabrication question for photojournalists and the designers of newspaper and magazine layouts. The SPJ code's standard says these photographs, which depart from the principles of documentary news photography, should be labeled.

These topics are discussed in more detail in Chapter 19.

Setting and Enforcing Standards

News organizations treat plagiarism and fabrication as more serious offenses than factual mistakes in reporting. These offenses frequently result in firing or forced resignation; 43 of the 76 journalists involved in Norman Lewis' plagiarism study lost their jobs.[44] In addition to disciplining the staff member, the news organizations usually disclose the offense. Their reasoning is that the audience, having been deceived, is entitled to know.

Newsroom leaders are perplexed over how to curb plagiarism and fabrication.

Their editing procedures are designed to catch and correct the human errors of honest journalists. Anyone who sets out to fabricate probably will succeed, at least for a while.

For the managers, then, the question is: Should we continue to operate on the basis of mutual trust? Or should we modify our procedures in order to catch the occasional rogue?

The consensus seems to be: Somewhere in between.

Trust is vital in a newsroom, and leaders undermine it if they treat everyone as a likely fabricator. Professor Russell Frank of Pennsylvania State University, a former newspaper journalist, said it would be hard to imagine the effect on morale in a newsroom in which every statement in every story is questioned. He told Lori Robertson of *American Journalism Review* that if a reporter was asked if he really went to the places mentioned in his story, he probably would respond: "Well for crying out loud, I wrote it. Of course I did."[45]

Still, newsroom leaders need to be alert to patterns of fabrication and, when they spot them, to investigate. They need to edit with a healthy sense of skepticism that picks up on quotes and scenes that seem too good to be true. The essence of skeptical editing is that reporters, veterans and rookies alike, are asked about crucial facts: "How do you know this?" This is a reality check for honest reporters who may be jumping to conclusions. It also could catch the rare fabricator.

As for plagiarism, leaders likewise should investigate promptly and thoroughly when they receive any hints of violations. Equally important, they should be clear to their staffs about how they define plagiarism. They should examine whether they are fostering plagiarism by condoning, for example, sports notebook columns based on notes shared by beat reporters in other cities.

Everyone in the newsroom should feel comfortable telling management in confidence when ethical violations are suspected, even if they are only hunches. In the Janet Cooke case, several *Washington Post* staff members doubted her story but did not go to the top editors. One of the doubters was reporter Jonathan Neumann, himself a Pulitzer winner. Neumann told the National News Council investigators in 1981, "[W]e felt it wouldn't be fair to put her on the carpet when we couldn't prove anything."[46] In the Jack Kelley case, *USA Today* staff members who challenged his veracity were rebuffed by editors, the blue-ribbon investigative panel concluded.[47]

In its 2005 ethics code, the *Los Angeles Times* told staff members that they have a duty to report unethical behavior. The code says, "If you know of anything that might cast a shadow on the paper's reputation, you are expected to inform a supervising editor. This can be an uncomfortable duty; under some circumstances, it can do harm to one's relationships with others in the newsroom. It is a duty nevertheless."[48]

Journalists who make wrong choices about plagiarism and fabrication may lose their jobs and careers. The pain of humiliation could last a lifetime.

Consider the lament of a journalist fired for plagiarism, a woman who was interviewed on condition of anonymity for Norman Lewis' research. Anyone doing a Google search of the journalist's name, Lewis wrote, will find "not a quarter-century of achievement, but the one time she forgot to paraphrase."

The journalist told Lewis: "With it out there on the Internet, it's out there forever."[49]

Notes

1 Leonard Pitts Jr., "Chris Cecil, plagiarism gets you fired," *The Miami Herald*, June 3, 2005.

2 Norman P. Lewis, *Paradigm Disguise: Systemic Influences on Newspaper Plagiarism*, 2007, https://drum.umd.edu/dspace/bitstream/1903/6803/1/umi-umd-4289.pdf, 162–6. In an adaptation of his thesis, Lewis published "Plagiarism antecedents and situational influences," *Journalism and Mass Communication Quarterly*, vol. 85, no. 2, Summer 2008, 313–30. In the adaptation, Lewis revised the number of appropriation plagiarism cases from five to four, and increased the number of research plagiarism cases from 66 to 67.

3 Lewis, *Paradigm Disguise: Systemic Influences on Newspaper Plagiarism*, 58–9.

4 Ibid, 166–82.

5 Ibid, 183–5.

6 Ibid, 182–3.

7 Roy Peter Clark, "The unoriginal sin," originally written for the March 1983 issue of *Washington Journalism Review* (now *American Journalism Review*). "The unoriginal sin" was posted on poynter.org in July 2000; http://www.poynter.org/content/content_view.asp?id=133454

8 Cynthia Gorney, "Getting it right," *American Journalism Review*, March 2001.

9 Howard Kurtz, "Ethics pressure squeezes a few out the door," *The Washington Post*, May 2, 2005.

10 Ibid.

11 Jack Shafer, "The Romenesko effect," *slate.com*, April 18, 2005.

12 Two surveys were conducted by the Freedom Forum Media Studies Center in September and October 1998. One survey involved a national sample of 1,016 adults, with a margin of error of plus or minus three percentage points. The other surveys were separate random samples of 400 adults in Boston and Cincinnati, with a margin of error of five percentage points. The results were reported by Michael White, "Survey: Public thinks journalists often guilty of ethical lapses," The Associated Press, Oct. 16, 1998.

13 Peter Johnson, "Media weigh in on 'journalistic fraud,'" *USA Today*, May 12, 2003.

14 Associated Press Managing Editors, "Readers respond: Why we don't alert media to mistakes," posted on poynter.org on May 19, 2003.

15 Clark, "The unoriginal sin."

16 Janet Cooke, "Jimmy's world: 8-year-old heroin addict lives for a fix," *The Washington Post*, Sept. 28, 1980.

17 *After Jimmy's World: Tightening Up In Editing* (New York: The National News Council, 1981), 16–25.

18 Sources for the Stephen Glass case: Buzz Bissinger, "Shattered Glass," *Vanity Fair*, September 1998; Lori Robertson, "Shattered Glass at The New Republic," *American Journalism Review*, June 1998;

Howard Kurtz, "Stephen Glass waits for prime time to say 'I lied,'" *The Washington Post*, May 7, 2003.

19 Sinead O'Brien, "Secrets and lies," *American Journalism Review*, September 1998.

20 O'Brien, "For Barnicle, one controversy too many," *American Journalism Review*, September 1998.

21 O'Brien, "Secrets and lies."

22 Matthew V. Storin, "Some practical advice from a crisis-buffeted editor," included in Robert H. Giles, ed., *Media Mistakes of '98*, a booklet published by the Freedom Forum Media Studies Center.

23 The Official Mike Barnicle Website, http://www.mikebarnicle.com/

24 Jacques Steinberg, "*Times* reporter resigns after questions on article," *The New York Times*, May 2, 2003; Howard Kurtz, "Reporter resigns over copied story," *The Washington Post*, May 2, 2003.

25 "*Times* reporter who resigned leaves long trail of deception," *The New York Times*, May 11, 2003.

26 Ibid.

27 Blake Morrison, "Ex-*USA Today* reporter faked major stories," *USA Today*, March 21, 2004.

28 Kurtz, "*USA Today* found hoax before writer confessed," *The Washington Post*, Jan. 13, 2004.

29 Blake Morrison, "Ex-*USA Today* reporter faked major stories," *USA Today*, March 24, 2004.

30 Rita Rubin, "Material without attribution," *USA Today*, March 21, 2004.

31 Bill Hilliard, Bill Kovach, and John Seigenthaler, "The problems of Jack Kelley and *USA Today*," a memorandum to publisher Craig Moon, published in *USA Today*, April 22, 2004.

32 R. Foster Winans, *Trading Secrets* (New York: St. Martin's Press, 1986), 140–61, 301–6.

33 Nicholas Bender, "Damage report: After the Chiquita story," *Columbia Journalism Review*, May–June 2001.

34 Bruce W. Sanford, "Chiquita lesion: Libel isn't weapon of choice," American Society of Newspaper Editors, Oct. 15, 1998

35 Lewis, *Paradigm Disguise*, 6.

36 Ibid, 206.

37 Lewis, "Plagiarism antecedents and situational influences," 323.

38 Trudy Lieberman, "Plagiarize, plagiarize, plagiarize … only be sure to always call it research," *Columbia Journalism Review*, July/August 1995.

39 Lewis, *Paradigm Disguise*, 216–17.

40 Author's telephone interview with Norman P. Lewis, Feb. 25, 2008.

41 Lewis, *Paradigm Disguise*, 155.

42 Edward Wasserman, "What is 'original' journalism anyway?," *The Miami Herald*, May 30, 2005.

43 Lewis, *Paradigm Disguise*, 210.

44 Ibid, 90.

45 Lori Robertson, "Confronting the culture," *American Journalism Review*, August–September 2005.

46 *After Jimmy's World*, 22.

47 Hilliard, Kovach, and Siegenthaler, "The problems of Jack Kelley and *USA Today*."

48 *Los Angeles Times* Ethics Guidelines, July 13, 2005. Accessed at http://www.asne.org/ideas/codes/losangelestimes.htm

49 Lewis, *Paradigm Disguise*, 138.

10 Conflicts of Interest: Divided Loyalties

Journalists owe their first allegiance to the audience

Learning Goals

This chapter will help you understand:

- the damage that a conflict of interest inflicts on a journalist's credibility;
- the definition of a conflict of interest, and the distinction between an *actual* and an *apparent* conflict;
- guidelines for avoiding conflicts of interest, actual or apparent; and
- situations that can lead to conflicts.

When investigative reporter Bill Dedman of *msnbc.com* ran a computer search of Federal Election Commission records in 2007, he turned up the names of 143 journalists who had made political contributions dating back to 2004.

Explaining the ethical significance of his finding, Dedman wrote: "There's a longstanding tradition that journalists don't cheer in the press box. They have opinions, like everyone else, but they are expected to keep those opinions out of their work. Because appearing to be fair is part of being fair, most newsrooms discourage marching for causes, displaying political bumper stickers, or giving cash to candidates."[1]

In an age when public records can be searched easily, making a contribution is not a private act – it's the electronic equivalent of putting a candidate's bumper sticker on your car.

William Powers of the *National Journal* scoffed at Dedman's report. With blogging, podcasting, and other kinds of "citizen journalism," Powers wrote in his magazine, "the curtain has been pulled back, revealing actual human beings. To the extent that media outlets deny this by pretending that their employees have no views on politics and other topics – or that those views don't influence the coverage – they come off as charlatans." He proposed that news organizations post their staff members' biases online so the audience could take them into account.[2]

Powers' idea appeals to some in the profession. But news organizations – newspapers, broadcast stations, and online news sites – are moving in the opposite direction. Through their ethics codes, they are telling journalists to avoid taking public positions on divisive issues and to shun involvement in the political process other than casting their votes in private. Their concern is that credibility suffers if it appears journalists put loyalty to partisan causes ahead of their duty to report the news fairly and impartially. As Dedman wrote, "appearing to be fair is part of being fair."

News organizations make no pretenses about whether their staff members have opinions. They know they do. But editors and news directors insist on two things:

- First, opinions must be filtered out of the reporting. Good reporters go where the facts lead them, not where their opinions would take them.
- Second, journalists must avoid taking public positions on controversial public issues – or *any* issues that they themselves cover or make news decisions about. To reveal one's opinions is to invite the audience to find bias in news coverage where it does not exist.

Consider this analogy: A football referee announces before the big game, "I'm going to call this game fair and square, but it's obvious to me that Team A is the best on the field today." Late in the game, a close play decides the outcome in favor of Team A. The referee called the play fairly, exactly the way he saw it, but he's not going to convince the fans of Team B that they weren't robbed.

Is it any wonder that referees keep their opinions to themselves? Shouldn't journalists, who wear the striped shirts in the news arena, be just as discreet?

The issue of reporters' political contributions offers an insight into the some-times-complex subject of conflict of interest.

Defining "Conflict of Interest"

Journalists owe their primary loyalty to the audience – the readers, listeners, viewers, and online users. Nothing should divert them from serving the audience to the best of their ability. Journalists have a *conflict of interest* if they allow self-interest, or a loyalty to any other person or organization, to take precedence over their duty to the audience.

A journalist who allows self-interest to interfere with his or her reporting is committing a flagrant violation of trust. Given the level of integrity in the profession, such instances are rare.

More often, what the audience sees is *an appearance* of a conflict. But appearances count. Knowing that a journalist makes political contributions – or otherwise asserts political opinions – can cause audience distrust even though the journalist, like the referee in the analogy, is doing an honest job.

Consider another analogy: If you are sick, you trust your physician to do what is best to help you get well. The physician owes primary loyalty to you. Several drugs might be effective in treating your condition, and let's say the physician chose the one he or she honestly thought to be most effective. Later, you learn that the physician earned a free vacation trip by writing a certain number of prescriptions of the drug you were given. Wouldn't you be suspicious? (In 2002, the federal government warned pharmaceutical companies not to offer financial incentives to doctors to prescribe certain drugs.)[3]

Just as a patient deserves the doctor's best medical judgment, the journalist's audience deserves news judgment that is not influenced by anything other than the journalist's own professional skill and experience. Avoiding conflicts of interest is all about carrying out the SPJ code's guiding principle of acting independently.

Some journalists – such as William Powers, whose opinion is quoted above – think an *apparent* conflict is nothing to worry about. Their reasoning is that only an *actual* conflict is a problem. Jeffrey Olen, in his 1988 book *Ethics in Journalism*, made the scholarly argument for this point of view:

> [C]onflict of interest problems for journalists can easily be overstated. The overstate-ment appears in the code, with the claim that journalists ought to avoid even the appearance of conflict. If media organizations wish to adopt that policy in order to project an enhanced image of trustworthiness to their audiences, that is one thing. But such a policy is not morally required. All that is morally required is that journal-ists, like anyone else, be trustworthy.[4]

With due respect, this text takes the opposite point of view. This text presumes that an editor or news director will not tolerate a journalist who is *not* trustworthy – that is, someone who commits an *actual* conflict of interest by distorting the news to fulfill a self-interest. However, the public usually lacks the concrete facts to judge whether a journalist is trustworthy. And so, if a journalist *appears* to have a conflict, the skeptical (or cynical) public is going to assume that he or she *does* have a conflict. For that reason, the majority view in the profession is that any hint of a conflict should be avoided. The profession collectively made that decision in the 1970s, when emerging newsroom codes banned the acceptance of gifts from news sources. Up to that time, journalists who took the gifts rationalized that they could still act independently. By banning the so-called freebies, the profession was saying that the only convincing way to assure the public of their independence was to say no to freebies. The concept of an apparent conflict, of course, applies to many situations besides the acceptance of freebies.

"We journalists, knowing that we are pure in heart, may dislike having to meet the unreasonable test of others' perceptions of us," the distinguished broadcast com-mentator Daniel Schorr wrote in 1983. "But isn't that the test we invented for those who wield influence in the society?"[5] "Men and women in the news busi-ness cannot allow their motives to become suspect," John L. Hulteng wrote in *Playing It Straight*.[6]

Both the news organization and the journalist bear a responsibility to act inde-pendently. They owe each other integrity.

To avoid conflicts, the news organization has an obligation to insulate its journalism from the commercial function, especially the sale of advertising, and to be careful that the company's civic activities do not compromise its journalism. Business-side conflicts are the subject of Chapter 11.

For the journalist, the responsibility to act independently means forgoing some privileges and even constitutional rights that other people enjoy. "Journalists have no place on the playing fields of politics," *The New York Times* declares in its ethics code. *Times* staff members may not run for office. They may not campaign for or give money to candidates, ballot causes, or efforts to enact legislation. They may not wear campaign buttons. They may not march in support of public movements or sign ads taking a position on public issues.[7] The *Times*' code, which generally reflects the values found in other newsroom codes but is far more comprehensive than the rest, is a supplemental text for this chapter and can be accessed at http://nytco.com/pdf/NYT_Ethical_Journalism_0904.pdf.

"We have no ideology in this newsroom," Leonard Downie Jr said in an online chat with readers after he had announced his retirement as editor of *The Washington Post* in 2008. "Our only bias is for a good story and accountability journalism. The only political activity our journalists are allowed to engage in is voting, and even that I don't do. No personal or financial support for candidates or issues. No demonstrating. No petition signing."[8]

The journalist might be conflicted – or appear to be conflicted – because of activities in these principal areas, which are discussed below:

- personal financial interests such as accepting gifts, holding a part-time job, or making investments;
- publicly stated opinions on controversial issues;
- involvement in off-the-job civic activities; and
- relationships with the subjects of news coverage.

Avoiding Conflicts of Interest

Journalists should be keenly aware that their acquaintances and news subjects see them in their professional role on a 24/7 basis. Even when they are off duty, they are judged by what they say or do.

Most newsroom codes make it clear that staff members can comfortably choose to be involved in community activities that are unlikely to attract news coverage – activities like parent-teacher associations, Little League sports, and neighborhood associations. However, the journalist should be conscious of his or her 24/7 professional role and use common sense to avoid likely conflicts. For example, it is perfectly acceptable for a journalist to be an active member of a church, synagogue, or other religious group. But the journalist should avoid serving on a committee protesting the location of a casino near the parish, because the committee's actions may well become a subject of news coverage.

When a conflict is unavoidable or insignificant, it should be disclosed to the audience. For example, the law firm representing a newspaper or broadcast station might receive news coverage for its work on behalf of other clients, and when that happens, it is appropriate to advise the audience that the firm also represents the news outlet. This brief mention tells the audience: "We're going to be fair in how we cover our law firm, but we're informing you of the association so that you can be the judge." This is called a *disclosure*.

If a conflict can be avoided, it should be. A disclosure in such a case is insufficient. Airlines and resorts might provide a free trip to a travel writer – an experience that the writer is supposed to evaluate for the benefit of potential paying customers. The writer's disclosure of the arrangement, while better than hiding it, does little to reassure readers. In the first place, the people providing the complimentary flight, lodging, and meals know that the writer is going to describe the experience, so they likely will lavish more attention on the writer than on the average customer. Another reason for the reviewer to be upbeat is the desire to get invitations to future junkets.

News organizations recognize that the actions of a staff member's spouse or "significant other" are beyond their control, but they require the staff member to inform them of any conflict that might arise from the relationship. "In a day when most families balance two careers, the legitimate activities of companions, spouses and other relatives can sometimes create journalistic conflicts or the appearance of conflicts," *The New York Times*' ethics code states. If, for example, a reporter is covering a political campaign and his or her spouse becomes a consultant to one of the candidates, the reporter has a duty to tell editors about the arrangement – and the reporter can expect to be reassigned.[9]

Like *The Times*, most newsrooms give their staffs written conflict-of-interest codes. Although such codes clearly cannot cover all situations that might arise, they are valuable because: (1) They provide guidance on dealing with the most common problems and set a tone for resolving problems that are not explicitly covered; (2) They inform the journalist in advance of the conduct that is expected, so that people are less likely to violate the code or to take personal offense when their activities are questioned.

Problem Areas for Conflicts

This section discusses several situations in which conflicts might occur. The four case studies accompanying this chapter – a larger-than-usual number because conflicts arise in such diverse ways – also are intended to give you a better understanding of the issues. In addition, you should also review *The New York Times*' ethics code. Bear in mind that not even *The Times*' extensive newsroom code can cover all situations that you might encounter, but even in these situations you can be guided by extrapolating from the code and applying common sense.

Freebies

Accepting gifts from people they cover is a onetime journalistic tradition now banned by newsroom codes. Although it is quite likely some freebies are accepted today, there is near-universal agreement that they are wrong.

To get an idea what it was like in the heyday of freebies, consider the tradition of "the divvy" among members of the Pennsylvania Legislative Correspondents' Association, an organization of Capitol reporters in Harrisburg. Every year during the holidays, the association received gifts of liquor from state officials, which the reporters then divided among themselves. The association ended "the divvy" in 1972, much to the dismay of veteran reporters who called themselves "the old guard." In a history, former reporter Gary Tuma reminisced:

> To most of the old guard, the divvy was one of the most cherished customs of a job they loved. The newsroom used to sponsor a legendary Christmas party in the Capitol, and in that season of good cheer the reporters annually received plenty of it, sent over from the Liquor Control Board by the case, brought in by lobbyists, and carried by state officials who strolled in smiling with both fists wrapped around the neck of a bottle. It was the good stuff, too.[10]

An editor who pioneered in banning freebies was J. Russell Wiggins, who was successively the managing editor, executive editor, and editor of *The Washington Post* between 1947 and 1968. When Wiggins died on November 19, 2000, Katharine Graham, chairman of *The Post*'s executive committee, wrote a tribute that was published in the paper. Graham wrote that on his arrival in 1947:

> Russ immediately made several changes that had a significant impact on the quality and integrity of the paper. First, he eliminated favors – free tickets for sports reporters, free admissions to theaters for critics, and parking tickets fixed by police reporters for people all over the building. This sounds elementary, but in those days it was done everywhere.[11]

The Times' code says: "Staff members may not accept gifts, tickets, discounts, reimbursements or other inducements from any individuals or organizations covered by *The Times* or likely to be covered by *The Times*. (Exceptions may be made for trinkets of nominal value, say $25 or less, such as a mug or a cap with a company logo.)"[12]

Secondary income

Newsroom codes generally allow journalists to do freelance work on their own time, with significant exceptions. The journalist cannot accept assignments that would interfere with his or her work for the primary employer.

Typically, the codes prohibit working for a competitor, or for a person or institution that the news organization covers.

Payments to a journalist from a third party, especially the government, pose a troubling question of divided loyalties. Kelly McBride of the Poynter Institute said, "Any time anyone gives you money, you have a loyalty to them, and that's a conflict."[13] The *Times'* code says:

> Staff members may not accept employment or compensation of any sort from individuals or organizations who figure or are likely to figure in coverage they provide, edit, package or supervise. ... Staff members may not accept anything that could be construed as a payment for favorable coverage or as an inducement to alter or forgo unfavorable coverage.[14]

In 2005, the conservative commentator Armstrong Williams was revealed to have received money from the federal government. A company owned by Williams received $241,000 from the Education Department to promote the No Child Left Behind law on his syndicated television show and to interview Education Secretary Rod Paige for television and radio spots.[15] Williams' company, in its billings to the government, showed he promoted the law at least 168 times in his syndicated columns and appearances on radio and television.[16] (He later repaid $34,000.)[17]

The Miami Herald reported in 2006 that 10 South Florida journalists had received thousands of dollars to appear on Radio Marti, a US government station whose radio and television broadcasts are aimed at undermining the communist regime in Cuba. Jesus Diaz Jr, publisher of *The Herald* and its Spanish-language affiliate, *El Nuevo Herald*, fired two *El Nuevo Herald* reporters and a freelance contributor who had received the government money. The dismissals led to a backlash in Miami's Cuban American community, prompting Diaz to resign three weeks later. Diaz said that in receiving the Radio Marti money, the journalists had committed "a breach of widely accepted principles of journalism ethics." But, he said later, the paper's policies prohibiting such conduct had not been clearly communicated in the *El Nuevo Herald* newsroom. Diaz said the reporters were offered their jobs back after credibly making the case that their editors had given them permission to appear on Marti. Carl Hiaasen, columnist for *The Miami Herald,* told National Public Radio that journalists in his newsroom would never have been allowed to accept money from the government, but it was different at *El Nuevo Herald*. "You're either the voice of the free press, or you're the voice of the government," Hiaasen said.[18]

Taking a public position on controversial issues

As noted in Bill Dedman's reporting on campaign contributions, newsroom codes discourage or prohibit journalists from taking public stands on controversial issues or getting involved in politics other than voting. Defining "controversial issues" is, of course, a judgment call. Can a garden columnist take part in a debate over a public school's sex-education course? While it is conceivable that a journalist might publicly express an opinion on relatively minor issues that he or she does not cover or make news decisions about, those exceptions should be rare. When members of the audience find journalists expressing opinions, they are not apt to make distinctions about who covers what.

Linda Greenhouse, who reported on the Supreme Court for *The New York Times,* participated in a 1989 abortion-rights march in Washington, which led to a reprimand from her editors.[19] In 2006, Greenhouse, whose coverage of the Supreme Court had won the 1998 Pulitzer Prize for beat reporting, was awarded the Radcliffe Institute Medal at Harvard University. On that occasion she made a speech in which she said:

> [O]ur government … turned its energy and attention away from upholding the rule of law and toward creating law-free zones at Guantanamo Bay, Cuba, Abu Graib, Haditha, and other places around the world. And let's not forget the sustained assault on women's reproductive freedom and the hijacking of public policy by religious fundamentalism.[20]

Four months after her Harvard speech, the then-public editor of *The Times*, Byron Calame, wrote a column saying that Greenhouse appeared to have gone beyond what she was allowed to say under the *Times'* ethics code, which cautions staff members not to "say anything on radio, television or the Internet that could not appear under his or her byline in *The Times*.[21] Calame quoted executive editor Bill Keller as saying in an email to him that the standard applies to all *Times* journalists "when they speak in public." Calame further quoted Keller as saying he had talked with Greenhouse about her remarks but would not disclose what he said.[22]

Interestingly, Calame's predecessor as *The Times'* public editor, Daniel Okrent, was outspoken in his defense of Greenhouse's speech. Okrent said that he handled thousands of complaints from the public during his term as public editor, but that not one of those complaints was about Greenhouse's reporting. "She demonstrates very clearly that no matter how strongly [she] feels about the issues … it doesn't affect the quality of her work or the way people perceive it," Okrent told National Public Radio.[23]

After retiring from *The Times*, Greenhouse gave her perspective on the two incidents in an interview in 2008 with a former *Times* colleague, Charles Kaiser, who posted the transcript online.

On the 1989 march, she said that before marching, "I made it perfectly clear in the office that I was doing this. Nobody raised an eyebrow. ... It was just obvious to everybody that, as a private citizen, I had a perfect right to do what I was doing. I went with three friends from my college class. You know, it wasn't under a banner that said 'New York Times Reporter For Choice.' We were just four women in a group of half a million." She said that after *The Washington Post* rebuked its staff members who had marched, *Times* editors expressed objections to her. "I just realized I was being thrown overboard as a sacrificial lamb for the greater good of journalistic ethics."

As for the 2006 speech, Greenhouse said: "I gave a kind of generational narrative. It wasn't a political rant at all. It wasn't intended by me to be a political speech, nor was it received by the audience that way." She said National Public Radio reported on "raw-meat sentences out of a half-hour speech" several months later, and "the editors failed to stand up for me."[24]

Journalists need to remind themselves that the Internet is a very public place; their web postings and even their email messages may be widely read. For that reason, they should be careful about expressing opinions about people and events in the news. Journalists could regret opinions they post informally on their own and friends' pages on Facebook and other networking sites, Also, on Facebook, people can declare themselves to be "friends" with other members – an appearance of conflict for a journalist if a "friend" is a news subject or source.

One of the political donors identified by Bill Dedman on *msnbc.com* was Calvert Collins, a reporter for the Fox television station KPTM in Omaha. In addition to giving $500 to Democratic congressional candidate Jim Esch, Collins posted a photo of her and Esch on her Facebook page with a caption: "Vote for him Tuesday, Nov. 7!" She told Dedman that she was trying to build rapport with the candidates and that her father wrote the check for the donation made in her name. She said she realized the photo was a mistake and removed it when her boss heard of it.[25] Soon after Dedman's article was posted, Collins left KPTM and joined KLAS in Las Vegas.

Rosemary Armao left her job as managing editor of the Sarasota (Florida) *Herald-Tribune* in June 2002 after she and a reader had an email exchange about the paper's lengthy profile of Katherine Harris, the ultimately successful Republican candidate for Congress. The reader complained to Armao that it was a "one-sided puff piece." Armao defended the article as balanced and fair, but then went on to write, "She's going to be the next congresswoman from this area, like it or not. ... I do not intend to vote for Harris. ... I blame the Democrats for not finding a better candidate." The email became public. Editor Janet Weaver told Armao that her response damaged the paper's credibility, but Armao argued that all journalists have opinions and should be straightforward and frank with their readers. Recognizing that the two editors were at an impasse, Armao resigned and moved to the *South Florida Sun-Sentinel* as state and investigations editor.[26]

Reporters who appear on television and radio talk shows are frequently invited to express their opinions on the news and to speculate on outcomes. The *Times'* code, in addition to stating that journalists may not say things they could not write under their bylines, discourages appearances on "strident, theatrical forums that emphasize punditry and reckless opinion-mongering."[27] Amy Goldstein, a Pulitzer Prize-winning reporter for *The Washington Post*, said: "It has become fashionable for reporters to go on TV and, when they do, they often are asked to give their opinions. There is a lot of pressure to do that. A reporter needs to say up front, 'I don't want to get those questions. If I do get them, I'm going to duck them.'" She said she prefers the practice of broadcast hosts like Gwen Ifill on Public Broadcasting Service, who, Goldstein said, invite guests "to tell what they know, not what they think."[28]

A manifestation of political opinion can be embarrassingly unprofessional even when it occurs within the confines of the newsroom. Editor David Boardman of the *Seattle Times* admonished his staff after there was cheering at the August 13, 2007, daily news meeting over the news that Karl Rove had resigned as a White House adviser. Boardman wrote:

> I ask you to leave your personal politics at the front door for one simple reason: A good newsroom is a sacred and magical place in which we should test every assumption, challenge each other's thinking, ask the fundamental questions those in power hope we will overlook. ... [I]f we allowed our news meetings to evolve into a liberal latte klatch, I have no doubt that a pathological case of group-think would soon set in.[29]

Civic activities

News organizations face complaints of favoritism if staff members cover organizations in which they are members or their bosses are members. This has led some journalists to refrain from joining anything. As a result, the journalists – whose career tracks usually have led them far from the places they grew up – find themselves isolated from their communities. They become distant from the people their news organizations are trying to serve.

In a manner similar to most newsroom codes, the *Times'* code states: "Staff members of *The Times* are family members and responsible citizens as well as journalists. *The Times* respects their educating their children, exercising their religion, voting in elections and taking active part in community affairs. Nothing in this policy is intended to infringe upon those rights. But even in the best of causes, Times staff members have a duty to avoid the appearance of a conflict."[30]

The question, then, is where to draw the line in community involvement. The first principle is that journalists should not cover or make news decisions about organizations in which they are members. In addition, they should avoid situations that could reasonably be expected to result in news coverage.

Jayne Miller, a reporter for WBAL for more than a quarter-century, is deeply involved in helping Baltimore's poor. She has served on boards of several not-for-profit groups that provide job training and promote homeownership in the city. She told David Folkenflik for a story in *The Sun* in 2001:

> I can't imagine living in this city and not getting involved as a citizen, because those are my true colors. Life is way too short to spend it working and going home here at night and closing the door and saying, "I'm done." I would be a poorer reporter if I weren't active as a citizen, because it brings perspective.

Folkenflik's story raised questions about the possibility of conflicts stemming from her board roles. The organizations lobby for and spend tax dollars, and several of Miller's fellow board members have been newsmakers she covers for the station.[31]

Miller said in a telephone interview in 2008 that she could avoid conflicts in her board work because she insists on three caveats: first, she will not ask for donations from people she covers or might be expected to cover; second, if a board's agenda includes a topic she covers, she will recuse herself; and third, she will not report on any issues involving the organizations she serves.

But what about the *appearance* of a conflict, since the public may not know of these caveats? Miller said that was not a concern. "My reputation is well established," she said. "People know I'm a no-nonsense reporter who is honest, open, and fair."

She said she had no problem covering her fellow board members. She said she could keep those relationships separate. "It's no different than if I lived next door to them as a neighbor."[32]

Relationships with sources

The *Times*' code takes note of the balancing act that reporters, especially beat reporters, must perform in their relationships with the people they write about. The code says:

> Cultivating sources is an essential skill, often practiced most effectively in informal settings outside of normal business hours. Yet staff members, especially those assigned to beats, must be aware that personal relationships with news sources can erode into favoritism, in fact or appearance. ... Though this topic defies firm rules, it is essential that we preserve professional detachment, free of any whiff of bias. Staff members may see sources informally over a meal or drinks, but they must keep in mind the difference between legitimate business and personal friendship. ... Scrupulous practice requires that periodically we step back and look at whether we have drifted too close to sources we deal with regularly. The acid test of freedom from favoritism is the ability to maintain good working relationships with all parties to a dispute.[33]

Reporter/source relationships are discussed in Chapter 13.

In recent years, newsrooms have been looking more closely at relationships of journalist organizations with the industries they cover. Max Frankel, as executive editor of *The New York Times*, was among the first news executives to take action in this area. In his memoir, Frankel wrote:

> A great uproar followed my discovery in 1989 that the reviewers of other papers were engaged in blatant politicking over the annual honors awarded by the New York drama and film critics. Since our critics routinely listed their favorite films, books and stage plays at season's end in *The Times*, I saw no reason why they should also join in a rival listing that provoked such unseemly behavior. ... By the same logic, I rejected the appeal of our leading sportswriters, who wanted to go on electing retired baseball players to the Hall of Fame.[34]

Frankel's bans on voting for those awards are embodied today in the *Times*' code.

This kind of voting puts journalists in the position of making the news that they then are expected to cover. The problem is compounded when huge sums of money ride on their decisions. The Associated Press for years has conducted a sportswriters' poll of the top college football teams, and it is popular with readers. In 2004, the AP told the Bowl Championship Series that it could no longer use the AP poll in its mathematical calculations of which teams would play in its bowl games, the most lucrative in the sport.[35] Member newspapers of the AP had complained that coaches were lobbying sportswriters for their votes.

Many baseball players have clauses in their contracts that entitle them to bonuses if the Baseball Writers Association of America gives them the Most Valuable Player Awards or the Cy Young Awards for pitching. But the biggest problem is the Hall of Fame. Because the association determines who goes into the Hall, the sportswriters now find themselves adjudicating the question of whether to grant the honor to players tainted by allegations of steroids-inflated statistics. Phil Sheridan, a columnist for *The Philadelphia Inquirer*, has called for the writers to bow out. He writes:

> The process has always been problematic. Writers have been known to snub players they didn't like or who didn't cooperate with them. Writers have deliberately left obvious Hall of Famers off their ballots because they wanted to prevent the dreaded unanimous selection. ... A lot of very questionable achievements are going to come before Hall of Fame voters in the next decade or so. There is no way that supposedly objective journalists should serve as arbiters who legitimize some careers and dismiss others.[36]

Questions of independence also come into play when industries hand out awards to journalists assigned to cover them. An example is the Eclipse Award, given for "outstanding coverage of thoroughbred racing." This award is conferred by the National Thoroughbred Racing Association, the National Turf Writers Association, and the Daily Racing Form.[37] In this instance, journalists not only vie for the approval of the people they cover, but they also help run the contest. The collaboration does not inspire an expectation of fearless coverage.

Case Study No. 5
Covering Police, Wearing Their Uniform

One evening in 1999, television reporter Caroline Lowe was speaking before a group of police trainees when one asked her what educational credentials she had to qualify her to speak about criminal justice. "He was glaring at me," she said.

Lowe, who has reported on the crime beat since 1977 for WCCO-TV in Minneapolis-St. Paul, was bothered by the question because she had dropped out of college to go to work. "I rattled off how many ride-alongs I had been on and that I done this for 20 years," she said in a telephone interview in 2003. "But he wanted to know what formal training I had had. I had to admit I had none."

The next day Lowe walked into the Metropolitan State University's School of Law Enforcement and signed up for her first criminal justice course. She planned then to take only a few courses to help her better understand the beat she covered. But 4 years and 61 credits later, Lowe graduated with a degree in criminal justice. As the outstanding student of her class, she made a speech at commencement exercises.

While she was working on her degree, Lowe went through 8 weeks of training, separate from the degree program, that would enable her to be certified as an officer. During training she learned how to shoot a gun and how to fill out police paperwork. WCCO broadcast a four-part series as she progressed through "cop school."

In August 2003, Lowe took a 12-day leave of absence to work as a police officer at Minnesota's State Fair. Lowe walked around the fairgrounds in uniform. In advance of the fair she also spent a few days getting familiar with the area so that she could direct people and get to places quickly. Nothing eventful happened while she walked the beat. She said that if she had encountered a crime, she would have responded like any other officer, but "I mainly just helped lost kids find their parents."

Lowe said she walked the beat at the fair to fulfill a requirement for becoming a certified police officer. "To get your Minnesota peace officer's license activated, you must actually have a job," she said. While walking the beat, Lowe was not paid by WCCO. She paid for her uniform and borrowed a gun and nightstick from another officer.

Her dual role stirred controversy in the Twin Cities journalism community in 2003. Some argued that walking the beat was a conflict of interest. Others maintained that she had proved her independence through her reporting, which includes reporting on corrupt police officers.

"I think I have a history in this town," said Lowe, an award-winning reporter. "I've done more tough stories on cops than anyone else." She said she was only increasing her expertise in the beat she covers. "I weighed the pluses and minuses of doing this and the pluses out-

Continued

weighed the negatives." She said that to avoid a conflict of interest, she decided never to cover any story involving an officer whom she has worked with or who works at the State Fair. "We don't usually cover the State Fair anyway, so it isn't really an issue," she said.

The Star-Tribune in Minneapolis conducted an online poll asking viewers how they felt about a reporter working in the beat she covers. Almost 70 percent either endorsed the idea or didn't care. Thirty percent thought it was a bad idea. Rob Daves of *The Star-Tribune* cautioned that the results could not be considered scientific. "Those polls are only for those who are motivated enough" to respond, Daves said.

Brian Lambert of *The* (St. Paul) *Pioneer Press* wrote two columns supporting Lowe. In the first column he dismissed the idea that "a reporter who covers the beat should never, ever assume the role of any person on that beat," saying it was "a one-size-fits-all view of the issue." His second column said Lowe's action was acceptable because she took an unpaid leave, she didn't have access to any secret files while on the job, and she had an established reputation as a reporter.

Another *Pioneer Press* columnist, Ruben Rosario, sent Lowe an email that said, "We need more journalists and newsroom decision-makers with diverse life experiences and backgrounds and less of the journalism school textbook-café latte crowd, which seems to dominate so many newsrooms I see."

Jane Kirtley, Silha Professor of Media Ethics and Law at the School of Journalism and Mass Communication at the University of Minnesota, said she knows and respects Lowe but disagrees with her decision. "Be a journalist or be a police officer," she told Lambert for one of his columns. "Either is fine. But not both at once. There are good reasons why the two don't overlap. Journalists have gone to jail to maintain separation between the two."

Lowe said she was aware that while certain WCCO colleagues "probably don't support what I did," most of those she works with have reacted positively. Maria Reitan, Lowe's news director at the time, supported her decision. The station's online biography of Lowe mentions her work as a police officer at the fair and says she may be the only reporter in the country who is also a certified police officer.

WCCO anchor Don Shelby also supported her. "For me, there's absolutely no difference in this case than having your court reporter get a law degree," Shelby told Lambert. "You can twist the argument any way you want if you're so inclined, but I see no difference."

Since walking the beat in 2003, Lowe has returned to the fairgrounds for police stints in 2004, 2005, 2006, 2007 and 2008. "Having the education, training, and experience have helped me ask better questions of the subjects … I encounter on the criminal justice beat," she said. Lowe also has received a master's degree in police leadership, become a marathon runner, and enrolled in cooking classes.

This case is adapted from a paper Lindsay Bosslett wrote while a student at Pennsylvania State University. Bosslett graduated in 2004 and now is a senior copy editor for *Woman's World* magazine.

Continued

Questions for Class Discussion

- Do you think that Caroline Lowe, as a police reporter, was in a conflict of interest when she took college courses in law enforcement?
- Was she in a conflict when she went through eight weeks of training and was certified as a police officer?

- Was she in conflict when she walked a beat in uniform at the State Fair?
- If you think she had a conflict, was it an actual conflict or an apparent conflict?
- What do you think of the arguments of Lambert, Rosario, Kirtley, and Shelby?

Case Study No. 6

Carrying the Torch, Stirring Controversy

When Dick Rosetta, a sportswriter for the *Salt Lake Tribune*, was asked if he would like to carry the Olympic torch for a ceremonial quarter-mile before the 2002 Winter Games, he accepted. "I've been a patriot from the get-go, and this is the American thing to do," Rosetta told The Associated Press. "You don't turn down carrying the torch for the Olympics. I don't care who you work for."

Rosetta's editor at the *Tribune*, James E. Shelledy, did care. He gave Rosetta the option of either covering the Games – he was scheduled to cover figure skating – or carrying the torch. Rosetta, who at age 60 had intended to retire before the Olympics but stayed on at his editor's request, chose the torch. He was relieved of his figure-skating duties.

"Our ethical guidelines state if you are directly involved in reporting or editing a news story, you can't be part of that event," Shelledy told The Associated Press.

Rosetta saw a distinction in the fact that the torch run was under the auspices of the US Olympic Committee while the Olympic athletic events, which he was supposed to cover, were overseen by the International Olympics Committee.

The Olympic torch-carrying ceremony, one of the most beloved rituals in sports, dates to the 1936 Games in Munich. Prior to its arrival in Salt Lake City, the torch had traveled more than 13,500 miles across the United States in 65 days in the hands of 11,500 bearers.

Many other media organizations allowed journalists to carry the torch, including NBC, whose "Today" show host Katie Couric made the run. Even the *Tribune* had runners in the event. A columnist and the publisher carried

Continued

the torch, and the paper defended this by saying the two were sufficiently distanced from reporting to maintain the paper's objectivity.

NBC telecast the Olympics from Salt Lake City. Brink Chipman, news director for KSL, the local NBC affiliate, told The Associated Press that this caused "an awkward situation" for the station's news staff. "We are a sponsor, but that has not stopped us from doing broad, intense coverage of the Olympics. If we didn't cover them honestly and legitimately, people would write about it … we'd be killed." KSL allowed "personalities" like the weatherman and anchors to carry the torch, but not reporters or editors.

Reporters for Salt Lake City's other newspaper, the *Deseret News*, got to carry the torch. *Deseret News* managing editor Rick Hall told The Associated Press, "The torch is not graft or bribery or a gift. … We didn't see this as a conflict because it won't change the way we cover the Olympics."

Deseret News columnist Lee Benson criticized Shelledy for removing Rosetta from the Olympics coverage. Benson wrote: "[T]aking ourselves too seriously is a journalist's nature. We spend so much time taking everybody else to task, we don't know honest from sincere. Give us long enough to think about it, and we probably wouldn't vote."

Mike Reilley, who runs *journaliststoolbox. com*, called the Olympic torch run "a rolling PR event" for the International Olympic Committee, the United States Organizing Committee, and the Salt Lake Olympic Committee. In a posting on the Society of Professional Journalists' online ethics forum, Reilley wrote that the *Tribune* made the right decision: "If it wants to maintain credibility in its community, it must maintain a distance from the event."

Herb Strentz, a professor at the Drake University School of Journalism in Des Moines, Iowa, expressed this opinion on the SPJ forum: "Really, not a thing is lost by *not* being involved, and that tips the scales for me."

Rosetta said he weighed the consequences of his decision. But in the end, he said, he "looked at all those people carrying the torch, holding it high … people who battled leukemia, people dying of cancer, the guy who coached the soccer team for 40 years, the World Trade Center survivors, and I said, 'Hey, maybe I do fit,' and I'll carry it with pride."

This case is adapted from a paper Jeff Rice wrote while a student at Pennsylvania State University. Rice graduated in 2003 and is a sports reporter for the *Centre Daily Times* in State College, Pennsylvania.

Questions for Class Discussion

- What are the arguments in favor of allowing the reporter to carry the Olympic torch? What are the arguments against?
- Do you agree with Rosetta that the paper should have recognized a distinction between the US Olympic Committee and the International Olympic Committee?
- If the conflict guidelines of *The New York Times* were applied in this case, what would the decision have been?
- Why do you think the Olympic officials asked sports reporters to carry the torch? Why do you think they asked Katie Couric?
- Do you think *The Tribune*'s decision on Rosetta was compromised by the fact that two other employees carried the torch?

Case Study No. 7
On Lunch Break, Defending Reagan
Michael Miner

AIDS came in and the Cold War went out with the 1980s. How people remember Ronald Reagan, who was president for most of that decade, could depend on which of those two great historic events touched them more profoundly.

Rick Garcia, political director of the gay rights group Equality Illinois, didn't join in the national mourning after Reagan's death in 2004. He happened to be in Springfield when a display of Reagan memorabilia was being dedicated in the Capitol's rotunda. The governor's office had organized the display and set out a public memory book that eventually would be given to the Reagan Library. With reporters and camera crews looking on, Governor Rod Blagojevich wrote the first inscription.

Garcia had come to Springfield to help welcome the Rainbow Riders, two consciousness-raising lesbian grandmothers who had been biking across the country. Afterward he went over to the Capitol to pick up a legislative directory and some newspapers. Passing through the rotunda, he noticed the Reagan display. The ceremony was over, and the crowd had dispersed. Garcia got in line behind a man and his two sons who were signing the memory book. When his turn came, he wrote:

My memory of President Ronald Reagan: Thousands of American men, women and children were dying from HIV and AIDS

during his administration. The president did nothing. The president said nothing. Not until the very end of his second term was he even able to utter the word "AIDS." Reagan's silence and his administration's policies contributed to the suffering and dying of thousands of men, women and children.

Two other people in the nearly empty rotunda had also decided to write in the book – Julie Staley, a reporter for WICS-TV in Springfield, and Curt Claycomb, her cameraman. Having covered Blagojevich, they were headed to lunch, but before taking off they wanted to pay their respects. Staley says, "So I walked up there and waited for this guy taking an immensely long time. And I thought, 'He must really love Ronald Reagan.'"

Garcia continued writing: "I mourn the president the way he mourned these men, women and children – with silence. May God forgive him, I can't. Rick Garcia." Then he went on his way.

Staley says, "I thought I'd sign right below him. I wanted to read what he wrote first. Oh my gosh! He totally defamed Ronald Reagan about his having no stand on the AIDS situation and HIV and all that. It was very cruel. It was inappropriate, and it made no sense whatsoever that he would do that. I was very incensed. I loved Ronald Reagan!"

It's not something she wants to discuss in any detail, but she says that over the years her

Continued

grandparents, parents, and husband have given Reagan "a lot of support." She fully shares their devotion. "I turned the page," she says. "I said, 'I'm not signing on *that* page.' I wrote my thing, and the photographer wrote his thing. As we were getting ready to leave we saw a security guard walking up, and the photographer mentioned it to him. He said, 'Some guy wrote something defamatory.' You know, you don't write hate messages in a public book."

Just then, Garcia happened to walk back into the rotunda. He saw a guard, a TV reporter, and a cameraman gathered at the memory book. He heard the guard say, "Was it the guy with two kids?" and the reporter responded, "No. It's signed 'Rick Garcia.'" He headed toward them.

Staley says, "He walked up and looked puzzlingly at us."

Garcia says, "She pointed at me and said, 'There he is!'"

Staley says, "I said, 'You're entitled to your freedom of speech, but this is an inappropriate place to do that.'"

Garcia emailed me his version of their confrontation. "She walked toward me and screeched, 'That is just tasteless and classless.' She repeated, 'You are tasteless!' I told her, 'Speaking the truth is not classless.' The cop said, 'Why don't you show some respect?' 'Why didn't President Reagan show some respect?' I replied and walked away. As I walked away, the reporter shouted at me, 'You are classless, totally tasteless. You are a big loser.' She repeated that a couple of times."

"I don't deny that I said that," says Staley. "If she had just been there to sign the book and didn't like what I had to say, fine, but she was *reporting* on the activities in the

rotunda," Garcia writes. "Any reporter worth her salt, upon seeing a non-complimentary entry, would look for other such entries, and then seek those folks out, because there is a story there."

Staley says, "We were out of tape. We had nothing more we could shoot. This was our lunchtime. This was on my personal time. I wasn't standing with a microphone in my hand. My equipment was set aside. I didn't sign the book 'Julia Staley, WICS.' I signed the book as Julia Heil Staley, someone who loved Ronald Reagan."

If you'd still been shooting tape, I ask Staley, would you have asked Garcia some questions?

"Oh, yeah, oh yeah, definitely," she says.

Do you want to try to reach him in Chicago?

"I don't want anything more to do with him."

WICS news director Susan Finzen says, "She had a right to express her opinion. Why does he consider it all right for him to express his opinion but not her?"

Garcia writes, "I called the station to complain. I was told that someone would call me back. No one did. I called again and said that I wanted to submit a formal complaint, and indeed I told the woman that I would not go away silently [and] that I would pursue this. No one from the station has called. ... In my thirty years of activism I have had many occasions to have interaction with reporters. Never have I encountered such unprofessional behavior. I want to lodge an official complaint."

Staley responds, "At that moment I was not representing the station. I was there as a private citizen. My company's backing me up on this. We're all stunned it's even an issue."

This case is a slightly edited version of a column in *The Chicago Reader* on June 18, 2004. Copyright © 2004, *The Chicago Reader*. Reprinted by permission.

Continued

Questions for Class Discussion

- Do you think Julie Staley acted appropriately when she:
  1 Decided to sign the memory book?
  2 Complained publicly about Rick Garcia's message in the book?
  3 Pointed out Garcia to the security guard?

- Is Staley's statement that she was on "personal time" relevant? Does it matter whether "at that moment I was not representing the station; I was there as a private citizen"?
- Do you agree with the station director's statement that Staley had as much right to express her opinion as Garcia did his?

Case Study No. 8
A Love Triangle on the Evening News

At 4 p.m. on June 8, Los Angeles Mayor Antonio Villaraigosa issued a terse statement announcing that he and his wife, Corina, were separating after 20 years of marriage.

Two hours later, Telemundo television anchor Mirthala Salinas delivered the story to her Spanish-language viewers on the Friday evening news.

"The rumors were true," she declared of the split after an introduction that described the story as a "political scandal" that had left "many people with their mouth open."

What Salinas, 35, did not say in the newscast was that she was the other woman. She and Villaraigosa, 54, had been in a relationship even though she had previously been the political reporter assigned to cover local politics and the mayor.

— *Los Angeles Times*, July 4, 2007

In separate announcements on July 3, Villaraigosa and Salinas (see Figure 10.1) confirmed the relationship, which had been the subject of Internet chatter. "I have a relationship with Ms. Salinas, and I take full responsibility for my actions," the mayor said at a news conference. Later in the day, Salinas said: "I first got to know the mayor at a professional level, where we went on to become friends. The current relationship grew out of our existing friendship."

Salinas was suspended, along with her station's news director and general manager. In September, she was reassigned to the station's bureau in Riverside, and the news director was reinstated. The general manager was replaced. Salinas resigned – "I wasn't going to Riverside," she told *Los Angeles Magazine* the

Continued

Figure 10.1 This photograph of Telemundo reporter Mirthala Salinas and Los Angeles Mayor Antonio Villaraigosa was taken on June 19, 2006, a year before they both acknowledged being involved in an affair
LOS ANGELES TIMES PHOTO BY ROBERT DURELL

next spring – and four months later she was hired for a talk show on AM radio.

Telemundo president Don Browne said that allowing Salinas to deliver the news about the separation of the Villaraigosa couple was a "flagrant" violation of the network's news guidelines.

Salinas said in the interview with Shawn Hubler of *Los Angeles Magazine* that she was filling in for an anchor at the station who was on maternity leave, so she got the assignment of reading the story about the Villaraigosas. "There was no way I could get out of it," she said. "I was shaking. I didn't want to be there. … I put myself like it wasn't me, like it was another person doing what I was doing. I pretended I wasn't reading it. At that moment, it was like it wasn't me sitting at the news desk, doing the newscast. It was something I wish I would not have done."

Salinas had worked for 10 years at Telemundo's KVEA, which ranks second in viewers among Los Angeles' Latino stations. She had won a Golden Mike broadcasting award, and the newscast she anchored had won two local Emmies.

Continued

Salinas said in the magazine interview that she and the mayor had a romantic relationship for six months, after she and Villaraigosa had seen each other frequently in social settings involving mutual friends. Villaraigosa visited her terminally ill mother and attended the mother's funeral in Phoenix in January 2007. Salinas said that when she returned to work after the funeral, she told her supervisors at the station "she should not do any more reporting on the mayor because he had done so much for her family that she could no longer be objective about him," according to the magazine. The station moved her off the politics beat to an assignment as backup anchor and general correspondent.

Salinas told the magazine her romance with mayor began in April 2007, several weeks after she made the request to her supervisors, and ended that October. "I think it just got to the point where we both realized that it wasn't working out as that kind of a relation-ship," she said. She later reconciled with a boyfriend she had been seeing before the relationship with the mayor, and they were planning to be married. She and Villaraigosa remain friends, she said.

Many newsroom codes assert that a romantic relationship with a news subject is an apparent conflict of interest, one generally resulting in a change of assignment for the reporter. *The New York Times*' code says, in Paragraph 24: "Clearly, romantic involvement with a news source would foster an appearance of partiality. Therefore staff members who develop close relationships with people who might figure in coverage they provide, edit, package or supervise must disclose those relationships ..." Although Salinas had made a disclosure of a close relationship with the mayor and was moved off the politics beat, she still was in the position of being the anchor who read the news story on Villaraigosa's marital breakup.

Questions for Class Discussion

- Why is Mirthala Salinas' relationship with the mayor an apparent conflict of interest for the reporter and her station?

- What should station executives have done when she reported the relationship to them?

Notes

1 Bill Dedman, "Journalists dole cash to politicians (quietly)", *msnbc.com*, June 25, 2007.

2 William Powers, "Who are we?", *nationaljournal.com*, July 6, 2007.

3 Robert Pear, "Drug industry is told to stop gifts to doctors," *The New York Times*, Oct. 1, 2002.

4 Jeffrey Olen, *Ethics in Journalism* (Englewood Cliffs, NJ: Prentice-Hall, 1988), 25.

5 Schorr is quoted in Charles W. Bailey, *Conflicts of Interest: A Matter of Journalistic Ethics* (Washington, DC: National News Council, 1984), 6.

6 John J. Hulteng, *Playing It Straight* (Washington, DC: American Society of Newspaper Editors, 1981), 25.

7 *The New York Times, Ethical Journalism: A Handbook of Values and Practices for the News and Editorial Departments*, September 2004, http://nytco.com/pdf/NYT_Ethical_Journalism_0904.pdf, Sections 62–5.

8 "*Post* newsroom leader to retire," an online chat between readers and Leonard Downie Jr, http://www.washingtonpost.com/wp-dyn/content/

discussion/2008/06/24/DI2008062401047.html, June 24, 2008.

9   *The New York Times, Ethical Journalism*, Sections 106–11.

10 Gary Tuma, *Covering the Capitol: A century of news reporting in Pennsylvania, centennial history of Pennsylvania Legislative Correspondents' Association, 1895–1995* (Harrisburg: Pennsylvania Legislative Correspondents' Association, 1996), 28–30.

11 Katharine Graham, "The evocation of excellence: Russ Wiggins, good steward, farseeing guide of *The Post* for 21 years, *The Washington Post*, Nov. 20, 2000.

12 *The New York Times, Ethical Journalism*, Section 33.

13 Jim Drinkard and Mark Memmott, "HHS said it paid columnist for help," *USA Today*, Jan. 27, 2005.

14 *The New York Times, Ethical Journalism*, Sections 34–5.

15 Greg Toppo, "Education Dept. paid commentator to promote law," *USA Today*, Jan. 6, 2005.

16 Greg Toppo, "Commentator says he may return fees," *USA Today*, Oct. 7, 2005.

17 Greg Toppo, "Pundit Armstrong Williams settles case over promoting education reforms," *USA Today,* Oct. 22, 2006.

18 David Folkenflik, "*Herald* publisher quits, reporters reinstated," National Public Radio, March 11, 2008.

19 Bill Kovach and Tom Rosenstiel, *The Elements of Journalism: What Newspeople Should Know and the Public Should Expect* (New York: Crown Publishers, 2001), 99.

20 Radcliffe Institute for Advanced Study, Harvard University, "Radcliffe Institute Medalist 2006: Linda Greenhouse," June 9, 2006, speech text at http://www.radcliffe.edu/alumnae/radday2006_greenhousespeech.aspx#

21 *The New York Times, Ethical Journalism*, Section 102.

22 Byron Calame, "Hazarding personal opinions in public can be hazardous for journalists," *The New York Times*, Oct. 8, 2006.

23 Folkenflik, "Critics question reporter's airing of personal views," National Public Radio, Sept. 26, 2006.

24 Charles Kaiser, "Full Court Press: Linda Greenhouse, legendary New York Times reporter looks back on three decades chronicling the Supreme Court – including her run-ins with the journalism ethics police," Oct. 10, 2008; http://www.radaronline.com/features/2008/10/linda_greenhouse_supreme_court

25 Dedman, "TV reporter who supported candidate is out," *msnbc*, July 11, 2007.

26 Paul Duke, "E-mail undoing," *American Journalism Review*, September 2002.

27 *The New York Times, Ethical Journalism*, Section 102.

28 Author interview with Amy Goldstein, Oct. 22, 2007.

29 "*Seattle Times* editor elaborates on newsroom cheering memo," Romenesko Misc., http://www.poynter.org/column.asp?id=45&aid=128555, Aug. 15, 2007.

30 *The New York Times, Ethical Journalism*, Section 60.

31 Folkenflik, "Citizen Jayne: Baltimore's best TV journalist believes she can balance her on-air reporting and her off-camera activism. But should she?" *The Sun*, Feb. 25, 2001.

32 Author's telephone interview with Jayne Miller, June 3, 2008.

33 *The New York Times, Ethical Journalism*, Sections 22–3.

34 Max Frankel, *The Times of My Life and My Life With The Times* (New York: Random House, 1999), 515–16.

35 The Associated Press, "AP made call with poll's integrity in mind," *espn.com*, Dec. 21, 2004.

36 Phil Sheridan, "Baseball writers wrong to exercise their right to vote," *The Philadelphia Inquirer*, Oct. 8, 2005.

37 National Turf Writers Association, "Eclipse Award for filly or mare sprinter added for 2007," Feb. 16, 2007, http://www.turfwriters.org/news/

11 The Business of Producing Journalism

News outlets' dual role: serving the public and earning money

┌───┐

Learning Goals

This chapter will help you understand:

- the tensions caused by technological and economic transition in today's news media;
- the fundamental elements of the business of journalism, and their ethical implications;
- how advertisers finance journalism but cannot be allowed to influence journalism;
- how some efforts to increase revenue for the media company, and to reduce expenses, have led to ethically questionable practices; and
- the delicate relationship between news and business executives of media companies.

└───┘

When John Carroll became editor of the *Los Angeles Times* in April 2000, he was eagerly welcomed by a newsroom staff that was reeling from the previous year's Staples Center debacle (see Case Study No. 9 "Sharing Ad Profits, Creating a Controversy") and uneasy about the paper's recent acquisition by the Chicago-based Tribune Company.

Given Carroll's sterling reputation as the leader of newsrooms in Lexington, Kentucky, and in Baltimore, few doubted that he would stabilize the newsroom. Even so, the *Times'* turnaround was astonishing. The new editor rallied morale and gave inspired direction to news coverage. In the next five years, the resurgent staff won 13 Pulitzer Prizes – meaning that, in the opinion of the Pulitzer judges, almost one-fifth of the nation's best newspaper journalism was being produced by the staff of a single paper.

And then Carroll quit.

While the *Times* was enjoying its profound journalistic success, Carroll was being worn down in the grueling battles that he and the publisher, John Puerner, were waging with Chicago executives who repeatedly demanded staff reductions. In deciding in July 2005 to retire at 63, Carroll followed Puerner out the door; the publisher had resigned a few months earlier to take a "self-imposed career break."[1]

The repetition of events that followed could have been scripted by the folks who gave us the movie *Groundhog Day*.

The editor Carroll had groomed as his successor, Dean Baquet, was in command 16 months. When he took the job, Baquet acknowledged the budget difficulties while saying he had every hope that he could make the paper better. But in August 2006, he and publisher Jeffrey Johnson publicly defied Tribune Company demands for another round of budget cuts that would eliminate more than 50 newsroom jobs. Both were soon forced out.[2]

The next editor lasted 14 months. The new publisher, David Hiller, had previously been publisher of the *Chicago Tribune*, and he tapped the *Tribune*'s managing editor, James O'Shea, to join him as editor of the *Times*. Because he was coming from the *Tribune*, O'Shea was expected to be more accommodating on budget matters. But in January 2008, this alliance, too, was history. O'Shea announced to the staff that Hiller was forcing him out because "we did not share a common vision for the future of the *Los Angeles Times*."[3]

A month later, the *Times* had another new editor: Russ Stanton, a 10-year *Times* veteran who in the previous year, with the title of innovation editor, had overseen the digital news report. "We in the newsroom," he told the staff, "need to figure out how to break this self-defeating cycle ... Our strategy of fight-lose-shrink is not working."[4]

Between 2000 and 2008, the *Times* reduced its news staff from about 1,200 to about 900, and its weekday circulation declined from around 1.1 million to around 800,000.[5] Adding to the turbulence, the *Times* had yet another owner. In December 2007, Chicago real-estate magnate Sam Zell won control of the Tribune Company and its string of newspapers and television stations in an $8.2-billion deal.[6] And on July 14, 2008, the same day that the *Times* began laying off 150 newsroom employees in the face of continued revenue declines, Zell ousted David Hiller as publisher.[7]

A Turbulent Period of Transition

The turnover of top executives at the *Los Angeles Times* between 2005 and 2008 – four editors and three publishers in less than 3 years – is highly unusual. But the tensions producing that turnover are common throughout the news industry.

The *Times'* saga illuminates the struggle involving all media platforms. Newspapers are hard hit, their circulation and advertising revenue plummeting. Television audiences are fragmented by the huge array of stations available from cable and satellite providers. Online news sites run by newspapers and broadcast stations, while adding an innovative dimension to journalism, have not yet devised a business strategy that could make them profitable enough to support adequate news staffs.

Statements of the *Times'* three departed editors and publisher David Hiller frame the debate over how news organizations should allocate resources in a time of technological and economic transition.

The editors all commented about what they saw as an absence of strategic focus by a newspaper whose operating-profit percentage was then still in double digits.[8] John Carroll: "The cutting became open-ended. And it was not accompanied by anything I could understand as a strategy for the future."[9] Dean Baquet: "[T]he cutting is not a part of anything. It's not moving toward anything. It's not part of a plan. It's to prop up [profit] margins that maybe cannot be propped up."[10] James O'Shea: "The way out of this is not retrenchment. If you don't invest in good, solid, accurate, fundamental journalism, you are just going to continue the decline and fall."[11]

In response to O'Shea, Hiller said the paper had looked for ways to "grow revenue" and had invested judiciously, most notably in the paper's web operations. But he also saw a duty to accept reality: "Last year, our operating cash flow went down by about twenty percent. Can you solve the newspaper industry's problems by spending more? It's an attractive theory, but it won't work."[12]

The editors thus argued that producing excellent journalism would attract readers, who in turn would attract advertisers; and that, conversely, reducing newsroom resources would only result in continued loss of readers and advertising. The publisher argued that when revenue goes down, so must expenses.

In the years that followed, however, even *The New York Times* and *The Washington Post* – newspapers that historically had invested heavily in news coverage – were forced to reduce staffing. For many newspapers, especially in big cities, the question became not whether they could achieve a desired profit level but whether they could turn a profit at all. Ironically, newspapers are facing those dire financial prospects at a time when their content, counting print and online, might be as well read as ever. Analyzing research by the industry, the Project for Excellence in Journalism calculated in 2007 that two out of three adults were reading their regional newspaper either in print or online at least once a week.[13]

Aspiring journalists reading this text need to be aware of the simmering dispute over media economics – not to frighten them away from the profession but to help them bring worldly wisdom when they enter it.

As this book has discussed, journalism performs a vital public service, and a journalism career has incalculable psychic rewards. But it should also be recognized that journalists' paychecks are drawn on the bank accounts of companies that cannot survive if they do not make a profit.

Although the news media are not the only industry under pressure in today's economy, theirs is an industry in which the public has an extraordinary stake.

Former newspaper editor Gene Roberts, in his Point of View "Tangoing Without a Partner," contends that the public interest must be a factor in the debate. He writes:

> Almost no one seems to be grappling with the fundamental questions of publishing and broadcast in a democratic society: What are a newspaper's (or television station's) obligations to its community? Does it have a societal duty to cover local government, state government, schools, courts and the major social and political issues of the day? What about foreign news and national news? ... Is there some point beyond which a publisher will not cut? Is there any public obligation at all, other than to public stockholders?

In Roberts' opinion, "staff reductions reduce a paper's ability to cover the news. And they raise the question of a paper's obligations to its community. ... It is an ethical question."

Media Economics: The Basics

In his 2004 book *The Vanishing Newspaper*, journalism scholar Philip Meyer cautions that for decades the newspaper business has been drifting in the direction of a strategy of "harvest market position." He writes:

> A stagnant industry's market position is harvested by raising prices and lowering quality, trusting that customers will continue to be attracted by the brand name rather than the substance for which the brand once stood. Eventually, of course, they will wake up. But as the harvest metaphor implies, this is a nonrenewable, take-the-money-and-run strategy. Once harvested, the market position is gone.[14]

The television industry similarly has reduced its investment in news coverage, while reshaping that coverage to meet the perceived tastes of the audience. Growing economic pressures on television journalism over the last generation have caused a lowering of journalism standards, according to former broadcast executive Av Westin.

Westin writes in the 2000 book *Best Practices for Television Journalists* that in television's early decades, news was a "loss leader" yielding prestige but little or no profit for the network or station. "But gradually, television news became the business of television news. Financial considerations ... began to edge their way toward becoming the paramount elements in decision-making, instead of good journalism."

Westin blamed those financial pressures for the "tabloidization" of television news. As the air time for network and local television news was expanded, "producers looked for material to fill the programs, [and] they discovered a growing demand for stories rooted in gossip, crime and glamour." That led, he wrote, to "tabloid television" shows and the proliferation of newsmagazines in prime time. As Westin saw it, all of these developments resulted in "dumbing down" television news.[15]

For online news sites, the key question is how to make the medium pay off in cash. Consumers have largely rejected the idea of paying for access to online news, making it necessary for online news sites, like broadcast stations, to depend on advertising to pay the bills and return a profit.

However, the traditional model of the news business may not work for news sites on the web. In print and broadcast media, the news coverage attracts an audience, which then is exposed to advertising adjacent to the news (see Figure 11.1, p. 167). Internet ad viewers, in contrast, are usually looking for something specific they want to buy. "People search narrowly for what they want, so accompanying news content may be beside the point – or even a distraction," media business analyst Rick Edmonds wrote for *poynteronline* in March 2008.[16]

So, even if news consumers ultimately move entirely online, the money may not follow. Print newsrooms historically have been by far the largest in the news media, and many of the most popular news sites on the web depend on the content produced by those print newsrooms. That raises another question, which unfortunately could be rhetorical: If print disappears, will the depth of news coverage be diminished?

The ownership of the news media, like that of other businesses, became concentrated in relatively few large companies in the second half of the twentieth century. The broadcast networks were bought by companies whose main business has nothing to do with news; for example, ABC is owned by Disney, a leading player in entertainment.

Adding to the difficulties for news operations, the owners of newspapers and broadcast stations typically are companies whose stock is traded on Wall Street. Public trading of stock makes it easier for the companies to raise capital, but it also puts pressure on company executives to produce favorable financial returns. If they don't, the institutional investors – those representing huge pension funds and mutual funds, to whom they owe a fiduciary responsibility – look for better investments elsewhere. Then there is the cyclical nature of the media industry, in which advertising revenues swing radically in response to the economy's ups and downs. A private owner might be inclined to protect the long-term health of the company by riding out the down cycles, accepting a lower profit. In contrast, the public owners – those holding stock – are looking only for maximum return on their investment, and they, unlike the best private owners, do not feel a civic responsibility to maintain quality news coverage for the communities where their companies operate. In deference to those stockholders, executives of publicly held companies feel compelled to reduce expenses whenever revenue declines, even if the company remains profitable. Not surprisingly, these cutbacks damage the news company's franchise. The diminished news coverage leads to losses of audience, which in turn lead to new losses of advertising. With the next revenue decline, the process is repeated. Intended or not, this pattern creates the "harvest market strategy" that Philip Meyer describes in *The Vanishing Newspaper.*

To reduce expenses when revenues decline, newspapers target salaries and newsprint (the paper that the newspapers are printed on). Salary savings are achieved in three different ways, singly or in combination: hiring freezes, in which staff members who resign or retire are not replaced; buyouts, in which bonuses are offered to staff members who will give up their jobs; and layoffs, in which staff members lose their jobs involuntarily, usually with some sort of separation payment. Newsprint reductions mean that each issue has less space for news (called the newshole). In broadcast, the expense savings are primarily in salaries, which means that a smaller staff has to fill the same airtime void – or possibly *even more* time, since many local stations have been increasing the amount of time for news. The reason: Newscasts cost the station less than buying syndicated shows to fill the slots on the schedule.[17] Whether the medium is print or broadcast, budget cuts mean that consumers get less substantive news; sooner or later, they realize it.

For newspapers, revenue almost certainly will never return to what the industry enjoyed in the pre-Internet days. Online sites like eBay, Craigslist and realtor.com have eviscerated newspapers' classified advertising, which once was lucrative and, compared with display advertising, easy to sell. In the third quarter of 2008, newspaper advertising had its worst decline in at least 37 years, according to the Newspaper Association of America.[18]

The early twenty-first century has seen a few exceptions to the long-term trend of more newspapers being owned by publicly traded media chains. Those exceptions, however, failed to reverse the trend of diminishing resources for journalism.

In buying the Tribune Company and its vast newspaper and broadcast holdings, Sam Zell took the company private, meaning that its stock is no longer traded on Wall Street. In Philadelphia, a group of local investors bought *The Philadelphia Inquirer* and *Philadelphia Daily News* in 2006, when McClatchy Newspaper Company, which had bought out Knight Ridder, put the Philadelphia papers up for sale. The investments by Zell and the Philadelphia group were highly leveraged with bank loans, and subsequent financial pressures led them to make drastic reductions in staff. Effectively, the new owners were answering to demanding overseers in much the same way that the executives of publicly traded companies have done. The publicly traded companies have to convince Wall Street that their earnings per share and share price will rise, as a result of some combination of higher revenues and profit margins. Owners in debt have to convince the bankers that they can earn enough cash flow to pay off their loans, and some bank loans have "covenants" requiring owners to maintain a ratio of debt to earnings.

In late 2008, Zell's Tribune Company – burdened by $13 billion in debt – filed Chapter 11 bankruptcy proceedings to protect the company from creditors while it restructured its finances. The Philadelphia newspapers did the same in early 2009, and board chairman Bruce Toll acknowledged that he and others who invested in the papers "will lose everything" because the newspapers were worth less than they owed.[19] Chapter 11 petitions also were filed in 2009 by *The Star Tribune* in Minneapolis, bought in 2007 from McClatchy by New York-based Avista Capital Partners, and by the Journal Register Company, which owns the *New Haven Register* in Connecticut and smaller papers in the suburbs of Philadelphia and Cleveland and throughout Michigan.

This chapter discusses several of the most significant ethical issues arising from the business of journalism. Those issues should be viewed in the context of the environment that has just been described: an environment of technological change, audience fragmentation, and a resulting scramble for resources.

The ethical issues are grouped under these categories:

- The role of advertisers in the business of news.
- Questionable practices that can result from efforts to increase advertising revenue, efforts to compensate for diminished newsroom resources, or both.
- The relationship of the news and business staffs in an organization that has both a quasi-civic duty to report the news and a marketplace obligation to earn a profit.

The Role of Advertisers

To understand the role that advertisers play in the mainstream news media, consider two kinds of publications that exemplify the two extremes in advertiser/news relationship. Call them the shopper model and the *Consumer Reports* model.

The shopper model

In most communities, people find their mailboxes stuffed with magazines that contain feature stories as well as a disproportionate volume of advertising. These are so-called "shoppers." Although the stories purport to give consumer advice, they are uniformly uncritical – or, to be more accurate, gushing in their enthusiasm – about the businesses that have bought ads. The stories are advertisements in a different format.

To the extent that you read shoppers, you take them on their own terms. Reading the display ads, you assume a "buyer beware" attitude. Reading the accompanying feature stories, you look only for services you want to check out for yourself. You are not fooled into thinking that the stories can be trusted as an independent evaluation of merchandise and services.

The *Consumer Reports* model

At the other end of the spectrum are a few niche magazines that depend entirely on the subscriptions paid by their readers. The reputation of *Consumer Reports'* product evaluations, for example, is built around the magazine's policy of accepting no advertising. Since there are no advertisers, readers can assume that what the magazine publishes is its own best judgment about the products. To head off suspicion that *Consumer Reports* might be secretly paid by manufacturers, the magazine prohibits companies and stores from using its product evaluations in posters or ads.

Strictly from a journalism standpoint, applying the *Consumer Reports* business model to the mass media is appealing but wildly impractical. Consumers have always demonstrated their resistance to paying directly for their news – most recently in rebuffing attempts to charge for online content. Newspapers' price-per-copy has historically paralleled the price of a restaurant's cup of coffee (at least until Starbucks popularized the idea of premium coffee at premium prices). Newspaper executives expect a decline in circulation whenever they raise prices. In any case, newspapers' revenue from circulation typically will not even pay the cost of the paper they are printed on. The tradition of free radio and free television, with advertisers paying the bills, is well established. Satellite radio and premium television channels buck that tradition by demonstrating that people will pay for *entertainment* uninterrupted by advertising.

The mainstream media

Like the shoppers, the news media depend financially on advertising. But like their counterparts at *Consumer Reports*, journalists who work for good news organizations demonstrate, day in and day out, that they owe their first loyalty to readers, listeners, viewers, and online users. They follow the SPJ code's guiding principle of acting independently. They put the audience ahead of the company that issues their paychecks – and ahead of the advertisers that provide the money to cover salaries and overhead. Moreover, the presence of advertising is so transparently evident that it serves as a daily disclosure of an unavoidable conflict of interest. The audience can and does hold the news organization accountable for being editorially independent of its advertisers.

In that respect, the companies that produce news are drastically different from other businesses. That difference is not easy for advertisers to understand or accept. The owners of a restaurant, for example, are accustomed to being treated with effusive courtesy by the company from which it buys food. But when the same owners buy an ad in a newspaper, they might be rewarded by a critic's negative review or news coverage of a city inspector's devastating hygiene report.

By establishing a reputation for delivering reliable news, the news organization assembles an audience.

The audience is now a valuable commodity that can be rented to advertisers.

Figure 11.1 A news organization's business relationship
GRAPHIC COURTESY OF BILL MARSH

Advertisers who try to influence news coverage – and executives of news organizations who allow them to do so – ignore the unique, fragile nature of the news business. That can be expressed as follows (and in Figure 11.1):

- First, thanks to the honest, fair news policies of the organization and the talent and energies of its journalists, a newspaper, broadcast station, or online news site attracts a loyal audience.
- Then, the audience becomes attractive to advertisers because it offers a mass of potential consumers of their products. Renting the audience to advertisers is a business transaction with benefits for both parties: The advertisers reach their potential customers, and the news company acquires the money it needs to pay expenses and make a profit.
- However, if advertisers tamper with the news policies and manipulate coverage, the audience dwindles as more and more consumers realize that the news coverage lacks integrity. The audience then is less valuable to the advertisers who did the tampering. In the end, both the advertisers and the news organization lose.

Barbara Cochran, president of the Radio-Television News Directors Association, explained the danger in an interview with *Columbia Journalism Review*: "If your viewers and listeners start to think your news content is for sale, you'll lose credibility and the value that advertisers want will be damaged."[20]

Online journalists also are twice as likely as print and broadcast journalists to say that owners and advertisers try to influence news coverage, according to a March 2008 report by the Pew Research Center for the People & the Press. The survey showed that about a quarter of print and broadcast journalists saw this kind of interference, while nearly half of the online journalists did. "This is especially notable, considering that most of the Internet journalists in the sample work for the online operations of traditional print and broadcast outlets," the survey analysts wrote.[21] Rick Edmonds, who helps to conduct seminars for online news executives at the Poynter Institute, said the survey confirmed "what we hear regularly ... lots of pressure to do deals and cut corners – worsened by the very foggy borders between news and ads in home-page design."[22]

Some Questionable Practices

The scramble to increase advertising revenue and to reduce newsroom expenses has resulted in some innovations that are ethically borderline or worse.

In-text advertising

As an online user, you are accustomed to seeing words with single blue underlines. They signal a link that can take you to another site providing information relevant to the story you are reading. So what happens if you see a word with two green underlines on a news website? The word is a legitimate part of the story, but if you move the cursor over it, an advertisement appears.

This is in-text advertising, a technique that has been a fixture in niche websites like those serving video-game buffs. In recent years it has found its way into the sites of some mainstream news organizations. The brokers who provide the service say they pose no problem to journalistic independence because, first, the journalists don't know what keywords have been sold; second, the user does not see the ad unless he or she moves the cursor; and third, the keywords are purposely marked with green double-underlines so that the user does not confuse them with links to related content.[23]

Those caveats did nothing to mollify former newspaper editor Tim McGuire. When he encountered in-text advertising for the first time on the *Arizona Republic's* website, he wrote in his blog:

> When the cursor floats over the words 'tennis' or 'athletic' a deodorant ad will pop up. That stinks! At that moment, a reader has to wonder whether they are reading real news or a conduit for advertising. It will not require conspiracy theorists to wonder if those words were necessary to the story or if they were inserted to maximize advertising opportunities.[24]

Advertising in nontraditional formats

In 2001, WFLA-TV in Tampa, Florida, started "Daytime," a show that went on the air each morning immediately after the NBC program "Today" and used a similar interview format. Unlike the guests on "Today," some of the guests of "Daytime" were paying for the privilege of being interviewed about their businesses. The fee was $2,500 for four to six minutes.

Reporting on the WFLA program in *The Washington Post*, media critic Howard Kurtz noted that the station's logo, including NBC's peacock, appeared at the bottom of screen during the show. The only indication that some guests were paying came at the end, when the words "the following segments were paid advertisements" appeared on the screen in small type for four seconds, along with a list.

Eric Land, WFLA's president and general manager, told Kurtz that he saw no ethical problem because the program was "a separate entertainment program," not a news program. He said, "This television station has a history of breaking new ground. It gives some local advertisers who might not have production capabilities a chance to come on and demonstrate their product or service in a different format than thirty-second spots."[25]

KUSA in Denver sells five-minute segments to advertisers to discuss their products and services, and in some segments the advertiser is interviewed. Community groups and other guests appearing on the same show do not pay. Each paid segment is acknowledged after the segment and at the end of the show. General manager Mark Cornetta of KUSA said that the paid appearances are "fully disclosed" and that the program is hosted by independent contractors, not the station's news staff. This is an advertising issue, not an ethical issue, Cornetta said.[26]

In West Virginia, Sinclair Media's WCHS-TV and WVAH-TV won a 2007 regional Emmy award in the health/science/environment news category for a 90-second "West Virginia Wildlife" segment. Later, *The Charleston Gazette* reported that the state's Division of Natural Resources pays for the series and approves the scripts. Station news director Matt Snyder said he had no problem with the arrangement. "This is not an issue-oriented endeavor," Snyder said. "This is a feature piece on West Virginia and all the great outdoors that it has to offer." The contract also requires the stations to cover a "hunting and fishing days" celebration and a hunt show.[27]

Those programs are a variation of "infomercials" on television and "advertorials" in newspapers, which, as the names suggest, are advertisements in a news format. Although such hybrids generally are plainly labeled, there is ample reason to suspect that the labels do not offset some consumers' visual impression that they are seeing real news. If the consumer misunderstands, the advertiser gains an advantage. The advantage is the perception that an independent third party, namely the station or newspaper, is endorsing the advertiser's product. The mistaken perception also erodes the credibility of the news organization as members of the audience become aware that the pseudo-news is inferior in quality, lacking a neutral point of view, or both.

In 2003, the Society of Professional Journalists ethics committee issued a statement calling for news companies to clearly label any advertising that resembles news. The SPJ committee said:

> These practices are a disservice to the public, eroding the trust the public must have to find the work of the press credible … Such phony 'news' stories not only offend the public trust, they also undermine the credibility of the news operation for advertisers. Legitimate advertisers pay to be associated with newspaper, magazine or news shows because their messages will appear in a trustworthy place. Permitting news to be bought destroys the very reason good advertisers want to advertise in the press in the first place.[28]

Content provided by outside sources

In January 2004, the federal government rolled out its Medicare prescription subsidy program. The George W. Bush administration had won congressional approval for the plan over Democrats' protests that it benefited pharmaceutical companies more than the elderly, and that the government-subsidized prescriptions would still be too costly for many people.

During a two-week period that month, millions of Americans saw a television segment extolling the benefits of the new prescription program. The 90-second segment, shown by more than 40 television stations in small and mid-size markets, included a pleasant conversation between a pharmacist and an elderly customer in which the two agreed that the new prescription plan was a good idea.

The narrator who provided the voice-over for that conversation — and for the segment's other upbeat scenes — signed off, "In Washington, this is Karen Ryan reporting."[29]

The *New York Times* revealed two months later that the video was not a real news story but a promotional piece produced by a public relations company for the federal government's Health and Human Services Department.[30] Critics of the administration denounced the use of taxpayer dollars for propaganda. Journalists were outraged that the local stations had aired the segment without identifying its source.

The Medicare segment was an egregious example of how television stations can misuse "video news releases" (VNRs). Smaller stations find VNRs appealing because their thin news staffs are struggling to produce legitimate news to fill the air time. When the news media cut corners, some public relations people exploit that weakness to get their message to the public in an uncritical fashion.

In the case of the Medicare VNR, federal spokesman Kevin W. Keane defended the government's action and said notifying Medicare clients of benefit changes was required by law. "The use of video news releases is a common, routine practice in government and the private sector," Keane told *The New York Times*. "Anyone who has questions about this practice needs to do some research on modern public information tools."[31]

Like a written news release, a VNR might contain information useful to the audience, and so it can be a starting point for additional reporting. Deborah Potter wrote in *American Journalism Review*:

> Some provide stations with newsworthy video they couldn't get any other way – like crash tests from the Insurance Institute for Highway Safety, or b-roll of a new medical procedure. But viewers deserve to know if what they're seeing is a handout from a commercial or government source. If a station is going to use any part of a VNR, even just the video, it needs to disclose where the material came from, either in the script or in a graphic.[32]

VNRs continue to get air time, with or without disclosures. They are so much a part of hospitals' marketing efforts that a 2004 headline in *Columbia Journalism Review* called them "the epidemic." That phenomenon, Trudy Lieberman wrote in the magazine, is "the product of a marriage of the hospitals' desperate need to compete for lucrative lines of business in our current health system and of TV's hunger for cheap and easy stories."

Lieberman wrote that in many of the TV-hospital partnerships, "the hospitals effectively co-opt the station's journalistic duties. How much control the hospitals get varies from partnership to partnership, but they often select the topics, choose the patients and doctors, and sometimes write or edit the script."[33]

The Radio Television News Directors Association's code of ethics states that electronic journalists should "clearly disclose the origin of information and label all material provided by outsiders." If the VNR is the only way that newsworthy video can be obtained, RTNDA says, news managers and producers have to decide whether its value outweighs "the possible appearance of 'product placement' or commercial interests."[34]

Targeted demographics

In a fairly common practice, news companies promote their ability to produce the affluent customers that blue-chip advertisers want to reach. When this business strategy is allowed to influence news coverage, it violates the concept of social responsibility that journalism should be championing. Not only are some citizens marginalized because of their poverty, but all members of the audience are deprived of news coverage that accurately portrays the entire community.

The authors of *The Elements of Journalism* call targeted demographics a strategy "to enhance profits by going after the most affluent or efficient audience rather than the largest." Bill Kovach and Tom Rosenstiel write:

> In television, that meant designing the news for women age 18 to 49 who make most household buying decisions. In newspapers, that meant limiting circulation to the more affluent zip code areas. Targeting the news meant a news company theoretically could get more out of less – higher advertising rates with a smaller audience. It also meant the paper or TV station could ignore certain parts of the community in coverage, which saved money. Isolation, in other words, became a business plan.[35]

One aspect of targeted demographics is the emergence of niche feature sections in the newspaper or separately printed magazines mailed directly to selected homes. These sections deal with such topics as gardening, gourmet dining, and health and fitness. They appeal to affluent readers and attract what is known in the business as "incremental advertising" – revenue that the newspaper otherwise would not obtain. From a news standpoint, the value of such sections is limited, and social-issue topics like problems of the homeless will never qualify for this kind of detailed treatment because they repel rather than attract advertisers.

Product placement

Moviegoers are accustomed to the distraction of brand-name products on the big screen, film producers having discovered long ago that they could make extra money by charging companies for the exposure. Now, some television news operations are copying the idea.

On the set of morning newscasts at KVVU in Las Vegas, two cups of what appeared to be McDonald's ice coffee were placed in front of anchors in the summer of 2008. Although the cups had the McDonald's logo, they did not contain real coffee. Each cup, with a straw, was a scale model weighing seven pounds.

KVVU news director Adam P. Bradshaw told the *Las Vegas Sun* that the cups were put out only after 7 a.m., when the newscast shifted to lifestyle news. "I stress the fact that it is being done on a program that is a combination of news entertainment and lifestyle programming," he said.[36]

Sponsored features

The Philadelphia Inquirer has sold sponsorship of two daily features to banks. The daily news summary runs across the back page of the sports section, adorned in the trademark color of TD Bank, whose advertisement usually is the only one on the page. More problematical is the Monday–Friday column, "Phillyinc," a column that appears on the front of the business section, surrounded by the trademark color of the page's only advertiser, Citizens Bank.

When the features began in 2007, *Inquirer* editor Bill Marimow said the bank sponsors would have no control over the content, which would be "a hundred percent based on our news judgment and prerogatives." In the first 11 months that the business column ran, Citizens Bank was mentioned only three times. Marimow said that he had fielded one complaint about news coverage from "one of Citizens' public-relations people, who is not an employee of the bank," and that he listened to the complaint but took no action on it.[37]

In 2008, *The Inquirer* added another sponsored feature: a column on the front of its weekly Travel Section. The sponsor was Apple Vacations, which sells packages of airline tickets and resort accommodations.

Sponsored newsrooms

Two Midwest radio stations sold naming rights to their newsrooms. Milwaukee's WISN-AM sold its naming rights to PyraMax Bank in 2005, and as of Jan. 1,

2006, the newscasts of WIBA-AM in Madison, Wisconsin, opened with this announcement: "From the Amcore Bank News Center." Both stations are owned by Clear Channel Communications.

Deborah Potter, who reported the transactions in *American Journalism Review*, commented, "Listeners who get their news from the Amcore or PyraMax Bank newsroom might legitimately wonder how impartial its reporters can be when covering the banking industry, not to mention a story involving one of the banks themselves."[38]

Jeff Tyler, vice president and market manager for WIBA-AM, said in 2008: "Many 'newscenters' both on radio and television have followed the pattern to provide a 'product placement' in this manner with no effect on news integrity."[39]

Seeking a government investment

As his newspapers were pressured by lenders, publisher Brian Tierney of *The Philadelphia Inquirer* and *Philadelphia Daily News* sought investment money in 2009 from Pennsylvania's two largest state-employee pension funds. He approached Governor Edward G. Rendell, who arranged a meeting with pension officials. Nothing came of the meeting, but it raised questions about whether a government agency's investment would undermine the newspapers' journalistic independence.

Tierney declared emphatically that "the editorial integrity of the product" would not be affected. "If newspapers are to play the vital role they do in a democracy," he said, "then they cannot be put into a special line where they alone stand barred from receiving the economic dollars that are available to every other business in the state."

Others said that, to the contrary, news organizations are a special kind of business in which a government stake is unacceptable. Bob Steele of the Poynter Institute, one of the critics of Tierney's move, said: "A newspaper's primary obligation is to the public ... and to shine the light of scrutiny on state government on behalf of the public."[40]

The Contrasting Cultures of News and Business

Two metaphors dealing with the relationships of business and news executives have attained mythical status. One metaphor holds that there should be a "separation of church and state" – with news as the church and business as the state. The second declares that "a wall" should separate the two.

Understandably, business executives take exception to the church–state metaphor. Jack Fuller, who was both an editor and a business executive, expresses his scorn: "The establishment of journalists as a kind of priesthood has introduced an element of insufferable self-righteousness in newsrooms that has aggravated the journalists' natural inclination to see themselves as living in a world apart from ordinary, mercenary concerns."[41]

The idea of a wall is impractical because there has to be communication between the news department and the business departments. The authors of *The Elements of Journalism* write that the fallacy of that metaphor was revealed in the *Los Angeles Times*-Staples Center crisis (see Case Study No. 9), when the publisher initially did not tell the editor that advertising revenue for the special Staples Center section would be shared with the center. "The wall, in other words, was kept intact," Bill Kovach and Tom Rosenstiel write. "When the arrangement was later discovered, both reporters and readers were outraged."[42]

But the Staples Center episode also suggests there was a flaw in the continual interaction between mid-level news and advertising executives, which had been ordered by the *Times'* parent company's chief executive, Mark Willes. In his exhaustive report on the episode, the late David Shaw wrote in the *Times* that the routine involvement of editors in efforts to build advertising revenue rendered them less sensitive to signals that there might be problems in the magazine edition devoted exclusively to the Staples Center.

Rather than a wall, some business executives have suggested that there should be a "picket fence" that people can talk through. After Staples, the *Times* developed a statement of principles, one of them acknowledging that there should be communication between departments, but at an appropriate level.

An appropriate level for a discussion of policy matters is the top managers in each department. For example, advertisers' complaints about news, if they are deemed worthy of the newsroom's attention, should be communicated only from the top advertising manager to the top newsroom manager. It is inappropriate for, say, an advertising manager who has lost a restaurant account to air his grievances with the restaurant critic he blames for having alienated the advertiser.

Some newsroom veterans fondly remember a day when owners didn't bother their editors with the problems of commerce. In *The Vanishing Newspaper*, Philip Meyer writes:

> The reason newspapers were as good as they were in the golden age was not because of the wall between church and state. It was because the decision-making needed to resolve the profit–service conflict was made by a public-spirited individual who had control of both sides of the wall and who was rich and confident enough to do what he or she pleased. In today's world, most leaders of the press do not have that kind of functional autonomy.[43]

Jack Fuller, for one, remembers differently. In his *News Values* (written 8 years before Meyer's book, so he wasn't responding to Meyer personally), Fuller asserts:

> Odd as it seems to some of us who can still remember what it was like to work for privately owned newspapers, there are journalists who appear to have forgotten some

of its worst qualities: the authoritarian management system in which editors were like children before the powerful father; the use of the paper's coverage for the owners' personal needs; ... the commingling of resources so that a photographer might find himself detailed to shoot the picture for the owner's Christmas card; the shameless willingness to give advertisers (and personal favorites of the owner) privileged access to the newspaper's news columns.[44]

In 1973, Ridder Publications bought the morning *Wichita Eagle* and the afternoon *Wichita Beacon* from local owners. In 1974, Ridder merged with Knight Newspapers to form Knight Ridder, and in 1975, Davis "Buzz" Merritt was sent from Knight Ridder's Washington bureau to be the editor of the two newspapers. What Merritt found in the editor's desk drawer – artifacts from the days of the authoritarian local ownership – offers a glimpse of how journalism can be distorted to serve commercial interests:

A folder marked "newsroom policies" contained a series of memos outlining some of the rules ... One, noting that *The Eagle* had reported the rape of a woman in the downtown Macy's department store parking garage, declared that henceforth, the address and location of crimes related to businesses would not be reported. ...

Another rule: Wichita's economy is heavily dependent on four aviation plants, Boeing, Beech, Cessna, and Learjet – and in the event of an airplane crash, the paper would not report the make of the plane, unless it was a Piper or some other brand built elsewhere.

Another was a list of ... prominent people whose names would not appear in a negative light in the newspaper without clearance from "the second floor." The newsroom was on the third floor; the business office on the second.

And there were instructions to make sure that some "good news" was on the front page of the newspapers every day, adorned with the round, yellow smiley-face icon then popping up elsewhere. Pointedly, the definition of "good news" included store openings and important new building permits.[45]

Although today's publishers ultimately make the decisions, policy for the newspaper company is influenced by the "operating committee," which consists of the vice presidents representing the company departments, including news. In this environment, the editor is outnumbered; all the other vice presidents are oriented toward the company's business function and tend to dismiss newsroom concerns about ethics and credibility.

Maxwell King, who was editor of *The Philadelphia Inquirer* between 1990 and 1997, said his business colleagues were disdainful of the arguments that he and Zachary Stalberg, editor of the *Philadelphia Daily News*, made in the operating committee's meetings:

Zack and I argued that the public's trust in the newspaper has a commercial value. We pointed out that in their relationship with advertisers, they would see that the customer's trust would deliver something of value. They wouldn't lie or misrepresent to an advertiser, so we should not do that to our readers. We said that if we are honest and ethical, people will buy our product. The business executives saw us as prissy and insulated from the harsh realities of the business world.[46]

Publishers' and station managers' civic activism sometimes places them at odds with their newsroom leaders. The business executives consider it an essential civic duty to be "good citizens" in the community like the top executives of other businesses. The newsroom leaders worry that the audience will associate the company's activism with news coverage and perceive favoritism toward the publishers' or station managers' causes.

News coverage also is clouded by an apparent conflict of interest when the news company or its chief executive holds ownership stakes in enterprises that make news. The Tribune Company's ownership of the Chicago Cubs is the prime example (the new owner, Sam Zell, has put the team on the auction block), but other news companies also have invested in sports teams or have paid to have their names placed on sports arenas. In Boston, the New York Times Company owns not only *The Boston Globe* but also a 17 percent share of the parent company of the Boston Red Sox. When the owners of the *St. Louis Post-Dispatch* owned a 4 percent share in the St. Louis Cardinals (the paper has since been sold), the *Post-Dispatch* editorially endorsed the Cardinals' successful campaign for government aid to help build a new ballpark.[47]

In Lancaster, Pennsylvania, the company that publishes the local daily and Sunday newspapers has invested in a hotel that is part of a convention center complex built mainly with local and state tax money. The city will own the 300-room hotel – meaning it will pay no local taxes – and will lease it to a company formed by Lancaster Newspapers Inc. and another business. After 20 years, the private company can buy the hotel. Molly Henderson, a county commissioner who opposed the project, lost a reelection bid in 2007 and afterward filed a lawsuit accusing the newspapers of biased coverage. Jack Buckwalter, chief executive of the company that owns the afternoon *Lancaster New Era*, morning *Intelligencer Journal*, and *Sunday News*, said every news story about the hotel and convention center had noted the company's involvement. "We bent over backward to be totally open and fair," Buckwalter said.[48]

In the worst form of the news–business relationship, some publishers and station managers abuse their authority by manipulating news coverage. Fortunately, that kind of direct interference is relatively rare today, far removed from the era that produced the policies Buzz Merritt found in the folder in the editor's desk at *The Wichita Eagle* in 1974.

Yet, in the twenty-first century, editors of the *Pittsburgh Tribune-Review* were keenly aware that publisher Richard Scaife would not tolerate anything about the Pittsburgh Pirates on the front page.[49]

Point of View
Tangoing Without a Partner
Gene Roberts

Having journalists discuss ethics and standards without the participation of business executives is like tangoing without a partner. No matter how expert, no matter how serious, half of the act is missing.

Business executives, of course, control the money, and without firm commitments from these executives, journalists cannot set meaningful standards on what they cover in a community and what they pass on to the readers in the news columns. And there is also the question of treating readers fairly and without confusion by clearly delineating news from advertising. Again, it takes two to tango.

It is more important today than in the past for key players on the business side to get exposure to discussions on ethics and professional standards. Why? The hierarchy of newspapers has changed dramatically in just a generation or so. As recently as the 1950s and 1960s, most daily newspapers were family-owned local institutions. There were good owners and bad owners in terms of feeling a sense of public responsibility, but they were in overall charge of both the newsroom and the business-side and usually had to give at least some thought to the problems of each side. Usually, the owner had an editor to run the newsroom and a general manager to head up the business operations. The owners could be absolute monarchs, but found it in their interest to have a separation of church and state.

Today, more than 80 percent of America's approximately 1,500 dailies are owned by groups and chains. And the chief executives of these organizations appoint publishers to run each local newspaper. Increasingly, as profit pressures mount, these publishers are far more likely to come out of accounting departments or advertising than out of newsrooms. And usually they have authority over the editor, but without having nearly as much exposure to the overall quandaries of publishing as the old local owners had.

As newspaper revenues fall, the business executives cope with one financial emergency after another and make little time, if any, for discussions of publishing ethics and standards. Almost no one seems to be grappling with the fundamental questions of publishing and broadcast in a democratic society: What are a newspaper's (or television station's) obligations to its community? Does it have a societal duty to cover local government, state government, schools, courts and the major social and political issues of the day? What about foreign news and national news?

For well over two decades now, the overall trend line at newspapers is down in newsroom staff and the space devoted to news coverage. Obviously this has an impact on a newspaper's ability to collect the news and pass it on to the readers. Is there some point beyond which a publisher will not cut? Is

Continued

there any public obligation at all, other than to public stockholders?

Newspapers operate under unique constitutional protections. Do these protections obligate newspapers to make any sort of minimal commitments to news coverage? None that America's publishers are willing to acknowledge through their professional organizations. Neither the Newspaper Association of America, which represents most dailies in the United States, nor the National Newspaper Association, which represents most weeklies and some family-owned dailies, have ethical codes or any sort of written standards of professional obligations. The National Funeral Directors Association has a code of ethics. So do airline pilots. And interior designers. And booksellers. And professional organists. And professional hypnotists. And wedding professionals. The fabric of civilized society is not likely to unravel if a wedding is mishandled or if an interior designer botches an apartment makeover. But if a newspaper fails to properly cover local government or the public schools?

We need codes. We need standards. But above all we need a sober assessment of our obligations to supply the news and enough of it to ensure that our readers can be knowing participants in our democracies.

Excerpted from the Neal Shine Lecture on Ethics delivered at Michigan State University, November 12, 2007. Gene Roberts is a professor in the Philip Merrill College of Journalism at the University of Maryland. He is former executive editor of *The Philadelphia Inquirer* and managing editor of *The New York Times*.

Case Study No. 9
Sharing Ad Profits, Creating a Crisis

The $400 million Staples Center, home of the Lakers and Clippers basketball teams and the Kings hockey team, was completed in 1999. To commemorate the arena's impact on Los Angeles' downtown, the *Los Angeles Times* published a 164-page special issue of its Sunday magazine on Oct. 10, 1999.

Two weeks later, the *Times* news staff was in revolt. It had been discovered that the *Times* had shared the magazine's considerable advertising profit with the Staples Center. That created a huge conflict-of-interest problem for the reporters and editors who worked on the section, because to the public it appeared that they were giving all that space to a business partner.

Although the magazine's content was not influenced by the Staples Center or the *Times'* advertising department, it had been unpopular in the newsroom from the beginning. Many of the journalists worked on the special magazine considered it as excessive. Alice Short, editor of the magazine, said, "I put in a couple of months of my life working on an issue of

Continued

the magazine I didn't want to do. We were told it was tough luck; we had to do it anyway."

The *Los Angeles Business Journal* broke the news of the deal, and *The New York Times* followed with a detailed article. Within hours of receiving the news, more than 300 *Times* staff members had signed petitions in protest. "In one swift blow," the petition said, "we communicated to our readers that we have undisclosed financial ties with our editorial subjects."

The staff got moral support from the paper's retired publisher, Otis Chandler, who in the 1960s and 1970s led the *Times* to a national reputation for quality journalism. In a letter that was read in the newsroom, Chandler denounced the profit-sharing deal as "unbelievably stupid and unprofessional." His statement said, "Respect and credibility for a newspaper is irreplaceable. Sometimes it can never be restored." Immediately, photographs of Chandler were posted throughout the newsroom.

Kathryn Downing, a lawyer with no newspaper experience before she was appointed publisher less than two years earlier, addressed a meeting of 200 angry staff members and acknowledged that the deal had been a mistake. She said she had thought she was "protecting the line" between the business and news sides of the paper, but "I missed completely the fallout from sharing revenue."

The Staples Center episode occurred in the context of a five-year campaign by Mark Willes, a former cereal executive who had been hired as chief executive of the *Los Angeles Times*' parent company, to demolish the so-called wall between the business and news sides. Willes appointed "general manag-

ers" for each news section and directed that the general managers and section editors work together on ideas to create new revenue streams. Robert G. Magnuson, a former *Times* business editor, assessed the Willes innovation afterward: "However well intentioned, the system broke down when overzealous GMs, intent on strutting their stuff and showing off their P&L [profit-and-loss] prowess, waltzed into the newsroom barking orders to editors and reporters."

Although editor Michael Parks initially opposed the idea of an internal investigation that would result in a detailed report for readers, he gave in and assigned the task to the paper's media critic, David Shaw. Shaw's 14-page report, edited by retired managing editor George Cotliar, was published on December 20. Shaw faulted publisher Downing for failing to comprehend the deal's ethical ramifications, and editor Parks for not stopping the magazine's distribution or disclosing the conflict when he became aware of the deal.

Shaw also criticized Willes' campaign to demolish the wall between the business offices and the newsroom and replace it with a line easily crossed. "Many in the *Times*' newsroom see the Staples affair as the very visible and ugly tip of an ethical iceberg of ominous proportions – a boost-the-profits, drive-the-stock-price imperative that threatens to undermine the paper's quality, integrity and journalistic purpose." Shaw conceded that a wall has its flaws, but "a wall is also impregnable and immovable; a line can be breached much more easily, moved so gradually that no one knows it has actually been moved until it's too late, and principles have been irrevocably compromised." Willes was quoted in Shaw's story as saying that the Staples Center

Continued

incident argues for more communication between newspaper departments, not less. People didn't talk to each other when they should have, Willes said.

The profit-sharing deal grew out of an agreement that the *Times* signed on December 17, 1998, making it a "founding partner" of the Staples Center. The *Times* would get exclusive signage rights to the arena, exclusive rights to sell the *Times* inside the arena, a news kiosk in the main entrance, and a 16-seat suite for all events. The *Times* agreed to pay the Staples Center $1,600,000 a year for five years – $800,000 in cash, and the rest from "ideas" that would generate revenue. The special magazine was one of those revenue-generating ideas.

The day before the Shaw report was published, Downing and Parks published a "to our readers" statement on the front page acknowledging that the Staples deal was a mistake and announcing a new set of ethical principles to guide the *Times*. The following are excerpts from the principles:

- The *Times* will not engage in any dealing with advertisers or other groups that require or imply coverage or restrict it in any way.
- The publisher will fully and promptly disclose the nature of relationships (partnerships, sponsorships) to the editor.
- Themed advertising sections must be readily distinguishable from news.
- The *Times* will not contribute to political candidates, parties or causes or to ballot measures.
- Editorial staff will not be involved in managing or promoting [events or festivals] but may provide advice on speakers and panelists.
- Contact between editorial and the business side is essential to publish on a daily basis. These contacts should come at a level appropriate to the function. On larger issues, such as themes of coverage, decisions require the approval of the editor or a managing editor.

In March 2000, the *Times* and other media holdings of the Times Mirror Company were sold to the Tribune Company of Chicago. Willes, Downing and Parks all left the company.

Questions for Class Discussion

- What is meant by the traditional "wall" between a news organizations news and business staffs? Do you think Mark Willes' effort to remove the wall was a contributing factor to the Staples Center episode?
- What was the ethical issue in the decision to share advertising profits from the special magazine with the Staples Center? What guiding principle of the SPJ ethics code is involved?

- What do you think of the *Times'* decision to publish a 14-page critical analysis of the affair? What guiding principle of the SPJ code is involved in this decision?
- Read the *Times'* new advertising/news guidelines in the case study. What do you think is the reasoning behind each of the guidelines?

Notes

1   Lori Robertson and Rachel Smolkin, "John Carroll bows out in L.A.," *American Journalism Review*, August/September 2005.

2   Sarah Ellison, "Tribune forces Baquet to leave as L.A. editor," *The Wall Street Journal*, Nov. 8, 2006.

3   Thomas S. Mulligan and Dawn Chmielewski, "*Times* editor to leave paper," Jan. 21, 2008.

4   Editor Russ Stanton's speech to the newsroom, http://articles.latimes.com/2008/feb/15/business/fi-stanton15, Feb. 15, 2008.

5   Mulligan and Chmielewski, "*Times* editor to leave paper."

6   Emily Steele, "Why *Los Angeles Times* can't keep an editor," *The Wall Street Journal*, Jan. 22, 2008.

7   Michael A. Hiltzik, "*Los Angeles Times* publisher David Hiller resigns," *Los Angeles Times*, July 15, 2008.

8   Richard Perez-Peña, "Parting shot from *Los Angeles Times* editor," *International Herald Tribune*, Jan. 22, 2008.

9   James Rainey, "A media match plagued by a clash of cultures," *Los Angeles Times*, Nov. 10, 2006.

10 Sridhar Pappu, "Reckless disregard: Dean Baquet on the gutting of the *Los Angeles Times*," MotherJones.com, March 1, 2007.

11 Emily Steele, "Why *Los Angeles Times* can't keep an editor."

12 Ibid.

13 Niki Woodard, "Newspapers try to count readers differently," Project for Excellence in Journalism, http:www.journalism.org/node/8415, Nov. 8, 2007.

14 Philip Meyer, *The Vanishing Newspaper* (Columbia: University of Missouri Press, 2004), 10. Meyer attributes the theory of "harvesting marketing position" to Michael E. Porter, *Competitive Strategy: Creating and Sustaining Superior Performance* (New York: Free Press, 1998), 311.

15 Av Westin, *Best Practices for Television Journalists* (New York: The Freedom Forum's Free Press/ Fair Press Project, 2000), 3–5.

16 Rick Edmonds, "State of the Media 2008: Decoupling blues," http://www.poynter.org/content/content_view.asp?id=139610, March 19, 2008.

17 Bruce Kirk, news director of WINK-TV in Fort Meyers, Florida., quoted in Deborah Potter, "Later news," *American Journalism Review*, February/March 2008.

18 Jenifer Saba, "NAA reveals biggest ad revenue plunge in more than 50 years," *Editor & Publisher*, March 28, 2008.

19 Steven Church and Greg Bensinger, "*Philadelphia Inquirer*'s bankruptcy costs owners group (Update 2)," Bloomberg.com, Feb. 23, 2009.

20 Trudy Lieberman, "The epidemic," *Columbia Journalism Review*, March/April 2007.

21 Pew Research Center for the People & the Press, "Financial woes now overshadow all other concerns for journalists," http://www.stateofthenewsmedia.org/2008/journalist_survey, March 17, 2008, 8. The survey of 585 reporters, editors, and news executives was conducted Sep. 17 to Dec. 3, 2007.

22 Rick Edmonds, email to author, March 25, 2008.

23 David Kesmodel and Julia Angwin, "Is it news … or is it an ad?", *The Wall Street Journal*, Nov. 27, 2006.

24 Tim McGuire, "Let's count to 100 and then decide we hate ads in news copy," *McGuire on Media*, http://Cronkite.asu.edu/mcguireblog, Nov. 7, 2007.

25 Howard Kurtz, "Florida TV station cashes in on interview 'guests.'" *The Washington Post*, Oct. 16, 2003.

26 Mark Cornetta, email exchange with Shannon Kahle and Gene Foreman, Sept. 25–30, 2008.

27 Andrew Clevenger, "DNR pays for control of outdoor TV segment," *The Charleston* (W.Va.) *Gazette*, March 28, 2008.

28 Society of Professional Journalists, "SPJ calls on news media to maintain clear separation of news and advertising," Nov. 10, 2003.

29 Neil Henry, *American Carnival: Journalism under Siege in an Age of New Media* (Berkeley: University of California Press, 2007), 149–50.

30 Robert Pear, "U.S. videos, for TV news, come under scrutiny," *The New York Times*, March 15, 2004.

31 Ibid.

32 Deborah Potter, "Virtual news reports," *American Journalism Review*, June/July 2004.

33 Lieberman, "The epidemic."

34 "RTNDA Guidelines: Video News Releases," http://www.rtnda.org/pages/media_items/guidelines-for-video-news-releases-vnrs244.php.

35 Bill Kovach and Tom Rosenstiel, *The Elements of Journalism: What Newspeople Should Know and the Public Should Expect* (New York: Crown Publishers, 2001), 57.

36 Abigail Goodman, "Eye-opener with a pitch: TV news program tries product placement as a revenue source," *Las Vegas Sun*, July 21, 2008.

37 Bill Marimow, email to author, March 18, 2008.

38 Deborah Potter, "For sale," *American Journalism Review*, April/May 2006.

39 Jeff Tyler, email exchange with Shannon Kahle and Gene Foreman, Sept. 27–30, 2008.

40 Mario F. Cattabiani, "Rendell tried to help Phila. papers," *The Philadelphia Inquirer*, Jan. 31, 2009.

41 Jack Fuller, *News Values* (Chicago: University of Chicago Press, 1996), 200.

42 Kovach and Rosenstiel, *The Elements of Journalism*, 62.

43 Meyer, *The Vanishing Newspaper*, 206–7.

44 Fuller, *News Values*, 197.

45 Davis Merritt, *Knightfall* (New York: American Management Association, 2005), 67.

46 Author's telephone interview with Maxwell King, Nov. 12, 2007.

47 Roy Hartmann, "Loving the Cardinals as they are," *The New York Times*, March 26, 2002.

48 Linda Loyd, "Tower sparks controversy in Lancaster," *The Philadelphia Inquirer*, Sept. 2, 2008.

49 Kimberly Conniff, "All the views fit to print," *Brill's Content*, March 2001.

12 Getting the Story Right and Being Fair

Newswriting skills of accuracy and fairness are ethical skills, too

Learning Goals

This chapter will help you understand:

- the ethical importance of being accurate and fair in news reporting;
- the need to keep an open mind as reporting progresses: the journalist's duty is not to a certain hypothesis but to the search for truth;
- the responsibility to prove the authenticity of documents used in reporting;
- other guidelines for avoiding inaccuracy, unfairness, or both; and
- the value of acknowledging and correcting errors in the news.

Richard Jewell, a security guard stationed in Atlanta's Centennial Park during the 1996 Summer Olympics, seemingly was in the right place at the right time in the early morning of July 27. Police had received an anonymous call at 12:58 a.m. warning that a bomb would explode in 30 minutes. Near his station in the park, Jewell noticed a suspicious backpack. After notifying an agent of the Georgia Bureau of Investigation, who summoned bomb technicians, Jewell helped to evacuate the area. The bomb exploded at 1:20 a.m., killing one person and injuring 111.

His rescue efforts made Jewell a media hero. Katie Couric interviewed him for NBC's "Today" show and told him, "You did the right thing, Richard."

His hero image was short-lived. On the afternoon of July 30, the *Atlanta Journal-Constitution* published an extra edition with the front-page headline: "FBI suspects 'hero' guard may have planted bomb."

In the interim, a former employer of Jewell's had tipped the FBI about Jewell's erratic behavior as a college campus security guard. One possibility the FBI was examining in its investigation was whether Jewell, who aspired to be a police officer, might have set the bomb himself in order to be seen as a hero in clearing people out of the area. *Journal-Constitution* reporters soon picked up tips from law-enforcement officers that Jewell was being viewed as fitting "a profile." Those tips led to the July 30 extra edition.[1]

Jewell never was charged. The FBI notified him three months later that he was not a target of its investigation. The Centennial Park bomb actually was planted by Eric Rudolph, who also carried out other bombings in the Atlanta area and in Birmingham, Alabama, that killed a police officer and maimed a nurse. Charged in the Centennial Park bombing in 1998, Rudolph eluded capture for five years in the mountains of North Carolina. He pleaded guilty and is serving life in prison.[2]

On Aug. 1, 2006, Gov. Sonny Purdue honored Jewell at the Georgia State Capitol for having saved lives at Centennial Park.[3] On August 30, 2007, Jewell died at age 44 after battling diabetes.[4]

The *Journal-Constitution*'s July 30, 1996, story about Jewell presents two ethical questions: First, should he be named, given that he had not been charged? Second, if the answer to the first question is yes, is the resulting story accurate and fair?

As for the first question, there is an element of risk whenever an uncharged suspect is identified in the media. Foremost, there is the risk to the subject of the story, whose reputation may be tarnished by the publicity, and this should be of grave concern to the journalists. And for the news organization, there is the possibility of a libel suit if the suspect is never charged; Jewell reached financial settlements with *The New York Post*, CNN, and NBC,[5] and his suit against the *Journal-Constitution* was pending when he died.

In most cases editors and news directors wait to see if law-enforcement officers have enough evidence to file a charge. However, an argument can be made that identifying Jewell on July 30 was appropriate given the case's high profile and the *Journal-Constitution*'s solid information that Jewell was under suspicion. (Not only did the paper receive multiple tips, but a reporter read the story before publication to a law-enforcement agent who did not object to any of the statements about the investigation. The agent also assured the journalists that publishing the story would not hinder the investigation.) In any case, Jewell's status as a suspect would have become known the next day when FBI agents with a search warrant combed his home for evidence of bomb-making. The *Journal-Constitution*, whose elaborately detailed coverage of the Olympics was widely admired in the profession, obviously felt itself under pressure not to be beaten by competitors in any news event pertaining to the Olympics.

If Jewell were to be identified, then the newspaper had a special obligation to be fair to the uncharged suspect. To begin with, its story should have prominently noted two important facts: that Jewell had not been charged and that investigators had not revealed any physical evidence linking him to the crime.

The *Journal-Constitution*'s headline and 10-paragraph story, which cited no sources, did not make those disclaimers. It contained other problems of fairness, accuracy, and completeness. Several of those problems were discussed in a case study that *Los Angeles Times* journalist Ronald J. Ostrow wrote in 2003 for the Project for Excellence in Journalism. Ostrow wrote that the *Journal-Constitution*'s reporting that day was "coverage being shaped to support a conclusion."[6]

The lead paragraph's description of Jewell as "the focus" of the investigation lent itself to interpretation that he was the only person under suspicion. Ostrow said the reporters and editors struggled over how to describe Jewell before settling on this wording; one thought "focus" was a less damning description than "suspect." The journalists were aware that law-enforcement agents were looking at other possible suspects.[7]

The story said Jewell "fits the profile of the lone bomber," including the characteristics of "a frustrated white man" and "a police wannabe." These prejudicial descriptions were gleaned from the reporters' conversations with investigators. The paper made a factual error in stating that Jewell had "approached newspapers ... seeking publicity for his actions," overtures that would have fit the presumed profile.[8]

The story said the warning call was made "on a phone a few minutes' walk from the park," an imprecise measurement given that 22 minutes elapsed between the call and the explosion. In fact, law-enforcement investigators had already concluded that the distance was too great for Jewell to have made the call and returned to the park to report spotting the knapsack, Ostrow wrote. Later, Jewell's attorney said, "The theory of a person setting off a bomb to become a hero doesn't work if you have an accomplice."[9]

The story contained subtle juxtapositions of fact that invite conclusions – including statements that, as a onetime deputy sheriff, Jewell received bomb training, and that he owned a knapsack similar to the one that contained the bomb. A conclusion also is suggested by conspicuously attributing to Jewell certain statements about his actions that were already established fact – that he spotted the knapsack, that he pointed it out to a law-enforcement officer, and that he helped move people from the area. The story stated ominously, "Agents have not seen Jewell in NBC tape of the 20 minutes following the blast."

The story does not include a comment from Jewell, although the paper did try to talk with him. A reporter was sent to his apartment complex, which was being watched through binoculars by several men in plain clothes, but Jewell would not come to the door when she knocked. The reporter said he asked her to come back later when his mother returned. It is not clear whether this reporter knew what was in the story that the paper was preparing. Before the story was published, another reporter made several unanswered phone calls to Jewell's apartment.

The *Journal-Constitution*'s story set off a media frenzy. On talk shows, commentators did not hesitate to speculate on Jewell's guilt.[10]

L. Lin Wood, Jewell's attorney, later filed court papers describing a news environment in which "the media struggles to fill air time with different faces, different stories or different angles to known stories. The competition is intense and the profit potential is enormous." As a result, Wood said, "mistakes about individuals are published with increasing frequency and instantaneously broadcast and published to the world."[11]

Even in such an environment, Ostrow wrote in his case study, the news media must continue "to meet their traditional standards of fairness, accuracy and professional responsibility." If they do not, he wrote, "then news reporting as we have known and honored it would almost certainly disappear. There would no longer be a compelling reason for it to exist."[12]

Accuracy and Fairness: Standards of Ethical Reporting

Accuracy and fairness are the essence of journalism. The two virtues are intertwined.

Accuracy starts with the basic reporting skills of getting the facts right and presenting them in context. Standards for accuracy appear in the SPJ code under the principle of "seek truth and report it":

- "Test the accuracy of information from all sources and exercise care to avoid inadvertent error." (One vital characteristic of the ethical journalist is being diligent in gathering information; it is unethical to be sloppy.)
- "Identify sources whenever feasible." (Although some important stories can only be reported if the source's identity is shielded, they are the exception. Stories are more authoritative if the sources are named, permitting the audience to make its own evaluation of their reliability.)
- "Give voice to the voiceless; official and unofficial sources of information can be equally valid." (In an earlier era of journalism, journalists depended solely on police reports for an account of, say, a street melee. Today, good reporting draws also from accounts of citizen eyewitnesses.)

Journalists should not be satisfied with merely being accurate – that is, correctly reporting facts. They should strive for *truth*, in which the facts are presented in a context that fosters an understanding of the event or issue being reported. Truth, or a humanly possible approximation of it, may not emerge from a single day's reporting. The Watergate case, for example, took more than two years (1972–74) to unfold.

Journalists should be dismayed that people with personal knowledge of a news story's subject frequently find errors. The American Society of Newspaper Editors' reader survey in 1998 showed that errors were found by 43 percent of those with personal knowledge. The most common complaints were that the reporter misinterpreted facts or context. Of ASNE respondents who said they had been quoted in a newspaper, nearly one-quarter said they were quoted incorrectly.[13]

Some news organizations spot-check their reporting by sending a questionnaire to the story subjects. Bill Marimow, a two-time Pulitzer Prize winner as a reporter before becoming a newspaper editor, "audited" his own stories by phoning the subjects after the stories were published to make sure he got the facts right. Marimow said his audits often produced added benefits. "If something has happened since your last conversation [with the source], the audit may yield a followup story for the web or the next day's newspaper. Most important – and this is a subtle benefit – your sources will begin to trust you and respect you more than most of the other journalists who cover them. … That trust and respect, in time, eventually lead to more exclusive stories for your news organization because, when your sources want to disclose something, they'll think of calling you first."[14]

Some magazines employ fact-checkers who essentially re-report the stories. They contact sources to ask if they were quoted correctly, and they conduct research to verify facts from archives. Time constraints make it impractical for newspapers, broadcast, and online sites to employ fact-checkers, but good editors develop a sixth sense that alerts them to facts in news stories that need to be double-checked. There is a saying in journalism: "If your mother says she loves you, check it out."

Fairness revolves around the journalist's moral obligation to be neutral and straightforward in reporting, rejecting favoritism or bias. Standards for fairness appear under two SPJ principles – "seek truth and report it" and "minimize harm":

- "Diligently seek out subjects of news stories to give them the opportunity to respond to allegations of wrongdoing."
- "Show compassion for those who may be affected adversely by news coverage."
- "Be judicious about identifying juvenile suspects or victims of sex crimes."
- "Be judicious about naming criminal suspects before the formal filing of charges."
- "Balance a criminal suspect's fair-trial rights with the public's right to be informed."

As the SPJ code states, it is essential to get a response from a person or institution criticized in a news story. In its manual of style and usage, *The New York Times* emphasizes that the subject must have a chance to reply to the criticism. "If the attack is detailed or occurs in a deeply researched article, time and space must be allowed for the subject's thoughtful comment. A reporter must make every effort to reach those criticized. If they cannot be found, the article should say what effort was made, over how long a time, and tell why it did not succeed."[15]

Sometimes, the subject's response is so convincing that the news organization kills the story once the response has been corroborated. At the other extreme, the response misstates or obfuscates. The journalist has a duty to ask followup questions. For example, in the aftermath of Hurricane Katrina's devastation of New Orleans in 2005, Chris Wallace of Fox News asked Homeland Security's Michael Chertoff: "How is it possible that you could not have known on late Thursday, for instance, that there were thousands of people in the convention center who didn't have food, who didn't have water, who didn't have security, when that was being reported on national television?"[16]

Fairness also means that news organizations should be conscious of how they handled comparable news developments in the past. If A's announcement of candidacy for mayor leads the evening newscast, so should B's. If a person is charged with a crime on the front page, his or her acquittal also should appear on the front.

Completeness is another essential reporting standard. Bill Marimow makes the point that a good news story is accurate, fair, and *thorough*.[17]

In some cases, journalists should acknowledge that their reporting is incomplete – that the audience's questions are the same questions the journalist is grappling with. Acknowledging these questions is an example of what is known as *transparency*. Butch Ward of the Poynter Institute writes:

> When you include in a story the questions that remain to be answered, you signal that the search for the truth is unfinished – and needs to continue. You also reduce the chance that the reader or viewer will come up with their own list of unanswered questions. And you head off any criticism of your work as careless, shallow, or biased by acknowledging that it is incomplete.[18]

Don't Fall in Love with the Story

The scientific method learned in chemistry class has application to journalism. Like the scientist, the journalist starts with a hypothesis – the premise that, if true, would result in a newsworthy story. Then, like the scientist who performs experiments to prove or disprove the hypothesis, the journalist gathers facts and dispassionately tests the premise. Neither the scientist nor the journalist is vested in *proving* the hypothesis. Instead, the goal of both is to *seek truth*.

On June 7, 1998, viewers of Cable News Network saw a documentary that made two stunning allegations: that the US military used lethal nerve gas in a commando operation in the Vietnam War, and that the target was American defectors.

The documentary, titled "Valley of Death," launched an early example of television–print convergence. The series "NewsStand: CNN & *Time*" was intended to produce blockbuster investigative reporting and to showcase it concurrently on the cable network and in the pages of the newsmagazine.

When the Pentagon vigorously disputed the two allegations, CNN's exposé quickly turned into an embarrassment for the network and its newsmagazine partner. CNN hired lawyer Floyd Abrams to conduct his own investigation. Abrams reviewed the evidence and reported on July 2 that the conclusions made in the documentary could not be substantiated. CNN retracted the story and apologized. The documentary's producers, April Oliver and Jack Smith, and their supervisor, Pamela Hill, lost their jobs. *Time* also retracted its printed version of the CNN story.[19]

What had gone wrong? The producers, CNN president Richard Kaplan said on his network's *Reliable Sources* program, had "fallen in love with their story."[20]

They had relied too much on evidence that supported their thesis and too little on evidence that indicated the thesis was not true. Kaplan's metaphor suggested that the producers, like anyone in love, magnified the positives and dismissed the negatives about the object of their passion.

Time managing editor Walter Isaacson made much the same assessment in an interview for *American Journalism Review*. The lesson to be learned, Isaacson said, was to be wary about "the dangers of reporters who zealously … believe in a particular story, grabbing at facts that support the story and ignoring those that don't."[21]

"Valley of Death" recounted a commando raid on a village in Laos in September 1970 that the military called Operation Tailwind. According to the CNN documentary, US pilots dropped sarin, a nerve gas, on the village one night, and 16 commandos attacked the village the next morning with automatic weapons and hand grenades. The documentary asserted that there were Americans in the village. To protect the commandos as they were being airlifted out of the area, CNN said, US pilots dropped sarin on approaching enemy troops.[22]

For confirmation, CNN relied most heavily on interviews with retired Admiral Thomas Moorer, who in 1970 was chairman of the Joint Chiefs of Staff and the nation's top military officer. The admiral's responses to questions, Abrams said, were "often cast in hypothetical terms," and he "simply does not come close" to confirming CNN's conclusions. For example, Moorer was asked on camera, "So you are aware sarin was used?" Moorer responded: "I am not confirming for you that it was used. You have told me that. But let me put it this way, it does not surprise me. In an operation of this kind, you must make certain your men are as well equipped for defensive purposes as possible. …"[23]

Another key figure in the documentary was Robert Van Buskirk, who was second in command of the Operation Tailwind commandos. In on-camera interviews former Lieutenant Van Buskirk said that "sleeping gas" was slang for "nerve gas" and that he and his men were warned to take gas masks because "this stuff can kill you." Van Buskirk wrote a book about Tailwind in 1983 that did not mention the use of nerve gas, an omission that the former officer said was necessary "because it was still top secret." Van Buskirk disclosed in an on-camera interview that he had been prescribed drugs for a "nervous disorder" for ten years. Abrams said that while Van Buskirk was an articulate, knowledgeable source about Tailwind, it was unacceptable for CNN to "ignore his medical history, the inconsistency between his book and what he said on air, and the ambiguity in his recollections of the gas."[24]

Abrams said CNN should have used more of its interview with former Captain Eugene McCarley, who led the commando unit. McCarley said on camera, "I never, ever considered the use of lethal gas, not on any of my operations." McCarley told the investigators CNN had not used his statement that the mission had nothing to do with killing American defectors. Abrams also said the two pilots who dropped the gas in question rejected the premise that it was nerve gas; one of the pilots found a journal notation he had written the day after the end of the mission saying that his plane had been stocked with tear gas. An Army medic who served on the ground in Tailwind said he told CNN producers three times that the gas was not sarin but tear gas: "[I]t burned like CS [tear gas] in the eyes, my throat felt like CS, and my skin felt like CS … once you are exposed to it, there is no question in your mind what it is."[25]

Abrams dismissed any possibility that the documentary was a fabrication. "The CNN journalists involved in this project believed every word they wrote," Abrams reported,

> If anything, the serious flaws in the broadcast … may stem from the depth of those beliefs and the degree to which the journalists discounted contrary information they received precisely because they were so firmly persuaded that what they were broadcasting was true.

Indeed, Oliver and Smith were not convinced that Abrams had disproved the conclusions in their documentary.[26]

If You Can't Prove It, You Can't Use It

A news story based on documents can collapse if the journalists cannot prove their authenticity. Establishing unequivocal proof is the responsibility of the journalist.

CBS's "60 Minutes Wednesday," in a report narrated by Dan Rather on September 8, 2004, asserted that President George W. Bush had received favored treatment while a Texas Air National Guard pilot during the Vietnam War era. As proof, CBS offered memos that it said were written by Bush's commanding officer in 1972 and 1973 and showed that the commander was disturbed over Bush's failure to take a physical exam to remain eligible for flight duty. The memos also purported to show that the commander thought he was being pressured to "sugar coat" Bush's officer evaluation and was displeased that Bush was asking for a transfer to Alabama so that he could help run a political campaign.[27]

Bloggers quickly disputed the authenticity of the memos, which contained a character (the raised "th" on a date) that the bloggers said was not available on the typewriters in use at the time. Citing this and other supposed discrepancies in the typeface, the bloggers said the memos must have been written not in the early 1970s but on a computer years later. They accused CBS of making a spurious allegation to damage Bush's reelection chances.[28]

As criticism mounted in the mainstream news media as well as in the blogosphere, CBS staunchly defended its reporting. But on September 20, CBS News president Andrew Heyward acknowledged that the network could not prove that the memos were authentic. "We should not have used them," Heyward said. "That was a mistake we regret."[29]

CBS ordered an investigation by former United States Attorney General Dick Thornburgh and former Associated Press president Louis D. Boccardi. On January

5, 2005, the panel reported that it had identified serious questions about the authenticity of the memos – "questions that should have been raised before the September 8 segment aired." The panel said these questions were ignored because of "a myopic zeal" to be the first news organization to broadcast what it believed to be new information about Bush's service in the Guard. The panel also deplored the network's "rigid and blind defense of the segment after it aired despite numerous indications of its shortcomings."[30]

Five days later, CBS announced that three executives had been forced to resign and that the producer of the segment, Mary Mapes, had been fired. Dan Rather had announced in November 2004 that he was stepping down as anchor of the network's evening newscast in March 2005.[31] In a lawsuit in September 2007, Rather said CBS had forced him to give up the anchor slot that he had held 24 years. His suit against CBS accused the network of violating its contract by subsequently giving him less airtime on "60 Minutes" than promised.[32]

The disputed "60 Minutes Wednesday" segment focused on four memos "taken from" the personal files of the late Lieutenant Colonel Jerry B. Killian, who was Lieutenant George W. Bush's commanding officer. CBS got the documents from Bill Burkett, a retired lieutenant colonel in the National Guard. How Burkett got the documents became a mystery; he gave Mapes the name of a chief warrant officer who provided them,[33] but on September 20 he admitted to Rather in an on-air interview that he had felt pressured and "simply threw out a name." Rather then told viewers that CBS could no longer vouch for the documents' authenticity.[34]

"60 Minutes Wednesday" viewers had been informed in the September 8 segment that a document expert "believes the documents are authentic." In fact, the investigative panel reported, the analyst had told the producers only that he believed Killian's signatures were authentic. According to the panel, he and three other analysts consulted by CBS had said that the documents themselves could not be authenticated because they were copies.[35]

As the bloggers attacked in the days after the broadcast, a retired Guard major general, Bobby Hodges, contacted Rather and Mapes. Hodges had been quoted on the broadcast, though not by name, as confirming the contents. He said that he had been misquoted and that, having seen the documents since the broadcast, he concluded they were not authentic.[36] Marian Carr Knox, a clerk typist who worked with Killian during the period in which he purportedly wrote the memos, told *The Dallas Morning News* that she did not think the memos were authentic but that the content reflected Killian's opinions. She said the same thing when Rather interviewed her on "60 Minutes Wednesday."[37]

The Thornburgh-Boccardi panel said the CBS team committed "a litany of missteps" in the rush to broadcast the content of the memos before any of its competitors:

• Failing to establish "the chain of custody" of the documents – that is, how they got from Killian's files to Burkett, whom the panel described as a "sometimes controversial source with a partisan point of view."

- Declaring that the memos had been authenticated by document experts, when only one of the four experts consulted would go so far as to say that Killian's signatures appeared genuine.
- Relying on Hodges as a "trump card" to confirm the memos, when he had not been shown the memos before the broadcast but instead had been read their contents over the telephone.[38]

The panel also faulted Mapes for agreeing to a request from Burkett to put him in touch with the campaign of John Kerry, the Democratic opponent of Bush in 2004. Passing Burkett's telephone number to the Kerry campaign, the panel said, "gave the appearance of a political bias and could have been perceived as a news organization's assisting a campaign as opposed to reporting on a story."[39]

The review panel said it could not conclude "with absolute certainty" that the documents were authentic or forgeries. Instead, the panel emphasized that the journalists should have realized that there were serious questions about authenticity and that those questions should have been resolved before broadcasting the story.[40]

The panel's report was disputed by Mapes in a statement immediately afterward and by Rather in his lawsuit in 2007. Mapes noted that the panel had not proved that the memos were false and asserted that the timing of the broadcast was not her decision. "If there was a journalistic crime committed here," she said, "it was not by me."[41] Rather's lawsuit called the investigation "biased" and incomplete and said it was commissioned by CBS to "pacify the White House."[42]

Other Accuracy/Fairness Guidelines

Report only what you know is true

That is a basic rule of journalism, and a corollary is that you never assume anything.

Print journalists sometimes have to write about events that may or may not have happened by the time the paper is delivered. The customary solution is to rely on phrasing like: "In the text of a speech prepared for delivery Saturday night, the president said ..." The prose may be awkward, but it has the unassailable virtue of stating no more than the journalist can swear will be so when the paper is delivered.

Mitch Albom, the *Detroit Free Press*' popular sports columnist, regretted not taking that approach when he composed a column on Friday, April 1, 2005, for a section that the paper would print in advance for its Sunday issue of April 3.

Albom interviewed Mateen Cleaves and Jason Richardson, players in the National Basketball Association who had starred earlier for Michigan State University. They told Albom they planned to be at Michigan State's semifinal game to be played on Saturday, April 2, the day after Albom needed to file the column but the day before readers would see it. When Albom interviewed them, they spoke wistfully about the fun they had as college players.

Drawing on details the players told him, Albom's column described Cleaves and Richardson as "they sat in the stands, in their MSU clothing, and rooted on their alma mater." Both had flown in "just to sit together Saturday," Albom wrote. "Richardson, who earns millions, flew by private plane. Cleaves, who's on his fourth team in five years, bought a ticket and flew commercial."[43]

Unfortunately for Albom and his newspaper, Cleaves and Richardson had changed their plans. Scheduling conflicts kept them from attending the game.

A correction was run, saying in part: "The *Free Press* should not have reported the players were at the game. We do not present as fact events that have not occurred."[44] Albom apologized in the paper. He also phoned in to a Detroit radio talk show to apologize to his colleagues at the *Free Press*. Albom said, "All I had to do was write the words, 'were scheduled to.' Jason and Mateen were scheduled to fly. Jason and Mateen were scheduled to be in the crowd. And the whole rest of the column would have made sense."

Editor Carole Leigh Hutton assigned a team of reporters and editors to examine more than 600 Albom columns to determine whether he had done anything like this in the past. The investigative report, published in the paper May 16, found no evidence of similar problems.[46]

Hutton said in a letter to readers that disciplinary action had been taken against Albom and four other staff members who "had some role" in putting the column in the paper.[47] As for how the column got past the editors, the investigative report quoted editors as saying they either missed the column's underlying problem or failed to follow through on their misgivings. "I could kick myself," said one editor who said she noticed the past tense but put aside her concerns.[48]

Frame your stories fairly

Framing is the term that journalists use to define or interpret events they report on. Steven Smith, former editor of *The Spokesman-Review* in Spokane, Washington, has described the frame as "the context or narrative theme through which the story is told."[49] When they write about the daily ups and downs of the stock market, journalists frame stories in terms of what likely caused the changes. Thomas Patterson and Philip Seib write:

> A news story would be a buzzing jumble of facts if journalists did not impose meaning on it. At the same time, it is the frame, as much as the event or development itself, which affects how the citizen will interpret and respond to news developments.[50]

Obviously, selecting the frame is highly subjective, and journalists should be alert to two traps – first, allowing their opinions to get in the way, and second, choosing a frame solely on the basis of audience appeal.

Conflict is a popular story frame but one that can be exaggerated. Although the conflict frame may result in provocative stories, that could ignore nuances and mislead the audience about context. An example is a tendency to frame stories about proposed business and residential construction projects as "environmentalists versus developers."[51]

A 1998 study by the Project for Excellence in Journalism concluded that the press:

> shows a decided tendency to present the news through a combative lens. Three narrative frames – conflict, winners and losers, and revealing wrongdoing – accounted for thirty percent of all stories … The penchant for framing stories around these combative elements is even more pronounced at the top of the front page and is truer still when it comes to describing the actions or statements of government officials.[52]

Michele McLellan writes in *The Newspaper Credibility Handbook* that conflict framing focuses on the most strident voices in the public arena, ignoring moderate perspectives. "[T]he extreme assertions of partisans strike people who are looking at the issue from the middle as simplistic and sensationalistic," she writes.[53]

When he talks with journalists about conflict framing, general manager Dennis Hetzel of *The Kentucky Enquirer* uses this hypothetical:

> [A] school board … votes unanimously without debate to implement a new reading program and then votes 4–3 to buy a new dump truck. What's more newsworthy, based on those facts? It clearly should be the reading program. Many young journalists pick the dump truck, however.[54]

The conflict frame also influences questions that reporters ask news subjects. Leslie Whitaker, a teacher and freelance writer, suggested in *American Journalism Review* that instead of encouraging conflict, reporters should ask questions likely to elicit thoughtful answers. As an example she cited a question a reporter asked Democratic presidential candidate John Kerry in 2004 after Kerry criticized President George W. Bush for not having attended a single funeral of a soldier killed in Iraq. The reporter's question was: "How can you go to 500 funerals and be president?" Whitaker considered the question overly contentious. She wrote that the reporter might have gained more insight into Kerry's thinking by asking: "As president, how would you handle the funerals of the soldiers who have died in Iraq? What do you consider important as you think about weighing the competing needs of honoring American soldiers and the limits on your time as president?"[55]

Insist on adequate sourcing

When the scandal of President Bill Clinton's involvement with White House intern Monica Lewinsky broke in January 1998, associate managing editor Martin Baron of *The New York Times* was out of the country on vacation. When he returned, executive editor Joseph Lelyveld asked him to critique the paper's coverage of January 22–30, a period of intense media competition during which some said *The Times* failed to meet its own standards. Baron's report was summarized in Marvin Kalb's book *One Scandalous Story: Clinton, Lewinsky and 13 Days That Tarnished American Journalism.*

Baron was especially critical of *Times* reporters' attribution, or lack of it – "omissions that were thinly disguised, often through the use of passive tense, with phrases like 'said to be' and 'reportedly were to be.'" In one instance, *The Times* attributed information to Linda Tripp's tapes of her conversation with Monica Lewinsky – tapes that the paper did not have. Baron cited other sourcing problems, including:

- Quotes we never heard but felt free to recount without attribution. *"I worked at the White House," Ms Tripp explained to Mr Starr's investigators. "I saw what happens when you go against them. They smear you. They crush their dissidents."*
- Repeating sensational reports of others without confirming them ourselves. *And ABC News reported tonight that she received a package for the President from Ms. Lewinsky believed to contain love letters.* Baron asked: "Believed to contain"? Who believed?
- Questionable exercises in mind-reading. *"She was in love with the guy," said the person after listening to the tapes. "She felt she was his soul mate."*[56]

Screen polls and surveys carefully

To protect their audience from junk data, journalists have a duty to give their audience certain essential facts about a poll. *The Associated Press Stylebook* lists them: who did the poll and who paid for it; how many people were interviewed and how they were selected; who was interviewed (likely voters? registered voters?); how the poll was conducted (by telephone interview or some other way); when the poll was taken; the sampling error; and what questions were asked and in what order.[57]

The results should not be overstated. If a poll shows Candidate A ahead a week before the election, the news organization should not project him or her as the winner. That is because the poll is only a snapshot in time. People can change their minds, and some of Candidate A's followers may not go the polls on election day.

Polls in which people vote by Internet or by telephone are worthless because they measure only the sentiments of people who are motivated enough to participate. They also are subject to manipulation. Barb Palser wrote in *American Journalism Review* that in 2000 the Republican National Committee urged supporters to vote in web polls conducted by the news media after a debate between the presidential candidates. The result was a 60–40 online verdict that George W. Bush "won" the debate, while scientific polls showed a dead heat.[58]

Be alert for hoaxes

The news media have always been a target of pranksters. In small towns across America, local papers and radio stations have learned to double-check obituaries and announcements of engagements and weddings. Failing to do so can result in embarrassment for the news organization, not to mention the anguish suffered by the subjects of the fake reports.

Sometimes the stakes are higher and the media victims bigger. The *Los Angeles Times* had to retract and apologize for a 2008 story based on purported FBI records in which a confidential informant accused two men of helping to arrange a 1994 attack on Tupac Shakur in which the rap star was pistol-whipped and shot three times. In the face of threats of lawsuits by the two accused men and a critical review by the investigative website *The Smoking Gun*, the *Times* concluded 10 days later that the FBI records appeared to be fakes.

The Smoking Gun showed that the records, which had been filed in court by a federal prisoner, looked as if they had been produced on a typewriter, though the FBI had been using computers for three decades. The *Times*' retraction said the website also pointed out "numerous misspellings and unusual acronyms and redactions that could have cast doubt on the documents' authenticity." The misspellings were similar to those in a lawsuit the same prisoner had filed.[59]

Use sound research techniques

The Internet and its search engines have made it easier to gather and verify facts, but journalists have to be discriminating in the sites they use. They should heed the admonition of David Cay Johnston, a *New York Times* reporter: "No matter who your sources are, when you sign your name you are responsible for every word, every thought, every concept."[60]

Wikipedia, the online encyclopedia started in 2001, should never be cited as a source in news stories because, as its own disclaimer says, "anyone with an Internet connection" can alter the content.[61]

Barbara G. Friedman, author of *Web Search Savvy: Strategies and Shortcuts for Online Research*, ranks Internet domains according to a "heirarchy of trust." Her rankings, in descending order, are: *gov* and *mil* (content on these domains is subject to "copious checks"); *edu*; *org* and *net*; and *com*.[62]

Blogs began as vehicles to express opinion, not to gather, verify and disseminate information. Although some blogs are factually accurate, journalists have a duty to assure themselves of a site's reliability before using it as a source.

Set the Record Straight

Corrections of fact are routine in the news media today. Acknowledging error is another product of the maturing of journalism in the second half of the twentieth century.

The late David Shaw, media critic for the *Los Angeles Times*, reminisced in 2004 about how, early in his career, editors regarded corrections as:

> the airing of dirty laundry that would, they feared, undermine their papers' credibility. Thus, newspapers generally printed corrections only when they were threatened with libel suits or when their errors were so egregious that they had no choice – and then they tried to bury those corrections in the back of the paper, next to the ads for athlete's foot powder.

Shaw credited the Louisville *Courier-Journal* and *Times* as being the first US newspapers, in 1967, to "institutionalize the practice of routinely publishing corrections in a prominent, designated place." By 1973, a quarter of the newspapers with more than 100,000 circulation had such a policy. The number grew in the 1990s, and the American Society of Newspaper Editors reported in 1999 that the practice was embraced by 93 percent of newspapers with more than 5,000 circulation.[63]

For newspapers, a "best practice" is to publish corrections in an anchored position – that is, in the same location each day, to be easier for readers to find. Another best practice is to write corrections in the most lucid prose, carefully explaining what was wrong with the original story and what the correct facts are. If the essence of a front-page story is proved wrong, the corrective story should also appear on the front. This was the case on March 27, 2008, when the *Los Angeles Times* apologized for and corrected its Tupac Shakur story mentioned earlier.[64]

For broadcast journalism, a problem is how to get a correction to the people who likely saw or heard the error, since the audience for subsequent newscasts may be different. In their book *Advancing the Story*, Debora Halpern Wenger and Deborah Potter recommend correcting the mistake in the next newscast and then repeating the correction the next day in the newscast aired in the same time slot that the mistake was broadcast. "The goal is to make sure the correct information reaches the widest possible audience as well as to let people know that accuracy matters to the news organization."[65]

When errors occur in online reporting, news organizations should correct the mistakes and indicate what was wrong in an earlier version. Simply removing the error without flagging the story means that users who saw the earlier version are not cautioned that they were misinformed. In *Advancing the Story*, Wenger and Potter advocate that news sites make their corrections policy clear to their users and provide an email address for reporting errors.[66]

Although it may seem a contradiction, the more diligently that journalists correct their errors, the more believable they become in the eyes of their audience.

Point of View

The Importance of a Second Look

William F. Woo

When you are assigned to a beat, it is important to maintain some independence, or distance, from it. It's easy to be captured by a beat and to assume that whatever officials tell you ought to go straight into the paper. That's especially so when the story is sensational and you have great access.

But there is never a moment when your critical thinking should be suspended, never a moment when it's enough to say, as a justification for printing something, that this is what the cops told me or the school officials told me or the "sources" at City Hall told me. There is no moratorium in journalism for checking it out yourself. Consider the story of Palestina Isa.

On an autumn day in 1989, Palestina, a 16-year-old Muslim girl, returned to her home in south St. Louis after her night shift at a fast-food restaurant. She and her parents lived in an apartment in what urbanologists call an ethnically changing neighborhood.

Back in the nineteenth century, it had been the home of German immigrants, who gave the area its name, Dutchtown. Then poor whites from the South moved in, and then blacks, and last came people from Asia, the Middle East, and Latin America. Newcomers to St. Louis, they found the sturdy brick apartments a good source of reasonable housing. The old-stock German Americans by then had long moved to St. Louis County.

Within minutes after she got home, Palestina Isa was dead, stabbed at least eight times by the hand of her father. According to the account in the *Post-Dispatch*, the girl had demanded $5,000 from her parents and had then gone berserk.

Here was our lede:

"Zein Hassa Isa explained Monday morning how some 12 hours earlier he took a knife away from his teenage daughter and then plunged it into her chest.

"*'She came at me with the knife. If she not dead, I dead,' said Isa.*"

There's no doubt in that account. He *explained* *how* he took the knife away from her. That she had a knife is assumed. As presented, that's beyond dispute and very different from, He *said* he had taken the knife away from her.

Explained tells us he was describing a reality. *Explained* tells us how it happened, not *that* it happened.

In rhetoric, this is called begging the question, in which the conclusion is assumed from the premise.

I remember the buzz at the morning news conference when the city editors promoted the story for page 1A, where it ran the next day. We have this exclusive interview with the father. Terrific quotes! Enterprise!

Continued

The killing in self-defense was the police version of the incident, which we had in detail and which was not available to other media. The problem was, none of it was true.

As it happened, Martha Shirk, my wife, was suspicious the moment she read the story. She covered children's welfare issues and knew that violence in the home usually has a history. It rarely happens out of the blue. This, after all, was an A student in high school. So Martha checked with the child abuse officials. Her follow-up story ran two days later. On page 4C.

It turned out that there was a record of hot-line calls about the Isa family. People who knew Palestina said she was a "girl you'd be proud to have as your daughter." She showed up at school with bruises on her face.

We come now to a divergence of the definition of enterprise. The original interview with the father, Zein Hassa Isa, was described as a real scoop. It was an exclusive, though the story had come about because police had made Isa available to our reporter. Working a beat, developing contacts, had resulted in a page one story. That's enterprise.

But Martha's piece was also enterprise. Nobody handed this one to a reporter. A beat reporter with sources had seen something that didn't ring true, and she had pursued it. I acknowledge a prejudice and personal interest here in the reporter, but I like the idea of journalists going beyond what official sources provide.

Unbelievably, here is what comes next. The father was suspected of being involved with the Palestine Liberation Front, and the feds had bugged the house. They recorded the killing and also other conversations.

Palestina Isa was going out with a black man. Her father was on tape saying his daughter was "a burned woman, a black whore, and there is no way to cleanse her except through the red color that cleanses her." To a caller, he had said, "Teaching her has to take place in the hotel under ground." In another conversation, he said, "I'll put a knife in her hand after she goes down, of course." Palestina Isa died in an honor killing.

The tape caught the terrible moments of the girl's death struggle. Eventually, her father and mother, who helped cover up the crime, were convicted of murdering their daughter.

In this case, the press enthusiastically, gleefully even, took the word of officials who were all to eager to place their own spin on events. Journalists failed to exercise critical judgment and failed to observe the requirements of fairness.

If you cover a beat, it's easy and comfortable to look at the world from the point of view of your sources and to ignore their biases. Now and then, a few journalists have the courage to say: Wait a minute. Let's examine this more closely.

Excerpted from *Letters from the Editor: Lessons from Journalism and Life* (Columbia: University of Missouri Press, 2007), 79–82. The book was compiled from the letters that William F. Woo wrote to his Stanford students. Woo was editor of the *St. Louis Post-Dispatch* for 10 years.

Case Study No. 10
Duke Lacrosse: One Newspaper's Journey

Rachel Smolkin

On March 24, 2006, Raleigh's *News and Observer* broke the news that "all but one member of the Duke lacrosse team had reported to the Durham police crime lab" for DNA testing.

Executive editor Melanie Sill says the story got front-page treatment because of the sweeping nature of "the roundup" of all members of a local college sports team. "We had never seen so many people brought in all at once for a cattle-call DNA test."

The story told the reason for the roundup: "Police think at least three of the men could be responsible for the sexual assault, beating, robbery and near-strangulation of one of two women who had an appointment to dance at the party March 13, according to a search warrant."

The police were investigating allegations by one of the two dancers that three team members forced her into a bathroom, where they beat her, raped her, and sodomized her. Two lacrosse players, Reade Seligmann and Collin Finnerty, were arrested on April 18, 2006, on charges of first-degree rape, first-degree sex offense, and first-degree kidnapping. Team captain David Evans was arrested on May 15, 2006. Evans spoke publicly before surrendering to police: "You have all been told some fantastic lies, and I look forward to watching them unravel in the weeks to come."

Duke canceled the men's lacrosse season, and coach Mike Pressler resigned.

District Attorney Michael B. Nifong pursued Seligmann, Finnerty, and Evans even as evidence of their innocence mounted. Two rounds of DNA testing of team members found no conclusive matches, and contradictions emerged in the accuser's account. As Nifong's case imploded, the North Carolina bar filed ethics charges against him. On April 11, 2007, State Attorney General Roy Cooper exonerated the three athletes. On June 15, 2007, Nifong was disbarred.

Through the episode, with admirable exceptions, the news media all too eagerly embraced the inflammatory statements of a prosecutor in the midst of a tough election campaign. Fueled by Nifong's frequent public pronouncements, the media quickly latched on to a narrative too seductive to check: rich, wild, white jocks had brutalized a working class, black mother of two.

National and international coverage tended to focus on strains between "town and gown," depicting an elite, largely white university colliding with the working-class, racially mixed city that surrounds it. The privileged nature of Duke's students, particularly its athletes, was frequently invoked; references to Duke's "Gothic" architecture and the schisms of the Old South were also popular.

"It was too delicious a story," says Daniel Okrent, a former *New York Times* public editor. "It conformed too well to too many preconceived notions of too many in the press: white

Continued

over black, rich over poor, athletes over non-athletes, men over women, educated over non-educated. Wow. That's a package of sins that really fit the preconceptions of a lot of us."

The lessons of the media's rush to judgment and their affair with a sensational, simplistic storyline rank among journalism's most basic tenets: be fair; stick to the facts; question authorities; don't assume; pay attention to alternative explanations.

The News and Observer, a McClatchy paper with a weekday circulation of 177,361, would quickly lead the media with probing, tenacious reporting that revealed numerous infractions in the investigation. But its "early coverage contributed to the narrative of racial/class/gender victimization that the local community and the national media seized upon," the paper's public editor, Ted Vaden, wrote on April 15, 2007.

A front-page, March 25, 2006, interview with the accuser, headlined "Dancer gives details of ordeal," did not name the woman, in keeping with the paper's policy on victims of alleged sex crimes. (*The News and Observer* did publish the accuser's name after the players were exonerated.) The one-sided, sympathetic portrayal, which several times referred to the accuser as "the victim," allowed her to make blind accusations. It wasn't made clear until deep into the story that the athletes could not be reached for comment.

A page-one story on March 28, 2006, disclosed that during the past three years, about a third of the men's lacrosse team had been charged with misdemeanors related to drunken and disruptive behavior. A similar front-page story on April 9 was headlined "Team has swaggered for years."

But the accuser's criminal record – stemming from a "2002 incident involving drunken driving, a stolen car and an attempt to flee

from police" – was not mentioned until April 7, 2006, low in a story on A14. No details were included. "It seemed to me there was some imbalance in publishing misdemeanor offenses of the students, but taking longer to publish the accuser's more serious offenses," public editor Vaden says. "And it was in a longer story about something else."

News and Observer metro columnist Ruth Sheehan produced an early conspiracy-of-silence rant. Her March 27, 2006, piece began: "Members of the Duke men's lacrosse team: You know. We know you know. Whatever happened in the bathroom at the stripper party gone terribly terribly bad, you know who was involved."

Sheehan reassessed as evidence of the players' innocence deepened. Her column on April 13, 2006, published three days after defense attorneys announced that DNA tests found no links between the accuser and the athletes, invoked the specter of Tawana Brawley, the black girl whose 1987 account of a gang rape by white law enforcement officers quickly unraveled. "There is no punishment on the books sufficient for a woman who would falsely accuse even the biggest jerks on campus of gang rape," wrote Sheehan.

Sheehan's deepening skepticism was reflective of *The News and Observer*'s coverage as a whole.

Executive editor Sill (now editor of *The Sacramento Bee*) calls the Duke case "a reminder of the need for skepticism when dealing with official sources and police and prosecutors. … It's kind of a case study of a lot of things that you know can go wrong in crime reporting if you don't heed that maxim 'innocent until proven guilty.'"

In spring 2007, Sill and her senior editors assembled the staff to talk about lessons learned. "A lot of the coverage held up," she

Continued

says. "I think there was a sense, though, that some stories were overplayed or lacked that sense of proportion." For example, "In reporting that storyline on the players' conduct, that's where we think that we overplayed things a bit and played to storyline a bit."

Sill notes the firestorm began as a local police story for the paper's Durham bureau, and "we likely didn't have as many person-to-person conversations" as staffers would have had if the story had broken in Raleigh, about 20 miles away. Also, while Nifong was talking, the players and their representatives initially were silent. That presented challenges for reporters trying to present balanced stories. "The first three or four days of coverage, that was a real hole in the reporting," Sill says. "In hindsight, we should have been much more emphatic much higher in the stories that we didn't have that other side."

Sill's reporters also watched in frustration as national media vied for their sources. "It was a messy story, and the outside media coverage, especially the cable television shows, the presence of every national media outlet here, made it much harder to report," she says. "People we would normally just go interview were having press conferences, or wouldn't talk, or would only talk in a leaking situation." But top editors told the staff that quoting unnamed sources was unacceptable.

Concerned about saturation coverage and the case's fluidity, senior editors also halted columns on the issue after Sheehan's second one, an April 3, 2006, piece demanding the firing of lacrosse coach Pressler. The respite gave staff a few days to get a better handle on emerging facts; when the ban was lifted soon after, columnists were told to use care, and top editors vetted all columns.

Joe Neff, a *News and Observer* investigative reporter, was one of a handful of journalists who dug deep into the evidence – some publicly available, some shared confidentially by sources – to debunk Nifong's case. These journalists bucked the pack and burrowed beneath an enticing narrative to raise questions about the case against the lacrosse players.

Sill assigned Neff to the story because "she had a gut feeling that it wasn't right," he says. "[W]e kept peeling back the layers of the onion. At first it just seemed like incompetence or tunnel vision on the part of the DA and cops. As we went along, it becomes less of the tunnel vision and more deceit."

He was struck by the absolute insistence of the defense lawyers, whom he'd known for years, that their clients were "innocent." He had expected to hear more routine assertions that "it didn't happen that way; it's a misunderstanding."

"In few criminal cases have the prosecution and defense stuck their necks out so far and so fast," Neff and Anne Blythe wrote April 8, 2006, on A1. On April 30, Neff, Michael Biesecker, and Samiha Khanna reported that the accuser "picked out her alleged attackers in a process that violated the Durham Police Department's own policy on identification lineups." Neff's August 6, 2006, story revealed that the "accuser gave at least five different versions of the alleged assault to different police and medical interviewers and made shaky identifications of suspects. To get warrants, police made statements that weren't supported by information in their files."

Looking back, Neff wishes he and his colleagues had paid more attention to two items available from the start. The first was a police-blotter entry published in the Raleigh paper on March 22, 2006, on page B3. The brief said a woman had told police she was raped and robbed March 13 during a party at 610

Continued

North Buchanan Boulevard. It cited Sgt Mark D. Gottlieb as saying that residents of the rental house were cooperating.

"[W]hen the story blew up and it became this huge mess, we never said, 'Wait a minute. The police sergeant said they were cooperating, and Nifong said they weren't cooperating,'" Neff says. "I wish we would have caught that."

The second set of facts involved the accuser, who told a *News and Observer* reporter for the March 25, 2006, story that she had just started working as an exotic dancer. On April 7, 2006, the paper reported that she had been arrested in 2002 after stealing a taxi and trying to run over a police officer. "If we had pulled that incident report, we would have seen that she was doing a lap dance at a strip club," Neff says. "Part of the reporting is just to go, 'Oh, let's go pull this and see if there's anything there.'" In this instance, it "would have really given us pause. She's someone who's saying she only just started dancing a couple of weeks ago, when four years before she'd been dancing at a strip club and stealing a car."

Beginning April 14, 2007, three days after the athletes were exonerated, *The News and Observer* published an exhaustive five-part retrospective by Neff examining Nifong's blunders. Each part appeared on A1; the first was headlined "Nifong's quest to convict hid a lack of evidence."

On April 23, 2007, columnist Ruth Sheehan apologized. "Members of the men's Duke lacrosse team: I am sorry," she began. She noted that she had written 14 columns on the case, moving well beyond her initial code-of-silence diatribe and her demand for coach Pressler's ouster. She had already acknowledged her errors, but for many readers that wasn't enough. They wanted an apology. And they got one.

"I decided I needed, just for my own conscience, really, to write the last column," says Sheehan, who regrets the damage that her first two pieces may have caused. "I will approach cases in a different manner now. I will be much more cautious. I had a visceral reaction to that case as it was being described by the prosecutor."

Excerpted and edited slightly, with permission, from Rachel Smolkin, "Justice delayed," *American Journalism Review*, August/September 2007.

Questions for Class Discussion

- How does this case illustrate how unfairness can result from the prevailing media practice of naming people accused of sexual assaults while withholding the identity of the accusers?
- What errors were made by *The News and Observer* in the early weeks of coverage?
- How did *The News and Observer* adjust its coverage as the news developed?
- What factors led many of the out-of-town media rush to judgment on the players' guilt?
- What lessons can be drawn from overall media performance in the case? From the performance of *The News and Observer?*
- Was *The News and Observer* accountable to its readers?
- What makes opinion columns a particularly sensitive journalism issue as major criminal cases develop? What can be learned from Ruth Sheehan's columns? Was she accountable to her readers?

Case Study No. 11
On TV, a 4-Year-Old's Visit to Death Row

Carolyn Mungo is a journalist who is always listening. In 2000, while working on a story for Houston's KHOU-TV about a woman who was angry that the local health department was providing vaccinations for children in certain neighborhoods but not others, she heard the woman say something that piqued her interest.

The woman mentioned how she had to fight for her daughter because the child's father was "DR," Mungo said. "Years ago, as a young reporter, I would have nodded, pretending I knew exactly what DR stood for. But I'm older and wiser. When she's done talking, I ask her what the heck DR is. She told me, 'Death Row.'"

Mungo sensed a story. So she went along with the mother and child as they made visits to Texas Death Row to visit Richard Cartwright, 4-year-old Ricki Cartwright's father. Brandy Thomas, the child's mother, told Mungo that Richard Cartwright regularly sends cartoon drawings and detailed, loving letters to the little girl.

(Cartwright, 31, was executed by lethal injection on May 19, 2005, for the robbery and murder of Nick Moraida, 37, at Corpus Christi in 1996. He had been on Death Row 8 years.)

When she reported on the visits to Cartwright, Mungo immediately saw an ethical question in whether to show the child's face and, if so, how much of it. "I didn't interview her for the piece," Mungo said. "She was clearly too young. I almost thought it might be better to hide her face. But her mother was determined to let others know the importance of the family bond. She didn't want to hide anything."

Even though KHOU-TV staffers were not allowed to witness the visitation, they were allowed to pay the prison system to take Polaroid photographs. A guard snapped five pictures for $5 each. The photos showed the inmate in a warm, laughing exchange with his daughter over prison telephones, separated by glass and steel.

After the story aired, viewers called the station to raise questions about fairness.

Some thought the story was sympathetic to Richard Cartwright while not giving the perspective of the Corpus Christi family who lost a loved one – the man Cartwright was convicted of killing. Mungo said, "They didn't like how I put a human face on a cold-blooded killer." But she said her story was about children of inmates on Death Row, not whether Cartright was guilty or the victim's family's reaction to the murder.

Other callers said the station was exploiting the child. Mungo said:

Viewers couldn't believe I would parade a little girl out like that for the sake of ratings. I was called insensitive to children. ... The criticism really hurt. I, for years, have specialized in children and family reporting. I have always felt I was very sensitive to what are often very upsetting stories involving children. The criticism caught me off guard.

Continued

Mungo had taken care to interview child psychologist Victoria Sloan for the piece. Sloan was concerned that the Death Row visitations might be too much for a 4-year-old to handle. But the Sloan interview was reduced to a single soundbite. It was followed by a similarly quick response from a member of the Inmate Families Association, who said such visitations are important to inmates and families.

The story ends with the mother reading a letter from the inmate to his child saying that even after he is executed, "I will watch over you and your mother, I promise."

Adapted from *Newsroom Ethics: Decision-Making for Quality Coverage*, 4th edn. (Washington, DC: Radio Television News Directors Foundation, 2006), 41–3.

Questions for Class Discussion

- Despite the viewer criticism, was this a legitimate subject for coverage? Does it influence your judgment to know that hundreds of thousands of children in America have a parent in prison, and that the number is growing?
- What respectful but tough questions might the journalist have asked the mother about whether these visitations might harm the child?
- Should the child's face have been shown? If so, what value might there have been in telling the public that the mother wanted viewers to see her face, and why? Should the mother's desire have dictated the journalist's decision?
- Should the station have shown the interview with the psychologist at a greater length? If it had, would the station be ethically obligated to give the Inmates Families Association representative an equal amount of time?
- Did the open (with music) and the close of the story set a sympathetic tone for the piece? Should they have done so?
- Should the station have interviewed the family of the murder victim?
- What lessons can be learned from viewer reaction to this story?

Notes

1 Ronald J. Ostrow's case study, "Richard Jewell and the Olympic Bombing," written for the Project for Excellence in Journalism and posted on Feb. 15, 2003, at http://www.journalism.org/node/1791. The case includes the text of the headline and story in the *Atlanta Journal-Constitution*'s extra edition on July 30, 1996. The bombing killed one person, not two as stated in the case study.

2 BBC News, "Man admits Atlanta Olympics bomb," April 13, 2005, http://news.bbc.co.uk/2/hi/americas/4441239.stm

3 The Associated Press, "Richard Jewell honored at Georgia Capitol for heroism during 1996," Aug. 2, 2006.

4 Kevin Sack, "Richard Jewell, 44, hero of Atlanta attack, dies," *The New York Times,* Aug. 30, 2007.

5   Ostrow, "Richard Jewell and the Olympic Bombing."
6   Ibid.
7   Ibid.
8   Ibid.
9   Ibid.
10 Ibid.
11 Ibid.
12 Ibid.
13 Christine D. Urban and Associates, *Examining Our Credibility: Perspectives of the Public and the Press* (Washington: American Society of Newspaper Editors, 1999), 74–5. The survey involved telephone interviews with a representative sample of 3,000 Americans.
14 Bill Marimow email to the author, Nov. 10, 2007.
15 Allan M. Siegal and William G. Connolly, The *New York Times Manual of Style and Usage* (New York: Times Books, 1999), 127–8.
16 Geneva Overholser, "On behalf of journalism: A manifesto for change," a project of the Annenberg Foundation Trust at Sunnylands, in partnership with the Annenberg Public Policy Center of the University of Pennsylvania, Oct. 12, 2006, http://www.annenbergpublicpolicycenter.org/Overholser/20061011_JournStudy.pdf, 10.
17 Marimow email, Nov. 10, 2007.
18 Butch Ward, "Time for transparency," June 15, 2007, http://www.poynter.org/content/content_view.asp?id=124790.
19 Susan Paterno, "An ill Tailwind," *American Journalism Review*, September 1998.
20 Richard Kaplan, comment made during an interview on *Reliable Sources*, Cable News Network, July 4, 1998.
21 Christopher Callahan, "An embarrassing time," *American Journalism Review*, September 1998.
22 Paterno, "An ill Tailwind."
23 Attorney Floyd Abrams' report on his independent investigation of CNN's broadcast "Valley of Death," July 2, 1998, accessed at: www.cnn.com/US/9807/02/tailwind.findings/index.html
24 Ibid.
25 Ibid.
26 Ibid.
27 Dick Thornburgh and Louis D. Boccardi, Report of the Independent Review Panel on the

September 8, 2004, "60 Minutes Wednesday" segment "For the Record" concerning President Bush's Texas Air National Guard Service, Jan. 5, 2005. Accessed at: http://wwwimage.cbsnews.com/htdocs/pdf/complete_report/CBS_Report.pdf, 1–2.
28 Ibid, 2.
29 CBS Statement on Bush Memos, Sept. 20, 2004. Accessed at: http://www.cbsnews.com/stories/2004/09/20/politics/main644539.shtml.
30 Thornburgh and Boccardi, 4.
31 CBS News release, "CBS ousts 4 for Bush Guard story," Jan. 10, 2005.
32 Jacques Steinberg, "CBS is sued by Rather over ouster," *The New York Times*, Sept. 20, 2005.
33 Thornburgh and Boccardi, 8.
34 Ibid., 25.
35 Ibid., 9–10.
36 Ibid., 11–12; 22.
37 Ibid., 24.
38 Ibid., 221–2.
39 Ibid., 26–8.
40 Ibid., 4.
41 Mary Mapes, statement issued after her dismissal by CBS. Accessed at: http://www.poynter.org/resource/public/20050110_182326_18354.pdf
42 Steinberg, "CBS is sued by Rather over ouster."
43 Mitch Albom, "Longing for another slice of dorm pizza," *Detroit Free Press*, April 3, 2005.
44 *Detroit Free Press*, correction, April 7, 2005.
45 Michael Hirsley, "No one's defending renowned journalist," *Chicago Tribune*, April 10, 2005.
46 David Zeman, Jeff Seidel, Jennifer Dixon, and Tamara Audi, "Albom probe shows no pattern of deception," *Detroit Free Press*, May 16, 2005.
47 Carole Leigh Hutton, "Letter to Readers: Albom's column to return," *Detroit Free Press*, April 23, 2005.
48 Zeman et al., "Albom probe shows no pattern of deception."
49 Quoted in Robert J. Haiman, *Best Practices for Newspaper Journalists* (Arlington, VA: The Freedom Forum's Free Press/Fair Press Project, 2000), 58.
50 Thomas Patterson and Philip Seib, "Informing the public," in Geneva Overholser and Kathleen Hall Jamieson, eds., *The Press* (Oxford: Oxford University Press, 2005), 193.

51   Richard Oppel, editor of the Austin (Texas) *American-Statesman*, makes this point in a quotation in Haiman, *Best Practices for Newspaper Journalists*, 58.

52   Framing the news: Triggers, frames and messages in news coverage," a study of the Project for Excellence in Journalism and Princeton Survey Research Associates, July 13, 1998. Accessed at: http://www.journalism.org/node/445

53   Michele McLellan, *The Newspaper Credibility Handbook: Practical Ways to Build Reader Trust* (Washington: American Society of Newspaper Editors, 2001), 81.

54   Quoted in Ibid, 83.

55   Leslie Whitaker, "Covering (and reinforcing) conflict," *American Journalism Review*, August/ September 2005.

56   Marvin Kalb, *One Scandalous Story: Clinton, Lewinsky, and 13 Days That Tarnished American Journalism* (New York: The Free Press, 2001), 154–6.

57   Norm Goldstein, ed., *The Associated Press Stylebook* (New York: Basic Books, 2007), 189–91.

58   Barb Palser, "All error, no margin," *American Journalism Review*, December 2004/January 2005.

59   James Rainey, "The *Times* apologizes over article on rapper," *Los Angeles Times*, March 27, 2008. The investigative report is "Big phat liar," http://www.thesmokinggun.com/archive/years/2008/0325081sabatino1.html, March 26, 2008.

60   Quoted in Donna Shaw, "Wikipedia in the newsroom," *American Journalism Review*, February/ March 2008.

61   http://simple.wikipedia.org/wiki/Wikipedia: Disclaimers

62   Barbara G. Friedman, *Web Search Savvy: Strategies and Shortcuts for Online Research* (Mahwah, NJ: Lawrence Erlbaum Associates, 2005), 166.

63   David Shaw, "Papers must write it up when they get it wrong," *Los Angeles Times*, June 13, 2004.

64   Rainey, "The *Times* apologizes over article on rapper."

65   Debora Halpern Wenger and Deborah Potter, *Advancing the Story: Broadcast Journalism in a Multimedia World* (Washington: CQ Press, 2007), 275.

66   Ibid., 276.

13 Dealing With Sources of Information

The fine line between getting close but not too close

Learning Goals

This chapter will help you understand:

- ethical issues in reporter/source relationships;
- the challenges of cultivating sources while maintaining independence in beat reporting;
- a journalist's ethical obligation to protect a confidential source;
- the debate over "tidying up" direct quotations of sources; and
- recurring situations that pose ethical issues in dealing with sources.

For more than 5 years, Nancy Phillips had cultivated Len Jenoff as a source in her reporting for *The Philadelphia Inquirer* about the 1994 bludgeoning murder of Carol Neulander, a rabbi's wife in suburban Cherry Hill, New Jersey. She had bought meals for Jenoff, had listened endlessly to his stories, and had given his wife her recipe for latkes. The couple sent her postcards from vacation resorts and holiday cards at Hanukkah.

Now, on December 9, 1999, Jenoff was giving her electrifying news: The rabbi had paid him to arrange the murder.

But there was no story in the next morning's paper. At Jenoff's insistence, Phillips' conversation with the self-styled private investigator had been *off the record*, meaning that she was bound by a reporter's honor not to publish what he told her.

"I can't believe I'm telling you this," Jenoff said. Moments later, he pleaded: "Please don't hurt me with this, Nancy. ... I may have to take this to the grave."

Phillips left his house shaken, suspecting that he might be telling the truth even though his conversations in the past had been riddled with lies. "But I was in a bind," she wrote in a first-person story in *The Inquirer* much later. "He would not give me permission to tell the story, and because I had agreed to keep his confidence, I had to honor that and could not tell the authorities." In keeping with the paper's policy, she did tell her editors what Jenoff had told her. They agreed that she should honor the confidentiality commitment, and they shared her skepticism of Jenoff.

Four months passed as Phillips anguished over the secret. She prodded Jenoff to go to authorities. On April 28, 2000, after she and Jenoff shared a pizza at a Cherry Hill restaurant, he asked her to ride with him to visit two places in Philadelphia that figured in the crime. As he drove, she urged him to go to the prosecutor's office right then. With his consent, she called Prosecutor Lee A. Solomon on her cell phone.[1]

For three hours, a hit man, a reporter, a prosecutor, and a homicide detective sat in a booth at a diner. They drank coffee (the prosecutor had six cups), and talked about murder.[2]

Jenoff's confession broke the case. He implicated the rabbi and named his accomplice, Paul Michael Daniels. The authorities had filed murder charges in 1998 against the rabbi, Fred J. Neulander, for arranging his wife's murder. But they had never found the weapon and had not charged anyone for carrying out the fatal bludgeoning. After the confession in the diner, police wired Jenoff and monitored a conversation he had with Daniels. When they heard the two men discuss the crime, they moved in and arrested them.[3]

Jenoff told Phillips at the end of the meeting in the diner: "You can now tell the story."[4] Nine days later, *The Inquirer* published Phillips' first-person account. It was the last story she has written about the case she had covered so long with skill and persistence. Having become a participant in the story, her editors determined that she could no longer cover it for *The Inquirer*.

Neulander, Jenoff, and Daniels all went to prison. The rabbi's motive for plotting his wife's murder was that he wanted to marry another woman but avoid the scandal of a divorce, which would probably have caused him to lose his synagogue. The hit men testified at his trial that Neulander had paid them $30,000 to kill his wife, and they had beaten her to death with metal pipes. Neulander was convicted and sentenced to life. Jenoff and Daniels pleaded guilty and were sentenced to 23 years each.[5]

For all its drama, the episode illustrates the ethical issues that reporters face regularly in dealing with their sources.

The first of these is Phillips' conviction that she should respect Jenoff's confidence. It would have been easy to rationalize that because he was certainly a liar and quite likely a murderer, she had no moral obligation to keep her off-the-record promise. That is not the way Nancy Phillips saw it.

"In this profession, we live and die on our ability to keep every promise we make to everybody, large and small," Phillips told *The Washington Post's* media writer, Howard Kurtz. "This, of course, was an extreme circumstance. ... When we laid down the rules, I obviously didn't know what was going to come out of his mouth."[6]

Another issue is the matter of who is entitled to the journalist's first loyalty. Prosecutor Solomon said that when journalists learn someone has committed a murder, they "have a moral and ethical obligation to step forward," Alicia C. Shepard reported in *American Journalism Review*. But *Inquirer* editor Robert J. Rosenthal told Shepard that journalists' duty is to publish stories for the people, not to help the police. "It's crucial for our long-term credibility to not be seen as a branch of law enforcement." Ethics scholar Louis W. Hodges of Washington and Lee University agreed that sources would evaporate if journalists were seen as working for the police, although there are exceptions, such as if a journalist knows someone is about to commit a serious crime.[7]

Then there is the matter of cultivating a source who might, as Jenoff eventually did, tell the reporter something of importance to the public. As discussed in Chapter 10, cultivating sources is "an essential skill, often practiced most effectively in informal settings outside of normal business hours ... but [reporters] must keep in mind the difference between legitimate business and personal friendship."[8] The process is something of a paradox – the journalist needs to get close enough to gain the source's confidence, even while maintaining sufficient distance from the source to be able to report as an independent observer. (Jeffrey Fleishman's Point of View "Sometimes, Different Rules Apply" relates a rare exception to the rule.)

Phillips' long conversations with Jenoff covered a range of subjects, including their shared Jewish religion. But throughout, she said, she made it clear to Jenoff that she was a reporter and not his friend. Even so, there were nasty insinuations. Before Neulander's trial, the rabbi's lawyers said Jenoff had told fellow jail inmates of having "a personal, physical relationship" with Phillips. To this, the reporter responded: "Let me be clear: As a reporter, I have conducted myself at all times as a professional."[9]

The Jenoff episode also raised a question that is unusual in reporter–source relationships: Though reluctantly, the reporter became part of the story she was covering.

The circumstance of Jenoff's off-the-record murder confession ultimately required Phillips to cross the line between observer and participant. She decided that she had to become an adviser to Jenoff, pushing him to tell the story to authorities. When he finally did this – and when he released her from her pledge of confidentiality – she wrote a detailed account of the entire episode for *Inquirer* readers, disclosing her own participation in the story.

Ethics in Reporter–Source Relationships

Unless they witness a news event themselves, journalists depend on other people for the information they report to their readers, viewers, listeners, and online users. Some of these *sources* saw the event themselves. Others possess expertise that could help the journalists' audience evaluate what is known about the event. This chapter discusses ethical issues in journalists' dealings with sources.

These are the pertinent ethical standards from the SPJ code, under the guiding principles of "seek truth and report it," "minimize harm," and "act independently":

- "Identify sources whenever feasible. The public is entitled to as much information as possible on sources' reliability. Always question sources' motives before promising anonymity."
- "Clarify conditions attached to any promise made in exchange for information."
- "Keep promises."
- "Recognize that private people have a greater right to control information about themselves than do public officials and others who seek power, influence or attention."
- "Be wary of sources offering information for favors or money; avoid bidding for news."

In selecting sources, journalists look for authority. They have to find sources who have first-hand knowledge, who are not merely repeating what they heard from others. Because a one-source story likely would be self-serving and reflect only a single perspective, journalists test a source's information by interviewing a diversity of people. A wide range of sources provides checks and balances.

Journalists have a responsibility to screen their sources on behalf of the audience, especially when the sources are nameless in their stories. "If your sources are wrong, you are wrong" was Judith Miller's explanation for her "totally wrong" stories about the likelihood that weapons of mass destruction would be found in Iraq when the United States invaded in 2003.[10] Miller's explanation offers little comfort for *New York Times* readers who were misled by her reporting. It also leaves the impression that reporters are stenographers who uncritically pass along what they are told.

Journalists must act independently, not allowing a relationship with a source, whether adversarial or friendly, to influence the story. Sometimes a journalist is dealing with a vulnerable person, sometimes with a crafty source seeking favorable treatment. Journalists have a moral duty not to exploit a vulnerable person for their own purposes, and they owe it their audience not to allow a crafty source to deflect them from the pursuit of the truth.

Sources who seek to manipulate may provide useful information; bad people, the saying goes, can give us good information. Mark Feldman, a former broadcast journalist who teaches at George Washington University, observed: "The public is the poorer if reporters get high-and-mighty and say, 'We accept only leaks with pure motives.'"[11] What is essential in these situations is a heavy dose of skepticism; journalists need to check out the information while being conscious of the source's motive. "[J]ournalists must take motive into account in weighing what sources tell them," Jack Fuller writes in *News Values*. "Motive gives a clue to the source's biases and reasons for lying or telling the truth only selectively."[12]

In general, a journalist should identify himself or herself to a person being interviewed. It is the journalist's responsibility to make clear what ground rules apply to reporting on the conversation. When interviewing ordinary citizens unfamiliar with the routine, the journalist should emphasize that what they say could appear in the newspaper, on the air, or on the Internet. If the story is to appear in multiple media, the source should know that, too.

The person being interviewed might ask what kind of story the journalist intends to write. That is a fair question, one deserving an honest answer. In outlining the premise that is being investigated, the journalist should also assure the interview subject that he or she will keep an open mind until all relevant facts have been gathered.

Should a source ever be deceived? There is sometimes a fine line between shrewd, resourceful reporting and unethical reporting. A deontologist-journalist would never deceive, of course. A teleologist-journalist might argue for misleading (read: *deceiving*) a source if the stakes are high enough – that is, the story is vitally important to the audience, and there is no other way to obtain it. This topic is discussed in Chapter 16.

Often, reporter–source issues revolve around confidentiality. Ideally, sources agree to be named and to allow their statements to be conveyed to the public. However, as discussed earlier in this book, valuable information sometimes might be obtained only if journalists protect the identity of the sources. It also might be useful, as in the Jenoff case described above, for a reporter to listen on an off-the-record basis in the hope that the source later will go on the record or that the information can be confirmed by named sources or by documents. This chapter discusses the responsibility of both the journalist and the news organization to honor a promise of confidentiality.

The Challenges of Beat Reporting

Most journalists are generalists. They have a broad range of knowledge and are quick learners, but they lack specialized knowledge in a given subject. To develop that kind of expertise, news organizations typically assign some of their reporters to what is known in the profession as "beats." Beat reporters cover a certain category of news: city hall, the police, the courts, a professional baseball team, the pharmaceutical business, and so forth. In addition to gaining an expertise in the subject matter, the reporter gets to know the newsmakers far better than a general-assignment reporter making a cold call on deadline to someone he or she has never met.

Emilie Lounsberry has covered courts nearly all of her newspaper career, starting when she was a college sophomore and a part-time court reporter for *The Daily Intelligencer* in Doylestown, Pennsylvania. Since 1982, she has reported on the courts for *The Philadelphia Inquirer*. She is sold on the value of beat reporting:

Being in a courtroom is as comfortable, for me, as being in my own living room. I know how events will unfold. I can recognize good lawyering and good judging. I am familiar with the language of the law — and it does not frighten me. The confidence and ease I've developed from covering the law has enabled me to go deeper and deeper into complex issues and investigative matters.

Along the way, I've also built a pretty good working list of sources — with cell phone numbers, home numbers, and even an occasional parent's phone number. Like building a beat, developing good sources is an essential component of good journalism. A good source is someone who can help a reporter figure out what is happening behind the scenes.[13]

When ethics scholar Edward Wasserman of Washington and Lee University looks at the beat-reporting system, he sees an inherent conflict of interest regarding sources. "If you deliberately set out to invent an arrangement less conducive to tough adversarial reporting, it would be hard to beat beats," Wasserman wrote in his column in *The Miami Herald*.

The wisdom of beats rests on the idea that journalism can flourish in a setting where a journalist's professional success utterly depends on the continuing cooperation of the same people that the journalist is supposed to badger, provoke, expose and, in sum, hold accountable on the public's behalf. And that is totally illogical.[14]

Wasserman identifies a genuine problem, but the crucial question is whether the problem is outweighed by the benefits of the beat reporter's expertise and wholesome source relationships. Lounsberry thinks a conscientious reporter can cope. "I try to keep a fair degree of independence from sources," she said. "I do not consider sources as 'friends'; when I meet with them, it is usually over lunch or coffee, rather than dinner or a social event. This helps keep some distance."[15]

Lounsberry's *Inquirer* colleague, Tommy Gibbons, a police reporter for almost 33 years, said mutual trust is the key to successful relationships on the beat. Even if the job occasionally requires writing a story that will not reflect favorably on a valued source, he said, "you'll be OK if you are trusted as being fair." When Gibbons retired, the Philadelphia police commissioner told a gathering of well-wishers that he "didn't always agree with what I wrote, but I was fair." That comment, Gibbons said, "was worth a million compliments."[16]

Protecting Sources Who Are in Jeopardy

Some people who secretly provide information for journalists' stories may be vulnerable professionally, economically, even physically. Journalists have a moral obligation not to place them in jeopardy.

Time and again, journalists have been threatened with jail or fines for contempt for refusing a judge's order to give up the identity of a source to whom they have pledged confidentiality. State shield laws provide some protection, but journalists still might be ordered to identify their sources if a judge determines that the information is vital in a criminal case and cannot be obtained in any other way. In addition, the federal government does not have a shield law.

Bob Mong, editor of *The Dallas Morning News*, instructs reporters to tell sources that while the paper will fight in court to protect their identity, "if at the end of appeals a judge rules against us, we would have to give up the name." Mong said nearly all confidential sources have agreed to that stipulation.[17] While Mong's protocol is a practical response to the environment that exists in the courts, other editors maintain that the only honorable course for a journalist in such a situation is to go to jail to protect the source.

The use of confidential sources places a heavy burden on journalists in addition to the duty to protect the identity. Journalists must go to extra lengths to corroborate information provided by confidential sources, because the audience has no way of assessing their authority or likely bias. Journalists should be reluctant to grant anonymity, agreeing only when convinced that the source is in jeopardy and that the source's information is both overwhelmingly important and unobtainable elsewhere on the record. Confidentiality should be invoked to protect a whistle-blower who comes forward to report abuse of power in government or business; it should not be granted to enable someone who wants to damage the reputation of a rival.

The New York Times adopted stringent guidelines on anonymous sources in 2004. At the request of *Times* public editor Clark Hoyt, a class at the Graduate School of Journalism at Columbia University read every word of every article in six issues of the paper published before the policy and six from the fall of 2007. The students found that the number of articles relying on anonymous sources fell by roughly half. Anonymous sources were much less likely to appear on the front page.[18]

Briefing staff members on the Columbia University study, *Times* executive editor Bill Keller wrote:

> The ability to offer protection to a source is an essential of our craft. We cannot bring readers the information they want and need to know without sometimes protecting sources who risk reprisals, firing, legal action, or, in some parts of the world, their lives when they confide in us.

Keller said some editors prohibit the use of anonymous sources. "This is high-minded foolishness," Keller said. "Without the option of protecting sources, with recourse only to an increasingly redacted public record, the coverage of government and other powerful institutions would tend more and more toward press-conference stenography."

Keller emphasized that anonymous sources, if they are to be quoted by *The Times*, must be in a position to know what they are talking about: "Was he in the room? Did she read the document?" He also prefers quality of sources over quantity. Instead of a "two-source rule" or a "three-source rule," *The Times*' policy relies on judgment. "One actual participant in an event may be better than three people who heard about it third-hand, or from one another. One neutral witness may be more valuable than a crowd of partisans."[19]

Journalists should give the audience as much information as possible about their unnamed sources without divulging their identity. It is a good idea to agree in advance with the source about how he or she is going to be described. For example, "a source in the administration" is better than "a government source"; "a source who works in the White House" is even better; and "a White House source with access to the memos in question" is better than any of the others.

Journalists must not mislead the audience about where their information came from. It is wrong to say that an official was "unavailable for comment" and then quote the official anonymously. And it is wrong to say that a statement came from "a league official" rather than an official of a certain team (it is rationalizing to argue that there is no deceit because the team is a member of the league).

Case Study No. 12, "*Newsweek* and the Flushing of the Koran," describes tragic events that followed publication of a news item based on an anonymous source. The reporters thought a second official was vouching for the item's accuracy, but there was a misunderstanding.

The Debate over Verbatim Quoting

When sources are quoted for print or online news outlets, journalists have three choices. They can:

- *Quote directly*. The words the source used are placed inside quotation marks. The quotation is, at least in theory, a verbatim transcript.
- *Quote indirectly*. The reporter paraphrases the source's statement, usually for brevity or clarity, but faithfully conveys the essence of what the source said. Quotation marks are not used.
- *Use partial quotations*. This is a combination of the first two. The quotation is paraphrased except for a few words of direct quotation that appear between quotation marks.

From the standpoint of newswriting technique, each of the three choices has strengths and weaknesses. This text deals only with their ethical implications.

Indirect and partial quotations are ethically sound if they are faithful to the essence of the source's statements, and if the phrases placed within quotation marks are the precise words the source used.

The ethics of direct quotations is a subject of debate in the profession. In theory, a direct quotation is verbatim; it is exactly what the source said, nothing more and nothing less. The controversy centers on whether practice follows theory.

Most newsroom ethics codes state the theory in unequivocal terms. *The Associated Press Stylebook* says: "Never alter quotations even to correct minor grammatical errors or word usage."[20] *The New York Times Manual of Style and Usage* says: "Readers have a right to assume that every word between quotation marks is what the speaker or writer said. *The Times* does not 'clean up' quotations."[21] *The Washington Post*'s policy is: "When we put a source's words inside quotation marks, those exact words should have been uttered in precisely that form."[22]

Strictly following those rules, a journalist would write direct quotations that record the source's every false start or stutter, every "you know," every "um" or "ah." In addition to humiliating the source, that would distract the reader.

The policy manuals offer a solution for the conundrum — use indirect quotations or partial quotations, or use direct quotations but insert an ellipsis (…) indicating that something inconsequential is missing. Usually those alternatives solve the problem.

Occasionally, though, the source's less-than-perfect utterance would, from a journalistic standpoint, make a highly desirable direct quotation. What is the ethical journalist to do?

The betting here is that in such a situation the journalist will, in the words of Roy Peter Clark of the Poynter Institute, "tidy up the quote rather than make someone look stupid."[23] Clark says, "I believe every writer, every journalist that I know, whether they're willing to admit it or not, cleans up quotes in some way."[24]

Regardless of how they feel about tidying up quotations, journalists reporting on news conferences should quote verbatim, false starts and all. Otherwise they may have to answer to an annoyed audience about why their quotations differ from what was heard on a broadcast sound bite or what was written in another journalist's account of the same news conference.

Some reporters drop "gonna" and "gotta" into direct quotations to add spice to their stories. Since almost no one slows down to pronounce "going to" and "got to" with perfect diction, reporters who selectively quote in this manner are unfairly portraying certain of their news subjects as being less than articulate.

It also is unfair to pick on people who are relatively uneducated, or for whom English is a second language. To grasp how humiliating that quoting in dialect can be, consider the way Roberto Clemente, a Puerto Rican who became one of major league baseball's early Latino stars, was quoted by some sportswriters when he joined the Pittsburgh Pirates in the 1960s: "I say, 'I 'ope that Weelhelm [Hoyt Wilhelm] peetch me outside, so I could hit to right,' but he peetch me inside and I meet it and hit it to right field. Willie runs to third and to home plate and the game is over. That make me feel real good." The headline over that story in the *Post-Gazette* was: "I Get Heet, I Feel Good." Clemente, who could be an eloquent public speaker in Spanish, was angered and hurt by the exaggerated phonetic spellings, biographer David Maraniss writes. The player told another sportswriter: "I know that I don't have the good English pronunciation because my tongue belong to the Spanish. But I know where the verb, the article, the pronoun, whatever it is, go."[25]

Athough repeated verbatim quotations should be avoided in these situations, lest they embarrass the story subject, neither should the subject be portrayed as an erudite speaker in English. In such a situation, indirect quotations with an occasional partial quotation are a better choice.

Occasionally, inserting a bracketed clarification into a direct quotation helps a reader understand the context, but this device can be overused. Liberally sprinkling bracketed phrases into extended direct quotations can produce two undesirable results. One is that the reader is distracted from the substance of the quotation. The other, more damning, is that the reporter seems to be suggesting that the speaker is so inarticulate that he or she needs the reporter's help to compose an intelligent sentence.

There is a consensus that quoting in slang and dialect should be avoided because it comes across as condescending. This stricture does not apply, however, when a speaker purposely uses slang or dialect. When Sylvester Croom took over as football coach at Mississippi State University in 2003, he acknowledged that he was the first of his race to hold that job in the Southeastern Conference. *The New York Times* cleaned up one of his remarks, quoting him: "'I am the first African American coach in the S.E.C., but there is only one color that matters here and that color is maroon,' referring to the Bulldogs' official colors, maroon and white, as the crowd applauded." Three days later, *The Times* published a correction. The coach, *The Times* reported, had said, "there *ain't but* one color that matters here and that color is maroon."[26]

National Public Radio cleans up after people who are interviewed on the network and even its own correspondents in the field.

In a good-natured *On the Media* show in 2007, NPR reporter John Solomon revealed that a producer working on the audio recording at an editing console can make a speaker sound more articulate without changing what the speaker meant to say. With just a few strokes of the keyboard, Solomon said, the producer "cleaned up and tightened the sound bites I was going to use, taking out sentences, words and even some of the pauses, making what are called internal edits. Then the various thoughts were woven together technically in a way that would be totally hidden to the listener."

To illustrate, Solomon ran an edited tape in which *The New York Times'* media reporter, David Carr, talked about how quotations are handled at *The Times*: "People have to speak in complete sentences or you don't use it." Then Solomon ran the raw tape of Carr's actual interview remark: "People have to speak in complete sentences or you – you – you – you don't – you don't – use it." (Carr quipped on the broadcast, "Everybody always sounds erudite and witty on NPR, and I've always wondered why.")

Also on the show, Solomon framed the larger debate over tidying up quotations:

> By making everyone sound better and increasing the amount of content in the broadcasts, it would seem to be a win-win-win for the network, its sources, and, most importantly, its listeners. Yet is there a small sin of omission? NPR may not be actively misleading listeners, but we all know that they don't know how we create the cleaner and more articulate reality.[27]

Frequently Asked Questions about Sources

Should children be interviewed?

"Understanding how young people see the world around them often demands that we hear what they have to say," Al Tompkins wrote for *poynteronline*. While giving young people a chance to be heard, journalists should be aware of their vulnerability. Tompkins noted that, especially in breaking-news situations, juveniles may not be able to recognize the ramifications of what they say.[28]

On April 20, 1999, Columbine High School near Denver was attacked by two students armed with guns; they killed 12 students and a teacher, then themselves. As broadcast journalists rushed to the scene, they conducted live interviews with young people fleeing the school. The combination of trauma and youthfulness produced some questionable interviews (a girl blurted the name of the one of the killers; fortunately, she had it right). A consensus best practice in conducting live interviews with juveniles is to conduct pre-interviews without cameras, recognizing that these young subjects can become emotional and make unpredictable statements. Because some journalists skipped the pre-interview to save time, the teenagers were put on the air without their interviewers' having any idea of what they would say.[29]

In his essay Tompkins suggested that the journalist try to secure parental permission for a child to be interviewed:

> Is it possible to have the parent/guardian present during the course of the interview? What are the parents' motivations for allowing the child to be interviewed? Are there legal issues you should consider, such as the legal age of consent in your state? If you conclude that parental consent is not required, at least give the child your business card so the parents can contact you if they have an objection to the interview being used.[30]

Should sources and story subjects see your copy?

Showing copy in advance of publication is a taboo in many newsrooms. No matter how clearly the journalist stipulates that only questions of accuracy will be considered, the practice can open the door to haggling. And the source/subject may feel betrayed if the story is changed in the editing process, even if cautioned about that possibility.

In spite of these hazards, a significant number of journalists consider some kind of source review – reading back quotations or showing entire story drafts – to be a valuable protection against inaccuracy. "I first showed a story to a source in 1985," Jay Mathews wrote in *The Washington Post*:

He was an old friend who worked as an economist for a Montana Indian tribe I was writing about, and I wanted to make sure I made no errors that might cause him grief. I woke up the next morning to find that the newsroom bogeyman had not gotten me and the story was better for having had that numerical error in the 19th paragraph corrected.[31]

If a reporter is writing about a highly technical subject, such as a complex surgical procedure, checking at least part of the story with the source seems a defensible practice. The goal is to get the facts right. A reporter, however, needs to comply with his or her news organization's policy on source review.

Should interviews be conducted by email?

Journalistically, this method is inferior to interviewing in person, Professor Russell Frank of Pennsylvania State University wrote in a 1999 *Quill* magazine article. Frank wrote that reporters "don't get enough of a sense of the person they're dealing with; e-mail doesn't lend itself to give-and-take, follow-up questions or serendipitous digressions; and e-mail responses sound canned, unspontaneous."[32]

However, the practice of email interviews has grown because of its sheer convenience. Reporters and sources don't have to take time to arrange an in-person interview or to play phone tag. Undoubtedly, some sources prefer email because it gives them a chance to write measured responses. The problems Frank identified persist today, and in terms of reporter preference, email interviews generally take third place to in-person interviews and telephone interviews. As a matter of disclosure to the audience, reporters should state if an interview was conducted by email or telephone rather than in person. In addition, reporters using information sent to them by email have an obligation to verify that the message was actually sent by the person whose name is signed.

Should sources be paid?

The SPJ code discourages payments, and the prevailing attitude in the profession is solidly against the practice.

Philip Seib and Kathy Fitzpatrick laid out the case against "checkbook journalism" in *Journalism Ethics*:

Digging for facts might require more effort than writing a check, but it is more honest. Buying news will create a marketplace for untruths in which the more lurid the story, the higher the payment. Money-hungry sources will be likely to embellish and fabricate to drive their prices higher. Also, this practice is likely to damage even further the public's opinion of how journalists do their job.[33]

A few journalists argue to the contrary. "It seems to me that news outlets need to get beyond their discomfort with paying *any* sources for *anything*," Tom Goldstein writes in *Journalism and Truth*. Goldstein observes that some news organizations have paid "consultants" for information, and that the practice of paying for quality information is well established in investing, the law, and other occupations. "Paid sources may have an incentive not to tell the truth," Goldstein writes. "But this does not seem terribly different from what is already the case: sources who are not paid may also have an incentive not to tell the truth."[34]

American correspondents have made payments abroad, though not without soul-searching. When Steve Stecklow was in Nicaragua covering the Sandinista–Contra conflict for *The Philadelphia Inquirer* in the 1980s, "I had to bring a carton of cigarettes to bribe soldiers at checkpoints to let me through." Stecklow, now with *The Wall Street Journal,* said bribing the guards was "the only way to get through. Also, many foreign news organizations routinely pay for information, and so the sources expect to be paid. It's hard to explain that we can't pay."[35]

Altruism is another reason that correspondents have paid for information. In Zambia, Michael Wines of *The New York Times* interviewed a group of stone-crushers, "a class of laborers who cling to the lowest social rung even in this, one of the world's poorest nations." He decided to pay them for their help on his story describing the misery of their lives.

After the interviews, Wines drove to a grocery store and bought $75 worth of cornmeal, cooking oil, rice, orange concentrate, bread, milk, and candy. "I returned and unloaded it to undiluted pandemonium – mothers' riotous joy; youngsters mobbing for sweets: actual dancing in the street for 30 people, a real live Christmas in July."[36]

Point of View
Sometimes, Different Rules Apply
Jeffrey Fleishman

I hated being in Children's Hospital of Oklahoma. I kept my notebook deep inside my pocket. When the mother next to me was told her child was dead, blown completely out of his sandals, some of her grief crawled inside of me.

What if it would have been one of my children? I quickly put that thought away, back someplace where I could collect it later. I looked at the clock: 5 p.m. Deadlines. I kept the notebook buried; to pull it out, I thought, would have been some kind of sin. My eyes

Continued

took in the details: Parents, their faces raw from worry, held up snapshots of infants and smiling toddlers. Nurses whisked by, their white shoes squeaking, their clip charts scant with answers.

Then she spoke. Jannie Coverdale spoke. "I need to know about my babies, no one's telling me anything about my babies." No one did. She had been to five other hospitals trying to find out about her grandsons Aaron, 5, and Elijah, 2. They had been in America's Kids day-care center. But where were they now? She walked outside with a cigarette. I followed. We talked for a few minutes. She asked who I was. I told her. There was that heavy silence reporters are used to. Then she said it was OK to tell her story. I reached for my notebook, slowly. Every word she spoke seemed to matter. In such agony, there is no falseness.

I thanked her. Deadlines. She said God would take care of her.

I rushed toward the hotel to file. All the way there I kept thinking that I have a 5-year-old son. His name is Aaron.

That night Dan Meyers, another *Inquirer* reporter, and I ate dinner together. His son, Jackson, had recently turned 1. We talked about Jackson and my kids, Aaron and Hannah. But soon we spun the conversation in another direction. Talking about our kids meant thinking about the bloody children from the day-care center, the ones zipped in body bags.

Before I went to bed that night I pulled out a picture of Aaron and Hannah. They were alive, small, in my palm. I turned the light off and sat with them in darkness.

It's strange to write like this. In the first person, no scenery to hide behind. We so often live out of our notebooks, using them as shields for feelings. Somewhere amid the truth-gathering, we've lost — necessarily so or not — a little of the ability to imagine. I guess that's why Hemingway said journalism is fine training for a writer, so long as the writer knows when to quit it. But Jannie Coverdale didn't have to imagine. She knew how to fit words to pain. And every time she spoke of her Aaron, I thought of mine.

Over the next five days I spent time with Jannie Coverdale. I stayed at a distance, coming only when invited, and found I was invited often. I saw worry wear her brown eyes down. I saw God lift her with hope, a spark across her wide, smooth forehead. I saw her, for a moment with clenched hands, grow strong in the belief that Aaron and Elijah were alive under some steel beam. Her fortitude rubbed off on me. And at times I hoped that when Jannie's ordeal was over, I'd write a story about how two little kids had survived in some crevice, some pocket of air.

"When I'm in bed and everything is quiet I see things," said Jannie. "I see the babies. One night I dreamt I saw Aaron and Elijah and there were angels holding them and God was blowing breath in their faces to give them life."

The angels had other plans.

Saturday night Jannie was told.

Aaron and Elijah were dead.

I had a picture of those boys in my hotel room. Every day I got up and looked at it. I placed it beside my computer when I wrote. They were the faces of my words, the boys who filled up my days. They held 90.53 inches of news space. Four days of coverage. Now, they were gone. There is power in innocent blood, whether it's that of the Coverdale

Continued

boys or the thousands of children – shriveled, hacked and dead – in Rwanda. You don't have to be a parent to feel that sorrow. You only have to be human.

On Sunday I did a story of Jannie picking out a casket. The funeral was on Wednesday. At the cemetery, the gravedigger twirled a hand-crank and the casket holding Elijah and Aaron descended into the clay with a mechanical finality.

Jannie cried: "They're taking my babies."
I put my sunglasses on.

I stood among the tombstones on the rim of the hundred or so people gathered around Jannie. My notebook was in my pocket. One of Jannie's sons came over to me. "My mom wants to see you," he said. I followed him through the crowd and stopped in front of Jannie. She opened her arms. I walked into them. A bomb had ripped away her grandsons, but her compassion was undiminished.

This essay about coverage of the 1995 bombing of the federal building in Oklahoma City was written for *The Philadelphia Inquirer*'s in-house newsletter.

Case Study No. 12
Newsweek and the Flushing of the Koran

In its issue distributed May 1, 2005, *Newsweek* magazine published a 10-sentence item in its "Periscope" column about abusive techniques used by American interrogators to "rattle" Muslim prisoners at the detention facility at Guantanamo Bay, Cuba. One sentence in the item said interrogators had flushed a copy of the Koran, the sacred Muslim text, down a toilet.

The item, quoting anonymous sources, said a forthcoming report by the US Southern Command in Miami was "expected" to mention the Koran incident.

Newspapers in Afghanistan and Pakistan republished the allegation. Anti-American demonstrations broke out in the Afghan city of Jalalabad, killing four protesters and injur-

ing more than 60. In the days afterward, the demonstrations spread across Afghanistan, Pakistan and other countries, leading to the deaths of about a dozen more protesters.

On May 15, *Newsweek* editor Mark Whitaker retracted the item and apologized. He told *The Washington Post*'s Howard Kurtz that the item was based on a confidential source, a "senior US government official," who after publication said he was not sure the story was true. Also after publication, Whitaker said, Pentagon officials and General Richard B. Myers, chairman of the Joint Chiefs of Staff, said investigators found "no credible allegations of willful Koran desecration."

"Whatever facts we got wrong, we apologize for," Whitaker said. "I've expressed regret

Continued

for the loss of life and the violence that put American troops in harm's way. I'm getting a lot of angry e-mail about that, and I understand it."

The item was principally reported by Michael Isikoff, *Newsweek's* veteran investigative reporter. Whitaker said *Newsweek* correspondent John Barry had showed a draft of the item to a senior Pentagon official before publication and asked, "Is this accurate or not?" According to Isikoff, the official told Barry, "We want to correct another part of it." Isikoff said later, "This was not, granted, the confirmation that we should have gotten, but it led to a misunderstanding on our part that they had reviewed what we were about to report and had no quarrel with the rest of the item."

If the military had asked the magazine to hold off, Whitaker said, it would have done so. He also said Pentagon officials raised no objection to the story for 11 days after it was published.

Kurtz, however, reported that the item raised anger at the Pentagon. Spokesman Bryan Whitman said the item was "irresponsible" and "demonstrably false." Whitman said the magazine "hid behind anonymous sources which by their own admission do not withstand scrutiny. Unfortunately, they cannot retract the damage that they have done to this nation or those who were viciously attacked by those false allegations."

"The fact that a knowledgeable source within the U.S. government was telling us the government itself had knowledge of this was newsworthy," Whitaker told Kurtz. "Obviously we all feel horrible about what flowed from this, but it's important to remember there was absolutely no lapse in journalistic standards here," he said. "We relied on sources

we had every reason to trust and gave the Pentagon ample opportunity to comment. ... We're going to continue to investigate what remains a very murky situation."

In a letter to readers that was published in the magazine, Richard M. Smith, *Newsweek's* chairman and editor-in-chief, announced a change in policy on anonymous sources. "From now on, only the editor or the managing editor, or other top editors they specifically appoint, will have the authority to sign off on the use of an anonymous source," Smith said. The identity of the source will be shared with the editor, he said. Smith promised that "the cryptic phrase 'sources said' will never again be the sole attribution for a story in *Newsweek*."

On June 3, the Pentagon made public the report foreshadowed in the *Newsweek* item. The Pentagon said a military inquiry had confirmed five cases in which guards or interrogators at Guatanamo Bay had kicked, stepped on, or splashed urine on the Koran. In another incident, a two-word obscenity was written in English on the Koran, but investigators could not determine who had written it.

The Pentagon said that the splashing was an accident. The investigators concluded that a guard urinated near an air vent, and the wind blew his urine through the vent into a cell. The report said the detainee was given a new uniform and a new Koran, and the guard was reprimanded.

Looking back on the *Newsweek* report about the flushing of the Koran, Isikoff said:

The original source for our item was a highly credible, senior U.S. government official who had reason to know what he/she was talking about. Had the editors known

Continued

the identity of the source prior to the item being run, they would have felt – and did, after the fact when they learned the person's identity – entirely comfortable in using this person as a main source for the item. In this case, much to everybody's regret, the source turned out to be wrong: The source confused a confirmed report of the urine-splashing incident with an unconfirmed FBI report of a Koran being thrown in the toilet.

In summary, Isikoff said, "*we* botched the confirmation. We thought they had confirmed it; in fact, they never focused on it. Neither they nor we recognized the explosiveness the half-sentence of the piece referring to the Koran ... was going to have in the Muslim world."

Questions for Class Discussion

- What guiding principles of the SPJ code are most involved in this case?
- With the benefit of hindsight, how should *Newsweek* have handled the item?

- What lessons can be learned from *Newsweek*'s experience?
- After its reporting was challenged, was *Newsweek* accountable to its readers and the public?

Case Study No. 13

Swimming in a Newsmaker's Backyard Pool

Friday, July 6, 2007, was a day off for Chicago television reporter Amy Jacobson. She was driving to her swim club with her two pre-school-age sons when she got a phone call inviting her to meet with a person she had been covering for WMAQ. That call set into motion a series of events that four days later would lead to her being fired.

The newsmaker was Craig Stebic, whose wife, Lisa, had disappeared April 30, 2007, in the midst of divorce proceedings. When she went missing, Lisa Stebic had been trying to get her husband evicted from the home.

Now Craig Stebic's sister, Jill Webb, was on the phone inviting her to the Stebics' home in suburban Plainfield to discuss the case. Day off or not, Jacobson was eager to talk with Stebic and seek his consent for an on-camera interview. Lucinda Hahn, who interviewed both Jacobson and Webb about the call for an article in *Chicago* magazine, described the conversation: "Jacobson replied that she had her two sons in tow; Webb didn't care. 'I live in Iowa,' Webb told *Chicago*. 'It's laid-back and family-oriented. I'm an emergency room nurse; I've had to bring my kids to work,

Continued

too.'" Webb said her own three children were swimming in her brother's backyard pool, and Jacobson and her sons could join them. Jacobson said later in an interview with Robert Feder of the *Chicago Sun-Times*, "It was a way for me to do my work and have fun with my kids."

Before driving to the Stebic home, Jacobson said, she phoned her husband, who agreed that by going there, she might be able to "advance the story." She did not, however, consult her supervisors at WMAQ.

While Jacobson, Stebic, his sister, and the five children gathered at poolside, they were captured on a video shot from a neighbor's home – a video that would be broadcast by rival station WBBM.

According to WBBM vice president and news director Carol Fowler, reporter Mike Puccinelli knocked on the door of the Stebic home that afternoon in an attempt to interview Stebic. "As he was turned away, he noticed people swimming in the backyard pool," Fowler said. "He asked a neighbor for permission to enter the home for the purposes of shooting video of Craig Stebic. In doing so, he recognized Amy Jacobson." The sequence of events was reported July 12 on WBBM's website, with this explanation: "[W]e'd like to provide information that we hope puts to rest concerns about the origin of the tape and claims that we were 'stalking' Jacobson out of professional jealousy or ran out to the home on a tip to 'catch her doing something wrong.'"

There is a dispute over who shot the video. WBBM says one its photographers, who accompanied Puccinelli, did so. In a lawsuit filed against WBBM and six individuals, Jacobson's lawyer contends that the neighbor shot the video and turned it over to WBBM. The lawsuit also says that before going to the neighbor's house, Puccinelli had asked his station's assignment desk to check out the license plate on a car parked in Stebic's driveway and learned that it was Jacobson's.

In her December 2008 article in *Chicago* magazine, Hahn wrote: "Puccinelli and his cameraman … left with the now-infamous videotape, took it back to their news truck, and beamed the images back to the newsroom in Chicago. There, the video was an instant hit. … Within an hour, word of the video buzzed through Chicago's journalism community."

The six-minute video shows Jacobson wearing a bikini-style top with a towel wrapped around the lower part of her swimsuit. Craig Stebic also appears in swimming attire.

WBBM held the video four days before broadcasting it. Fowler said on camera, "Once we got this video, it was clear it was provocative, but there were so many questions. For sure we could have thrown it on the air, but it wouldn't have been the right thing to do because there was no context."

In her televised statement, Fowler said: "Once … we learned that both of the major newspapers in Chicago were taking the matter very seriously and [WMAQ] was taking the matter very seriously, that met the threshold of a news story in my judgment." She also said, "The degree to which this feeding frenzy detracts from [the investigation of Lisa Stebic's disappearance] is really very unfortunate."

WMAQ fired Jacobson the day the video aired.

In an interview July 11 with Spike O'Dell on WGN, Jacobson said going to Stebic's

Continued

home was "a horrible mistake," but not a mistake that should have caused her to be fired from the job she had held for 11 years, a tenure during which she won four local Emmy awards. She also emphasized that Stebic had never made any improper advances and that "another mother was there with her children." (Jacobson's lawsuit stated that she and Stebic were never in the pool together.)

O'Dell asked, "Had you not been in a swimming suit, had you been out there in your work clothes or a casual outfit, would it be a story today?"

Jacobson: "No."

O'Dell: "So the bathing suit put it over the top?"

Jacobson: "That's how I feel, yes."

Jacobson also said in the interview, "If I was a man, this wouldn't be an issue."

In the midst of the controversy over the swimming video, Plainfield Police Chief Donald Bennett disclosed on July 12 that "Amy Jacobson has in the past informed the Plainfield Police Department of her prior conversations with Mr. Stebic." Bennett was answering a written question submitted prior to a press conference in which he announced that police had named Stebic as "a person of interest" in his wife's disappearance.

Carol Marin wrote in the *Chicago Sun-Times* about her WMAQ colleague: "Being poolside in a bathing suit with a likely suspect in a 'foul play' investigation is monumental bad judgment. But being a police informant? That's unethical."

Columnist-blogger Eric Zorn of the *Chicago Tribune* said Jacobson told him that her bosses thought she was "getting too close to police" in her investigation of the Stebic case. He quoted her as saying that she shared information occasionally with police. "Here's a good example," he said she told him. "The police couldn't talk to Craig Stebic. So when a story ran in the *Naperville Sun* saying there were blood droplets on a tarp found in his car, I went to his door with a cameraman. I said, 'Where did the blood come from?' He said it was animal blood. So I called the police and told them what he said. Then I did my live shot."

According to Zorn, Jacobson said: "I talk to cops and sources all the time. They call me. I call them. You give news to get news."

Zorn also spoke with Chief Bennett, who told him: "Amy Jacobson advised us on a couple of occasions that she had talked to Mr. Stebic. That was it. It wasn't like she was doing something in conjunction with us."

Zorn, whose columns and blogs were generally supportive of Jacobson, wrote that she was wrong "to blur the line between detective and reporter." He wrote that unless there is an emergency – "the kidnapper went that-a-way!" – reporters should never give information to police before they give it to their audience.

Bob Steele of the Poynter Institute also thought Jacobson should have given her WMAQ viewers whatever information she had about the Stebic investigation. Sharing information with police, he wrote, is "a very serious violation" of ethical principles. "Independence is the linchpin principle for journalists. Journalists have a primary and essential obligation to serve the public. Journalists should not be collaborating with law enforcement agencies. … [S]he was compromising her credibility and that of her station."

Continued

Jacobson filed her lawsuit on July 7, 2008, asserting that the video subjected her to "enormous public humiliation and disgrace." The suit said the video invaded her privacy and resulted in her losing her job and her home. In late 2008, Jacobson and her husband were in divorce proceedings.

Questions for Class Discussion

- Should Amy Jacobson have phoned her news director before accepting the invitation to join the gathering at the Stebic home?
- Do you agree with Jacobson that if she had not been in swimming attire, there would have been no controversy? Do you agree with her contention that a male reporter in the same circumstances would not have been fired?
- Was it ethically improper for Jacobson to inform the police about her conversations with Craig Stebic? What guiding principle of the SPJ code is involved? Should reporters exchange information with their sources?
- Examine WBBM's role in the case. Should WBBM have broadcast the video? What do you think of the station's explanation of its involvement?
- Compare this case with the episode involving Nancy Phillips in the opening of Chapter 13. What similarities are there? What differences?

Notes

1   Nancy Phillips, "Tale of murder took years to unfold," *The Philadelphia Inquirer*, May 7, 2000, supplemented by an email exchange with the author on Feb. 2, 2009.
2   Alicia C. Shepard, "The reporter and the hit man," *American Journalism Review*, April 2001.
3   Ibid.
4   Howard Kurtz, "Reporter kept her promise," *The Washington Post*, May 11, 2000.
5   Robert Hanley, "2 hit men get 23-year terms for killing wife of rabbi," *The New York Times*, Jan. 31, 2003.
6   Kurtz, "Reporter kept her promise."
7   Shepard, "The reporter and the hit man."
8   *The New York Times, Ethical Journalism*, Sections 22, 23.
9   Shepard, "The reporter and the hit man."
10 Don Van Natta Jr., Adam Liptak and Clifford J. Levy, "The Miller case: A notebook, a cause, a jail cell and a deal," *The New York Times*, Oct. 16, 2005.
11 Bob Egelko, "BALCO case has journalism in a quandary," *San Francisco Chronicle*, Feb. 18, 2007.
12 Jack Fuller, *News Values* (Chicago: University of Chicago Press, 1996), 41.
13 Emilie Lounsberry, "Beats, courts and sources," a paper written for the author, Aug. 20, 2007.
14 Edward Wasserman, "The insidious corruption of beats," *Miami Herald*, Jan. 8, 2007.
15 Lounsberry, "Beats, courts and sources."
16 Author's telephone interview with Tommy Gibbons, Sept. 18, 2007.
17 Author's telephone interview with Bob Mong, Sept. 10, 2007.
18 Clark Hoyt, "Culling the anonymous sources," *The New York Times*, June 8, 2008.
19 Bill Keller, "Memo on anonymous sources," *The New York Times*, June 9, 2008.
20 *The Associated Press Stylebook*, 203.
21 Allan M. Siegal and William G. Connolly, The *New York Times Manual of Style and Usage* (New York: Times Books, 1999), 278.

22   The policy was quoted in Deborah Howell, "Quote, unquote," *The Washington Post*, Aug. 12, 2007.

23   Quoted in Fawn Germer, "Are quotes sacred?", *American Journalism Review*, September 1995.

24   Quoted in Hallie C. Falquet, "Verbatim," *American Journalism Review*, October/November 2006.

25   David Maraniss, *Clemente: The Passion and Grace of Baseball's Last Hero* (New York: Simon and Schuster, 2006), 155, 174.

26   Ray Glier, "College football: Pioneer sees a coach first and foremost," *The New York Times*, Dec. 3, 2003, with correction appended on Dec. 6, 2003.

27   John Solomon, "Pulling back the curtain," National Public Radio, http://www.onthemedia.org/yore/transcripts/transcripts_123104_curtain.html, May 25, 2007.

28   Al Tompkins, "Guidelines for interviewing juveniles," http://www.poynter.org/content/content_view.asp?id=4571, May 17, 1999.

29   Alicia C. Shepard, "Columbine shooting: Live coverage," in Tom Rosenstiel and Amy S. Mitchell (eds.), *Thinking Clearly: Cases in Journalistic Decision-Making* (New York: Columbia University Press, 2003), 64.

30   Tompkins, "Guidelines for interviewing juveniles."

31   Jay Mathews, "Sources of accuracy," *The Washington Post*, May 31, 2003.

32   Russell Frank, "You've got quotes!", *Quill*, October 1999.

33   Philip Seib and Kathy Fitzpatrick, *Journalism Ethics* (Fort Worth, TX: Harcourt Brace, 1997), *Journalism Ethics*, 109–10.

34   Tom Goldstein, *Journalism and Truth: Strange Bedfellows* (Evanston, IL: Northwestern University Press, 2007), 118.

35   Author interview with Steve Stecklow, Oct. 19, 2007.

36   Michael Wines, "To fill notebooks, and then a few bellies," *The New York Times*, Aug. 27, 2006.

14 Making News Decisions About Privacy

The public may need to know what individuals want hidden

> **Learning Goals**
>
> This chapter will help you understand:
>
> - the tension between the public's legitimate need to have certain information and the desire for privacy by the individuals involved;
> - the legal restraints on publicizing private information;
> - a three-step template for making decisions in privacy cases; and
> - how journalists should approach situations in which privacy is central to decision-making.

As the 2001 spring semester neared an end at Pennsylvania State University, the leader of the campus Black Caucus was the target of a viciously racist letter that threatened her death. To protest what they perceived as an inhospitable racial climate at Penn State, a group of students and their supporters rushed onto the field on April 21 just before the annual Blue-White football scrimmage attended by 40,000 spectators. Twenty-six protesters were arrested and briefly taken into custody.[1]

In its report on the demonstration, the *Centre Daily Times* listed the names and addresses of those arrested. That provoked a torrent of criticism from letter writers who argued that, by publishing those details, the State College local newspaper had made it easier for the protesters to be found by anyone who wished to do them harm.

"The lives of members of our community have been directly threatened, and their most vocal advocates already fear too much for their own lives," one letter read. "Now their homes, the places that they should feel most safe to them, have suddenly become the places most dangerous for them to be. I understand that the law allows for the release of that information, but any sense of moral decency, compassion or humanity does not."[2]

Editor Bob Unger reprinted that letter in a column he wrote to defend his decision. He wrote that the paper always reports the identity of people charged with crimes; that addresses are always used to avoid confusion with people whose names are similar; and that the names and addresses of the protesters were already available to anyone who took the time to go to the police station.

Unger wrote that he admired the students' purpose. Their actions, he wrote, "were in keeping with the great tradition of civil disobedience that inspired a generation of Americans for whom the civil rights movement of the 1950s and '60s was among the noblest times in our nation's history." But he reminded his readers that those who choose civil disobedience take a risk. "These young people have chosen the public arena to express their deepest worries and to help bring changes to an institution they love. They have become public figures by their own choice. They cannot have it both ways."[3]

By framing the question in terms of the paper's policy, Unger was taking a rule-based, deontological stance. In his view, the rule of publishing names and addresses has a logical basis, and it should apply in every situation. Everyone is treated the same.

The letter-writers were making an ends-based, teleological argument. They contended the paper should have recognized that the protest was all about safety, and that it should have been obvious that publishing the names and addresses would compromise their safety further. They argued that, under the circumstances, the paper should have made an exception to its policy – an exception that it could easily defend.

After their arrest at the Blue-White game, the 26 demonstrators slept for the next 10 nights at the student union while their leaders negotiated with Penn State administrators. More threats were received, and the university stepped up security. The demonstration at the student union ended when the school agreed to double the number of faculty members teaching African and African American studies; provide scholarships for students who double those studies with another major; and create an orientation course on diversity.[4] The school year came to a close without further incident, although graduates and guests had to pass through metal detectors at commencement.

Public Interest vs. Individual Desire for Privacy

The debate over publishing the Penn State protesters' names and addresses illustrates an important ethical issue for journalists, who frequently must decide whether the public has a legitimate need for information that the people involved would prefer to keep private.

This is a classic conflict of the SPJ code's guiding principles of *seeking truth* vs. *minimizing harm*. The tensions are summed up by Philip Patterson and Lee Wilkins in *Media Ethics: Issues and Cases*: "The challenge for journalists is to be courageous in seeking and reporting information, while being compassionate to those being covered."[5]

The law does give individuals an ability to sue to shield certain information from the public, and of course journalists must be aware of these legal limits. However, as a practical matter in these decisions, journalists look to their ethical standards rather than to a rule of law.

In privacy cases, the audience's perception of journalists' conduct again comes into play. The audience appears jaded by the slogan "the public's right to know," seeing it as an excuse to invade someone's privacy to sell newspapers or raise broadcast ratings. Nevertheless, journalists frequently do have a responsibility to inform the public of matters that the participants could argue are none of the public's business.

Like "the public's right to know," an individual's "right to privacy" is a phrase that does not appear in the Constitution. However, Professor Louis W. Hodges of Washington and Lee University considers it "reasonable to claim that privacy is assumed as necessary to the guarantee of other rights."[6] Hodges writes of individuals' "moral right to privacy" and defines it as "the power to determine who may gain access to information about oneself."[7] He writes, "Privacy plays a central role in human affairs. Without some degree of privacy, civilized life would not be possible."[8] However, he also asserts:

> But the right of privacy is not absolute. It stands beside a countervailing right of others to know quite a lot about us as individuals. Those two legitimate rights – the individual right to a measure of privacy and the right of others to know something about the individual – frame the moral issues.[9]

In the broadest sense, individuals' desire for privacy is trumped by the media's duty to report on the public performance of public officials, crimes, and accidents.

- *Public performance of public officials.* Although the officials may try to evade the media's scrutiny, it is an axiom of our democracy that the people's business should be conducted in public. Governments at all levels have enacted laws to enforce this concept – laws that require governing bodies to debate and vote in public, and courts to be open.
- *Crimes.* Citizens need to know about crimes in order to protect themselves and to evaluate the performance of the police. But coverage of crimes could result in some invasion of privacy.
- *Accidents.* For the same reasons that they need to be informed about crimes, citizens have a clear interest in knowing about events that cause loss of life, injuries, and property damage. As in the case of crimes, news coverage could divulge facts that those involved want to keep private.[10]

The issues, however, are more complex than the above list would make it appear. Journalists have to decide questions like these: Should public officials have some zone of privacy in their personal lives, and if so, how wide should it be? What entitlement to a zone of privacy do celebrities have? When their decisions affect the public welfare, should not the owners of private businesses be scrutinized just as officeholders are? When journalists report on crimes and accidents, how much private information should they make public? If an ordinary citizen commits suicide in private, should the death be reported as a suicide?

The Legal Restraints in Privacy Cases

Although the courts commonly rule in favor of the news media in privacy cases, practicing journalists need to know how privacy law might restrict their reporting. The legal concept of privacy was articulated in 1890 in a *Harvard Law Review* article by Samuel D. Warren and Louis D. Brandeis. Reacting to scandal-mongering in American newspapers of the period, they proposed that citizens be able to sue "an unrestrained and unrepentant press." Over the next century, the law on privacy evolved into four distinct categories, or torts, in which subjects of news coverage might sue news organizations: intrusion into a person's solitude or private affairs; publication of embarrassing facts; false light; and appropriation.

- *Intrusion into a person's solitude or private affairs.* Journalists cannot trespass into a person's home or personal papers. The tort takes place with the act of intruding, even if nothing is published. In his memoir, former *New York Times* executive editor Turner Catledge reminisced about how "picture snatching" was an accepted practice when he was a reporter in the 1920s: "The best way to get the pictures [of murder victims] was just to snatch them off the walls and tables and mantels and out of family albums at the scene of the action."[11] In modern times, the courts have held that even when invited by police to accompany them on a raid on private property, journalists can be sued by the property owners. This category of law also bars the harassment of a person or disrupting his or her private life.
- *Publication of embarrassing private facts.* Journalists cannot delve into a person's past to report notorious information if that information has no bearing on the person's present life, or if it is something that the public has no legitimate interest in. In today's computerized society, that kind of information is particularly easy to find in the databases of government and business. (See "*public records*" below.)
- *False light.* Journalists cannot create an erroneous, unattractive impression about a person. Newspapers sometimes do this when they use a file photo to illustrate a current story with an entirely different context – for example, using a routine classroom photo of students taking an exam to illustrate a story about cheating on exams. Television stations have the same problem with file video.
- *Appropriation.* If a person's name or photograph is going to be used for commercial purposes, the subject must give approval (and presumably be compen-

sated). Tiger Woods has to agree to the use of his likeness to sell golf apparel and automobiles.

The law otherwise is permissive. As a result, the journalist has to discern the difference between legally acceptable conduct and truly ethical conduct. In *Ethics in Media Communications: Cases and Controversies*, Louis A. Day addresses two areas in which these decisions frequently are made: public places and public records.

- *Public places*. "The general rule is that anything that takes place in public view can be reported on. The idea is that activities that transpire in public are, by definition, not private." Day cautions that journalists ought to use restraint. Before taking a photo of two lovers on a bench in a public park, he suggests, a news photographer first ought to ask permission: First, as a matter of decency, because the photographer is intruding in a private moment. And second, to avoid acute embarrassment, if the lovers happen to be married, but not to each other.[12]
- *Public records*. Day notes that journalists have a right to report embarrassing information that appears in the public record. "Any citizen could conceivably examine this record," he writes.

> Thus, the press is merely providing publicity for what individual citizens could see for themselves if they wished. This is a convincing argument from a legal standpoint. From an ethical perspective, it is less so. The reality is that most private facts committed to public records remain unknown to society unless publicized by the media.[13]

On the Internet, either by mining free sites or by subscribing to a search website, journalists and others can access huge quantities of sensitive information, including: the amounts of mortgages people owe on their homes, the salaries of public employees in some jurisdictions, the amount of taxes people have paid (or failed to pay), bankruptcies, criminal records, marriages and divorces, and political contributions. The availability of this information confers power on the journalist, along with the responsibility of deciding whether the benefit of disseminating the information outweighs the potential embarrassment to the individuals involved.

Making Decisions: A Three-Step Template

Journalists must recognize that their decisions about intruding into people's privacy can cause profound harm in their lives. In these situations, there is a conflict between the SPJ code's guiding principles of reporting truth and minimizing harm.

The decision-making process (see Box 14.1) calls for a careful, sensitive application of ends-based thinking and the Golden Rule. The process involves three steps: assess the information, calculate the likely harm, and then weigh those two factors to arrive at the decision.

Box 14.1   Making decisions in privacy cases

Step 1: Analyze the information

- Is the information something the public needs to know or merely something the public is curious about?
- Is the information important?

Step 2: Analyze the likely harm

- Does the publication, broadcasting, or posting of the information inflict harm? If so, how much?
- Is harm inflicted by merely gathering the information?

- What degree of privacy can the news subject reasonably expect?
- Did the news subject deliberately create news?

Step 3: Make the decision

- Does the value of the information to the public outweigh the harm that might be inflicted on the news subject?
- Can the public be sufficiently informed if certain harmful details are omitted?

Step 1: Analyze the information

Journalists first evaluate the public's need to know the information that the subjects of the news coverage want to keep private. In doing so, they distinguish between what the public is *interested in* and what it has a legitimate *need to know*. While this decision obviously is subjective, a simple test is to ask whether the information fulfills journalism's primary duty – providing citizens with the information they need to go about their daily lives and to make governing decisions about their community.

People are interested in a lot of things that they do not have a need to know. Louis Hodges notes that people are capable of such things as morbid curiosity and prurient interest – factors that "are not grounds for invading someone's privacy, although they are the criteria that gossip sheets use." In Hodges' standard, the reported information should be "of overriding public importance" and "the public need cannot be met by any other means."[14]

The fact that something is "a good story" – which in newsroom parlance is any story, good news or bad, that people will eagerly receive – is not a sufficient criterion. Working under intense deadlines and competitive pressure, journalists may not make a sound distinction between what the public is interested in and what it needs to know.

Applied ethics in journalism is *not* about reflexive decision-making; it is about critical thinking. To arrive at a decision they can defend, journalists must go beyond reflex and weigh concrete factors pro and con about whether to use a story.

Especially in their decision-making about privacy, journalists must be on guard against rationalizations. Their passion is to tell good stories. They feel pressure from their bosses and colleagues to deliver good stories. It is tempting to reveal private information, even if it harms the subjects. It takes discipline to test whether a decision to publish is self-serving.

Step 2: Analyze the likely harm

If the information is deemed to have met the importance standard in some degree, journalists next assess the harm that the reporting might inflict on the subjects of the story. The *gathering* of the information, aside from the *publication* of it, can itself be intrusive and cause harm. Louis Day cautions that journalists need to respect their news subjects as autonomous individuals whose dignity "should not be arbitrarily compromised for the sake of some slogan such as 'the people's right to know.'"[15]

This step also involves comparing the degree of harm to the degree of privacy that the news subject can reasonably expect. Public officials doing the public's business have the least claim to privacy, and ordinary citizens have the greatest.

Celebrities – "public figures" in legal terms – often protest that the media invade what they consider to be a zone of privacy. During the 1980 World Series, *The Philadelphia Inquirer* sent a reporter to the suburban neighborhood of the Phillies' star third baseman, Mike Schmidt. The resulting feature story portrayed Schmidt as a friendly neighbor who, among other kind gestures, autographed the cast of a teenager's broken arm. Although he was portrayed in favorable terms, Schmidt was not pleased. "*Write what you want about what I do at the ballpark*," he told sportswriters emphatically, "*but leave my private life alone.*"[16]

It also is pertinent whether the subjects deliberately decided to create news or whether they were drawn involuntarily into the news.

Step 3: Make the decision

In this step, journalists consider what they have learned in steps one and two, and they arrive at a decision they can defend. They construct a scale in which the importance of the news is weighed against the harm inflicted on the subject of the coverage, as modified by the degree of privacy the subject can expect under the circumstances. They consider whether they can fulfill their duty to inform the public while omitting some of the harmful private details.

News Situations in Which Privacy Is a Factor

People thrust into the news

People who involuntarily become newsmakers typically have survived some sort of disaster, or they are relatives of people tragically killed. Of all the people journalists deal with, this group has both the most entitlement to privacy and the least experience in coping with the media. The SPJ code cautions: "Recognize that private people have a greater right to control information about themselves than do public officials and others who seek power, influence or attention. Only an overriding public need can justify intrusion into anyone's privacy."

News consumers *want* to know about how these news subjects are coping with their ordeals, but this does not meet the *need* standard. The same consumers are likely to be scornful of reporters who appear to violate privacy.

In *Best Practices for Newspaper Journalists*, Robert J. Haiman writes:

> The public … disapproves of newspaper photographers and television camera crews who "catch" private citizens in moments of grief and shock. [The public characterizes] spot news photography as often unnecessarily invasive, insensitive, and unfair. That powerful images of sorrow or tragedy are newsworthy and are captured openly, utilizing traditional photojournalism practices, does not persuade those who believe people in such circumstances are entitled to a zone of privacy from the press. The public sympathizes strongly with victims of tragedy who sometimes seem to be revictimized by their encounters with reporters and photographers at a moment when they are most vulnerable.[17]

Victims of sex crimes

A common practice in journalism is to withhold the names of victims of sex crimes. This practice is based on the principle of minimizing harm. Kelly McBride of the Poynter Institute, writing in *Quill* magazine, gave these specific reasons:

- "Rape is different from any other crime. Society often blames the victims. Studies show rape victims suffer from the stigma of being 'damaged' by the experience."
- "Rape victims are less likely to report the crime if they know their names will appear in the newspaper. Rape is already the most underreported crime in the country."
- "Because rape victims are treated with insensitivity by society, they deserve a level of privacy not afforded other crime victims."[18]

Exceptions to the rule have been made if the victim is murdered, if the victim has been abducted, or if the victim agrees to be identified. Case Study No. 15, "Identifying a 13-Year-Old Rape Victim," presents questions that journalists should consider in an abduction/sexual molestation case, especially when the victim is a juvenile.

Journalists who disagree with the prevailing standard make these points:

- It is not fair to name the accused without also naming the accuser, since the accusation may prove false – as it did in Case Study No. 10, "Duke Lacrosse: One Newspaper's Journey."

- Names are part of the story and add credibility, and journalists should not allow the person making the news to dictate how the news will be covered.
- By withholding names in these cases, journalists reinforce the notion that the victims have disgraced themselves.

These arguments obviously have merit, and there is no clear-cut answer. The author sees the "minimizing harm" principle as more compelling. In an effort to offset the unfairness implicit in naming only the accused, news organizations are obliged to report with equal prominence if the accused is acquitted. As for the argument that the newsmaker is dictating the terms of coverage, there is no indication that the public sees a sinister departure from normal reporting standards when sex-crime victims go nameless. And while it makes sense to combat the idea that a stigma attaches to rape victims, it is ethically questionable to enlist an unwilling victim in that cause.

Politicians' private lives

Until the 1980s, politicians' sexual affairs outside marriage were generally ignored unless they affected the politicians' performance of official duties. That was the policy that the Washington press corps followed when President John F. Kennedy engaged in multiple affairs that drew no press notice, even though one of his partners was a girlfriend of a Mafia leader. Professor Larry Sabato of the University of Virginia wrote, "In the press reports, Jack Kennedy, champion philanderer, became the perfect husband and family man."[19] In retrospect, even by the standard of the 1960s, Kennedy's promiscuous conduct exacted a cost in his performance of official duties, and by omission the press created a false impression of the president.

Sometimes, politicians' affairs did make news when the old standard prevailed.

In 1974, Arkansas Representative Wilbur D. Mills' affair with a burlesque dancer, Fanne Foxe, was reported because Washington police stopped him one night for speeding and driving with his headlights out, and Foxe dashed from his car and jumped into the Tidal Basin. Although reporters had been aware that Mills – who chaired the House Ways and Means Committee – had a drinking problem, they did not cover his personal life until he became a police item.[20]

In 1976, journalists reported on Ohio Representative Wayne L. Hays' affair with Elizabeth Ray, because she was paid $14,000 a year as a staff member without having to do any Congress-related work. That was news because Hays had abused his office by paying his mistress with taxpayers' money. "I can't type. I can't file. I can't even answer the phone," Ray told *The Washington Post*.[21]

The climate changed in 1987 when *Miami Herald* journalists staked out the Washington townhouse where Colorado Senator Gary Hart, a leading candidate for the 1988 Democratic presidential nomination, met with an aspiring actress named Donna Rice. Amid the ensuing publicity, Hart withdrew from the race.

Alicia C. Shepard reported in *American Journalism Review* about what happened in the years after that:

> An obscure lounge singer named Gennifer Flowers held a press conference in 1992. Flowers claimed that for 12 years she had carried on an affair with Bill Clinton, at the time a presidential candidate. The story paralyzed the Clinton campaign briefly. The source, Flowers, had been paid by the *Star*, a supermarket tabloid, and the story was not entirely verifiable. It played itself out after the candidate, with wife Hillary Rodham Clinton at his side, deflected the charges on "60 Minutes." (In 1998 Clinton admitted that he had sex with Flowers, but just once.)
>
> Two years later, an Arkansas state employee named Paula Jones accused Clinton of crudely propositioning her when he was governor of the state. Jones' press conference was largely ignored by the media, although her charges gained attention after she filed a suit against the president. Then, on January 21, 1998, Monica Lewinsky entered our lives. Before long, semen-stained dresses, kinky acts with cigars, oral sex performed on a president while he chatted with a congressman – all found their way into print and onto broadcasts. Some news organizations relied on firsthand reporting; others picked up what was being reported elsewhere.[22]

Contemporary journalists continue to debate whether a politician's sex life is a private matter or a public concern. Journalists who say that it is a legitimate subject of coverage argue that it illuminates a character issue that their audience is entitled to know about. Journalists also point to hypocrisy if the office holder has campaigned as happily married or is an ardent supporter of so-called "family values." Other journalists argue that the old standard should continue to apply – an extramarital affair by a politician is none of the public's business unless there is a pattern of sexual harassment or a problem with the way the politician conducts his or her public office.

During the 1996 presidential campaign *The Washington Post* prepared a story about an affair that Bob Dole, the Republican candidate, had in the late 1960s with a university employee while he was a congressman and still married to his first wife, Phyllis Holden. Several editors at *The Post* wanted to publish the story because of what they said was the Dole campaign's effort to cast him as a morally superior alternative to Bill Clinton. Ultimately, *Post* editor Leonard Downie Jr killed the story. Downie decided that the story did not meet his standard – that "the revelation of a love affair from a quarter century earlier had to be justified by its relevance to the candidate's suitability for the presidency or his past conduct in public office."[23]

North Carolina Senator John Edwards' affair with Rielle Hunter presents a noteworthy case study because the mainstream news media did not mention the affair for months after the *National Enquirer* reported it. Finally, in August 2008, Edwards admitted in an ABC News interview that he had been involved in 2006 with Hunter, a videographer who then was working in his campaign for the Democratic presidential nomination. He denied that he was the father of Hunter's child, born in February 2008. He acknowledged meeting with Hunter in a

California hotel room in July 2008 at her request because "she was having some trouble; she just wanted to talk," and "I wanted her not to tell the public what had happened."[24]

Although the *National Enquirer* had been reporting on the affair since October 2007, Edwards had denied the allegations, dismissing one *Enquirer* story as "tabloid trash."[25] The *Enquirer* disclosures were followed by silence in the mainstream media, but not in the blogosphere and on talk shows, where "the MSM" was denounced for trying to protect Edwards. "The new media really kept this story alive," *Enquirer* editor David Perel said.[26] Although some mainstream organizations chose not to pursue the story – "I'm not going to recycle a supermarket tabloid's anonymously sourced story," said executive editor Bill Keller of *The New York Times*[27] – others tried to check it out, with little to show for their efforts. Then, in August 2008, *The Charlotte Observer* and *The* (Raleigh) *News and Observer* in Edwards' home state started publishing stories; *The Charlotte Observer* found the birth certificate of Hunter's child with no father's name listed. As ABC News investigated the case, Edwards agreed to the interview in which he confessed.[28]

Media writer Howard Kurtz wrote in *The Washington Post* about "the box" mainstream journalists found themselves in, not reporting on a subject that was common knowledge. Kurtz wrote, "When critics, especially on the right, accused the media of protecting a Democrat because of liberal bias, journalists were unable to respond, because to do so would be to acknowledge the very thing they were declining to report."[29]

One reason the traditional media were leery of the Edwards story is that the *Enquirer* paid for information on Edwards. Perel said the paper's policy was no different from that of police, who have been known to pay informants. "The thing to remember is we only pay for information once it's verified and accurate," Perel said. "So, if somebody tells us that John Edwards is going to show up at the Beverly Hilton to meet Rielle Hunter, and he does, well, that information is verified."[30]

Ombudsman Michael Getler of Public Broadcasting Service criticized PBS's *NewsHour With Jim Lehrer* for making no mention of the Edwards story on Aug. 8, 2008, the day he admitted the affair. To Getler, that didn't make sense, especially when *NewsHour* three days later broadcast a lengthy segment examining why the mainstream media had remained silent on the story for so long. When Getler asked why the newscast itself had declined to report the story once Edwards confirmed it, he was told that Edwards was no longer a candidate for public office and was not on a short list for the vice presidential nomination. In his ombudsman column, Getler explained why he disagreed:

> a startling, nationally televised confession by a very high-profile public and political figure; a former senator who has twice campaigned for the presidency and who was campaigning at the time of the affair; who was the vice-presidential candidate in 2004; who withdrew from the 2008 race only early this year; who used campaign funds to hire the filmmaker; [whose] wife is suffering from cancer; who used his family and the importance of character and values in his campaigns; who was a

possible speaker at the forthcoming Democratic nominating convention; and who campaigned surely knowing that this affair could blow up the party if he became successful and if it became known, which it almost always does …[31]

Kelly McBride of the Poynter Institute wrote an essay discussing another sensitive question – when, if ever, are journalists justified in disclosing a politician's homosexuality? Journalists commonly argue that disclosure is justified if a politician has consistently voted on public policy issues that appear to undermine the rights or the political agenda of gay and lesbian citizens, and there subsequently is evidence that the politician is gay. McBride wrote that she favored a higher threshold. "Merely voting a certain way on issues doesn't quite cut it. The only time the hypocrisy argument really works is when an individual has railed against gays and lesbians as a campaign platform." She also doubted that voters deserve to know if the politician says he's not gay and it turns out that he is. Again proposing a higher standard, McBride asked: "Has he deceived a spouse? Has he actively created a false impression?"[32]

McBride dismissed the argument that "we don't care whether he's gay; we report on the effect the story has on the political scene." This, she wrote, is "a cop-out, a great way to back into a salacious story without taking responsibility for the information at the heart of the story."[33] Her answer, of course, could apply as well to stories about politicians' extramarital relationships that are heterosexual.

Suicides

Journalists generally agree that a suicide ranks low on the scale of news, particularly when the person involved is not a news figure and when the suicide occurs in private. There also is a consensus, however, that coverage is necessary if a suicide takes place in public or if the person involved is well known.

The suicide of Budd Dwyer in Harrisburg, Pennsylvania, on January 27, 1987, met both criteria: Dwyer, the state treasurer, shot himself to death in front of reporters and photographers at a news conference after he had been sentenced to prison for fraud. Even given those powerful news values, many readers objected to the broadcast of an unedited video by one station and to front-page coverage with graphic photographs in newspapers. The objections focused not on privacy but on matters of taste. The Dwyer suicide is discussed in detail in Case Study No. 17, "Covering a Public Official's Public Suicide."

When non-celebrities commit suicide in a spectacular way – say, by leaping from a bridge while a crowd watches – most editors and news directors will opt for subdued coverage rather than appearing to glamorize the act and thus encouraging copycats.

A more common problem is faced by news outlets of all sizes is deciding whether to include the cause of death in the obituary of a private citizen who has committed suicide in private. The anguish of the deceased's family is intensified when the obituary mentions suicide, no matter if it is a single sentence: "Police said the cause of death was a self-inflicted gunshot wound." Seeking to minimize harm, some journalists readily omit any reference to suicide, even if they list the cause of death in other obituaries. Other journalists object that this is censoring the news and that credibility suffers because, by omission, the news outlet is implying the death was due to natural causes. They reason that relatives and friends are well aware of the cause of death and might infer from the omission that other news is censored as well.

However, a news organization intent on reporting suicides may be thwarted by funeral directors and medical examiners who suppress the cause of death as a gesture of compassion to the families.

The way that the news media report suicide can contribute to copycat suicides, according to a study published in August 2001 by the American Foundation for Suicide Prevention, the American Association of Suicidology, and the Annenberg Public Policy Center of the University of Pennsylvania. The study found that people in the audience might identify with the suicide victim if the news media:

- portray suicide as a heroic or romantic act;
- report the suicide method, especially if the description is detailed; or
- present suicide as the inexplicable act of an otherwise healthy or high-achieving person.

The study showed that more than 90 percent of suicide victims have a significant psychiatric illness, which often is undiagnosed, untreated, or both. "The cause of an individual suicide is invariably more complicated than a recent painful event such as the break-up of a relationship or the loss of a job." An example of a problematic headline cited in the study was "Boy, 10, kills himself over poor grades."

The study's authors urged the news media to produce more stories on such topics as trends in suicide rates, recent treatment advances, myths about suicide, and warning signs of suicides.[34]

Juveniles accused of crimes

Advocates in the criminal justice system urge that underage offenders should be shielded from publicity. Although names of the accused are routinely publicized in other crimes, these advocates argue that this is inappropriate when the defendants are juveniles. They say the public's desire to know the names should yield to the possibility that these young people can rebuild their lives if they do not also have to cope with the notoriety.

Few journalists disagree with that principle, and the practice is to withhold names (even in the rare instances that authorities provide them) when crimes like burglary or shoplifting are involved.

The decision-making is more complicated when children are accused of homicides or other major felonies. These situations do not lend themselves to a blanket rule, but many editors and news directors will identify children who are accused of multiple murders, as in the 1998 shooting deaths of four students and a teacher at a school in Jonesboro, Arkansas. The reasoning is that in such high-profile events, the need of the public to be completely informed outweighs the desire not to interfere with the rehabilitation of the offenders. Bill Keller, then managing editor of *The New York Times*, said that in the Jonesboro case, the boys' lives were forever "turned upside down," making their identification in the newspaper "inconsequential."[35]

Adult relatives of the prominent

Louis Hodges thinks the public may be interested in what these relatives do, but he considers that to be questionable justification for reporting on them against their will. "Like other citizens," Hodges writes, "they should be reported on because of the significance of what they do."[36]

The cases of two presidential brothers are illustrative. In the late 1970s, the drinking problem and resulting outrageous behavior of Billy Carter of Plains, Georgia, would not have received national attention if his brother Jimmy had not been president.[37] Likewise, the fact that Roger Clinton served a year in an Arkansas prison on a conviction for drug charges was reported nationally because his half-brother Bill became president in 1993.[38]

However, Billy Carter and Roger Clinton also made news *precisely* because their brothers were in the White House. Billy Carter received a $220,000 loan from Libya and was briefly a "registered agent" of the Libyan regime (federal investigators found no evidence that the younger Carter had influenced American policy).[39] During the Clinton administration, Roger Clinton was investigated for allegedly taking money from convicted felons in exchange for promising to make pardon requests to his brother. (Roger Clinton denied this, but he did submit six names to President Clinton to consider for clemency.)[40]

While it is common to see reporting on the relatives of the prominent, this reporting is generally done in an understated fashion. The arrest of college students for underage drinking is not usually national news, but in May 2001 it was – when President George W. and Laura Bush's 19-year-old twins, Jenna and Barbara, were arrested at a Texas restaurant. Most of the coverage was subdued, although there were exceptions, notably *The New York Post*'s front-page headline, "Jenna and Tonic."

White House spokesman Scott McClellan declined to discuss the arrests, saying, "If it involves the daughters in their private lives, it is a family matter."[41] The Society of Professional Journalists' ethics committee disagreed. "If we failed to report these incidents the public would quite rightly accuse us of covering for the Bush family," committee chair Gary Hill said in a news release. "But … journalists should continue to place these events in the proper context. These are not serious crimes. … These events do not mean journalists should now have a field day with all aspects of the Bush family's private lives."[42]

Reporting based on social networking websites

MySpace, Facebook and other social networking websites provide an online connection for groups such as college students, business partners and friends. They have become a routine source of background and tips for many journalists, especially when young people are involved in the news. It is smart reporting, but it also presents ethical questions of accuracy and fairness: The posting may not be authentic, and the posting probably was intended for a private audience even though it is in a public space.

Mike Pride, retired editor of the *Concord* (New Hampshire) *Monitor*, offers an example:

> You have a young murder victim, and it's hard to get information about the victim. Then you discover a page on MySpace. How can you be sure the victim actually wrote it? Is it fair to publish it? It is in public and it is legal, but [the victim's] putting it on the web is not the same as putting it on the front page of the newspaper.[43]

Jason Spencer of the *Herald-Journal* in Spartanburg, South Carolina, gave advice to fellow reporters in an article in *American Journalism Review*:

> Never use MySpace or Facebook data without double-checking its authenticity. E-mail MySpace or Facebook "friends" to verify information or arrange interviews; always identify yourself as a reporter. Remember: The information people post on a social networking page is self-selected. It could be biased, exaggerated or just plain wrong.[44]

Butch Ward, Distinguished Poynter Fellow at the Poynter Institute, wrote an essay for *poynteronline* about the need for verification. The essay was inspired by his daughter Caitlin's experience in having her web comment used by the news media. Caitlin Ward, a student at Lafayette College, posted a memorial message on the MySpace page of a friend who was killed in the Virginia Tech massacre on April 16, 2007. A few days later, a friend told her that she had been quoted on *The New York Times*' website. No one from *The Times* had called for confirmation before her message was included in one of its mini-profiles of the Virginia Tech victims.

When Butch Ward contacted *The Times* while preparing his essay, an editor responded that the newspaper had concluded the risk in this instance was low. Ward ended his essay with the question: "Are we really willing to risk even further damage to our credibility by abandoning traditions as old and honored as verification?"[45]

Case Study No. 14
Revealing Arthur Ashe's Secret

Arthur Ashe was born July 10, 1943, in Richmond, Virginia. Early in life, he learned that the color of his skin could create barriers for him. Richmond's segregated park system afforded few opportunities for a black child to play tennis, so Ashe often practiced his game using a wall or through visualization. But he got a break when collegiate player Ron Charity recommended Ashe to Dr Robert Walker Johnson, a wealthy instructor. Ashe quickly became a prized pupil and, after eight years at Johnson's camps, earned the first scholarship given a black tennis player by UCLA. In 1965, he won the NCAA tennis championship.

He graduated from UCLA in 1966. After he served two years in the Army, his professional tennis career exploded. He was ranked No. 1 in the world in 1968 and 1975. He was the first black man to win a Grand Slam event, and the only black man to win the US Open (1968), the Australian Open (1970) and Wimbledon (1975). Ashe was the first black member of the US Davis Cup team and the first black man inducted into the International Tennis Hall of Fame.

Off the court, Ashe had a tougher opponent: racism. And he fought back. He was instrumental in getting South Africa banned from the Davis Cup because of its apartheid policies. Ashe was also a leader in creating minority-group youth tennis programs.

His tennis career came to a sudden end in 1979, when he suffered a heart attack at age 36 and had quadruple-bypass surgery. He had a second bypass four years later but suffered another heart attack in 1992. The turning point in Arthur Ashe's life came in 1988, when tests revealed that he had contracted the AIDS virus through a blood transfusion. He got his transfusion 18 months before blood supplies first were tested for the AIDS virus.

Ashe's family and closest friends kept the secret of Ashe's health condition for three years. "I was with Arthur at the hospital in '88 when he found out," said Donald Dell, one of Ashe's closest friends for more than 20 years. "But I honored his wish for privacy this whole time. He has always wanted to continue with his work and to live like a normal human being."

On April 7, 1992, a *USA Today* reporter called Ashe and asked if he had been diagnosed with AIDS. Ashe would neither confirm nor deny it. Editors at the paper told Ashe that while they would not report his AIDS condition without on-record sources, they intended to pursue the story over his objection. The paper took the stance that a well-known, although retired, sports figure with AIDS was important news. *USA Today* did not publish a story immediately, but Ashe realized that his request for privacy was not going to be granted. He held a news confer-

Continued

ence the next day and announced that he had AIDS. Ashe said, "It put me in the unenviable position of having to lie" to protect his privacy, and added, "No one should ever have to make that choice." He went on to say: "I am sorry that I have been forced to make this revelation at this time. After all, I am not running for some office of public trust, nor do I have stakeholders to account to. It is only that I fall in the dubious umbrella of 'public figure.'"

USA Today received several hundred letters and telephone calls expressing disapproval of the paper's position. Lucie Roane of Vienna, Virginia, said, "The story was horrendous. It was invasion of privacy and it is not the public's right to know everything about everybody because they happen to be a public figure." Jeff Breitenfield of Madison, Wisconsin, said, "So how about a little compassion and respect for a guy who's not only been a model athlete but a model citizen, as well?" Colleen Bodgan of East Amherst, New York, said, "The fact that Arthur Ashe contracted AIDS is not a shock … What is shocking is *USA Today*'s lack of sensitivity in investigating and reporting what Ashe clearly held as a private confidence."

Ashe's wife, Jeanne, was angry that he had been forced to go public, but she also was relieved. She said, "You feel like you're hiding something. It's not so much you're hiding the disease than it is you're hiding your privacy. I hope that they will see that his life has been an example of dealing with adversity and positive thinking. It's a picture of hope."

In a column in *The Washington Post* the Sunday after the press conference, Arthur Ashe discussed his right to privacy versus the public's right to know. Here is a passage:

I know there are trade-offs in life. I understand that the press has a watchdog role in the maintenance of our freedoms and to expose corruption. But the process whereby news organizations make distinctions seems more art than science. I wasn't then, and am not now, comfortable with being sacrificed for the sake of the "public's right to know." Doctors, lawyers and journalists have gone to jail rather than expose a client or source without his or her permission. Perhaps sportswriters' organizations should take another look at the currently accepted rationale for making these decisions.

USA Today defended itself. Gene Policinski, the managing editor/sports, wrote for *The Bulletin* of the American Society of Newspaper Editors: "The news was that one of the great athletes of this century had a fatal illness – and that the illness was AIDS. By any journalist's definition, that's news."

The editor of *USA Today*, Peter Prichard, said in a column that the paper investigated a tip about Ashe's illness not just because he was an admired athlete. He said the paper was also motivated because Ashe had fought against racism, had been an advocate for good health, and was an intelligent and graceful human being. Prichard also pointed out that Ashe was on the board of Aetna Life & Casualty, "a company involved in controversy over insurance for AIDS patients."

Prichard's column continued: "If in fact Ashe had AIDS, we thought it was news. If it came from a transfusion, that might revive concerns about the blood supply's safety." Prichard argued that if the paper had failed to check out the tip, it would have been sharing Ashe's secret. He thought it was a mistake for journalists to keep secrets or to

Continued

protect some people but not others. "Sweeping Ashe's secret under the rug would have contributed to the public ignorance of AIDS and done nothing to reduce the disease's stigma," Prichard wrote.

> This is not to say that the media ought to make every AIDS sufferer a public issue. In the end, journalists serve the public by reporting news, not hiding it. By sharing his story, Arthur Ashe and his family are free of a great weight. In the days ahead, they will help us better understand AIDS and how to defeat it. Then some good will have come from all of this.

The Arthur Ashe case divided the journalistic community, even within *USA Today*. DeWayne Wickham wrote a column entitled, "Stop the voyeurism and gossip-peddling." He said that journalism "teeters on the edge of a very slippery slope" in confronting Ashe, forcing him to go public or lie. He said Ashe deserved the same privacy that the newspaper gives rape victims. "Like them, he, too, should not be twice victimized by being made to suffer the harsh glare of the public spotlight."

Jack Shafer, then the editor of *City Paper* in Washington, wrote that he was sympathetic to Ashe and the anguish that he felt, but that "news stories cause anguish all the time." Mike Berardino, a columnist for the *Sun-Sentinel* in Fort Lauderdale, Florida, wrote: "Call me sentimental, but I believe there are some things that should remain private, at least until after one's death. Ashe's terrible misfortune seems to qualify under these terms."

Arthur Ashe died February 6, 1993, but the ethical dilemma posed by his case continues to cause debate among journalists.

Reflecting on the case in 2008, Peter Prichard said that if Ashe had not chosen to reveal his illness, it was "highly unlikely" that *USA Today* would have reported it. "We had told him we would only print it if we could get it on the record," the former editor said. "For me that meant we would have to learn it from Arthur, or from his doctor, or from his wife."

Policinski said in 2008 he had told Ashe directly that he would require "two on-the-record, identified sources" and that these would have to be people who could "produce verifiable evidence – his physicians, for example."

In today's environment, Prichard said, "it almost seems quaint that a news source would choose to withhold a story." He elaborated:

> Almost nothing is withheld today; once talked about among friends, almost any story always gets into the news stream, whether it is born as a rumor on a blog or a website, or an unsourced line in a gossip column, or, glory be, it matures into a legitimate, occasionally well-sourced scoop in a mainstream medium. So I think our restraint in insisting that we would only print this news if we had the story on the record was rare in 1992, and it seems almost unimaginable in today's media world.

This case is adapted from a research paper that Jaime Fettrow wrote while a student at Pennsylvania State University. She graduated in 2000 and is a sports anchor and reporter for WHP-TV at Harrisburg, Pennsylvania.

Continued

Questions for Class Discussion

- Do you think the story about Ashe's illness would be eagerly read by the public? (If you're not familiar with Ashe because he was before your time, think of another famous athlete who retired just a few years ago. As a hypothetical example, would you be *interested* in reading such a story if it involved Michael Jordan?)
- If you think the story would be eagerly read, would you publish it against his wishes?
- What reasons did *USA Today*'s editors give for publishing the story over Ashe's objections? Do you think those reasons are persuasive?
- What do you think of DeWayne Wickham's argument that Ashe deserved the same right to privacy that journalists routinely give to rape victims?
- If you would have kept Ashe's secret, would you have disclosed the cause of death when he died in 1993 even if the family still objected?
- If the family of former President Ronald Reagan had wanted to keep his illness with Alzheimer's disease a secret, would you have complied? If there is a difference in your position on the two cases, why?
- What rights to privacy does a person give up when he or she becomes a public official? A public figure?

Case Study No. 15

Identifying a 13-Year-Old Rape Victim

On New Year's Day 2002, 13-year-old Alicia Kozakiewicz walked out of her house in suburban Pittsburgh and got into a car driven by a Virginia man she had met in an online chat room. That was the beginning of a nightmare. For the next four days, she was tortured, sexually assaulted, and chained to the floor of the basement of the man's townhouse.

While she was missing, Pittsburgh news media outlets ran her photograph and stories about her disappearance. Those media notices helped lead to her rescue. A Florida man saw an online video of Alicia being held captive, then found the missing-person news stories. The tipster notified the FBI. Agents traced the abductor's screen name, determined her location, and came to her rescue.

Returning home after her rescue, Alicia and her parents, Mary and Charlie Kozakiewicz, found the place surrounded by reporters and photojournalists. Before going inside, they spoke briefly with the media. Mary Kozakiewicz said their only purpose

Continued

was to allow Alicia "to say thank you because everyone had done their job. In this community, when you get help, you say thanks." She added, "But many said that by allowing her to say thanks … we gave a press conference."

Indeed, that was the way some of the journalists saw it, and the perception contributed to their decision to continue naming the girl in their coverage of her abduction and rescue, even though her abductor had been accused of sexual assault. (The abductor, Scott Tyree, then 38, was convicted and sent to prison.)

Johnna A. Pro, a *Pittsburgh Post-Gazette* staff writer, told student journalist Alissa Wisnouse in 2002:

> I think they thought this was her 15 minutes of fame. I think we might have hesitated had her parents brought her back and hidden her at her grandmother's house. But they were making no attempt to shield her from the onslaught of the media.

It would be years before any members of the Kozakiewicz family spoke to journalists again. As the incessant coverage continued in the print and broadcast media, they disconnected their telephones and would not answer the door. Mary Kozakiewicz said her daughter felt she was "being forced into hiding."

This case study focuses on the *Post-Gazette*, although the *Pittsburgh Tribune-Review* and at least some of the local broadcast outlets also continued using the girl's name.

Like most news media, the *Post-Gazette*'s policy is to shield the identity of sexual-assault victims. But in this case, reporters and editors were already inclined to continue using her name because it was "out there" as a result of the two missing-person stories.

They reasoned that it would have been futile to try to pull her name back.

The parents' behavior seemed to assuage any doubts. Pro said in 2002 she felt bad for the girl "because I think she was wronged by her parents, not us. It's her parents' job to protect her, not ours. I think once she was found, they could have and should have shielded her from the media. And they didn't." Put simply, Pro said, "I'm not her mother, I'm not her dad. I'm a journalist with a job to do."

After the initial stories about rescuing the girl, the *Post-Gazette* stopped using her photograph. However, the newspaper continued to use her name in 13 news stories, 5 columns, and 2 letters to the editor, according to the numbers Wisnouse reported in a thesis at Pennsylvania State University that spring.

The coverage continued for a month. The topics included updates on criminal proceedings against Tyree, Internet safety for teens, and whether the girl's parents owed tuition payments for Alicia because she was attending a public school outside her home district (Mary Kozakiewicz said they did not owe tuition). One column discussed how, before her abduction, the girl had a website "replete with sexually provocative phrases and pictures of herself" (Mary Kozakiewicz characterized the pictures as "simple family photos").

On January 20, more than two weeks after the girl was rescued, the *Post-Gazette*'s editor, John Craig, wrote a column discussing the newspaper's decision to name her:

> If the *Post-Gazette* has a firm policy on not identifying the names of victims of sexual crimes, and is at particular pains to protect the identity of children, how is it that the newspaper continues to print [her] name

Continued

and picture? We had a lively internal debate on that question over several days last week. … I acknowledged that withholding the names of sexual-abuse victims of all ages is a popular position and it was unlikely that there would be complaints if we stopped using her name. … In my opinion, electronic databases being what they are, unless there is a fundamental change in the laws of the United States, anyone visiting the *PG*'s files years from now will be able to find the name and the stories. That is a long-term privacy risk.

Craig invited readers to share their thoughts with him, and Pro said there was no public outcry about using the girl's name. "People were upset with her parents. The public reaction was against her parents, not the media," Pro said. The parents, of course, were not talking, so that perception went unchallenged.

Looking back on the case in 2008, Pro said:

Did we do a disservice to Alicia? The nurturing, empathetic side of me says yes. Even so, I believe my job as a journalist covering the story was to report it fairly and accurately, which I did; to debate the necessity of using her name with my colleagues and superiors, which I did; and serve my readers, which I did.

The disconnect between the parents and the journalists proved to be emotionally costly. After a girl has been rescued from a predator, Mary Kozakiewicz said, "you should not use her name. Give her time to heal."

Mrs Kozakiewicz said, "Things would die down a bit, but every time her name was mentioned on television or in the newspaper, people would be pointing again." As a result, she chose to home-school Alicia for the remainder of the school year. "When she attended a public high school the following year, kids still treated her differently."

In the fall of 2007, college freshman Alicia Kozakiewicz began conducting weekly multimedia presentations at elementary and middle schools in the Pittsburgh region. "Given the awful power of her tale, she's been inundated with requests to speak," Nicole Weisensee Egan wrote in *People* magazine. Egan described a presentation she made before 400 students: "Projected behind her on a screen is her missing poster. 'That's me about five years ago,' she tells the kids, who listen with rapt attention. 'I was almost another body in the morgue. So please: Listen to me.'"

Mary Kozakiewicz said her daughter's experience with the news media was a factor in her decision to speak to the school groups. Mrs Kozakiewicz said she, too, is speaking out. She travels with Alicia to speak with law-enforcement officers, educators, and legislators. To families with missing children, she said her message is: "Be very careful of the media because though they may be instrumental in the recovery of your child, you must also be aware of the harm they can do."

Should the *Post-Gazette* and other Pittsburgh media have continued using Alicia's name in 2002?

In an email to Wisnouse, Bill Mitchell of the Poynter Institute addressed the question of whether the parents invited publicity:

The parents' views should certainly be considered but not necessarily considered determinative. A parent in such case might urge a newsroom to use a child's name – who knows why? – but the newsroom would still be faced with making its own best decision in the interest of the child and its own principles.

Continued

This case is adapted from an honors thesis that Alissa Wisnouse (now Alissa Barron Stranzl) wrote while a senior at Pennsylvania State University. The case uses Alicia Kozakiewicz's name because she is now an adult and is making public presentations on her experience.

Questions for Class Discussion

- Do you think the fact that the girl's name was "out there" in the missing-person stories gave the *Post-Gazette* no choice but to continue using her name?
- If you favor continuing using her name, do you think it was appropriate to write enterprise stories on such topics as her Internet site and whether the girl's family owed tuition payments?
- If you think the *Post-Gazette* should have stopped using her name, how would you have explained your decision to the readers?
- Should the parents' apparent willingness to allow the girl to be interviewed have guided the journalists' decision to continue covering her?
- In writing his column, was editor John Craig being accountable to *Post-Gazette* readers?

Notes

1   Adam Gorney, Gwenn Miller, and Alex Weininger, "Racist mail spurs demonstration," *The Daily Collegian*, April 23, 2001.

2   Leah Milito, letter to the editor of the *Centre Daily Times*, April 29, 2001.

3   Bob Unger, "Why we published protesters' addresses," *Centre Daily Times*, April 29, 2001.

4   Diana Jean Schemo, "Penn State students end sit-in over threats against blacks," *The New York Times*, May 4, 2001.

5   Philip Patterson and Lee Wilkins, *Media Ethics: Issues and Cases*, 5th edn. (New York: McGraw-Hill, 2005), 135.

6   Louis W. Hodges, "The journalist and privacy," *Journal of Mass Media Ethics*, vol. 9, no. 4 (Mahwah, NJ: Lawrence Erlbaum Associates Inc.), 202.

7   Ibid., 197.

8   Ibid., 200.

9   Ibid., 202.

10 The three topics were identified in Jay Black, Bob Steele, and Ralph Barney, *Doing Ethics in Journalism: A Handbook With Case Studies*, 3rd edn. (Boston: Allyn & Bacon, 1999), 238.

11 Turner Catledge, *My Life and the Times* (New York: Harper & Row, 1971), 38.

12 Louis A. Day, *Ethics in Media Communications: Cases and Controversies*, 5th edn. (Belmont, CA: Thomson Wadsworth, 2006), 139.

13 Ibid., 139.

14 Hodges, "The journalist and privacy," 203.

15 Day, *Ethics in Media Communication*, 153.

16 Author's recollections as managing editor of *The Inquirer*.

17 Robert J. Haiman, *Best Practices for Newspaper Journalists* (Arlington, VA: The Freedom Forum's Free Press/Fair Press Project, 2000), 29.

18 Kelly McBride, "Rethinking rape coverage," *Quill*, October/November 2002, 9.

19 Larry J. Sabato, *Feeding Frenzy: How Attack Journalism Has Transformed American Politics* (New York: The Free Press, 1991), 40.

20 Gail Collins, "A candidate's 'irrelevant' past," *The American Editor*, December 1999, 16.

21 Marion Clark and Rudy Maxa, "Closed session romance on the Hill," *The Washington Post*, May 23, 1976.

22 Alicia C. Shepard, "Gatekeepers without gates," *American Journalism Review*, March 1999.

23 Leonard Downie Jr and Robert G. Kaiser, *The News About the News* (New York: Alfred A. Knopf, 2002), 56–62.

24 Rhonda Schwartz, Brian Ross, and Chris Francescani, "Edwards admits sexual affair; lied as presidential candidate," http://abcnews.go.com/Blotter/Story?id=5441195&page=1, Aug. 8, 2008.

25 Michael Calderone, "Why I also didn't write on John Edwards," http://www.politico.com/blogs/michaelcalderone/0808/Why_I_also_didnt_write_on_John_Edwards.html, Aug. 10, 2008.

26 Russell Adams and Shira Ovide, "Mainstream media notes *Enquirer* scoop," *The Wall Street Journal Online*, Aug. 11, 2008.

27 Clark Hoyt, "Sometimes, there's news in the gutter," *The New York Times*, Aug. 10, 2008.

28 Adams and Ovide, "Mainstream media notes *Enquirer* scoop."

29 Howard Kurtz, "Affair put press in a touchy situation," *The Washington Post*, Aug. 11, 2008.

30 David Perel's comment on *Reliable Sources* on Cable News Network, Aug. 10, 2008.

31 Michael Getler, "The Edwards confession: unfit for NewsHour viewers?", http://www.pbs.org/ombudsman/2008/08/the_edwards_confession_unfit_f.html, Aug. 13, 2008.

32 McBride, "Thresholds of coverage: When to say he's gay," http://www.poynter.org/content/content_view.asp?id=129197, Aug. 30, 2007.

33 Ibid.

34 American Foundation for Suicide Prevention, "Reporting on suicide: Recommendations for the Media," http://www.afsp.org/index.cfm?fuseaction=home.viewPage&page_id=7852EBBC-9FB2-6691-54125A1AD4221E49

35 Quoted in "Naming kid criminals," *Columbia Journalism Review*, July/August 1998, 18.

36 Hodges, "The journalist and privacy," 210.

37 PBS.org, *The American Experience*, "Jimmy Carter: People and Events/Billy Carter," http://www.pbs.org/wgbh/amex/carter/peopleevents/p_bcater.html.

38 CNN.com. "Roger Clinton now target of pardon probe," *Inside Politics*, http://archives.cnn.com/2001/ALLPOLITICS/02/22/burton.rich.02/.

39 Robert Hershey Jr, "Billy Carter dies of cancer at 51: Troubled brother of a president," *The New York Times*, Sept. 26, 1988.

40 Viva Novak and Michael Weisskopf, "New questions about Roger Clinton's slippery schemes," Time.com, June 30, 2001.

41 "It's a family affair," msnbc.com, May 31, 2001.

42 Society of Professional Journalists news release, "SPJ urges ethical reporting of First Family's personal lives," http://spj.org/news.asp?ref=126, June 1, 2001.

43 Author's telephone interview with Mike Pride, Sept. 18, 2007.

44 Jason Spencer, "Found in (My)Space," *American Journalism Review*, October/November 2007, 36–9.

45 Butch Ward, "From MySpace post to NYT quote," http://www.poynter.org/content/content_view.asp?id=123419, May 21, 2007.

15 Making News Decisions About Taste

The conflict between reflecting reality and respecting the audience

Learning Goals

This chapter will help you understand:

- the choices that journalists have to make when reporting the news could offend a significant segment of the audience, and why those choices have ethical implications;
- a two-step process for making decisions about news content that is likely to offend;
- the problem of perceived insensitivity by the media;
- the problem of offensive words in the news; and
- the problem of offensive images in the news.

Two days after Seung Hui Cho massacred 32 fellow Virginia Tech students and shot himself to death, a package arrived at NBC news headquarters in New York at 11 a.m. Wednesday, April 18, 2007.[1] The package contained 25 minutes of video, 45 photographs, and a 23-page manifesto in which the mass murderer sought "to use the media as his personal platform."[2]

Cho mailed the package during the two hours that elapsed between the murder of two people in a dormitory and 30 others in a classroom building. He sent it by overnight delivery, but the package was delayed because he entered the wrong zip code. The network notified the FBI and held off reporting on the package until the agency's experts could examine it.

That evening on "NBC Nightly News," the network broadcast 2 minutes of video, 7 photographs, and 37 sentences from Cho's manifesto. The images showed Cho pointing guns at the camera and profanely denouncing rich "brats" and their "hedonistic needs." In an excerpt shown by NBC, Cho said:

> You had a hundred billion chances and ways to have avoided today. But you decided to spill my blood. You forced me into a corner and gave me only one option. The decision was yours. Now you have blood on your hands that will never wash off.

Anchor Brian Williams told viewers, "We are sensitive to how all of this will be seen by those affected and know we are, in effect, airing the words of a murderer here tonight."[3]

Parts of the same video appeared on cable news programs that evening and on the three networks' morning shows on Thursday. Newspaper front pages displayed photographs of Cho waving the guns. Online news sites around the world posted various versions of Cho's package overnight.

The reaction of the public was swift and overwhelmingly angry. In protest, the families of several Virginia Tech victims canceled scheduled appearances on the NBC "Today" show.[4] Expressing the view of many, one comment posted on NBC's website said, "I am totally appalled that NBC News has chosen to broadcast the videos of a psychopath according to his wishes."[5] A reader wrote to the *Houston Chronicle* to object to its front-page photo of Cho: "Are you trying to glorify or vilify this tormented young man? And are you giving fodder for others who might … get their '15 minutes of fame' …?"[6]

A theme of the public's outrage was that the news media were paying too much attention to the killer and not enough to the innocent victims. Some made the point that the image of Cho with his guns was the last thing those victims ever saw.

As the complaints poured in on Thursday, television organizations sharply reduced their use of the video. According to a content analysis by the Project for Excellence in Journalism, "By Thursday night, some of the cable shows were showing brief excerpts of the videos while others were not showing anything at all. And by Friday morning, it appears that almost all of the TV outlets decided to stop airing the footage."[7] NBC anchor Williams said he would broadcast more material only if it shed more light on the killings.[8] Fox News announced that it would stop showing the video, saying "sometimes you change your mind."[9] ABC News spokesman Jeffrey Schneider said, "It has value as breaking news, but then becomes practically pornographic as it is repeated ad nauseam."[10]

WSLS-TV, the NBC affiliate in Roanoke, decided after the first day to stop airing audio of Cho's "ranting death tape" or images of Cho pointing weapons at the camera. "We realize that would only further cause pain to the Virginia Tech community," executive producer Jessica A. Ross said in a statement.[11]

On April 24, Williams and NBC News president Steve Capus flew to Chicago to appear on "The Oprah Winfrey Show" to defend their decision. "Sometimes good journalism is bad public relations," Capus said. "Remember, this was days after the incident. The largest question out there was 'Why?'" Williams said the images were too much for his own family to watch but too important not to give to the public. He and Capus said the network showed restraint in selecting which of Cho's material it would broadcast.[12]

The ethical issue that journalists faced in Cho's hate-filled package pivoted on balancing the fundamental principles of truth-telling and minimizing harm. It involved choices about *taste* – choices between reporting certain information because it is in the public interest, or withholding it or toning it down out of respect for the sensibilities of the audience. Respect for the audience is an ethical responsibility. So is a concern for the people involved in the stories and pictures.

Despite the protests, journalists were right to inform the public about the contents of Cho's multimedia package, although the quantity of coverage is open to debate. "I believe that the video and Cho's so-called manifesto add pieces to a complex puzzle, albeit a very painful puzzle," said Bob Steele of the Poynter Institute. "We may not know more about why he did what he did, but his tape and his writings might give us more understanding of what happened on Monday and why it happened as it did."[13]

What is beyond dispute in the Cho case is that many in the audience thought their values were not shared by the news media. This may be a gross misreading of the media's intent, but it reinforces the axiom that editors and news directors should approach taste decisions with care and explain those decisions thoughtfully. Even then, they can expect complaints.

A Two-Step Decision Process on Taste Issues

To make decisions about taste – how to handle offensive content – journalists should be aware that the media can offend in three ways:

1   With words or images that can be perceived as insensitive, as the Cho package was.
2   With words that are obscene, vulgar, or profane, are sexist, or disparage ethnic or racial groups.
3   With images that portray graphic violence and nudity.

In general, the mainstream news organizations police their content to avoid *unnecessarily* offending their audiences. Editors and news directors want to build a loyal audience. They know that many news consumers will go elsewhere if they are regularly offended by what they read, see, or hear, or if they are concerned about exposing their children to content of this kind. That is a powerful incentive for news organizations to avoid offensive content. Unlike the motion-picture industry, whose rating system cautions customers about the kind of language and scenes they will see if they go to a certain movie, mainstream news outlets assume that their audience expects nothing more startling than a PG or PG-13 product.

A two-step process (Figure 15.1) can guide you to a thoughtful decision on whether to publish, broadcast, or post offensive content:

Step 1: Recognize words or images that are likely to offend a significant number of the audience

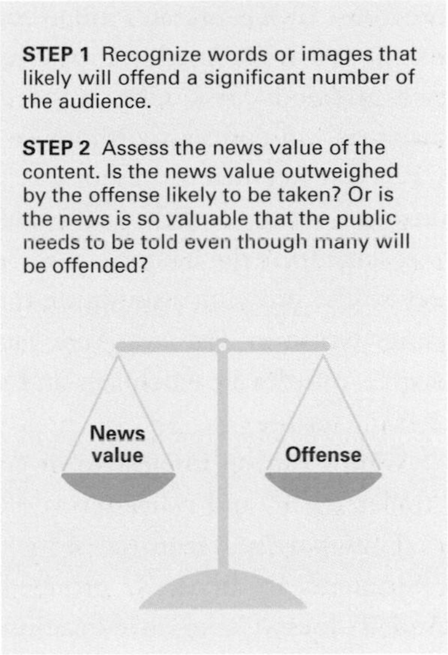

The three categories listed above should help you identify problematic material. So should your observations about audience reaction in the past to material that your organization and other organizations have used. Pay attention to a furor like that generated by the Cho package, because the audience is sending a message.

Apply what some journalists call "the Wheaties test": deciding whether a typical news consumer can handle watching, hearing, or reading the news while eating breakfast. Rule-based thinking would lead you to discard any content that fails the Wheaties test. That could be the easiest choice, but it might not fulfill your responsibility to inform the public.

Figure 15.1 Making decisions on offensive content GRAPHIC COURTESY OF BILL MARSH

Step 2: Assess the news value of the content

In this step, ends-based thinking is involved. You may decide that the news value does not outweigh the offense likely to be taken. Or you may decide that the news is so valuable that the public needs to be told even though many will be offended.

If you decide to use the offensive content, make careful decisions about how to present it – that is, apply Aristotle's Golden Mean. Consider the amount of time to allot on a broadcast; the size and location of photographs in a newspaper; and cautionary notices that can be posted with links used in online coverage. Think about how to explain your decision.

When the Audience Might See Insensitivity

As discussed above, the Cho multimedia package offended a sizable segment of the audience primarily because of the perception that news organizations were glorifying a mass killer. The media were criticized for perceived insensitivity, not for vulgar language or obscene images (Cho's profanities in his videotape were bleeped by broadcasters).

Another example of what some perceived as insensitivity was CBS's decision to broadcast on "60 Minutes" the videotaped moment of death for a terminally ill man whom Dr Jack Kevorkian injected with potassium chloride. CBS's broadcast of Kevorkian's video on November 22, 1998, was widely criticized, and six network-affiliated stations refused to air the segment. The criticism was two-pronged: First, CBS was faulted for giving Kevorkian a platform for airing his views on euthanasia (the network said it was illuminating the debate). Second, CBS was accused of using exclusive video of a man's death to boost ratings during a sweeps week (CBS said the show was not rushed).[14] "That this death was staged for the cameras is the most unsettling aspect of the story, a dark corollary to the growing assumption that the untelevised life is not worth living," Caryn James wrote in *The New York Times*.[15] Later, Kevorkian was convicted of second-degree murder in Michigan and served 8 years in prison before being paroled in 2007.[16]

Words can be insensitive in context even if they are not vulgar. Examples are "trailer trash" and other terms of class identification.

This passage, from a story about public schools, is gratuitously hurtful: "[S]tudents are 'tracked,' grouped by their perceived abilities into separate classes. And it doesn't take an education expert to see when a teacher … is stuck in a class period where the school's discipline problems, throwaways and dumb kids have been sent to learn."[17]

Offensive Words in the News

Although taste decisions are usually a matter of judgment than of law, broadcast news organizations are subject to the scrutiny of the Federal Communications Commission. The FCC prohibits what it calls "indecent" or "profane" material between the hours of 6 a.m. and 10 p.m. local time, when the FCC says there is "a reasonable risk" that children will be in the audience. There is no FCC list of words that are always indecent or profane; the FCC says it decides on a case-by-case basis and is influenced by the context in which the words are uttered.[18]

Print and online news outlets answer exclusively to their audiences, and their policies are guided by what they think their audiences will deem appropriate.

Newspapers and magazines seeking a mass-circulation audience have the greatest reluctance to use offensive content. These publications presume that readers do not expect to find offensive content and that they will react negatively if they do.

Alternative papers and specialty magazines allow themselves greater freedom to use offensive content in describing the people and events they cover. The reasoning is that their audiences are composed of adults willing to tolerate coarse language if that results in realistic reporting and robust commentary.

On the Internet, there are widely varying standards. The websites of mainstream news organizations generally reflect the same standards as the originating newspaper or broadcast organization. However, the online magazine *Salon* has been described by one of its top editors as being aimed at an adult audience and consequently "reflects the vernacular of the general population."[19]

Journalists producing the mass-circulation publications are confronted with a delicate balancing act when news of importance has an unsavory element. Clarity may be sacrificed as they try to convey news while minimizing offense. Case Study No. 16, "Reporting on a Vulgar List in the News," illustrates the compromises that have to be made.

The compromises also provoke spirited newsroom debates. An incident on the floor of the United States Senate on June 24, 2004, illustrates the diversity of opinion:

> *The Washington Post* reported that Vice President Dick Cheney told Senator Patrick Leahy of Vermont: "Go fuck yourself." In its version, *The New York Times* said Cheney had used "an obscenity." The *Los Angeles Times* reported Cheney said, "Go … yourself."[20]
>
> Media writer Howard Kurtz told his *Post* readers that the paper's then-executive editor, Leonard Downie Jr, explained the decision to use the vulgarity: "When the vice president of the United States says it to a senator in the way in which he said it on the Senate floor, readers need to judge for themselves what the word is because we don't play games at *The Washington Post* and use dashes."[21]

The three newspapers diverged again when the Rev. Jesse Jackson said bitterly on July 6, 2008, that Barack Obama was "talking down to black people" and "I want to cut his nuts off." The vulgarity was captured by a Fox News microphone that Jackson thought was turned off, and Jackson subsequently apologized. The *Los Angeles Times* printed in full what Jackson said; *The Washington Post* said "he wanted to castrate the presumptive Democratic nominee"; and *The New York Times* described Jackson's remarks as "critical and crude" without specifying what was crude. *The Post*'s website provided a link to the video of Jackson's remarks.[22]

The Jackson incident led Clark Hoyt, *The Times'* public editor, to write a column musing about the difficulty that news organizations have in dealing with coarse language uttered by subjects of news coverage. Hoyt wrote:

> As potty-mouth language spews from the president of the United States, the vice president of the United States, from rappers, rock bands, Hollywood movies, the Broadway stage, modern literature, cable television, the Internet and people on the sidewalk talking into their cell phones, *The Times* and other news media face a tough choice – where to draw the line on words once thought unfit for what used to be called polite company.

Hoyt wrote that *The Times* wants neither to be a holdout against modern culture nor at the forefront of defining new standards of what is acceptable. He quoted Craig Whitney, the newspaper's standards editor, as saying, "We don't want to cheapen ourselves. But we don't want to be so prissy we're out of touch."[23]

As for the Jackson "nuts" quotation, Hoyt would have used it if it had been his call. His reasoning:

> Jackson is a major figure on the public stage. His comment, accompanied by a vig-
> orous slashing motion, spoke to a deep anger toward Obama and a fascinating
> generational schism among black leaders. By failing to report what Jackson said, or
> even find a way to describe it more delicately, *The Times* left readers to wonder and
> speculate. Better to quote Jackson and move on.[24]

Some editors will make exceptions in their language policies to quote verbatim when vulgar language is used by a high-ranking official or a public figure on a public occasion. *The Plain Dealer* in Cleveland also made an exception on July 7, 2007, when its front-page story quoted verbatim what witnesses said a man shouted before he shot three neighbors to death: "I'll bet you guys won't be doing this shit again." The editors thought that, given the violence that followed, readers were entitled to know exactly what the man said.[25] In both Washington and Cleveland, some readers voiced objections. "Does this mean all bars are down at *The PD* and we can expect to see other obscenities and vulgarities in the paper now?" a Cleveland reader asked.[26]

Although *Post* editor Leonard Downie Jr and others see it as playing games, some publications will use initials followed by dashes in direct quotations to indi-cate which vulgar expression was used without spelling it out. Some will use an ellipsis. The *New York Times* allows the use of the bracketed "[expletive]" in quota-tions. In what is probably the least satisfactory way to sanitize quotations, some papers insert in brackets what is thought to be a less offensive slang term, such as "[butt]" instead of "ass," a technique that may soften the language but still conveys the questionable imagery. All those efforts to avoid giving offense run the risk of confusing readers about what actually was said.

There is no perfect solution. Something news organizations can do, however, is to opt more often for paraphrased indirect quotations. If they severely limit the use of direct quotations containing offensive words, a decision has to be made only when such a quotation would accomplish an important journalistic purpose. Ethical journalists limit their use of racy language to quotations that meet this demanding standard. They do not use such language except when quoting, and they do not exploit vulgarity by, for example, using it or coyly hinting at it in a headline.

Obviously, the concept of "journalistic purpose" can be fiercely debated. Reporting, in some manner, the statements of Vice President Cheney, Reverend Jackson and the angry shooter in Cleveland fulfilled a journalistic purpose. Reporting verbatim the locker-room comments of a professional athlete, uttered in an environ-ment where vulgarity is commonplace, just as clearly does not. Unfortunately for the decision-makers, there are many cases between those extremes.

When the *Los Angeles Times'* standards and practices committee issued a new taste and obscenities policy on August 28, 2008, the committee emphasized that the restrictions on crude language apply to both print and online content. In her cover memo to the staff, deputy managing editor Melissa McCoy acknowledged that "in the Wild West of the web … practices differ from the relatively staid world of print." She wrote, "A less formal voice may be appropriate in online stories and on blogs (as is often the case in feature stories too), but a conversational style is not an invitation to abandon *The Times'* high standards by introducing gratuitous obscenities."[27]

In 1998 many newspapers printed "sexual descriptions and slang" that appeared in documents that independent counsel Kenneth Starr submitted with his recommendation that President Bill Clinton be impeached. *The New York Times* included the expressions in texts of the Starr documents but omitted them from its news stories.[28] "The Starr Report raised questions about what content is suitable for family newspapers and live broadcasts," online expert J. D. Lasica wrote. "Many news organizations resolved this dilemma by heavily editing its content in print and on air and then making the entire report available on their web sites, accompanied by prominent warnings about the report's graphic content."[29]

Offensive Images in the News

Photographs or video showing graphic violence, nudity, or perceived invasion of privacy are more likely than coarse words to disturb members of the audience. If everything else is equal, images affect people more viscerally. People can be expected to react angrily when they encounter offensive images without warning, on television or on the front page of a newspaper. The subject of offensive images is discussed in more detail in Chapter 19.

Case Study No. 17, "Covering a Public Official's Public Suicide," is a classic example. In this case, the public protested instances in which broadcast or print media were thought to have gone too far in depicting what happened at the convicted Pennsylvania state treasurer's news conference in 1987. There also was widespread self-restraint, as nearly all the Pennsylvania television stations stopped the videotape before R. Budd Dwyer fired the fatal shot, and few newspapers published the still photograph showing that moment.

Live coverage of breaking news could result inadvertently in televising a death on camera. In 1998, a KTLA-TV helicopter covered an incident in which a man with a rifle was sitting in a truck on a Los Angeles freeway, standing off police and backing up traffic for miles. Suddenly the truck burst into flames and the man, later identified as Daniel Jones, a 40-year-old AIDS patient, emerged and took off his scorched pants. Then he ran back to the truck and pulled out the rifle, while news managers at the station screamed to pull the cameras back. "But the order came too late, as KTLA viewers saw Jones blow his brains out," the magazine *Brill's Content* reported.[30]

The Radio-Television News Directors Association has created guidelines for evaluating graphic video and sound. The RTNDA notes, "Television news managers understand that the visual images always overpower the spoken word. Powerful pictures can help explain stories better or they can distort the truth by blurring the important context of the report." The RTNDA guidelines urge journalists to identify their journalistic purpose in broadcasting graphic content and to consider whether there are alternative ways to tell the story.[31]

On questions of taste, online news sites have another advantage over the older media: When these sites post offensive but newsworthy images, they can require users to click a hyperlink in order to access them.

"TV, radio and print don't allow the audience to avoid the content if they so choose," said Jonathan Dube, editor of *Cyberjournalist.net* and a president of the Online News Association. "If you air a video or print a large photo, your audience will see it. The web, on the other hand, enables the news organization to post the video, but behind a warning, so that only those who seek it out will see it."[32]

Case Study No. 16
Reporting on a Vulgar List in the News

When a document circulating among students at Mount Lebanon High School rated the school's "Top 25" girls, the episode made the front page of the *Pittsburgh Post-Gazette*. The document's vulgar language did not.

Challenged to depict the document accurately but within the bounds of taste that restrain a family-oriented newspaper, the *Post-Gazette* wrote on April 26, 2006:

> The document, titled "Top 25 in 2006," ranks the girls in order from 1 to 25. It includes their names, grade levels and photos.
>
> Each girl is assigned a letter grade for her breasts, buttocks and face, followed by a brief description of each girl in crude and vulgar terms.
>
> There are references to girls performing oral sex and comments about their height and weight.

The paper quoted the father of one of the girls rated in the list – not named to protect the girl's identity – as calling it "the equivalent of a written rape on our daughter."

The *Post-Gazette* put its coverage online in the same form that appeared in the print version. That attracted a volume of reader postings exceeded only by comments on major stories about the Steelers, Pittsburgh's pro football team. The reader reaction was fairly evenly divided between people expressing outrage over the list and those baffled by why such adolescent conduct was reported at all, much less on the front page.

The online magazine *Salon*, with more liberal standards for an audience it considers primarily of adults, reported on May 5 that "while the *Post-Gazette*'s description was technically accurate ... it had the effect of

Continued

downplaying the list's vulgarity." *Salon* continued:

(Heads-up: The next couple of paragraphs quote from the list itself, including graphic and offensive descriptions.) The list actually awards each girl a "titty grade" and an "ass grade" along with her face grade, and gives an approximate 100-word "Reason Top 25" explanation for each. A representative description notes that "Despite her egocentric views," one top scorer's "beauty and her big round ass makes this quality easily forgettable. … We all know we want to lather up that ass with some ketchup and dip our hot dog into it." Another girl is praised for doing "a great job in using the brain cells she has to cordially select her outfits to illustrate her many positive aspects of her body. All the boys in the senior class are just counting the days when her and [name deleted by *Salon*] break up so they can move in for the kill on her luscious, fresh, and splendid vagina."

Other girls are described as being "a strong 'freshman 15' candidate," "the perfect height to suck a dick" and, in the case of a Latina on the list, using "a perfume to keep the taco smell off of her." The list also includes an entry for the girl voted least attractive, who's described as a "cottage cheese filled disgusting thing" with a "maggot filled pussy."

The *Post-Gazette*'s managing editor, Susan L. Smith, said the staff wrestled with the list's terminology before arriving at "a fairly clear consensus" that the paper had to adhere to its language standards. Executive editor David Shribman ruled: "I can identify no real journalistic purpose at this time in violating our own standards of good taste by pub-

lishing these crude and demeaning personal descriptions, no matter how shocking the impact of those words might be on our own readers."

Columnist Sally Kalson said she understood the editors' decision. But, she wrote in her column:

we still have a dilemma. Anyone who dismisses the list with "boys will be boys" has not seen the actual document. … Comments from readers on our website indicate that some are defending the boys in a vacuum. If they knew the actual content, many would hang their heads in shame.

The *Post-Gazette* considered putting the list online with a link from its website warning users of its explicit content. Deputy managing editor Mary Leonard said that idea was discarded, noting that for mainstream media like the *Post-Gazette*, "standards for the web are still evolving."

The newspaper and its website continued to cover the Mount Lebanon incident through the spring and summer. A single male student was suspended, and his name was published in the *Post-Gazette* after the parents of one of the girls sued him for defamation. The police investigated but did not file criminal charges. The school district conducted a day-long sexual harassment training session for its teachers. The district was cleared in a sexual harassment complaint, filed by a parent, when the US Department of Education's Office of Civil Rights found that district officials had investigated the incident promptly and thoroughly.

In a May 15 editorial, the *Post-Gazette* wrote:

Continued

Students, and not just those in Mount Lebanon, must learn two … lessons. One is to leave their vulgarity at home – along with guns, knives and other weapons. The other is that cyberspace, for good or evil, gives them the kind of power wielded by any media mogul. Like the owner of a newspaper chain or a TV network, list makers are protected in this country by free-speech guarantees. What students may not know, however, is they lose some of those rights when they walk through schoolhouse doors. Courts have ruled that schools may prohibit lewd, profane and vulgar speech.

Questions for Class Discussion

- Why does a mainstream newspaper like the *Post-Gazette* adopt restrictive standards on language?
- Did the *Post-Gazette's* language standards result in imprecise or ineffectual reporting of the offensive nature of the list?
- If you think it did, is this an acceptable trade-off for a mainstream newspaper?
- Do you think the *Post-Gazette* should have put the list online for readers to see its contents for themselves? If so, would you have required readers to consider a disclaimer warning them of the vulgar language before linking to the list's explicit content? Would you have deleted the names?
- Why do you think *Salon* decided to go beyond the boundaries that the *Post-Gazette* thought it had to observe?
- Do you agree with *Salon's* decision?

Case Study No. 17
Covering a Public Official's Public Suicide

A day before he was scheduled to be sentenced to prison for fraud, Pennsylvania State Treasurer R. Budd Dwyer called a news conference. The three dozen reporters and photographers who assembled at Dwyer's Harrisburg office on Thursday, January 22, 1987, were expecting Dwyer to announce his resignation. Still and video cameras recorded the scene as the embattled treasurer read a rambling, half-hour-long statement criticizing the criminal justice system.

When a camera crew started to pack up its equipment, Dwyer told them to stay, saying, "We're not done." Dwyer reached inside a manila envelope and pulled out a .357 Magnum. After waving back the horrified journalists, Dwyer placed the pistol in his mouth and fired.

Continued

The public suicide of the disgraced public official presented a grim decision for television news directors and newspaper editors around Pennsylvania: What images of the incident should they pass along to their viewers and readers?

The raw video showed Dwyer reading the statement, taking the gun from the envelope, cautioning the people in the room to stay back, putting the pistol in his mouth, and pulling the trigger. In some versions, he falls out of the frame; in others, the cameras follow him to the floor. The versions showing him on the floor are the most graphic, as blood pours from his mouth, nose, and forehead.

Photographers of the print media also kept their cameras trained on Dwyer. Paul Vathis of The Associated Press wrote for *Editor and Publisher* magazine that he acted instinctively: "From professional experience, I just kept taking pictures."

In addition to head-and-shoulders "mug shots" of Dwyer, images offered to editors for newspapers that afternoon and the next morning showed Dwyer reaching into the envelope (Figure 15.2), holding the pistol in his right hand while waving people back with his left (Figure 15.3), holding the pistol in both hands in front of his chest (Figure 15.4), placing the pistol in his mouth (Figure 15.5), collapsing in a blurred moment immediately after the gunshot (Figure 15.6), and lying dead on the floor while his aide directs the journalists to leave the room (Figure 15.7).

Deciding for television

The suicide occurred just after 11 a.m. and tape was fed by satellite to television stations around the state within 30 to 40 minutes, according to a study by Professors Patrick R. Parsons and William E. Smith of Pennsylvania State University.

Their analysis, published in the *Journal of Mass Media Ethics*, showed a remarkable similarity in the way that the videotape was edited by 16 of the 20 stations that broadcast news:

> They showed a soundbite from the news conference followed by the moments just before the actual suicide. Most stations stopped the tape as Dwyer held the gun pointing upward in front of him. Half a dozen stations froze the video at that point, letting the audio track continue through the gunshot; the rest cut back to the anchor or went to black. At least two stations, during their noon newscasts, showed Dwyer placing the gun in his mouth, but stopped the tape before that point on subsequent newscasts.

Three stations showed the moment of death in the noon newscasts. They ran the tape until just after Dwyer pulled the trigger but did not follow his body to the floor, thus eliminating a scene of gore. The stations defended their decision on the grounds of newsworthiness and immediacy, and they noted that the images they showed were, in the words of the researchers, "not particularly graphic or bloody."

Two of these stations, WPXI in Pittsburgh and WPVI in Philadelphia, did not show the gunshot on their later newscasts. The news director of WPXI, who was out of state at the time, said later he regretted that this part had been shown at noon. He phoned from the West Coast to order that the gunshot be eliminated in the subsequent newscasts.

The other station showing the gunshot was WHTM in Harrisburg. Its initial bulletin,

Continued

Figure 15.2   R. Budd Dwyer's
suicide 1
PHOTO BY PAUL VATHIS. REPRINTED BY
PERMISSION OF THE ASSOCIATED PRESS

Figure 15.3   R. Budd Dwyer's
suicide 2
PHOTO BY GARY MILLER. REPRINTED BY
PERMISSION OF THE ASSOCIATED PRESS

Figure 15.4   R. Budd Dwyer's
suicide 3
PHOTO BY PAUL VATHIS. REPRINTED BY
PERMISSION OF THE ASSOCIATED PRESS

Figure 15.5   R. Budd Dwyer's
suicide 4
PHOTO BY PAUL VATHIS. REPRINTED BY
PERMISSION OF THE ASSOCIATED PRESS

Figure 15.6   R. Budd Dwyer's
suicide 5
PHOTO BY PAUL VATHIS. REPRINTED BY
PERMISSION OF THE ASSOCIATED PRESS

Figure 15.7   R. Budd Dwyer's
suicide 6
PHOTO BY PAUL VATHIS. REPRINTED BY
PERMISSION OF THE ASSOCIATED PRESS

Continued

without a cautionary disclaimer, broke into children's programming, which had a larger audience than usual because many schools were closed as a result of a heavy snowstorm. The station later apologized. The station showed the videotape again at its regular newscasts in the evening, this time warning viewers about its graphic nature. The video then was accompanied by a studio discussion of suicide by mental health officials.

The twentieth station did not run video on any of its newscasts. This was WLYH of Lancaster, whose news director, Cliff Esbach, said the pictures did not add anything to the description in the story. He also said that showing the tape "just wouldn't be the decent thing to do."

Professors Parsons and Smith concluded that the "standard version" – stopping the video before the gunshot – was an easy decision for the news directors. "There was little agonizing over the issue. Even those journalists who did have trouble making the decision eventually came to the majority conclusion." The news directors who chose this standard version said the moment of death was in bad taste. "We want good video," one news director told the researchers, "but we want the video for its news value. We're not looking to shock people."

Deciding for newspapers

For their Thursday afternoon and Friday morning editions, editors at Pennsylvania daily newspapers selected from images supplied by The Associated Press and United Press International. Their choices were tabulated in a study published in the *Newspaper Research Journal* by Professor Robert L. Baker of Pennsylvania State University. For this case study, Baker's totals for similar images offered by both AP and UPI are combined.

The most frequently used image, on front pages and overall, was a photograph of Dwyer holding the pistol in one hand while waving back onlookers with the other. Baker's study showed that the AP and UPI versions were used in 43 papers, including 31 on the front page. From a taste standpoint, this image has the advantages of suggesting the tension and violence of the incident but without showing anything graphic.

Thirty-eight newspapers chose a head-and-shoulders mugshot of Dwyer, including 28 that used such a picture on the front page. Nearly all these newspapers also published one or more additional photographs from the news conference.

The third most frequently used image was that of Dwyer with the pistol in his mouth before he pulled the trigger. Thirty-nine newspapers used that photo, including 18 on the front page. Many readers deemed this photo to be too graphic, especially if it appeared on the front. The other images, in order of frequency of use are:

Reaching into the envelope: Thirty-five newspapers, including eight on the front page.
Pistol in both hands: Nineteen newspapers, including seven on the front page.
Collapsing after the impact: Six newspapers, including five on the front page. This is the most graphic of the still pictures of the news conference.
Body on the floor: Twelve newspapers, including two on the front page.

Continued

The largest newspaper in the state, *The Philadelphia Inquirer,* ran two photographs on the front page. One showed Dwyer holding the pistol and waving people away, and the other showed him with the pistol in his mouth. On an inside page, *The Inquirer* ran the body-on-the-floor image. About 500 readers telephoned the newspaper the next day to complain, especially about the pistol-in-mouth image. A common complaint was that if a graphic photo runs on the front page, there is not much parents can do to shield their young children from seeing it.

The two Pittsburgh dailies, the *Post-Gazette* and *The Press,* both decided against showing either the pistol-in-mouth photo or the collapsing-after-impact photos. "I thought both of those were sensational and gruesome, without much value," said Madelyn Ross, managing editor of *The Press.*

The *Meadville Tribune,* published in Dwyer's hometown, ran only a mugshot. Managing editor John Wellington told a researcher, Professor Robert C. Kochersberger of North Carolina State University, that the paper's decision was immediate and instinctive. "Would anyone with half a whit of common sense want graphic suicide pictures imposed on his children?"

Questions for Class Discussion

- This text has made the point that suicides generally are not treated as significant news stories. In the case of R. Budd Dwyer's suicide, what news values argued for extraordinary treatment?
- Are you surprised that 16 of the 20 stations chose to edit the raw videotape in a similar fashion (stopping before the gunshot)? Why do you think all those news directors came to the same conclusion independently of each other?
- Did WHTM make a mistake in how it broadcast its initial news bulletin on the suicide? If so, how?
- Do you agree with WLYH's decision not to show any of the video?
- Why do you think so many newspapers chose a version of Dwyer holding the pistol and waving for people to stand back?
- Do you think a newspaper should have run a version of Dwyer holding the pistol in his mouth? If you do, should the newspaper run the photo on the front page or on an inside page?
- Was the *Meadville Tribune* right to run only a mug shot of Dwyer? Regarding the editor's statement about children, consider: Should a newspaper be edited for children, or should it be edited for adults with the likelihood that children may see it? (To use the movie industry's terminology, the difference is between editing for a G audience or a PG audience.)

Notes

1   The Associated Press, "NBC News: Airing Cho video 'good journalism,'" April 24, 2007.

2   Kim Pearson, "Cho manifesto highlights challenges for online journalism," *Online Journalism Review*, http://www.ojr.org/ojr/stories/070502, May 3, 2007.

3   David Folkenflik, "NBC cites an obligation to air Cho materials," National Public Radio, http://www.npr.org/templates/story/story.php?storyId=9692304, April 19, 2007.

4   Ibid.

5   Pearson, "Cho manifesto highlights challenges for online journalism."

6   James T. Campbell, "Right choice to use killer's photos on Page One," *Houston Chronicle*, April 20, 2007.

7   Project for Excellence in Journalism, "Campus rampage is 2007's biggest story by far," http://ww.journalism.org/node/5197, news coverage index for April 15–20, 2007.

8   Folkenflik, "NBC cites an obligation to air Cho materials."

9   David Bauder, "Backlash leads to pullback on Cho video," The Associated Press, April 19, 2007.

10 Ibid.

11 Jessica A. Ross, executive producer of WSLS-TV in Roanoke, VA, statement issued April 19, 2007.

12 AP, "NBC News: Airing Cho video 'good journalism.'"

13 Campbell, "Right choice to use killer's photos on Page One."

14 Franklin Foer, "Death in prime time," *U.S. News & World Report*, Dec. 7, 1998.

15 Caryn James, "'60 Minutes,' Kevorkian and a death for the cameras," *The New York Times*, Nov. 23, 1998.

16 Kathy Barks, "Kevorkian leaves prison after 8 years," The Associated Press, June 1, 2007.

17 Cited in Doug Kim, Melissa McCoy, and John McIntyre, "Charged language," a paper presented to the American Copy Editors Society in Portland, OR, September 1998.

18 FAQ on Federal Communications Commission's website, http://www.fcc.gov/eb/oip/FAQ.html

19 Lori Robertson, "Language barriers," *American Journalism Review*, November 2000, 41.

20 Howard Kurtz, "*Post* editor explains decision to publish expletive," *The Washington Post*, June 26, 2004.

21 Ibid.

22 Clark Hoyt, "When to quote those potty mouths," *The New York Times*, July 13, 2008.

23 Ibid.

24 Ibid.

25 Ted Diadiun, "The s- word," *The Plain Dealer*, July 15, 2007.

26 Ibid.

27 "Readers' representative journal: a conversation on newsroom practices and standards," *Los Angeles Times*, Sept. 3, 2008. *The Times*' taste and obscenity policy can be accessed at: http://www.latimes.com/news/local/la-times-taste-guidelines,0,1543340.story

28 Allan M. Siegal and William G. Connolly, The *New York Times Manual of Style and Usage* (New York: Times Books, 1999), 241.

29 J. D. Lasica, "The Starr investigation," in Tom Rosenstiel and Amy Mitchell (eds.), *Thinking Clearly: Cases in Journalistic Decision-Making* (New York: Columbia University Press, 2003), 39.

30 D. M. Osborne, "Overwhelmed by events," *Brill's Content*, July/August 1998, 67–8.

31 *Newsroom Ethics: Decision-Making for Quality Coverage*, 4th edn. (Washington, DC: Radio Television News Directors Foundation, 2006), 86–7.

32 Pearson, "Cho manifesto highlights challenges for online journalism."

16 Deception, a Controversial Reporting Tool

A collision in values: Lying while seeking the truth

Learning Goals

This chapter will help you understand:

- the importance of recognizing an intention to deceive and not rationalizing it;
- the exacting conditions that a news organization should meet before engaging in undercover reporting;
- other situations, short of going undercover, in which journalists deceive or could be perceived as deceiving; and
- why even journalists who say it sometimes is proper to deceive a source are opposed to deceiving the audience.

He was lying on the floor, curled up in a ball, his knees doubled into his stomach and his hands clasped over his head.

Then the big, black leather shoe came crashing down on top of his shaved head and his face ricocheted off the shiny, gray concrete floor.

Another foot slammed into his stomach with all the force of a football kicking specialist. Another foot dug into his back and another into his legs and another into the top of his head.

For nearly three minutes, the four white-suited attendants – three stood more than 6 feet tall – towered over the huddled figure on the floor, kicking every part of his defenseless body.

On a spring day in 1965, readers opened their copies of *The Plain Dealer* in Cleveland to find this vivid account of what happened to a young man incarcerated at Lima State Hospital for the Criminally Insane. They also learned what had led to the punishment: The man had *whispered* in a ward where the "patients" were forced to sit together for 11 hours a day, a rule of utter silence enforced by beatings or by canceling a man's privilege to buy candy or tobacco "and other small things that are his last tie with the outside world."[1]

Plain Dealer readers learned this — and much more disturbing information about Lima State Hospital — because reporter Donald L. Barlett had gained employment as an attendant at the hospital.

As a new employee, Barlett was assigned an orientation tour of nine wards. He and another attendant were with a group of patients who were sweeping out cells and mopping halls on a ward's first floor when a teenage patient rushed up and shouted, "Someone's gettin' it upstairs." With that, the other attendant raced up the stairs to the second floor, and Barlett followed. They arrived to find the beating under way.

Barlett's job brought him in contact with the hospital's assortment of criminals and teenage runaways. He talked with patients and other attendants. After working days in the hospital, he spent his evenings compiling notes on what he had seen and heard.

Those notes were turned into a series of stories in *The Plain Dealer* that revealed a practice of housing young runaways with adult sex criminals; treatment for mental illness that consisted almost entirely of heavy doses of sedatives; incarceration based on psychiatric evaluations lasting all of 10 minutes; therapy that consisted of spending all day tying bits of string together; punishment meted out to patients who had epileptic seizures; and almost nonexistent educational and occupational training programs.

"For nearly seven weeks, a *Plain Dealer* reporter worked in the dark imprisoned world of Ohio's most troublesome criminals and sex criminals," the newspaper announced in a sidebar to the first story in the series. The newspaper also disclosed that, to get hired, Barlett had used a version of his own name "but a fictitious background."[2]

It wasn't Barlett's idea to pose as a hospital attendant. His city editor simply told him what he was going to do. "See what's going on inside," Barlett remembers the editor's instructions. He was told to collect information and follow where it led.[3]

After Barlett's series of stories, the governor of Ohio ordered institutional reforms at Lima State Hospital.

What Barlett did at Lima State Hospital is known as undercover reporting. Gathering information while pretending to be someone else is the ultimate act of journalistic deception.

Deception is a paradox in journalism because it represents a collision in values. Journalism's purpose is to reveal truth, and deception is making someone else believe what the deceiver knows to be untrue.

A strictly *deontological* journalist would never practice deception, because a universal rule of behavior requires truth-telling at all times. A *teleological* journalist, considering the potential results of the reporting, might conclude that deception is acceptable if it will lead to a greater good. Anecdotal and some empirical evidence suggests that most journalists take the teleological approach.

Retired editor Reid MacCluggage is on the teleological side. In the president's column for the newsletter of the Associated Press Managing Editors in 1998, MacCluggage wrote:

Readers will support editors who make intelligent, thoughtful and empathetic decisions, and they will condemn editors who shoot from the hip. ... There are times when we need to bend the rules to break an important story. But those times should be rare, the stories must be profound, and editors need to proceed with great caution.[4]

Ethics scholars also refrain from an absolute position on deception. Louis W. Hodges has expressed the journalist's moral choice in these terms: "[D]eceit is morally wrong ... but ... circumstances can arise in which deceit is relatively less wrong than other possible courses of action." In some newsgathering situations, then, "deceit is morally acceptable." However, journalists must not deceive unnecessarily, and they have a moral obligation to give good reasons for deceiving. In contrast, Hodges says, a decision not to deceive requires no justification.[5]

As Don Barlett sees it, a failure to deceive could itself be morally wrong. He thinks that if deception is the only way that journalists can inform the public about important facts – such as the sweeping dysfunction at Lima State Hospital – they have a moral obligation to deceive.

Barlett said, "A decision to withhold critical information from readers by refusing to document it is every bit as deceitful as gaining access to information under false pretenses – but without serving any greater good."[6]

Defining Deception and Avoiding Rationalizations

Whether a certain act of journalistic deception is acceptable can be decided only on a case-by-case basis. The decision must take into consideration both the degree of deception and the news value of the information that might be obtained.

To make a reasoned decision, journalists must first acknowledge that they are contemplating deception. Then they should ask themselves if the information to be gained for the public is important enough to justify the deception. Applying the Golden Rule, they should ask themselves how they would feel if they were deceived in the same way. They should consider what they would do if their deception is discovered. When they report to the audience, they should be willing to disclose their deception.

The first step in the decision process – acknowledging an intention to deceive, whether verbal or nonverbal – is not easy. It is human nature to rationalize, to call it something else, like smart reporting. At one of his ethics seminars for journalists, Michael Josephson posed a hypothetical question, and the give-and-take went like this:

JOSEPHSON: What would you do if someone stole a highly newsworthy document from the mayor and gave it to you?

REPORTER: I prefer to say that my newspaper "obtained" the document.
JOSEPHSON: Then you don't know the definition of stealing?[7]

So, definitions are needed.

In her seminal book *Lying*, the ethicist Sissela Bok defines *deception*:

> When we undertake to deceive others intentionally, we communicate messages meant to mislead them, meant to make them believe what we ourselves do not believe. We can do that through gesture, through disguise, by means of action or inaction, even through silence.[8]

For a communication to be deceitful, it must be intentional. Giving someone misinformation through honest error does not meet Bok's definition.[9]

In their Watergate investigation in 1972–74, Carl Bernstein and Bob Woodward falsely told potential sources that "a friend [at the Nixon reelection committee] told us that you were disturbed by some of the things you saw going on there, that you would be a good person to talk to. ..." Bernstein and Woodward acknowledged that this approach, though it seemed to work best, was "less than straightforward." Right or wrong under the circumstances, it was deception.[10]

To the extent that journalists will consider deception, deceiving the audience is not what they have in mind. "Never lie to the audience" is as close to an absolute rule as you will find in journalism ethics, an example of Kantian deontology. That is because seeking truth for the public is the profession's reason for existence.

Deceiving a journalist's colleagues likewise is out of the question, because the resulting lack of trust would make that journalist ineffective and, quite likely, soon out of a job.

By a process of elimination, then, the only acceptable targets of journalistic deception are sources and story subjects. Does that mean it is open season on these people?

It had better not be, the ethics scholars say. They argue that acts of deception damage journalism's credibility and that consequently the bar for engaging in them must be kept high.

Sissela Bok writes in *Lying* that journalism is one of several professions – others include medicine, the law, and the military – in which practitioners find themselves "repeatedly in straits where serious consequences seem avoidable only through deception." But resorting to deception in a crisis can lead to using those tactics more casually, she warns. In journalism and the other professions she mentions, achievements in a competitive environment are rewarded. "Cutting corners may be one way to such achievements, and if deception is pervasive and rarely punished, then it will be all the more likely to spread. The accepted practices may then grow increasingly insensitive, and abuses and mistakes more common ..."[11]

For Deni Elliott, sleight of hand is a tool for a magician, not a journalist. She writes that deceptive newsgathering techniques "cause more harm than good to the profession of journalism as a whole."[12]

Michael Josephson cautions that journalists' credibility and trustworthiness can be undermined by misrepresentations, trickery, impersonation, and the use of hidden audio recorders or cameras in newsgathering. These practices, he writes, "are outside the bounds of generally accepted journalistic behavior" and require thorough discussion. Josephson would require the approval of the highest authority in the newsroom for any act of deception.[13]

A High Threshold for Undercover Reporting

Although today's print media rarely engage in undercover reporting, the technique has flourished – in the form of hidden cameras – in television reporting.

In *The Elements of Journalism*, Bill Kovach and Tom Rosenstiel outline three formidable standards that should be met for undercover reporting:

1   The information is vital to the public interest.
2   There is no other way to get the story.
3   The deception is disclosed to the audience.[14]

Louis Hodges adds this standard: The deception must not "place innocent people at risk." A journalist posing as a firefighter probably would fail this standard by being unable to deliver as a firefighter in case of an actual fire, endangering other firefighters and possibly civilians in a burning building.[15]

The authors of *Doing Ethics in Journalism* add other caveats:

- The journalists and the news organization must "apply excellence" through solid reporting and by committing the time and money needed to be thorough.
- The harm prevented by the deception must outweigh any harm caused by the act of deception.
- The journalists must conduct "a meaningful, collaborative and deliberative decision making process" in which they weigh such factors as their motivation and the consequences of the deception.[16]

Four decades later, Don Barlett's cameo role as an attendant at Lima State Hospital passes those tests. His information was vitally important, as he documented that the hospital was a dumping ground for more than a thousand people who under the law could be incarcerated wrongly and indefinitely. To report in a convincing way, he had to get inside and see the abuses firsthand. *The Plain Dealer* told its readers how he got inside, including lying in his employment application. Barlett's job as an attendant did not put other people at risk. Excellence in reporting and writing are in evidence throughout the series, as Barlett demonstrated the skills that later would make him a two-time recipient of the Pulitzer Prize. The subsequent reforms at Lima State Hospital are evidence that his masquerade prevented harm. Barlett thinks his superiors considered possible consequences of his assignment and found them outweighed by the value of giving their readers an eyewitness account. Almost certainly, however, an undercover assignment would be undertaken with much more deliberation in a newsroom today.

Undercover reporting was a tradition in newspaper investigative reporting through the 1970s. A familiar name in journalism lore is that of Nellie Bly, the 21-year-old reporter who got herself committed to Blackwell's Island in 1887 and reported for *The New York World* about what she saw in the notorious asylum.[17] Bly's masquerade is memorialized in a 3-D film of journalist exploits that visitors can see today at the Newseum in Washington.

The noted journalist Ben Bagdikian persuaded the Pennsylvania attorney general in 1972 to allow him to be a prisoner in the state prison at Huntingdon so that he could take "a serious look at the whole system." After three months of observing men behind bars, Bagdikian wrote an eight-part series about the experience for *The Washington Post*. In the series, he wrote that other kinds of research – interviewing former prisoners and reading books and reports – "had not prepared me for the intellectual impact of maximum security incarceration."[18]

The reluctance of today's print media to use undercover reporting can be traced to the anti-deception arguments made by two influential editors in blocking a Pulitzer Prize for an elaborate ruse staged by the *Chicago Sun-Times* for a series of 25 articles published in 1978.

To document its suspicions about shakedowns by city inspectors, the paper ran a bar – aptly named The Mirage – for four months in late 1977. The *Sun-Times* history of the episode tells what happened next:

> There was a payoff parade of city and state inspectors, hands out, in search of health and safety violations to wink at. Six accountants offered to keep, and kept, endless crooked books for the tax man. It was all put down on paper by the reporters … and made vivid by *Sun-Times* photographers … snapping quietly from a hidden loft.

The *Sun-Times* history credits the series with "serious" reforms – new procedures in city inspections, revisions of the city code, and investigations by the city, state and federal agencies.[19]

When the Mirage story became a finalist for a Pulitzer Prize, it was vigorously and successfully opposed by two members of the prize board. Benjamin Bradlee of *The Washington Post* and Eugene Patterson of *The St. Petersburg Times* argued that reporters ought to operate in the open. Patterson said the *Sun-Times* reporters could have interviewed bar owners.[20] That was not practical, according to the *Sun-Times* history, which states that the paper's investigative reporters had been hearing for years from business people complaining about being shaken down. "But … nobody would go on record. Everyone was afraid of City Hall."[21]

Such was the influence of Bradlee and Patterson that undercover reporting went out of favor in newspapers in the years that followed. There were exceptions, however, and one of them – Tony Horwitz's posing as a worker in a chicken-processing plant in 1994 – won a Pulitzer Prize for the *Wall Street Journal* reporter. Horwitz's bosses ordered him to tell no lies, and on his application form he listed Columbia University as his education and Dow Jones & Company as his employer, without specifying that it published *The Journal*. He was hired immediately.[22]

In the spring of 1992, ABC producers lied about their work experience and gave phony references to gain employment as meat wrappers at Food Lion super-markets, where they used cameras hidden in wigs to expose unsanitary food handling and labor-law violations. ABC broadcast its findings on "PrimeTime Live" in November 1992 during a sweeps period.

Food Lion sued the network, not for libel but for fraud and trespass. A North Carolina jury returned a $5.5 million judgment, and jury foreman Gregory Mack said afterward: "You didn't have any boundaries when you started this investigation. … You kept pushing on the edges … It was too extensive and fraudulent."[23] First Amendment lawyer Bruce W. Sanford observed:

> The jury felt that reporters shouldn't misrepresent themselves or use other deceptive practices to obtain news, even when the "news" amounted to truthful reporting about serious health and safety violations at one of America's largest grocers.[24]

On appeal, the Food Lion verdict was overturned.

Walter Goodman defended ABC's deception in a *New York Times* essay after the jury verdict:

> Yes, the reporters were out to catch instances of unappetizing behavior and the most flagrant and unfragrant of them were played up, as is the way in exposes. But the program made a strong case that tricks like repackaging outdated fish and prettifying unsold chicken with barbecue sauce were common at two Food Lion Stores at least. Employees seemed to be doing such refurbishment as a matter of course.

Goodman said ABC could have bought the food and subjected it to laboratory analysis, but such findings "would have been no substitute for the on-the-spot evidence of malpractice."[25]

Beginning in the 1980s, undercover reporting has been a staple on television, Susan Paterno wrote in "The Lying Game" in *American Journalism Review* in May 1997. "Local news teams try to outdo one another during sweeps weeks," she wrote, while national newsmagazines have proliferated on the networks. "[T]elevision needs pictures. And pictures drive reporters undercover for dramatic, indisputable evidence of wrongdoing." Paterno quoted Ira Rosen, ABC's senior producer in the Food Lion case: "In television, pictures provide a level of truth as much as the spoken word. You can't separate the two. People need to see."[26]

The authors of *The Elements of Journalism* worry that journalism's watchdog role can be diminished as the networks' primetime magazines and local stations' newscasts focus on consumer topics instead of monitoring the powerful.

> [T]oo much of the new "investigative" reporting is tabloid treatment of everyday circumstances. … Consider the Los Angeles TV station that rented a house for two months and wired it with a raft of hidden cameras to expose that you really can't get all the carpeting in your house cleaned for $7.95. … [E]xposing what is readily understood or simply common sense belittles investigative journalism. The press becomes the boy who cried wolf. It is squandering its ability to demand the public's attention because it has done so too many times about trivial matters.[27]

Bob Steele of the Poynter Institute also has deplored "the glut of hidden camera stories focusing on small-scale consumer scams, 'gotcha' pieces targeting someone for a minor breach of behavior, or weak investigative reports that don't justify deception." He praises hidden-camera reporting that has "exposed systemic racial discrimination, critical weaknesses in airport security, gross incompetence by law enforcement officers, and abhorrent patient care in nursing homes and hospitals."[28]

Steele would limit hidden cameras to stories that reveal "exceptionally important information … of vital public interest, such as preventing profound harm to individuals or revealing great system failure." Hidden cameras should be a tool of last resort, after journalists have tried or have ruled out obtaining the information through conventional techniques. When hidden-camera reporting accuses someone of wrongdoing, Steele wrote, "we must insure that the tone and emphasis of hidden camera video meet standards for factual accuracy and contextual authenticity." He also observed that hidden-camera journalism sometimes traps "the little guy who happens to be easily accessible," instead of the higher-ranking people who are truly responsible.[29]

Other Reporting Techniques Involving Deception

In 1964, Harry Pearson was a reporter for the *Pine Bluff* (Arkansas) *Commercial*. From an Army sergeant, the paper got a tip that certain officers in the Arkansas National Guard had worn the incumbent's campaign bumper stickers on their helmets when they marched in the annual "Governor's Day" parade, with Governor Orval E. Faubus on the reviewing stand. This blatantly violated the fundamental rule that the Army stands above partisan politics, and the sergeant was indignant that ranking Guard officers had done nothing about it. Although the sergeant was certain that the offending officers were the commander and three top staff officers of an artillery battalion, he didn't know which of the five artillery battalions it was.

Pearson obtained a list of the artillery commanders. He decided to place his first call to the commander of a battalion in eastern Arkansas, where Faubus' political support was strongest. When the colonel answered the telephone, a dialogue like this ensued:

> PEARSON: Colonel B—, why did you and your staff officers wear Faubus bumper stickers in the parade at Fort Chaffee?
> THE COLONEL: Well, it was the Governor's Day parade, after all. We were just honoring the governor on his day.

With the colonel's confirmation, Pearson had nailed his story.

By insinuating to the colonel that he knew he was the violator, Pearson was, of course, practicing deception – namely *misrepresentation*. Was it justified? Though the story could not be called vital to the community, it was interesting and revealing. It confirmed for *Commercial* readers what many considered to be an open secret: that the National Guard was enmeshed in politics on the state level. (The bumper-sticker-wearing colonel, incidentally, went on to a long career in the state legislature.)[30]

If the colonel had not been the one who wore the bumper sticker, he could have set the reporter straight. Bluffing averted the possibility that all five of the colonels, when they realized Pearson did not know who wore the stickers, could have answered "no comment" and possibly left him without a story.

Pearson's editor congratulated him on his shrewd reporting. Years later, the editor (who happens to be the author of this book) asked several journalists if they thought Pearson's bluffing was an acceptable reporting technique. The verdict of this sampling of journalistic opinion was *yes* – then and now. "You don't always tell all you know," said Roy Reed, a former *New York Times* reporter. "At other times, you indicate that you know more than you do. The public needs to know the information, and the source may not be forthright."[31]

Homer Bigart of *The New York Times* was a reporter who habitually pretended to know less than he did. It was a technique he used skillfully to get reluctant sources to tell him more than they intended. Bigart practiced the technique when he was sent to Philadelphia, Mississippi, in 1964 to cover the investigation into the killing of three civil rights workers. "Couldn't have a normal conversation with the man," one of his interview subjects complained to another *Times* reporter. "He didn't know anything. I had to explain *evvvverything* to him."[32]

Reporter Jack Nelson flew to Orangeburg, South Carolina, in February 1968 to investigate a melee at South Carolina State College in which police and National Guardsmen killed three black students and wounded more than two dozen others. The authorities said they had fired when students charged at them, throwing bottles and bricks. As Gene Roberts and Hank Klibanoff write in their book *The Race Beat*, Nelson went directly to the hospital where the wounded students had been treated.

With an air of authority underpinned by his business suit and crew-cut hair, he introduced himself as "Nelson, with the Atlanta bureau. I've come to see the medical records." Nelson's bureau was, of course, the *Los Angeles Times* bureau, not the FBI's Atlanta bureau.

The records Nelson inspected showed that sixteen students had back wounds, and that some who had lain on the ground to escape the gunfire had wounds on the soles of their feet. Nelson's story in the *Times* authoritatively disputed the official version that the shots were fired in self-defense.[33]

While covering a murder case around 1960 for *The News and Observer* in Raleigh, North Carolina, Gene Roberts picked up a stethoscope from a desk and "walked nonchalantly into the emergency room where police were interrogating a suspect who confessed." Years later, as executive editor of *The Philadelphia Inquirer*, Roberts told the story to Penn State professor H. Eugene Goodwin for his ethics textbook. "I didn't lie to anyone," Roberts said. "We're not obligated to wear a neon sign."[34]

In his 1985 book *The News at Any Cost*, Tom Goldstein described how Athelia Knight of *The Washington Post* reported in 1984 on the ease with which drugs could be surreptitiously taken into Lorton Reformatory near Washington. Knight sat silently on a bus that was headed for the prison and listened as other passengers talked about smuggling marijuana and other illegal drugs to inmates. She said, "I must have seemed like just another woman with a husband or boyfriend locked up." If asked, she would have identified herself as a reporter. Her editor, Ben Bradlee, considered the situation vastly different from the Mirage reporting he had criticized in 1978. He said, "I see a really seminal distinction between planning any kind of deception, however much the end might seem to justify the means, and embarking on a project where your occupation as a journalist is not advertised."[35]

Jack Fuller writes in *News Values*:

> I do not believe that the journalistic obligation of truth-telling requires reporters to wear their press passes on their chests. When a reporter in the course of his ordinary human activity and without lying gets into a position to witness newsworthy events (when a building inspector solicits a bribe at the reporter's own home, for example, or if a city work crew goes to sleep on the job along his route to the office) he does not need to interrupt the action with a disclosure of his affiliation.[36]

Mayhill Fowler, a blogger for *The Huffington Post*, was invited to a fundraiser in San Francisco for presidential candidate Barack Obama two weeks before the important Pennsylvania primary in April 2008. She got the invitation because she was an Obama contributor. It was at this gathering that Obama said small-town Pennsylvania voters "cling to guns or religion or antipathy to people who aren't like them" as a way of expressing their bitterness over economic hardships. After Fowler reported the statement in her blog, the mainstream media picked it up. Obama had to explain, especially to voters in Pennsylvania, that "I didn't say it as well as I should have."[37]

Fowler was hardly concealed as she did her reporting at the fundraiser. Obama, she said later, "was looking at 350 strangers, many of whom were using cell phones and small video cameras and flips to record the event." Her invitation, press critic Jay Rosen noted in his own blog, didn't say "you can't blog about this."[38]

Many journalists have long held the position that they have no moral obligation to identify themselves at a gathering as large as the one Obama addressed in San Francisco. At an occasion like that, they reason, it is absurd for speakers to expect to keep secret what they say. (Although some Obama followers complained that Fowler was unfair to report his remark, Rosen gave the candidate credit for neither challenging Fowler's right to report nor questioning her accuracy.)

Deceiving the Audience Is Rejected Nearly Universally

Journalism's purpose is to inform the public; to achieve that purpose, news organizations must gain the public's trust. That hard-earned trust is squandered if the organization knowingly circulates misinformation.

That journalists reject deceiving the audience was confirmed in a survey of 740 members of Investigative Reporters and Editors in 2002. Those experienced journalists were asked about 16 deceptive practices on a seven-point scale, from "not at all justified" to "very justified," based on the question, "Given an important story that is of vital public interest, would the following being justified?"

Asked if they would make an untrue statement to readers/viewers, 99 percent rated the practice "not all justified" or "mostly" not justified. The respondents also rejected other scenarios in which the audience would be deceived: "using nonexistent characters or quotes in a story" (97 percent) and "altering quotes" (96 percent).

In contrast to the near-unanimous rejection of making an untrue statement to readers/viewers, a significantly lower 80 percent rejected making an untrue statement to news sources. Forty percent rejected withholding information from readers/viewers, compared with 10 percent rejecting withholding information from sources.

Analyzing the survey results, Seow Ting Lee of Illinois State University saw a pattern: that journalists "reacted more favorably to deceptive practices targeting news sources than to those targeting news audiences."

Lee also noted another pattern: that the journalists generally "were more approving of deceptive practices that involved *omission* (withholding information, surreptitious recording of information) than of deceptive practices involving *commission* (impersonation, lying, tampering with or falsifying information)."[39]

When journalists are asked to lie to their audience, the request most often comes from police who seek their help in solving crimes or protecting innocent people from harm.

One newspaper that intentionally published a false story was the *King County Journal* in Washington State. In 2003, the authorities had been tipped by a jailhouse informant that a former prisoner supposedly had been hired for arson by his cellmate, a man in prison for murdering his wife. If the former prisoner burned the house where the murderer's mother-in-law and his 13-year-old son lived, the murderer would pay even more to have the family of his prosecutor killed. Before placing the second contract, the murderer wanted to see a story in the paper stating that the arson had been carried out.

Acting on the informant's tip, authorities arrested the former prisoner, who cooperated to avoid a murder-conspiracy charge. Then a deputy prosecutor and the sheriff's office told *Journal* editor Tom Wolfe that they could trap the murderer if the paper published a story stating falsely that the house was torched. Lives were at stake, they said.

Wolfe's first reaction was that deliberately publishing the fake story would erode the paper's credibility. But he concluded that what he was being asked to do was not very different from withholding certain information about a crime that might endanger someone. "We know the people involved quite well," he said. "It was not a theoretical concern, it was an actual concern."

The sheriff's office said the ruse helped them trap the murderer, who was caught discussing his plans in a secret recording after reading the fake story.[40] "We very much appreciate the *King County Journal* for printing [the story] for us," a spokeswoman for the sheriff said.[41]

Journalism ethics teachers criticized the *Journal*. "It was a lie. The newspaper deliberately told a falsehood, not just to the guy in the prison cell, but to all its readers," said Michael Parks, then the director of the School of Journalism at the University of Southern California's Annenberg School for Communication. Publishing a bogus story undermines "the foundation of trust the newspaper has with its readers," said Aly Colon of the Poynter Institute's ethics faculty.[42]

Later, the top King County prosecutor said that if he had known about it, he would have vetoed his subordinates' decision to ask the *Journal* to publish the fake story. "It was not sensitive to the traditional role of the press," Prosecutor Norm Maleng's spokesman said. "It just wasn't appropriate."[43]

Case Study No. 18

Rumsfeld's Q&A With the Troops

Secretary of Defense Donald Rumsfeld took questions from the troops December 8, 2004, while visiting Iraq and Kuwait. One question in Kuwait made worldwide news: "Why," asked Specialist Thomas Wilson of the Tennessee National Guard (Figure 16.1), "do we soldiers have to dig through local landfills for pieces of scrap metal and compromised ballistic glass to uparmor our vehicles?" Rumsfeld's response proved

Continued

Figure 16.1 Specialist Thomas Wilson directs a question (provided by a reporter) to Defense Secretary Donald Rumsfeld at a base in Kuwait
PHOTO BY GUSTAVO FERRARI. REPRINTED BY PERMISSION OF THE ASSOCIATED PRESS

controversial. He said that the Army was trying to improve the armor on its vehicles in Iraq, and that the delay was not a matter of money or of intent, but of production limitations. In the days afterward, Army suppliers disputed the statement about production limitations. One result of the question – and the public attention focused on it – was that the shipment of armored humvees to the troops was sped up.

Rumsfeld also said in his response: "As you know, you go to war with the Army you have. They're not the Army you might want or wish to have …" His critics back in the United States saw this comment as condescending and pointed out that Rumsfeld had had many months to prepare for the military operations in Iraq.

The question was popular with the troops assembled for the secretary's visit. From the audience of 2,300 soldiers came an outburst of "hooahs" and applause so loud that Rumsfeld had to ask Specialist Wilson to repeat his question.

A day later, there was a postscript: The question that the soldier asked turned out to have been written for him by a *Chattanooga Times Free Press* reporter who was "embedded" with the soldier's unit. The question's origin became known because the reporter, Edward Lee Pitts, wrote about it in an email to a colleague at the paper, and someone leaked the email to Internet sites. That led to criticism of the reporter. "He created news in order to cover it," Rush Limbaugh said on his radio talk show. Limbaugh called it "a setup." In the story Pitts wrote for his newspaper about the question and Rumsfeld's answer, Pitts had not disclosed that he was the author of the question.

In his email, Pitts said he had wanted to ask the question himself but was denied a chance to speak to Rumsfeld at what the Pentagon called a town hall meeting for GIs. In his email, he wrote: "I just had one of my best days as a journalist today. As luck would have it, our journey North was delayed just long enough so I could attend a visit today here by Defense Secretary Rumsfeld." Pitts wrote that he and two soldiers "worked on questions to ask Rumsfeld about the appalling lack of armor their vehicles going into combat have." Pitts said he "found the Sgt. In Charge of the microphone for the question and answer session and made sure he knew to get my guys out of the crowd." Pitts wrote that Wilson told him he "felt good b/c he took his complaints to the top."

Continued

President George W. Bush and Secretary Rumsfeld said they welcomed the pointed questions that the soldiers raised. Bush said the military was addressing the issue of lack of armor for its vehicles in the combat zone and said he didn't blame the soldier for asking the question. "If I were a soldier overseas wanting to defend my country," the president said, "I would want to ask the secretary of defense the same question." Rumsfeld said it was "good for people to raise questions."

Tom Griscom, publisher and executive editor of the *Times Free Press*, supported Pitts, with a caveat. "I am supportive of his trying to find a way to get the question asked," he said. He said it was a mistake not to have told readers about the question's origin. The paper disclosed Pitts' role on the front page of the next day's paper.

Griscom said "the soldier asked the question" and could have turned Pitts down. "Because someone's in the media who's embedded with them, does that mean they don't have the same opportunity to make a suggestion of something that might be asked?" Griscom said. "Is that what makes it wrong, because a journalist did it? ... That response from the troops was a clear indication that this is an issue on their minds."

Don Fost wrote in the *San Francisco Chronicle* that the incident "raised questions about journalistic objectivity and whether the press manipulates the coverage of events." Jane Kirtley, professor of media ethics and law at the University of Minnesota, told Fost that Pitts broke the rules. "I don't like it," she said. "Not because they're not good questions, but because we have to play by the rules."

On his network's "Reliable Sources" program, Jamie McIntyre of CNN said he might have suggested a question for a soldier who asked, but he thought actually writing the question "does cross a line." On the same program, Matt Cooper of *Time* magazine supported Pitts, calling the question "clever" and saying it was validated by the troops' enthusiastic reaction. McIntyre and Cooper both said Pitts should have told readers about his involvement.

Other ethics experts supported Pitts.

Tom Rosenstiel, director of the Project for Excellence in Journalism, said that Pitts "may have emboldened soldiers to ask questions that citizens are often a little more timid about asking." He said that Pitts may have helped frame the question "in a more provocative way" but that there was "no sleight of hand."

Alex Jones, director of Harvard University's Joan Shorenstein Center for Press, Politics and Public Policy, said Pitts' role "makes me uncomfortable" but "I don't consider this to be a setup because it was a legitimate question as far as the soldier was concerned."

Stuart Loory, who holds the Lee Hills Chair in Free Press Studies at the University of Missouri, said,

Reporters don't have the same access any longer that they did to ask their own questions. And planting a legitimate question with somebody who may have the access, I think, is an acceptable practice. The question is whether or not the soldier who asked the question really believed in it, and my guess is that he did, or he wouldn't have asked it.

Bob Steele of the Poynter Institute said the question was legitimate. "The soldiers were not deceived. They knew what was going on."

Pentagon spokesman Larry Di Rita had a different view. He said in a news release:

Continued

"Town hall meetings are intended for soldiers to have dialogue with the secretary of defense. … The secretary provides ample opportunity for interaction with the press. It is better that others not infringe on the troops' opportunity to interact with superiors in the chain of command."

Questions for Class Discussion

- Did Edward Lee Pitts engage in deception by helping the soldiers write their questions and arranging for the sergeant at the microphone to call on them? If you think it was deception, do you think it was justified?

- In his first story on the town hall meeting, should Pitts have told readers that he wrote Specialist Wilson's question?
- If you were Pitts, how would you respond to Rush Limbaugh's criticism that you "created news in order to cover it"?

Case Study No. 19

Spying on the Mayor in a Chat Room

Reporters for *The Spokesman-Review* in Spokane, Washington, interviewed an 18-year-old high school graduate in the fall of 2004 about a dinner date the teenager said he had a few months earlier with a 53-year-old man he had met in an online gay chat room.

This is what the teenager told the reporters: After dinner, he was given the keys to a convertible in the restaurant parking lot. As he drove curvy roads north of the city, he asked the older man what he does for a living. "[H]e says, like, I'm the mayor of Spokane." Until that moment, the teenager had no idea he was on a date with Mayor Jim West – a date that ended with consensual sex.

When reporters interviewed the high school graduate after police tipped them about him, *The Spokesman-Review* had spent two years investigating West, a Republican with an anti-gay rights record. But the newspaper did not immediately publish the teenager's account of a date with West.

At the time, the newspaper was seeking interviews with two men who had told police that West sexually abused them when they were children and West was a sheriff's deputy and Boy Scout leader. In the winter and spring of 2005, reporters interviewed those men and heard the accusations themselves.

Steven A. Smith, then editor of *The Spokesman-Review*, wanted proof of West's

Continued

conduct "beyond a shadow of a doubt." In an online Q&A with readers later, Smith reviewed the evidence that the paper had at the time:

- There was the account of the eighteen-year-old who said he had chatted with a person while on gay.com, that the person turned out to be Mayor West, and that the conversations resulted in a date and a sexual encounter.
- And there were the accounts of the two men alleging that West abused them as children, but both were felons and one was in prison at the time on a drug conviction.

"The problem in the cyberworld is that there was no backup evidence," Smith said in the Q&A. "If we had published that allegation [of the teenager who had the date with West], it would have elicited an immediate denial from the mayor, and that would have been that. The screen names would have disappeared, the mayor would have dropped out of the chat rooms, and we'd be guilty of either improperly sullying his reputation or guilty of letting him off the hook."

Smith said the only way to confirm the story was to go online and engage the mayor in the chat room. To do this, *The Spokesman-Review* hired a forensic computer expert, a former federal agent whom it did not identify. The expert registered on gay.com as "Moto-Brock," a fictitious high school senior questioning his own sexuality and eager to met older gay or bisexual men.

"It took two months of chatting with the mayor online in a variety of ways to get him to the point where he trusted us enough to reveal himself," Smith said.

Ultimately West thought he was communicating with a teenager, Smith said, adding: "He showed up for a meeting that he set up, and at that point, we knew we had the mayor."

On May 5, 2005, *The Spokesman-Review* published its story about the 18-year-old high school graduate's 2004 date with the mayor; the allegations of the two men who said West abused them as children – and the details of his online conversations with the paper's computer expert.

"Once in the chat room, which has a policy that all participants be 18, the consultant changed his age to 17 because the newspaper wanted to know whether West was using the Web to meet underage children," the newspaper reported. "Within two months, Moto-Brock and RightBi-Guy [who turned out to be the mayor] were discussing sex in the gay.com chat room, and the dialogues were being recorded by the newspaper's consultant."

The paper said that when West was interviewed the day before its story was published, he admitted his online relationships with the 18-year-old and Moto-Brock. After a long pause in the interview, he said, "They were both adults, and I was in public office when I dated women in this community. So what's your point?"

The paper said the transcripts of the online conversations showed that RightBi-Guy was the first person to raise the issue of sex. The *Spokesman-Review* report continued:

He also suggested that he and Moto-Brock switch their conversations from the gay.com chat room to America Online instant messaging, which is transitory in nature and disappears quickly unless steps are taken to record chats. Over a period of several

Continued

months, RightBi-Guy offered Moto-Brock autographed sports memorabilia, prime seats for Seahawks and Mariners games, help getting into college, an internship job in the Spokane mayor's office and the promise of trips to Washington, DC. In mid-March, Moto-Brock told RightBi-Guy that he'd turned 18.

The paper said it confirmed West's identity when he showed up for a golf date with Moto-Brock at Indian Canyon at 10 a.m. April 10. Earlier, in order that Moto-Brock would know whom to look for, RightBi-Guy had emailed him his picture. "The picture was of West," the paper reported.

> He also e-mailed Moto-Brock a link to the mayor's Web page on the Spokane City Hall site. Three people affiliated with *The Spokesman-Review* reported seeing West arrive at the course in his blue Lexus at 9:45 a.m. April 10. ... The two never met in person. Shortly after that failed meeting, the consultant was asked by the newspaper to stop communicating online with RightBi-Guy. But West subsequently sent the consultant two more e-mails, including a final message sent April 28. Sent from the mayor's office, the e-mail has 'internship' in its subject line. The e-mail asks Moto-Brock, 'Still interested?'"

Days after publishing its story, *The Spokesman-Review* reported that Ryan Oelrich, 24, said he was appointed by West to the city Human Rights Commission in April 2004 after apparently meeting him in a gay.com online chat room. Oelrich said that after he was appointed to the commission, West made several sexual advances online and once offered Oelrich $300 to swim naked with him. Oelrich said he declined the offer.

Oelrich, who heads a gay youth organization in Spokane, said he knew of five or six young gay men who also received inappropriate sexual advances from West. Oelrich said he left the Human Rights Commission in January 2005 after West "hounded me for months, telling me I was cute and asking me out on dates."

At a news conference, West said: "I categorically deny any allegations about incidents that supposedly occurred 24 years ago as alleged by two convicted felons and about which I have no knowledge. The newspaper also reported that I had visited a gay Internet chat room and had relations with adult men. I don't deny that."

An ethical issue for *The Spokesman-Review*, in addition to its use of deception, was whether West's sexual activity warranted news coverage. Editor Smith said in an online Q&A with readers on May 9:

> This is not about being gay. As we were working on our actual stories, I kept rewriting them in my mind as if the issues involved hetero sex – that is, a scenario in which the 50-plus-year-old mayor was chatting up 17- and 18-year-old high school girls and then initiating cyber-sex and soliciting real-life sex when they turned 18. As a parent of teenagers, including a teen-age daughter, I decided it would absolutely be a story. ... I think this story is about behavior most in our community would find repulsive – gay or straight.

Another questioner wanted to know why the paper faked the age – 17, almost 18. Smith responded:

> The website requires a simple declaration of age to register. And those who use the site tell us it is replete with youngsters. If you go

Continued

into the chat rooms, you'll often find more underage kids than adults. We're also told this is a site where older men seek out minors. We wanted to know if the mayor would approach someone underage (he did without prompting), if he'd turn the conversations to sex (he did, without prompting). But as soon as we moved the character to 18, the mayor's intent became overtly sexual.

David Zeeck, editor of *The News Tribune* in Tacoma, Washington, was one of several newspaper editors who criticized *The Spokesman-Review*'s decision to use deception. Zeeck wrote in a column May 8: "Without the expert's ruse, they had their 53-year-old mayor trolling for sex online and admitting to having consensual sex with an 18-year-old he met through a chat room. Gay or straight, that's not the sort of behavior I want my mayor engaging in."

When *Editor and Publisher* magazine asked 10 top editors about *The Spokesman-Review*'s using the computer expert to engage the mayor online, no one endorsed the idea. That led Steve Lovelady, then managing editor of *CJR Daily*, an online service of *Columbia Journalism Review*, to defend *The Spokesman-Review*'s reporting on West as "public service journalism at its best." He criticized other editors who

> piously declare that they wouldn't have taken the measures that Smith took to make his story airtight. … What exactly is Steve Smith supposed to be guilty of? Having the prudence and caution to hire an expert to ascertain the mayor's online identity before *The Spokesman-Review* went into print? Where I come from, we don't call that entrapment; we call it responsible journalism.

After the newspaper's revelations, a petition was circulated to oust Mayor West. The recall petition contended that West used his political office for personal benefit by offering a city internship to someone he thought was an 18-year-old man he had met in a gay online chat room and with whom he had conducted sexually explicit chats. West, who was not charged with any crime, acknowledged making mistakes in his personal life but asked voters to give him a second chance. On December 6, 2005, the mayor was recalled from office in a special election, with the electorate voting by a two-to-one ratio to oust him. On July 22, 2006, West died of colon cancer.

Questions for Class Discussion

- Was *The Spokesman-Review* justified in investigating and reporting on Mayor West's sex life?
- If you think the paper should have reported on that subject, would you have published the story solely on the basis of the statements of the 18-year-old high school graduate and the two men who said West abused them as children?
- If you didn't think that was enough evidence, would your decision have changed when Ryan Oelrich, whom West had appointed to a city commission, made his statements to reporters?
- Was the paper justified in using deception by hiring a computer expert to pose as a high school student and engage in an online conversation with the mayor?
- Was the paper accountable to its readers after publishing the allegations?

Notes

1 Donald L. Barlett, "Patient at Lima beaten and kicked for whispering," *The Plain Dealer*, May 27, 1965.

2 *The Plain Dealer*, "PD reporter got job 'inside Lima' for data," May 23, 1965.

3 Author's telephone interview with Donald L. Barlett, April 23, 2007.

4 Reid MacCluggage, "Should we ever deceive?", *APME News*, Winter 1997–98.

5 Louis W. Hodges, "Undercover, masquerading, surreptitious taping," *Journal of Mass Media Ethics*, Fall 1988, 26–36.

6 Barlett, email to author, June 24, 2008.

7 Author's recollections as managing editor of *The Philadelphia Inquirer*, for which Josephson conducted seminars in the early 1980s.

8 Sissela Bok, *Lying: Moral Choice in Public and Private Life* (New York: Vintage Books, 1978), 13.

9 Ibid., 8.

10 Carl Bernstein and Bob Woodward, *All the President's Men* (New York: Touchstone, 1974), 60.

11 Bok, *Lying*, 120.

12 Deni Elliott, *Montana Journalism Review* 26 (Summer 1997), 3–6.

13 Michael Josephson, "Declaration of ethical standards," written for the Associated Press Managing Editors, 1993.

14 Bill Kovach and Tom Rosenstiel, *The Elements of Journalism: What Newspeople Should Know and the Public Should Expect* (New York: Crown Publishers, 2001), 83.

15 Hodges, "Undercover, masquerading, surreptitious taping."

16 Jay Black, Bob Steele, and Ralph Barney, *Doing Ethics in Journalism: A Handbook With Case Studies*, 3rd edn. (Needham Heights, MA: Allyn & Bacon, 1999), 163.

17 Public Broadcasting System, "Nellie's madhouse memoir," http://www.pbs.org/wgbh/amex/world/sfeature/memoir.html

18 Stephen Klaidman and Tom L. Beauchamp, *The Virtuous Journalist* (New York: Oxford University Press, 1987), 195.

19 *Chicago Sun-Times*, http://www.suntimes.com/news/metro/history/798307,CST-NWS-high17.stng

20 Philip Seib and Kathy Fitzpatrick, *Journalism Ethics* (Fort Worth, TX: Harcourt, Brace & Company, 1997), 90.

21 *Chicago Sun-Times*, http://www.suntimes.com/news/metro/history/798307,CST-NWS-high17.stng

22 Susan Paterno, "The lying game," *American Journalism Review*, May 1997.

23 Ibid.

24 Bruce W. Sanford, *Don't Shoot the Messenger: How Our Growing Hatred of the Media Threatens Free Speech for All of Us* (New York: The Free Press, 1999), 145.

25 Walter Goodman, "Beyond ABC v. Food Lion," *The New York Times*, March 9, 1997.

26 Susan Paterno, "The lying game."

27 Bill Kovach and Tom Rosenstiel, *The Elements of Journalism: What Newspeople Should Know and the Public Should Expect* (New York: Crown Publishers, 2001), 121–2.

28 Bob Steele, "High standards for hidden cameras," http://www.poynter.org/content/content_view.asp?id=5543, Aug. 1, 1999. This article was originally published in *Hidden Cameras/Hidden Microphones: At the Crossroads of Journalism, Ethics and Law*, a 1998 publication of the Radio-Television News Directors Foundation.

29 Ibid.

30 Author's personal recollections as managing editor of the *Pine Bluff Commercial* and confirmed in email correspondence with Harry Pearson, May 14, 2008.

31 Author's telephone interview with Roy Reed, Sept. 10, 2007.

32 Gene Roberts and Hank Klibanoff, *The Race Beat: The Press, the Civil Rights Struggle, and the Awakening of a Nation* (New York: Alfred A. Knopf, 2006), 363.

33 Ibid., 402.

34 Ron F. Smith, *Ethics in Journalism*, 6th edn. (Malden, MA: Blackwell Publishing, 2008), 195. Roberts' account of walking into the emergency room wearing a stethoscope is familiar to the author and other *Philadelphia Inquirer* editors of the period (1972–90) that Roberts led the paper.

35   Tom Goldstein, *The News at Any Cost: How Journalists Compromise Their Ethics to Shape the News* (New York: Simon & Schuster, 1985), 143–4.

36   Jack Fuller, *News Values: Ideas for an Information Age* (Chicago: University of Chicago Press, 1996), 51–2.

37   Jay Rosen, "The uncharted: From Off the Bus to Meet the Press," http://www.huffingtonpost.com/jay-rosen/the-uncharted-from-off-th_b_96575.html?view=

38   Ibid.

39   Seow Ting Lee, "The ethics of journalistic deception," in Lee Wilkins and Renita Coleman, *The Moral Media: How Journalists Reason About Ethics* (Mahwah, NJ: Lawrence Erlbaum Associates, 2005), 98–100. Lee's web survey was conducted Feb. 2–23, 2002. Of the 3,795 members of the Investigative Reporters and Editors to whom the survey was delivered, 740 responded, a rate of 19.4 percent.

40   Aly Colon, "Faking the news: Weighing the options when the stakes are high and important principles are at stake," http://www.poynter.org/content/content_view.asp?id=30941, April 22, 2003.

41   Sara Jean Green and Ian Ith, "Ethics of paper's fake arson story debated," *Seattle Times*, April 18, 2003.

42   Ibid.

43   Robert L. Jamieson Jr., "A question of ethics: Fake story is news not to print," *Seattle Post-Intelligencer*, April 25, 2003.

17 Covering a Diverse, Multicultural Society

An ethical duty to be sensitive in reporting on minority groups

---

Learning Goals

This chapter will help you understand:

- the ethical dimensions of covering a diverse, multicultural society;
- the complexity of stories about racial and ethnic conflict;
- techniques that help journalists do a better job of covering cultures other than their own;
- ethical issues in the coverage of new immigrants;
- when racial identifications in news stories are justified, and when they are not;
- ways to make coverage more inclusive of the entire community;
- the need to eliminate any disparity in how different races and ethnicities are covered; and
- the need for accuracy and sensitivity in covering gays and lesbians in the news.

On December 14, 1995, 17-year-old Cynthia Wiggins rode a local transit bus from the east side of Buffalo, New York, to her job at a fast-food restaurant in the Walden Galleria Mall in suburban Cheektowaga. The bus stop was on Walden Avenue, a seven-lane highway that went past the mall. The curb where the bus stopped was covered by a snowdrift eight feet high, and there was no crosswalk. Threading her way through the busy Christmas-season traffic, Wiggins walked alongside an 18-wheel dump truck. The driver couldn't see her.

As she started to cross in front of the truck, the traffic light turned green. The driver of a nearby van watched helplessly as "both sets of tandems went over the girl." The witness said, "[T]here's no way she could get out of the way of the wheels."

To many people – particularly those who are white – nobody was to blame for Cynthia Wiggins' tragic death.

To many other people – particularly those who are black, as Wiggins was – she was surely a victim of racism.

A few months after Wiggins was fatally injured on Walden Avenue, Ted Koppel of ABC News took his *Nightline* camera crews to Buffalo to try to sort out the controversy.

"Remember now, we're talking about a traffic accident," Koppel told his viewers when the *Nightline* report aired on May 22, 1996. "No one has charged that Cynthia Wiggins was run down deliberately. No one has even suggested that she was killed intentionally because of her race. So why do feelings run so high?"

The ABC journalists interviewed white residents who said the accident had nothing to do with race. One of these, radio talk-show host Gary MacNamara, said: "There have been many cases, many things that happen in our society, where automatically racism is thrown out, that it's got to be racism, it's got to be racism, without any proof. Well, that's crying wolf."

This is what *Nightline* reported in its documentary, titled "The Color Line and the Bus Line":

> After giving birth to a son, Wiggins was studying part-time to get her high school diploma. She received some public assistance but needed a part-time job. With no jobs available in her depressed neighborhood, she found work in the Galleria in the nearly all-white Cheektowaga. To get there required a half-hour ride on the Number 6 bus.

But the Number 6 bus did not stop in the mall, a circumstance that became the crux of the controversy over Wiggins' death.

Koppel told his viewers that when the Galleria was built in 1988, "there was clearly some nervousness about the crime rate at the Thruway Mall, just down the road."

Ken Cannon, a former executive of the company that developed the Galleria, said in reference to Thruway Mall: "There had been some knifings, and there had been some other instances related to drugs, and alcohol, which we were not interested in moving down the highway. And nor was the town, for that matter."

"I was surprised," said Gordon Foster, a former transit official, "but they had mentioned one route that they did not want to have serve the mall, which was Route 6, which ... at that time, went right by the area where they were building the mall, and had been there for many years."

Cannon said the transit officials "did ask us about access for the bus traveling down Walden Avenue, and I said to them that we had these concerns about security."

Also interviewed for *Nightline* was Bud White, a merchant who had talked with the Galleria's managers about locating a store in the mall. He said that at a meeting with Tim Ahern and Mark Congell of the mall management, he asked about "the black community" and was told: "You know, don't worry about the black communities. ... We don't want 'em, and we're not going to let 'em ... [W]e're not going to let the buses come in."

Ahern said he and Congell remembered the meeting with White, and "those statements are emphatically false."

Professor Henry Taylor of Buffalo University, an African American, told ABC:

> It sounds so innocent. Don't let the buses roll into the suburban regions. Don't let the buses roll into the malls. Don't let the buses roll into the industrial parks. But there are major consequences to this. That's why I refer to those transportation issues as racist. Sanitized, guiltless racism, the kind of ... racism that people can engage in in the quietness of their suburban homes.

At the end of the documentary, Koppel told his viewers that after Cynthia Wiggins' death, the transit company and the mall had agreed on a new bus stop on the grounds of the Galleria. "Passengers on the Number 6 bus will no longer have to dodge traffic on Walden Avenue," Koppel said. "It is, in a manner of speaking, Cynthia's legacy."[1]

The *Nightline* editor and producer who initiated the Buffalo story was Eric Wray, an African American, who had immediately sensed its importance. Until the reporting in Buffalo began, Koppel himself had doubts about whether the story about a traffic accident was worthy of national attention.

Wray wrote later that ABC's reporting in Buffalo was an example of the Rashomon approach, named for the film of the same name by the Japanese film-maker Akira Kurosawa. It involves looking at a story through multiple perspectives. Each observer has "a different perspective that leads to differing conclusions and reveals different 'truths' about what actually happened."

Wray saw the Rashomon approach as especially important in stories involving racial or ethnic conflict. He continued:

> In many ways, the Cynthia Wiggins tragedy is its own Rashomon. Clearly, white and black Buffalo area residents had different opinions about the circumstances that led to her death. Differing notions about the placement of the bus stop – sinister to some; incidental to others – point up different perceptions of racism. Buffalo's, and to some extent, America's stance on racial justice issues appears quite adequate to some but unfair to others.
>
> For journalists, this is a major point of conflict in the story. The same event was viewed by many people differently and was clearly based on their vantage points. ...
>
> Each perspective has its own biases and prejudices. The "truth," if there is such a thing in journalism, can only be determined by looking at an event from multiple points of view.[2]

In 2006, the *Nightline* documentary was praised by the authors of a book that celebrates and analyzes exemplary reporting on America's cultural diversity. "The story teaches how to question assumptions by using a variety of voices and perspectives to examine a racially divisive issue," write Arlene Notoro Morgan, Alice Irene Pifer, and Keith Woods in *The Authentic Voice*. "It also teaches the value of using street reporting to combine a variety of conflicting viewpoints, creating a narrative that allows the audience to reach its own conclusion through the facts that are laid out."[3]

Ethics in Reporting on a Multicultural Society

Providing accurate, fair, and sensitive coverage of a diverse, multicultural society is an essential dimension of ethical journalism.

Until the last half of the twentieth century, that kind of coverage was rarely an acknowledged goal of the American news media. In 1947, the Hutchins Commission challenged the news media to "give a comprehensive picture of constituent groups in society, avoiding stereotypes."[4] In 1968, the Kerner Commission painted a picture of an American society divided along racial lines and said the division was strikingly evident in the news media, whose workforce then was nearly all white and nearly all male.[5] The civil rights movement of the 1960s put pressure on news media executives to end hiring discrimination and begin actively recruiting members of racial and ethnic minority groups.

Today, the news media are consciously striving to bring members of those minority groups into the ranks of journalists and to broaden their news coverage to include all elements of a diverse community.

The news media still have a long way to go before they truly are representative of society as a whole. Members of minority groups made up 23.6 percent of the television news workforce and 11.8 percent of the radio news workforce as of the last quarter of 2007.[6] Among journalists working at daily newspapers in 2008, 13.5 percent were members of minority groups.[7] Contrast this with the Census Bureau's estimate on July 1, 2007, that members of minority groups accounted for one-third of the national population of 301.6 million. The Census Bureau uses the following classifications of minority groups: Hispanic (who can be of any race), black, Asian, American Indian, and Native Hawaiian and Pacific Islander.[8]

Still, diversity in hiring has done much to inform the reporting that goes into newspapers, broadcast stations, and online sites. Although no journalist should be expected to speak for his or her entire ethnic group, journalists of color exert a valuable influence on newsroom decision-making that was missing in the past. And, increasingly, journalists of color are the people making the decisions.

The Society of Professional Journalists' ethics code, under the guiding principle of "seeking truth," tells journalists to:

- "Tell the story of the diversity and magnitude of the human experience, even when it is unpopular to do so."
- "Examine their own cultural values and avoid imposing those values on others."
- "Avoid stereotyping by race, gender, age, religion, ethnicity, geography, sexual orientation, disability, physical appearance, or social status." (A stereotype is "a fixed mental image of a group that is frequently applied to all its members.")[9]

- "Give voice to the voiceless; official and unofficial sources of information can be equally valid."

The Challenge of Covering Other Cultures

A challenge for journalists, irrespective of their own racial or ethnic groups, is to write knowledgeably about another culture. Specifically, the challenge is to rise above "superficial, ordinary and, in important ways, harmful journalism," wrote Keith Woods, dean of faculty at the Poynter Institute.[10] It requires conversation about a subject that makes many journalists uncomfortable. It means taking the initiative.

As the United States population continues to diversify, the ability to report on multiple cultures becomes an ever more important skill. The Census Bureau predicted in 2008 that so-called minority groups would collectively become a majority in 2042 (see Figure 17.1).[11]

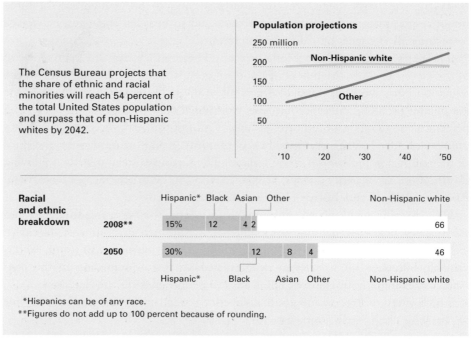

Figure 17.1 US demographics
REPRINTED BY PERMISSION OF *THE NEW YORK TIMES*

The Census Bureau projects that the share of ethnic and racial minorities will reach 54 percent of the total United States population and surpass that of non-Hispanic whites by 2042.

*Hispanics can be of any race.
**Figures do not add up to 100 percent because of rounding.

Source; Graphic by *The New York Times,* based on data from the US Census Bureau

Joann Byrd, former ombudsman of *The Washington Post*, wrote *Respecting All Cultures: A Practical Ethics Handbook for Journalists* in April 2002 when she was chair of the Ethics and Values Committee of the American Society of Newspaper Editors. Here is some of the advice she gave:

Challenge our stereotypes. These scraps of shorthand are often pejorative, and since stereotypes are almost never accurate, they can be counted on to get in the way of a trustworthy report. The cure for stereotypes is becoming informed about people as individuals.

Ask about cultural traditions. Remember that cultural values influence each of us. … [S]hared ideas can reveal what the people themselves see as their "community." And if they serve as glue for families and groups of people, traditions are inherently interesting to people who practice them and those who have different traditions of their own. Besides, talking about values can move us beyond the superficial in short order.

Learn protocols and courtesies. Appropriate dress and customs about such things as shaking hands and eye contact will help us avoid inadvertently insulting a new acquaintance.[12]

For more of Joann Byrd's recommendations for covering other cultures, read her Point of View, "Gaining Respect by Showing Respect."

Aly Colon, who taught ethics at the Poynter Institute for many years, suggests ways that a journalist could connect with people of other cultures:

Make it a point to go out into the many different communities in your city. Stroll their streets. Shop in their stores. Eat in their restaurants. Study their history. Learn their culture. Show them your face. Have a conversation with them. Listen. Listen. Listen.[13]

Techniques for coverage of race relations and ethnic diversity have been refined through a "Let's Do It Better!" program launched in 1999 at the Graduate School of Journalism at Columbia University. The program, led first by professor Sig Gissler and then by associate dean Arlene Notoro Morgan, recognizes the nation's best reporting on the subject. As winning journalists discuss their projects in conferences conducted by Columbia, they share their successes and failures. From their experience, teaching tools for the profession evolve.

A group of journalists led by Keith Woods and Arlene Notoro Morgan met at the Poynter Institute in 2001 to analyze about 150 of the best entries in the Columbia program, a trove that included print, radio, and television journalism. The panel wanted to know what worked best in this sensitive area of reporting.

Woods summarized what they learned: "The best stories … seem to be written *from* communities, not *about* them. The stories are intellectually curious, not merely voyeuristic. They answer some questions and raise others. They challenge, inform, and are delivered with authority."[14]

Woods wrote that four fundamental measures of excellence emerged from the study:

1 *The story provides context,* offering historical and supporting information that helps the audience understand. The reporter assigns race its appropriate place in the story.

2   *The story embraces complexity*. It rises above "one-dimensional explanations and the polarized, black-or-white, saints-or-sinners framing to reveal the gray truths of race relations."

3   *We hear the voices of the people*. The quotes and sound bites are "purposeful and clear"; they "advance the story, convey character and personality, reveal new truths, or otherwise add value to the piece."

4   *The story has the ring of authenticity*. The reporting is "broad and deep enough, the details fine enough, the opinions open enough to provide true insight." The writing is clear, direct, and free of euphemisms. The sources are representative of the group, not "assigned an undue leadership role by the media or by themselves."[15]

When Freedom Forum researchers conducted town meetings with news consumers in its Free Press/Fair Press Project in 1998–99, they repeatedly encountered complaints from members of minority groups that news outlets were sending reporters into black and Hispanic communities mostly to cover crime, violence, poverty, or drugs. They said positive developments efforts in minority communities rarely were covered.

Robert J. Haiman, whose *Best Practices for Newspaper Journalists* draws on the ideas gathered in the town meetings, wrote that minority participants were disturbed that newspapers persisted in "anointing" minority community leaders. These presumed leaders, Haiman writes, were not necessarily regarded as leaders by the people who lived in those communities, nor had they been empowered to speak for the communities.

Haiman quotes one black participant: "You have got to stop looking for two or three people to speak for the black community; it can't be done any more than two or three people can speak for the entire white community. And, besides, too often you get the wrong ones, anyway."[16]

For newspaper editors and broadcast directors, a perplexing question is which reporters and photojournalists should cover minority communities. One goal is to *get the story right*, with all its nuances. Another is to *get the right story*, because stories can be technically accurate, yet lacking the diverse viewpoints that are critical to completeness.

So who should get the assignment?

It would seem logical that an African American reporter would be more likely to gain rapport with African American news subjects than a white reporter. Or that a Latino reporter would be more successful with Latinos, especially in overcoming a language barrier.

But journalists who are members of minority groups can feel isolated and stereotyped if they only, or usually, cover their own communities. Some of these journalists told Haiman they felt pressured to "conform to dated newsroom standards that hampered them in suggesting or assigning stories outside traditional white awareness and sensitivities."[17]

Deciding who gets a certain assignment "can be a controversial judgment call," former network producer Av Westin writes in *Best Practices for Television Journalists*.

Westin would not assign stories automatically on the basis of race. But he also writes:

> In newsrooms where racial and ethnic diversity exists, take advantage of the mix of backgrounds and interests, because the issues in their communities will then work their way back into the broadcasts ... A well-rounded reporter should be able to handle any subject matter. On the other hand, in a complex story involving sensitive community feelings, it can be productive to assign a reporter who brings special insights or experience to the story. The decision of whom to assign should be influenced, finally, by who can do the best job.[18]

Issues in Covering New Immigrants

Gabriel Escobar, an immigrant from Colombia who is now metropolitan editor of *The Philadelphia Inquirer*, has reported extensively on immigrants for *The Washington Post*. "These stories are a way to shed light on the complex process of assimilation, and executed well, they will add texture and dimension," he writes in an essay for *The Authentic Voice*.

But this coverage "will not always be greeted with applause," Escobar writes. People in the immigrant community complain that the media seldom go beyond the superficial feature. But these same people, he writes, will object "when the attention becomes probing and, in the process, reveals something that someone will construe as a negative." Escobar offers this case in point:

> Several years ago, I suggested to a colleague who covered transportation that he examine why so many Latino immigrants were getting killed crossing streets in suburban Washington. His analysis proved something irrefutable: immigrants were far more likely to die than any other group.
>
> Several theories were offered, and one of the most perceptive was that these immigrants had settled in neighborhoods built and designed for commuters. By necessity and circumstance, they were pedestrians in places ill suited for walking.
>
> When the story ran, [*The Post*] received numerous complaints from Latino activists and others who said the reporters had stooped to a new low: accusing immigrants of being so ignorant that they did not understand something as elementary as crossing the street. Instead of pressing local communities to improve pedestrian access and educate the public, the reaction to the story removed any impetus to address what clearly was a safety issue.[19]

Escobar also found that while his Spanish fluency could be an asset, it had a downside. Instead of perceiving him as a neutral reporter, the people he was covering saw him as an ally. "To them, I was on their side, and the bond was sealed by my ability to talk to them in Spanish. What I saw as a very effective tool employed in the act of reporting, they saw as some manifestation of cultural solidarity."[20]

In a situation in which his news subjects took his neutral reporting to be a betrayal, Escobar learned a lesson: "It was part of my job, paradoxically, to maintain some distance even as language brought us closer. Just as critical, however, was recognizing that cultural perceptions often trumped the ability to communicate in the language of the subjects being covered."[21]

The issue of undocumented immigrants is a news story of growing importance. A wave of immigration that gained momentum in the 1970s has made Hispanics the country's largest minority group with about 15 percent of the population. The Census Bureau estimated in 2007 that there were 45.5 million Hispanics in the US.[22] Also in 2007, the Pew Hispanic Center estimated that about one-fourth of Hispanic adults are in the US illegally.[23]

When journalists report on undocumented immigrants, they run the risk that their story subjects may be deported. This presents an ethical dilemma: The Society of Professional Journalists' principle of seeking and reporting truth would argue that the names should be used, and there is no question that credibility suffers when the people in news stories are nameless. But the SPJ principle of minimizing harm would guide journalists to omit names in order to protect their sources.

For these stories, the detailed standards in the SPJ code also are at odds. The code says that journalists should "identify sources whenever feasible." It also says journalists should "show sensitivity" when dealing with inexperienced sources and "show compassion for those who may be adversely affected by news coverage."

Although private citizens may choose to notify authorities if they encounter an undocumented immigrant, journalists must not. As neutral observers gathering information, they do not take sides in the dispute over illegal immigration. They avoid being perceived as an arm of law enforcement, a concern that was discussed in Chapter 13. At the opposite extreme, they could be seen as protecting law-breakers. So, the question remains: How much information should journalists tell the audience about someone who is in the US illegally – and how much should be withheld?

Reporters who cover immigration are struggling with that question.

Daniel Gonzalez, who covers the immigration beat for *The Arizona Republic* in Phoenix, told Lucy Hood of *American Journalism Review* that he always tries to name people – but he doesn't always give the full names. "Mexican people have two last names. Sometimes we might use the least common of the two names." On other occasions, Gonzalez said, he uses the first name only, or the first name and an initial.[24]

For "Enrique's Journey," a series of articles tracing a Honduran boy's arduous trip to join his mother in North Carolina, Sonia Nazario of the *Los Angeles Times* omitted the last names of the boy and his mother. The decision was made reluctantly after the *Times* ran their names through a computer search and determined that the two could be located online. Nazario's account, which won the 2003 Pulitzer Prize for feature writing, was accompanied by this explanation: "The *Times*' decision in this instance is intended to allow Enrique and his family to live their lives as they would have had they not provided information for this story." Nazario said, "The readership reaction confirmed that we made the right decision. I didn't get any response from the readers asking why we hadn't put his last name in. I did get messages saying: 'Thank you for not listing his last name. That was the right thing to do.'"[25]

Kelly McBride of the Poynter Institute told *American Journalism Review*'s Lucy Hood that journalists must be aware of the risks when they report on undocumented immigrants, and they need to ask themselves questions: Is the source likely to be fired, deported, or harassed? Is the source capable of assessing the risk? Does he or she understand the legal implications? "You have to ask a lot of questions," McBride said, "including what your journalistic purpose is."[26]

It is essential that the subject of the story give what is known as "informed consent" — that is, he or she fully understands the terms of the agreement. Gonzalez, of *The Arizona Republic*, said he always tells his sources what his story is about and clearly explains the possible consequences to them. "Once you've done that," he said, "you've done your job."[27]

Case Study No. 20, "When a Story Gets Its Subject Arrested," tells about an undocumented grocery worker, Julio Granados, who was arrested by the Immigration and Naturalization Service after he was the subject of a detailed, illustrated feature story in *The News and Observer* of Raleigh, North Carolina.

When to Identify News Subjects by Race

Through the mid-twentieth century, newspapers — especially in the South — routinely identified people by race in all kinds of news situations. More precisely, nonwhite people were identified by race; a person whose race was not mentioned was understood by readers to be white. The practice both reflected and encouraged stereotypes.

Although routine racial identification has disappeared, journalists sometimes are confused about when it serves a purpose to specify the race of the people involved in the news.

Keith Woods of the Poynter Institute urges journalists to "flag every racial reference" and ask these questions:

1 *Is it relevant?* Race is relevant when the story is about race. Just because people in the conflict are of different races does not mean that race is the

source of their dispute. A story about interracial dating, however, is a story about race.

2   *Have I explained the relevance?* Journalists too frequently assume that readers will know the significance of race in stories. The result is often radically different interpretations. That is imprecise journalism, and its harm may be magnified by the lens of race.

3   *Is it free of codes?* Be careful not to use *welfare, inner-city, underprivileged, blue-collar, conservative, suburban, exotic, middle-class, Uptown, South Side,* or *wealthy* as euphemisms for racial groups. By definition, the White House is in the inner-city. Say what you mean. [See Woods' Point of View "In Writing About Race, Be Precise."]

4   *Are the racial identifiers used evenly?* If the race of a person charging discrimination is important, then so is the race of the person being charged.

5   *Should I consult someone of another race/ethnicity?* Consider another question: Do I have expertise on other races/cultures? If not, broaden your perspective by asking someone who knows something more about your subject. Why should we treat reporting on racial issues any differently from reporting on an area of science or religion that we do not know well?[28]

Physical descriptions of suspects in crimes are a nettlesome issue. If a description includes race and little else, minority-group news consumers often protest that the description is merely a device for mentioning the race of a person who supposedly committed a crime.

For this reason, many news organizations have adopted a policy of using descriptions of suspects only when they are sufficiently detailed to be of help in apprehending the suspect. This calls for applying common sense. If the police say the suspect is "a black male adult wearing a yellow sweatshirt," the description could fit many people.

If a description is to be published, broadcast, or posted online, skin color is an essential element. It is illogical to list gender, age, height, weight, attire, and other identifying characteristics while omitting race. Though often misunderstood by even seasoned journalists, the purpose of the policy is not to keep race out of a description but to establish a high standard for using a description in the first place.

When *The Eagle-Tribune* in Lawrence, Massachusetts, announced such a policy in 2005, internal emails denounced the policy as misguided political correctness. One of the newsroom dissenters wrote: "Are we to write that 'Three men from east Texas were convicted of dragging James Byrd behind a pickup truck until he was decapitated' without mentioning that the thugs were white and the victim black?"[29]

This reference to a 1998 murder in Jasper, Texas, revealed a misunderstanding of the policy and its intent. No responsible news organization would have published a news account of the racially motivated Texas killing that failed to identify the race of the killers and the victim.

Making Coverage More Inclusive of the Entire Community

For reporters, an important dimension of achieving diversity in news coverage is to broaden their so-called Rolodex list – the expert commentators they consult about news developments – to make sure that they are truly representative of the community.

Members of racial and ethnic minorities still tend to be quoted most often in stories about race or ethnicity. Robert J. Haiman's *Best Practices in Newspaper Journalism* recounts a comment by a black participant in one of The Freedom Forum's workshops: "[W]here is the story that quotes a black doctor on some medical [advance] that has nothing to do with race?"[30]

"Look closely at your Rolodex," professor Yanick Rice Lamb wrote in *Quill* magazine. "If you sorted your sources roughly by age, gender, race, geography and so on, where would you come up short? … This is not about being politically correct; it's about doing good journalism." Lamb, a former reporter who teaches journalism at Howard University, wrote that "good experts are everywhere, and they're easy to find." Among her suggestions: visit neighborhood churches, restaurants, community centers, and schools; ask existing sources for other contacts; and check out community papers, radio stations, and websites.[31]

Encouraging reporters to diversify their source lists should be a goal of newsroom managers, but experience suggests that an informal approach is best. Applying quotas – such as quoting a minimum of one minority-group member on a newspaper's front page each day – can be counterproductive.

Keith Woods says the goal should be "mainstreaming," or the inclusion of oft-excluded groups in stories that are not about their race or ethnicity. "Journalists have complained at times – legitimately – that the mindless pursuit of mainstreaming has led to tokenism, where people with little expertise and less to say have been forced into stories simply because they fit a demographic quota," he said. A better course, he said, is for journalists to learn enough about their communities to be able to "draw on a fuller palette of people."[32]

Eliminating Racial and Ethnic Disparity in Coverage

After half a century of striving for diversity and enlightened news coverage, the news media still occasionally reveal a double standard.

Editorial-page editor Cynthia Tucker of the *Atlanta Journal-Constitution* wrote a column in 2005 that noted the disparity in news coverage of two young, middle-class women who vanished after planning a wedding.

Jennifer Wilbanks, a Georgia white woman, drew intense media attention when she ran away before her wedding. In contrast, there was only media silence about Stacy-Ann Sappleton of Tecumseh, Ontario, a black woman who disappeared after flying into New York City's LaGuardia Airport and catching a taxi that was supposed to have taken her to her future in-laws' home in Queens. Her fiancé, his parents, and Sappleton's mother spent a frantic weekend searching before her bullet-riddled body was found in a trash receptacle in Queens. "When she first disappeared, we tried to contact the media, and they wouldn't help us," the fiancé told *The New York Times*.[33]

Tucker wrote:

> The frenzy surrounding Wilbanks' disappearance once again highlights a peculiar feature of early 21st century American culture: a fixation on pretty, young, middle-class white women. … Heaven knows, my industry ought to come in for a heaping dose of criticism for the sensationalist coverage given one small drama – the Wilbanks disappearance – without broader societal implications. But the fact is that the run-away-bride soap opera attracted loads of interest from readers and viewers. As American news consumers, are we discriminating about the sort of victims worthy of our concern: pretty, middle-class, young, white – yes; old, ugly, poor, black, brown – apparently not.[34]

On August 30, 2005, soon after hurricane Katrina devastated New Orleans, two wire services sent their clients similar photographs of people wading through chest-high water and carrying food and belongings. The caption for an Associated Press photograph of an African American man said he was photographed after "looting a grocery store."[35] The caption of an Agence France-Presse/Getty Images photograph, showing two white people, a young man and woman, said they were photographed after "finding bread and soda from a local grocery store."[36] Bloggers quickly protested the disparity.

Three Pennsylvania State University researchers analyzed 1,160 photographs relating to five weeks of Katrina coverage in four newspapers: *The New York Times*, *The Washington Post*, *USA Today*, and *The Wall Street Journal*. The researchers concluded:

> Photographs consistently put Anglos [non-Hispanic white people] in the role of helper and African-Americans in the role of helpless victim, supporting previous stereotyping. … The overwhelming representation of White military and social service personnel "saving" the African-American refugees may be one of the most significant themes in images of people in the coverage.[37]

Educating fellow journalists on fairness and accuracy in covering racial and ethnic groups is a top priority for the professional organizations formed in recent decades by journalists of color. Through their websites, these groups offer stylebook supplements and background information. The groups include:

- The National Association of Black Journalists (NABJ), founded in 1975 (http://nabj.org).
- The Asian American Journalists Association (AAJA), founded in 1981 (http://www.aaja.org).
- The National Association of Hispanic Journalists (NAHJ), founded in 1982 (http://www.nahj.org).
- The Native American Journalists Association (NAJA), founded in 1984 (http://www.naja.com).
- The South Asian Journalists Association (SAJA), founded in 1994 (http://saja.org).

Every four years beginning in 1994, members of NABJ, AAJA, NAHJ, and NAJA have held a joint convention called UNITY: Journalists of Color, Inc. (http://www.unityjournalists.org/). The 2004 convention in Washington, DC, was attended by 8,100 people, making it the largest gathering of journalists in American history.[38] UNITY describes itself as "a vehicle for the different ethnic groups to work through differences while supporting and collaborating on a common agenda." That agenda is to advocate fair and accurate coverage of people of color, and to challenge the news industry to reflect the nation's diversity in its staffing.[39]

Covering Gays and Lesbians in the News

When *The Washington Post* wrote in 2008 about the burial at Arlington National Cemetery of an Army intelligence officer killed in an explosion in Baghdad, the paper reported poignantly on many aspects of the soldier's life.

Donna St. George's story recounted that Major Alan G. Rogers had been awarded two Bronze Stars; that in the fatal explosion he shielded two fellow soldiers who survived; and that his commanding officer in Iraq called him "an exceptional, brilliant person – just well-spoken and instantly could relate to anybody."[40]

What the published story did not say was that Rogers was gay.

St. George's story originally had mentioned that Rogers was a former treasurer of the American Veterans for Equal Rights and that several of his friends had confirmed his sexual orientation. These friends told St. George he hadn't been allowed to share that information in the military because of the "don't ask, don't tell" rule. (The military, which once discharged service members found to be gay or lesbian, adopted a policy in 1993 saying that it would not ask members about their sexual orientation and that members would not be permitted to tell others about their orientation.)

Ombudsman Deborah Howell wrote that after an "agonizing" newsroom discussion, *Post* executive editor Leonard Downie Jr made the decision to omit the information about Rogers' sexual orientation. According to Howell's account, Downie concluded "there was no proof that Rogers was gay and no clear indication that, if he was, he wanted the information made public."[41]

The editor's ruling was in line with *The Post*'s stylebook policy, which states:

> A person's sexual orientation should not be mentioned unless relevant to the story. … Not everyone espousing gay rights causes is homosexual. When identifying an individual as gay or homosexual, be cautious about invading the privacy of someone who may not wish his or her sexual orientation known.[42]

The debate that *Post* staff members had about the Rogers story is an example of how a stylebook provides a valuable starting point for discussion but does not necessarily dictate a final decision. In her column, Howell wrote that *The Post* was right to be cautious, but she differed with the decision: "[T]here was enough evidence – particularly his feelings about 'don't ask, don't tell' – to warrant quoting his friends and adding that dimension to the story of his life. The story would have been richer for it."[43]

The Post's experience illustrates a problem that many gay men and lesbians say they have with the news media. They perceive a double standard: If people are "straight," spouses and families are typically mentioned in stories about their lives; if they are openly gay or lesbian, the comparable basic facts tend to be omitted.

Robert Dodge, who in 2001 was the president of the National Lesbian and Gay Journalists Association (NLGJA), made the double-standard argument about stories about heroes of September 11. He wrote that the media should have mentioned their sexual orientation while recounting the lives of a priest who was killed while administering the last rites to injured rescue workers at the World Trade Center; one of the passengers aboard United Airlines Flight 93 who tried to overpower hijackers planning to crash the plane into targets in Washington, DC; and the first officer of the airliner that hijackers crashed into the Pentagon. Dodge continued:

> Some journalists may embrace outdated ideas that identifying openly gay and lesbian heroes will cast a negative image on their memory. This decision is based on a presumption that being gay or lesbian is wrong, a bias that works completely against news objectivity. Withholding relevant details about their lives, their partners and families is unfair and hurtful to the people they loved. In our mission as journalists, it also denies readers and viewers information about the true identity of those who are in the news. It is the same as withholding information about the spouse, children and other features about the heterosexual heroes.
>
> What about legitimate concerns about "outing" someone, or disclosing the sexual orientation of someone who deserved privacy? We suggest more and better reporting.
>
> Instead of asking whether the victim was married, it might be better to ask if he or she had a partner. This basic question may open the door to find out more about the subject of your story – including the chance that they were heterosexual and had a significant, romantic relationship outside of traditional marriage.[44]

Biographical stories like the one about Major Rogers and the gay heroes of 9/11 call for a level of personal detail that is not appropriate in routine news accounts, where a person's sexuality – along with his or her race, ethnic background, or religious beliefs – is usually irrelevant.[45]

Because this is an issue of fairness and sensitivity, it deserves the attention of journalists.

The National Lesbian and Gay Journalists Association (http://nlgja.org) was founded in 1990. Like the professional organizations of journalists of color, NLGJA offers online resources to help fellow journalists be fair and accurate in their reporting – in this case, on stories involving lesbian, gay, bisexual, and transgender issues.

The stylebook supplement states, for example, why *sexual orientation* is better than *sexual preference*: Sexual orientation is "innate sexual attraction." Sexual preference is "a politically charged term implying that sexuality is the result of a conscious choice."[46]

NLGJA has conducted panel discussions and workshops at UNITY conventions. However, despite encouragement from some within the UNITY fold to make the quadrennial gathering more inclusive, NLGJA has not been invited to membership in UNITY, which is keeping its focus on issues relating to race and ethnicity. The arm's-length distancing of NLGJA illustrates how complex – and important – it is to report on racial, ethnic, gender, religious, and other divisions in the diverse, multicultural society.

Point of View
Gaining Respect By Showing Respect
Joann Byrd

Let's say that among people in this particular community, common courtesy requires an exchange of gifts. Enter American journalists who've been told it's unethical to accept gifts, and to offer anything as payment for information.

This is a collision of values.

Here's another one: Most people we want to interview expect to build trust over a long period before they tell us anything; they don't respond favorably to a stranger demanding a quote for the first edition.

Whether they are white business people or Native American tribal elders or Vietnamese immigrants, their expectations and our journalistic needs do not seem, at the moment anyway, compatible.

Such conflicts occur when we are defining news in our communities, when we are pursuing enterprise, and when we are racing the clock.

But the fact that there may be conflicts ahead cannot deter us from covering stories across cultures. Unless we do those stories, we

Continued

are not meeting our ethical obligation to reflect all the people who live in the region where we report the news. The trick will be providing that coverage with a minimum of damage to anybody's values.

It's our responsibility as journalists to make this work.

To begin, let's define culture, also known as "community." This is a group of people who share an ethnic heritage or a language, a faith, a physical characteristic, a history, a profession, an interest, or some other quality that brings them together.

It might clarify things if we think of journalism as a culture. Journalism certainly has unique rules and procedures, assumptions, and values. Those conventions are the reasons we run into ethical challenges when we are acting as journalists in a world inhabited by people who aren't.

This is actually the lede: Show respect. When we respect people, we hold them in esteem and treat them as honorable equals.

The people we are meeting, interviewing, writing about, and photographing are worthy of our respect just because they are human beings.

These new sources, then, are not merely means to our own journalistic ends. They are autonomous individuals with their own interests and integrity.

Unless they're elected officials, public employees, or executives of publicly traded companies, the people we encounter as we cover the news are not obligated to talk to us, to have their picture taken, or to do even one thing to help us tell a story. And if they decline – which seems more likely in a community not thoroughly immersed in the ways of the mainstream news media – we just find someone else.

We demonstrate respect by honoring the courtesies expected in a culture, by being straightforward with people about what they are getting into, and by acknowledging their concerns. We treat them as thinking adults who deserve a voice in what transpires.

Showing respect is the minimum behavior that people require of each other. To build relationships, we should do more than what's required.

We've wisely absorbed the caution that no culture is a monolith, and that all the people in a group we define will never – OK, *almost* never – act or think alike.

If we're behaving with respect toward the individuals we are covering, we will naturally use the right framework. If we respect an individual, we don't think of her as merely a part of a whole, as a carbon copy of anyone else.

And if we cover individuals, their stories will convey the complexity of their culture.

The goal is not happy, lightweight stories. Our audience knows when we are pandering to them, and they're apt to be pretty skeptical about our expanding our coverage to produce fluff.

No source objects to looking good, but candy-coated pieces also can feel patronizing to the subjects of the stories who are grown-ups with serious lives and concerns.

Holding back on serious journalism in other cultures does not demonstrate respect.

Quality journalism does.

Adapted from *Respecting All Cultures: A Practical Ethics Handbook for Journalists*, written by Joann Byrd for the American Society of Newspaper Editors, April 2002.

Point of View

In Writing About Race, Be Precise

Keith Woods

A cornerstone of great writing is precision. A great wrecking ball of precise writing is the word *race*. It foments fear. It breeds euphemisms and codes that slip unchallenged into our vocabulary. It engenders a universal, pathological discomfort with difference that comes stuttering from our keyboards in inane, insulting, and inexplicable ways.

Take the phrase "inner-city youth." What does that mean? Does it mean young people who live in the innermost core of the city? In the euphemistic lingo of race, conflated as it often is with class and geography, the precise answer is: not exactly.

We use "inner-city youth" to mean young people who are poor, black, Latino, Asian, or Native American – though it is most often reserved for the first two. It never means "white."

If you mean black children who are poor, then write this: *black children who are poor*. If you're referring to the innermost core of the city, then write: *inner city*. If you mean both, then say so. But if you can't be sure which of those phrases covers the group you're describing, don't pull out another label. Do more reporting.

Race, class, and geography morph into one phrase in other ways: "blue collar" and "soccer mom" are generally euphemisms for white people, the former living in the city, the latter in the suburbs. Check the language (*grassroots*) and notice how many ways (*diverse people*) we have for using race (*mainstream people*) without ever (*underprivileged*) actually (*at risk*) using race.

What, for example, does "minority" mean? Here's what my dictionary says: "1. the lesser part or small number; less than half of a total; opposed to majority. 2. a racial, religious, national, or political group smaller than and differing from a larger, controlling group of which it is part."

"Minority" defines people in relation to other people. In Congress, members of one party are minorities at any given time. In the world, Christians are minorities. But journalists use the word interchangeably with race, transforming people into "lesser" numbers even in places where they are the majority.

"Minority" is not a synonym for someone's race. Precision demands that you use it when referring to numbers. Even then, write what you mean: *racial and ethnic minorities*. If you're only talking about Latinos, don't switch to the ubiquitous "minorities" on second reference. Say: *Latinos*. And that reminds me. "Latino" is not a separate racial category. ... Latinos are an ethnic group of many races, including mainstream people.

Oops. I meant to say non-black people. Uh, non-minorities? Okay, non-diverse people. That's another of our hang-ups around writing race. We have a tough time saying "white." It's understandable, given the way that word is quickly translated to "racist" in the language of modern race relations: White flight. White leader. Angry white

Continued

male. I suppose it's one reason why no one wants to call a gang of white youngsters a "white gang," since our racial codebook so easily transforms "white gang" into "skinheads," even when they're fighting other white males.

"Minority" is not a synonym for someone's race. And if you'll tolerate one last racial rant, here goes. Why, in the name of melanin, do boys and men, whether they're toddlers, teens, or tottering octogenarians, get reduced to their naked gender – males – when we're writing about race? White males. Asian males. Two males. Ten males.

Somewhere along the way, journalism adopted the veterinarian way of referring to some people, which doesn't require us to reference the fact they're people at all. They're just males. Like my cat. Or my fish, which is, best I can tell, a black male.

Lost in that language is our humanity. When you think about it, that's the problem with all the euphemisms and dodges of our racial codes and idiosyncrasies. They strip people of an identity and reduce their lives to a shorthand that is as imprecise as it is insulting.

Maybe in the history of our linguistic evolution, there were good intentions, honorable efforts to get away from even worse ways of referring to people. That does not mean journalism should engender with its prose the kind of distrust and conversational dysfunction that comes when you don't say what you really mean.

It takes just a few more words to be respectful. Just a little more thought to be complete. Just a little better journalism to be precise.

Keith Woods is dean of faculty at the Poynter Institute. This essay originally appeared on March 4, 2003, at http://www.poynter.org/content/content_view. asp?id=22934, and has been modified slightly for this text.

Case Study No. 20

When a Story Gets Its Subject Arrested

Sharyn Vane

Julio Granados allowed *News and Observer* reporter Gigi Anders to come into his life – to the bodega where he worked, to the home he shared with other Mexican immigrants, to the shrine he'd built in a nearby thicket of trees. He told her all about sending money home to his family in Mexico and his lonely life in America.

On March 8, 1998, the Raleigh, North Carolina, daily published "Heart Without a Home," (see Figure 17.2) two full pages on Julio's life. And two weeks later, readers learned of the postscript: Granados, 21, and five others at the El Mandado market had been arrested by the Immigration and Naturalization Service. Agents in Charlotte had seen *The News and Observer*'s article – which mentioned Granados' undocumented status and included details about where he lived and worked – and decided to arrest him.

Continued

Part of a surge of Latino immigration to North Carolina, Julio Granados sought to help his family in Mexico. But his success has a price — a life often alone.

As a young teen, Julio Granados learned to play the guitar while attending seminary. Although he left behind the dream of being a priest, he finds playing his acoustic guitar a familiar, comforting way to pass the time.

STAFF PHOTOS BY ROBERT MILLER

Heart without a home

BY GIGI ANDERS
STAFF WRITER

RALEIGH

On this Monday, as he does on alternate weeks, Julio Granados is sending $500 to his mother, Amalia, in Mexico. It's half of what he has made in the past two weeks of 11-hour days, but it's much more than that, too. The money — and the opportunity to earn it — is what brought Granados to Raleigh almost 20 months ago, and it's what sustains him.

"It's a good feeling not to have to depend on your parents," Granados says. "Without my help, they'd have to sacrifice a lot."

Granados and his family have been apart since he left Guadalajara on foot on a soft Friday evening, late in June 1996. He kissed and embraced his parents and stepped into the night, carrying a battered duffel bag with only a change of clothes. He had his Mexican voter ID and 600 pesos in

his wallet, not even $100. But it was enough.

Walking along the road, his brown leather work boots kicking up the yellow dust, Granados looked at the slowly darkening sky, trying to memorize this twilight and what it held: the long, thin cirrus clouds that turned from pale to deepest gray, a thousand white stars that shared their scattered light with the yellow moon. Mexico is yellow, he thought, and America will be green.

Granados knows that working in America without proper papers is a risk. But he's willing to take it on.

He works six-day weeks at La Bodega El Mandado, a Hispanic supermarket in North Raleigh that is one of the busiest sites of electronic money transfers in the Triangle. It sends thousands of dollars a day by wire to mothers, fathers, wives in towns and cities throughout Mexico and Central America.

This morning, Granados already has alerted Amalia that the money is coming, using a prepaid phone card he bought at the bodega. At

See GRANADOS, PAGE 20A

Granados looks at an old family picture taken at a birthday party; he is the boy at left in the snapshot. Now 21 and living in North Carolina, he finds that recalling the good times eases his loneliness.

Figure 17.2   Heart without a home
REPRINTED BY PERMISSION OF *THE NEWS AND OBSERVER*

Incensed, the Hispanic community blamed *The News and Observer*. And some of the paper's own reporters and editors were asking whether the newspaper had weighed the ramifications of its actions before publishing the story.

In the weeks after the story ran and Granados was arrested, Anders received dozens of calls – including death threats – at home and at work. The paper published letters decrying the story as "irresponsible journalism" that "destroyed this young man's life." Anders and her editors met with the staff as well as with members of the Latino community to talk about what the paper did

and why it did it. Executive editor Anders Gyllenhaal (now editor of the *Miami Herald*) wrote a column praising the piece but acknowledging there were things editors might do differently next time.

Central to the story of Julio Granados and its aftermath is the paper's role. How much responsibility do journalists have in ensuring that their sources – particularly those who aren't media savvy – fully understand the potential consequences of a Page One story?

"Our goal here was not to do anything but try and explain this person's life," Gyllenhaal said. "We certainly didn't mean for this to happen."

Continued

News and Observer features editor Felicia Gressette had noted an increase in the numbers of immigrants working in and around the city. Gressette thought it made sense to humanize these faceless workers. "[F]or an awful lot of people, middle-class whites, it's outside of their frame of reference," she said. "We wanted to do a story that would get inside the life and world of someone who had come to the Triangle," as the cities of Raleigh, Durham, and Chapel Hill are called.

Gressette assigned the story to Anders, a Cuban-born features reporter fluent in Spanish who had profiled other Hispanics in the community. Anders knew exactly where to look: the El Mandado bodega in north Raleigh, a sort of crossroads for the area's growing Hispanic population. Over lunch, she explained to proprietress Ana Roldan what she was looking for and asked Roldan if she knew anyone who might fit that description.

"She didn't hesitate," Anders recalled. "She said, 'Julio. He's perfect. He's exceptional.'"

And he *was* exceptional, Anders would find out. Though a bit bemused as to why *The News and Observer* would be interested in him, he gamely let Anders and photographer Robert Miller join him at work at El Mandado as he unpacked crates of mangoes and stocked shelves with stacks of tortillas, at home as he strummed his acoustic guitar and hummed "Ave Maria," and in the woods behind his house as he struggled through the brambles to a makeshift altar with a statue of the Virgin of Guadalupe. A former seminary student, he was articulate and thoughtful in their Spanish-language interviews, detailing memories of Mexico made painful by their distance from his current life.

Anders knew she had the makings of a great profile. But she admitted to being worried when she asked Granados about his US work status and he told her he had no papers.

"I felt my heart sinking because I thought, 'He's going to pull out,'" Anders remembered. "But he didn't. I said, 'OK, do you understand that your name is going in this story? And your picture? Do you understand what this means?' And he asked, 'Do they read the *N&O* in Charlotte?' Charlotte is a synonym for the INS. And I said, 'Yes.'

He said, 'Might I get deported?' I said, 'You might.' And he said, 'Well, if that's what happens, then I guess it's my destiny.' That's the word he used – destiny."

Granados said he didn't remember it that way: He told another *News and Observer* reporter in April that he gave Anders permission to use his name but not his status. "My name, yes. But not the fact that I'm here without papers."

Anders responded that she had given Granados fair warning. "This is, to my mind, a full-grown person making his own decision," she said.

When Anders' story became a contender for Sunday front-page play, projects editor Rob Waters wondered aloud at a meeting exactly what Granados had been told. "I remember thinking that this would be at least an implicit invitation to the INS to come get this guy," Waters said. "I was simply raising one question, and I think I remember being told that those questions were being raised."

The story went to press.

"I think that there was some naiveté on our part about what the reaction would be," executive editor Gyllenhaal said. "Part of what happened was that a lot of people in the community are divided on the whole

Continued

question of undocumented workers, and some of them who are opposed called the INS and said, 'You look at this, you've gotta do something about this.' ... We just didn't think the thing through."

Sixteen days after the story ran, INS agents arrived mid-morning at El Mandado, loading Granados and the five others into a van for the trip to jail. Anders got a hysterical call at home from Roldan and promptly called Gressette to let her know what had happened. Word began filtering through the newsroom, and Gyllenhaal and managing editor Melanie Sill called a meeting. Fifty to 60 staffers showed up for the hour-long session.

"It was not a relaxed meeting," Anders says, describing pointed queries on how much Granados really understood about what might happen to him after the story ran. Had a trusting 21-year-old immigrant been exploited? How much had she talked with Granados about the INS? And what had she told the Roldans?

One of those who had concerns was state government editor Linda Williams. She said that when she read Anders' story that Sunday morning, she instantly thought, "Oh my God, he's going to be deported." While Anders may have talked with Granados about the potential repercussions of the profile, Williams said, she also should have talked with Roldan and her husband, Marco, about the story's implications for them.

"The people who own the store – why were they not quoted in the story about why they were hiring people illegally? How do they justify hiring him?" Williams asked.

If the newsroom was concerned, some readers were downright angry. They barraged the paper with letters, and they weren't fan letters. "Irresponsible journalism resulted in

the arrest of Julio Granados, the hard-working Mexican featured in your March 8 article," fumed Eunice Brock and Charles Tanquary. "This feature story could have been written equally forcefully without showing Granados' face or revealing his name and place of employment." Charlie Ramirez wrote, "I am sure he will enjoy being back in his homeland, courtesy of the *N&O*. Whatever happened to journalistic integrity?"

The Roldans said Anders misled them about how much detail she would include in her story. "She said, 'I will not write something like that. I will not write something to put Julio or your business in any trouble,'" Marco Roldan insisted. Anders said she made no such pronouncements to the couple.

INS agents said they received copies of the Granados article from two sources. But Charlotte-based agent Scott Sherrill said it was more than just the front-page play that triggered action. "There were some things in there that made us feel like it was important that we do this," Sherrill said. "The fact that he claims he was smuggled across the border ... It implies in there that he eluded arrest by the Border Patrol by running after he was smuggled across the border. That makes it a little more of a serious violation."

Gyllenhaal tackled the controversy in a column on March 29, "Lessons in a story gone wrong." He defended the piece as a "powerful package." But he acknowledged that the fact that the story was so detailed led INS agents to Granados at El Mandado. And he said that *The News and Observer* didn't think hard enough about the impact of such a story on "one largely powerless, fairly ordinary young Mexican."

He said the paper could have left out the name of the market, a crucial detail that

Continued

might have kept the INS from acting. However, Anders pointed out that because the story was indeed so acutely detailed, leaving out the name of the market would have made the newspaper look as if it was deliberately trying to hide Granados from the INS – something the paper wouldn't do for other lawbreakers.

Roberto Suro, author of *Strangers Among Us: How Latino Immigration is Transforming America*, said:

> One thing that makes me uncomfortable is this idea that someone who is just a straightforward illegal alien, basically for economic reasons, somehow deserves some kind of protection. How much do you get in the business of making judgments? What if you're writing about

people who use and sell drugs – you won't ID a user, but you would ID a seller? You're making a judgment that one violation of the law is somehow less serious than another.

Suro also questioned whether someone like Granados was truly ignorant of the backlash potential of such a story:

> He was certainly conversant with the law as it applies to be here illegally. To have gotten as far as he did – to go across the border all the way to North Carolina, he had to have had a fair knowledge of the law as it applies to the foreign-born and what's required to avoid getting caught. I mean, he may not have understood the U.S. tax code, but where it mattered, he knew.

Excerpted from Sharyn Vane, "Too much information?", *American Journalism Review*, June 1998.

Questions for Class Discussion

- How does this case illustrate a conflict between reporting truth and minimizing harm?
- What responsibility did *The News and Observer* owe to Julio Granados?
- What responsibility did the paper owe to the owners of the market where he worked?
- Should journalists protect their sources and story subjects even though they are violating the law?
- Is there an Aristotle's Golden Mean in this case? Would it have been practical to omit some crucial details, as the executive

editor says? Or would that have signaled to readers that the paper was trying to hide Granados from the INS, as the reporter says?
- What ideas do you have about how the paper could have reported this story without endangering Granados or appearing to go out of its way to protect him?
- In the aftermath of the arrest of Granados and the others, what did *The News and Observer* do to be accountable to its readers? To its staff?

Notes

1   This account of the Cynthia Wiggins case is constructed from Chapter 5, "The Color Line and the Bus Line," in Arlene Notoro Morgan, Alice Irene Pifer, and Keith Woods (eds.), *The Authentic Voice* (New York: Columbia University Press, 2006), 105–26. The chapter includes the transcript of the *Nightline* broadcast on May 22, 1996.

2   Eric Wray, "Reporting the Rashomon way," *The Authentic Voice*, 126.

3   Morgan, Pifer, Woods, *The Authentic Voice*, 106.

4   Commission on Freedom of the Press. *A Free and Responsible Press: A General Report on Mass Communication: Newspapers, Radio, Motion Pictures, Magazines, and Books.* (Chicago: University of Chicago Press, 1947), 26–7.

5   United States National Advisory Commission on Civil Disorders. Report of the National Advisory Commission on Civil Disorders. (Washington, DC: US Govt. Printing Office, 1968), 211–12.

6   Bob Papper, "2008 women and minorities survey," Radio-Television News Directors Association's *The Communicator*, July/August 2008.

7   "Newsrooms shrink; minority percentage increases slightly," American Society of Newspaper Editors news release, April 13, 2008.

8   US Census Bureau, "U.S. Hispanic population surpasses 45 million, now 15 percent of total," news release, May 1, 2008. The bureau gave the following estimates as of July 1, 2007: Hispanic, 45.5 million; Black, 40.7 million; Asian, 15.2 million; American Indians and Alaska Natives, 4.5 million; and Native Hawiian and Other Pacific Islander, 1 million.

9   Charles Zastrow and Karen Kirst-Ashman, *Understanding Human Behavior and the Social Environment* (Chicago: Nelson-Hall, 1987), 556.

10   Keith Woods, *The Essence of Excellence: Covering Race and Ethnicity (and Doing It Better)*, a report for the Columbia University Graduate School of Journalism, 2001, 3.

11   US Census Bureau, "An older and more diverse nation by midcentury," news release, Aug. 14, 2008; http://www.census.gov/Press-Release/www/releases/archives/population/012496.html

12   Joann Byrd, *Respecting All Cultures: A Practical Ethics Handbook for Journalists* (Washington, DC: American Society of Newspaper Editors, 2001), 7–11.

13   Aly Colon, "Making connections with diverse communities," *Quill*, July 2000, 70–1.

14   Woods, *The Essence of Excellence*, 4.

15   Ibid.

16   Robert J. Haiman, *Best Practices for Newspaper Journalists* (Arlington, VA: The Freedom Forum's Free Press/Fair Press Project, 2000), 43–4.

17   Ibid.

18   Av Westin, *Best Practices for Television Journalists* (Arlington, VA: The Freedom Forum's Free Press/Fair Press Project, 2000), 23–4.

19   Gabriel Escobar, "The making of 'The Other Pro Soccer,'" in Morgan, Pifer, Woods, eds., *The Authentic Voice*, 326.

20   Ibid., 328.

21   Ibid., 328–9.

22   US Census Bureau "U.S. Hispanic population surpasses 45 million, now 15 percent of total," news release, May 1, 2008.

23   Pew Hispanic Center, "2007 national survey of Latinos: As illegal immigration issue heats up, Hispanics feel a chill," Dec. 19, 2007.

24   Lucy Hood, "Naming names," *American Journalism Review*, April/May 2006.

25   Sonia Nazario, "Ethical dilemmas in telling Enrique's story," *Nieman Reports*, Fall 2006, 27–9.

26   Hood, "Naming names."

27   Ibid.

28   Keith Woods, "Guidelines for racial identification," http://www.poynter.org/content/content_view.asp?id=4343, Feb. 25, 2000.

29   Jay Fitzgerald, "Paper's edict draws dissent," *Boston Herald*, July 15, 2005.

30   Haiman, *Best Practices for Newspaper Journalists*, 44.

31   Yanick Rice Lamb, "Take time to examine your sources," *Quill*, October/November 2002, 38.

32   Woods, *The Essence of Excellence*, 7.

33   Shaila K. Dewan and Sherri Day, "Police wonder if cabby erred before a killing," *The New York Times*, May 14, 2004.

34 Cynthia Tucker, "Our opinion: Media blackout for this bride," *The Atlanta Journal-Constitution*, May 8, 2005.

35 The Associated Press caption: "A young man walks through chest deep flood water after looting a grocery store in New Orleans on Tuesday, Aug. 30, 2005."

36 The AFP/Getty Images caption: "Two residents wade through chest-deep water after finding bread and soda from a local grocery store."

37 Shannon Kahle, Nan Yu, and Erin Whiteside, "Another disaster: An examination of portrayals of race in Hurricane Katrina coverage," *Visual Communications Quarterly*, vol. 14, Spring 2007, 86.

38 Keith Woods, "The meaning of unity," http://www.poynter.org/content/content_view.asp?id=69836, Aug. 11, 2004.

39 UNITY: Journalists of Color, Inc., "UNITY's history," http://www.unityjournalists.org/mission/history.php

40 Donna St. George, "Army officer remembered as hero," *The Washington Post*, March 22, 2008.

41 Deborah Howell, "Public death, private life," *The Washington Post*, March 30, 2008.

42 Ibid.

43 Ibid.

44 Robert Dodge, "Gays and lesbians on September 11," http://www.diversitywatch.ryerson.ca/media/archive01/02.htm.

45 Bao Ong, "Is sexuality part of the story?" http://nlgja.org/resources/toolbox_outing.html.

46 National Lesbian and Gay Journalists Association, "NLGJA's stylebook supplement on LGBT terminology," http://nlgja.org/resources/stylebook.html

Ethics Issues Specific to Web Journalism

Online, there are huge opportunities – and pitfalls

The lives of nearly 200 people were "suddenly and irrevocably linked" – the words are those of the *Star Tribune*'s website – when the Interstate 35-W bridge in Minneapolis collapsed into the Mississippi River during the evening rush hour on August 1, 2007. Thirteen people were killed and 144 injured.

"They were stuck in Minneapolis traffic on their way home from work," *startribune.com* wrote.

> They were bound for the Metrodome to see the Twins play the Royals. They were going to spend time with in-laws, work out, pick up a child from the sitter, teach a folk dancing class, eat at an African restaurant, deliver a truckload of bread to Iowa. Alongside the cars were workers in hard hats, laying down a new surface of concrete on a nondescript 40-year-old highway bridge.

In the days and weeks that followed, *startribune.com* told the stories of those people through the techniques long practiced in the print and broadcast media, while also exploiting the Internet's unique powers of interactivity, nearly endless capacity, and on-demand availability.

"13 Seconds in August" opens with ambient sound from the scene and one of the early 911 calls while website visitors see stunning photography of the disaster. Then an aerial photograph of the collapsed bridge appears. Each vehicle in the photo is labeled with a number. Other numbers are placed over the water or in the bridge's rubble. The numbers represent the people who were on the bridge when it fell. By clicking on the numbers, website visitors can learn their identities and their stories. Some of the survivors tell their stories in video interviews.[1]

"Click by click, you read, hear and see the individuals themselves, in their own voices, tell the story of what happened to them," *Star Tribune* editor Nancy Barnes wrote in the newspaper in December 2007. "Collectively, these stories, told in multiple media, present a powerful human documentary …"[2]

Many viewers of this "living document" were continuing to contribute their stories. Invited by *startribune.com* to "help us fill in the missing pieces," these online users had identified the drivers and occupants of 78 of the 84 cars, trucks and other vehicles in the aerial photo.[3]

A year after the bridge collapse, the project's lead designer, Dave Braunger, told Sara Quinn of *poynteronline* that the site gives users "a sense of community that … developed among complete strangers." Some users spend as much as two hours on a visit. "The most gratifying feedback has been from the survivors themselves," Braunger said. "It's been somewhat of a cathartic process for them … A lot of them say it's been really hard for them to hear these stories, but it made them feel less alone. They felt like there were others who could understand what they'd gone through."[4]

The impressive work of the Minneapolis staff is just one of a growing list of journalistic feats that illustrate the Internet's ability to transform the way the news is reported – through text, audio, still photography, video, and a two-way conversation with the audience.

Remember that this kind of innovation in storytelling is being carried out by people who for the most part got into journalism to report the news in newspapers and on television or radio. This transition generation has moved beyond the mindset of simply converting print stories and broadcast scripts into an electronic form. Imagine what can be done by a generation that grew up with the Internet – such as the college students who are reading this text.

The journalism of the future, former newspaper editor John Carroll told a group of journalism students in 2008, "will have tools unlike any imagined by earlier generations. You will have tools for finding things out, and tools to send your stories to the entire world at the speed of light."[5]

Ethics Standards Apply to News on All Platforms

In the history of journalism, going back four centuries or so,[6] the Internet era is a blink of the eye. As recently as the early 1990s, most people didn't know the web existed. Until the first graphic web browser was released in 1993, computer users had to enter complicated text commands to move from one site to another. Not many people were interested.[7]

Once the browser changed how people went online, the Internet took hold in everyday life. To get an idea of how fast that happened, consider the statistics compiled by the UCLA Center for Communication Policy on how long it took to equip 30 percent of American homes with modern technology. For electricity, reaching this benchmark required 46 years; for telephones, 38 years; for television, 17 years. It took the Internet only 7 years.[8]

A milestone event for the Internet as a news medium was independent counsel Kenneth Starr's report on President Bill Clinton's affair with Monica Lewinsky, made public by the House of Representatives on September 11, 1998. Millions of users accessed the report on the web – "unfiltered by the news media," as J. D. Lasica pointed out. As late as 1995, Lasica wrote, "such a document could have been conveyed to the public only by journalists. Now it was instantly available to anyone with an internet connection to read, dissect, forward to others, debate in an online forum, or print out and share with friends and neighbors." Online columnist Jon Katz told Lasica, "People reached their own conclusions about the document fairly quickly, without the Washington press corps, the pundits, and the Beltway politicians telling us what to think."[9]

As the web became popular, the old media took notice. Although they didn't know whether a website could turn a profit, newspaper and broadcast executives sensed that if they didn't stake out an online news presence, other entrepreneurs would. The old media had a decisive advantage in this race: They already had the journalists to provide the content, while competitors would have to assemble comparable staffs from scratch.

Twenty newspaper websites were operating as 1994 began, increasing to about 100 by the end of the year and to 300 by mid-1995.[10] As the twenty-first century began, more than 4,500 newspapers and 1,400 television stations around the world had websites.[11]

In the adolescent era of online journalism, its practitioners are not just exploring its potential for reporting the news. They also are grappling with how the time-honored principles of journalism apply to the special challenges of the new medium.

One of the pioneer online journalists of the 1990s was Fred Mann, who led *philly.com*, the website of *The Philadelphia Inquirer* and *Philadelphia Daily News*, through its first 11 years. In a paper written in 1998 for *poynteronline*, Mann underscored the importance of staying true to the principles of the profession:

> If journalistic organizations are to become serious players online, then the journalistic core values they hold dear are going to have to move onto the web with them. To allow a diminution of the values online such as accuracy, credibility, balance, accessibility, news judgment, and leadership would be to risk undermining the good name – and the economic value – of the mother ship.[12]

Online expert Dan Gillmor writes in his 2004 book, *We the Media*, that journalism's ethics apply to all publishing platforms: "No matter which tools and technologies we embrace, we must maintain core principles, including fairness, accuracy, and thoroughness. These are not afterthoughts. They are essential if professional journalism expects to survive."[13]

Ethical challenges abound in the new medium. Some of these are intrinsic to the nature of online journalism, such as the propriety of linking their users to other sites containing graphic images or hateful text. Some are old problems that take on added significance on the deadline-a-minute web, such as balancing the need for speed with the duty to verify facts. Some result from skimpy staffing that allows content, both news accounts and reader comments, to be flagged onto the web without editorial oversight. And some of these challenges exist because the news websites too eagerly adopt questionable practices found elsewhere on the web – for example, allowing reporter blogs to stray from fact into opinion.

This chapter discusses five of those ethical issues: keeping the facts straight; blogging by journalists; monitoring user comments; deciding when to link; and dealing with requests to alter the online archives.

Keeping the Facts Straight in a Medium Built on Speed

In a fiercely competitive medium that posts news accounts instantly, there is a danger that the verification process will be neglected in the rush to be first. This problem is compounded by tight budgets. Most news websites have small staffs that are unable to give the news the kind of scrutiny traditional in print. For one thing, most online sites do not have copy desks as newspapers do.

In addition, traditional journalists may be tempted to rely on what citizen bloggers call the self-correcting nature of the web: Put your first draft out there and let the audience correct it. Bob Steele of the Poynter Institute scorns this approach as "morally bankrupt," noting that the initial posting, even if corrected later, could cause serious harm.[14] Because search engines like Google and Yahoo! crawl the web and archive content, original versions of stories may stay online even if they have been corrected later.

The issue of speed-versus-verification did not begin with online news, of course. Wire-service reporters have always worked on the assumption that every minute of the day or night, a client newspaper is going to press somewhere. In the heyday of afternoon newspapers, an era that ended in the 1960s, reporters battled the clock as multiple editions were printed during the late morning and early afternoon while the news was being made. Contemporary radio and television journalists do the same when they report live.

Robert H. Giles, curator of the Nieman Foundation's midcareer journalist fellowships at Harvard University, is concerned about the combination of speed and small staffs in many online operations. "As we cut corners," he said, "we haven't built into online the capacity to edit. We are going to regret it, as mistakes are made."[15]

Joann Byrd, former ombudsman of *The Washington Post*, also is troubled about online editing.

> Good journalism is defined by the assumption that we have verified the facts to the best degree humanly possible. We cannot let loose of the verification process and our obligation to keep people informed. ... I'd rather wait a half-hour and put out something that readers can trust.[16]

Kinsey Wilson, former executive editor of *USA Today* and director of its website, said candidly that online journalism requires reporters who can function without the backstopping of layers of editors.

> In the traditional newspaper model, there are checkpoints along the way to publication of the story. Online, you have to rely on the individual to take more care. You need people with high degrees of judgment, maturity, and training. People who know when they can safely work solo and who know when they need another set of eyes on a story or a blog post.

Wilson offered an example of how speed comes into play. In *USA Today*'s print newsroom, as many as a half-dozen photo editors go through a deliberative process of selecting and cropping photos. "For online," Wilson said,

> the selection is made much more quickly; there's less expertise involved and less editing. This gives rise to the criticism that online does not place the same value on quality. However, our ultimate goal is to have credibility with our readers, and one component of credibility is speed. If we are always late, our readers will have moved on. I don't say that speed trumps those other values, but it is one piece of the puzzle of credibility.[17]

David Zeeck, executive editor of *The News Tribune* in Tacoma, Washington, compared posting news online to doing a live broadcast. "You correct as you go. It would be great to have the same level of verification as the print newspaper does, but you have to get the news out there. You don't have eight hours to do three levels of editing and have conversations about news stories. Your job is to get it online. It's about immediacy."[18]

At *The Oregonian*'s website, Michael Arrieta-Walden said,

> accuracy is still the primary value. That requires us not to publish some things, and we may publish other stories that are incomplete. It is an ongoing struggle. A key factor is fairness. If a person is accused and does not respond immediately, we have until the end of the day to do the story in print. We can go online immediately, but we have to consider whether we should reach the accused person for comment.

We need to weigh the possible harm that can be done if we post the story immediately.

Arrieta-Walden said *The Oregonian* schedules editors, including copy editors, in the early morning whose duties include reviewing online copy, but that review may take place after the copy has been posted on the web.[19]

Copy editors, of course, do more than check facts; they also correct reporters' grammar and punctuation. In focus groups and surveys, such as those conducted by the American Society of Newspaper Editors in 1999,[20] readers have said language errors undermine their trust in the news they are reading. If news stories are posted on the web without a review by a copy editor, they may well contain language errors even if factually accurate.

John McIntyre, former assistant managing editor of *The Sun* in Baltimore, discussed editing for the Internet in his blog on February 20, 2008: "[T]he conventions of electronic publication are in flux. Decisions are being made by people who do not grasp how the work is done and how it ought to be done. Time is running short, and a good deal of damage has already been done." McIntyre does not think it is necessary to transfer the newspaper editing model, with multiple layers of editors, to the web. He wrote:

> I assigned a single copy editor to work with the assigning desks on daytime copy for *baltimoresun.com*. This editor catches errors and clarifies cloudy passages quite adequately, and the web offers the opportunity for continual updating and further correction. We need the additional strength for the print edition, because once those papers are on the trucks, they are beyond remedy.[21]

Ethics Issues in Blogging by Journalists

Blogging as part of the job

To connect with the audience, news sites have sought to duplicate the popularity of free-wheeling citizen blogs. Those sites have encouraged their staff members to write blogs, and many journalist blogs have attracted loyal followings.

"More and more journalists are realizing that blogging can help them increase their transparency — and their credibility — with their audience," Bob Steele and Bill Mitchell of the Poynter Institute wrote in 2005. "They're opening their eyes to a fact of life that Dan Gillmor has taken up as something of a creed: the readers (at least some of them) know more about a story than its author does."[22]

Keven Ann Willey, editorial page editor of *The Dallas Morning News*, launched the nation's first editorial-page blog in 2003. She says blogging increases readership and provides a window into the editorial board's thinking. Her advice to bloggers: "Be brief and informal. Breezy, conversational tone is good. ... Go for the quick hit, light touch, witty aside. Attitude required. ... Don't write anything you wouldn't want your mother to read in the paper."[23]

Another of the early journalist bloggers, *Chicago Tribune* columnist Eric Zorn, considers blogging to be the purest form of journalism. He told *American Journalism Review* in 2003 that he carries his notebook everywhere so he can share his thoughts instantly in his "Change of Subject" blog for *chicagotribune.com*. "You start thinking about life in this whole new way," Zorn said. "Your brain is turned on all the time."[24]

As a columnist, Zorn also expresses opinions in the print *Tribune*. Other journalist bloggers, however, are expected to write from a neutral point of view for their newspapers or to report neutrally in broadcasts. Aiming for a gossipy tone in their blogs, some of these journalists have been known to express opinions about the people and events they cover. This issue is explored in Case Study No. 21: "For a Reporter/Blogger, Two Personalities."

The Washington Post says in its web principles that "reporters and editors should not express personal opinions unless they would be allowed in the newspaper, such as in criticism or columns."[25]

Editing – how much of it, and when it occurs – is another issue as print and broadcast journalists move to the web. Consider this paradox in how the same organization treats print and online copy: When a newspaper reporter writes a just-the-facts news story for the print edition, the copy may be reviewed by three or more editors checking factual accuracy, quality of prose, spelling and grammatical correctness, and inadvertent expressions of bias. When the same reporter writes a blog in which risk-taking commentary is encouraged, the reporter quite likely posts it directly to the Internet with no editor intervention.

To Bob Giles of the Nieman Foundation, putting blogs on the web without editing poses a threat to credibility. If the reporters reveal their biases in the blogs, the audience may perceive bias in the supposedly neutral news stories that appear in the print edition. "Blogs can be very effective, giving behind-scenes information and more information, but they have to be kept in bounds," Giles said. "There has to be a review process. There has to be accountability."[26]

These are the reasons that editors most frequently give for posting blogs first and editing later: Editing detracts from the spontaneity of the blog (editors would "beat the life out of them," one blogger said); writers are encouraged to blog at all times of day and night, and editors are not always available; there is a bottleneck as blogs await editing; and bloggers know the guidelines and can be trusted to follow them.

At *The Oregonian*, Michael Arrieta-Walden said bloggers are expected to notify a designated editor when they have posted, so that the blog can be checked.

On some occasions, blogs have been offensive. ... We are always reminding bloggers that we want them to be conversational, but it is still up to the paper to establish boundaries, and we don't compromise on them. If a blogger repeatedly violated the guidelines, the editors would respond.[27]

The *South Florida Sun Sentinel* appointed a blogs editor to oversee the paper's 40 staff blogs. Howard Goodman, who got the assignment, edits some blogs line by line before they are posted, mostly "high-profile work where errors would be costly." In a concession to speed, other blogs are posted first and reviewed soon afterward.

"There's too much competition from 24-hour news sources to avoid taking some of the risks that blogging requires," Goodman said.

> We are no longer competing only with that other paper that comes out the next morning, not even with that TV station and its 11 p.m. broadcast. We're in a climate of 24-hour TV news and constantly updating websites. The business pressure for immediacy is quite intense.

Goodman said and other *Sun Sentinel* editors wrestle every day with questions about balancing the business pressure for speed and the journalistic need for editorial review. "This version of media is so new, so untested, that we're forced to navigate without the benefit of a completed map. We're relying on our instincts and experience to guide us, knowing full well we might hit the rocks."

He said the assistant city editors were becoming more engaged in editing online content, a recognition of the growing importance of the paper's website.

For the blogs that go into cyberspace as soon as their writers have finished them, Goodman back-reads them, using his BlackBerry if he is not at his computer. "One of the beauties of blogs is that you can change them after publication if you see a misspelling or a badly worded sentence or add important information if it's missing." He said a blog can be taken down if it proves to be seriously flawed, though he worries that a copy of it could linger somewhere on the Internet.[28]

Blogging by the news organization

As discussed in Chapter 7, blogs can help a news organization be accountable to the audience by allowing journalists to explain their decisions, answer questions from the audience, and solicit tips for future news coverage.

The blog form also can be effective in covering breaking news, as *The Roanoke Times* demonstrated in the Virginia Tech massacre on April 16, 2007. Rather than taking the time to put their information into the format of news stories, *Times* reporters filed bulletin after bulletin. The time-stamped items were posted on roanoke.com with the most recent always at the top. In a paper prepared for the Associated Press Managing Editors in October 2007, *Times* reporter Mike Gangloff gave these tips for a breaking-news blog: "Don't be afraid to flood the site with info. That's what the readers are coming for. ... [G]ive a snapshot of how our community is being affected. ... Work in vignettes from around the community that show how people are responding."[29]

Blogging as a hobby

There is another genre of journalist blogs: those written for the journalist's pleasure. Such a hobby can cause problems for the news organizations that employ the journalists, either on grounds of perceived bias or on grounds of competition.

The Dallas Morning News allows its staff members to create their own blogs or participate in online forums, but insists on these caveats:

> Staff members ... must remember at all times that they are participating in a public activity. All the rules that apply to any public activity apply here. Staffers are responsible for reflecting well on the organization, for avoiding situations that would raise questions about credibility or fairness, and to honor our standard policies in matters such as libel, privacy, political involvement, and conflicts of interest.[30]

When he was editor-in-chief of *The Washington Times*, Wesley Pruden required that topics discussed in the private blogs be different from those the staff members cover for the paper. He also cautioned about bias: "Employees ... should recognize that even though their comments may seem to be in their 'private space,' their words are a direct extension of the newspaper. This is because search engines, and particularly other blogs, can locate their posts."[31]

Occasionally, personal blogs have created controversy.

Steve Olafson, a reporter for the *Houston Chronicle*, was fired in 2002 because a blog he wrote under the pseudonym Banjo Jones expressed opinions about the people and events he covered.[32] After leaving the paper, Olafson continued his blog and, in an ironic twist, the *Chronicle* website decided in 2006 to post a link to his blog.[33]

Daniel P. Finney resigned from his reporting job with the *St. Louis Post-Dispatch* in 2004 after his bosses discovered that, under the pseudonym Roland H. Thompson, he occasionally wrote about his paper and about the topics of his *Post-Dispatch* stories before they appeared in the paper.[34] Reflecting on the incident four years later, Finney expressed regret about a "self-indulgent, silly blog" and said he had rebuilt his career. After freelancing and working in public relations for 18 months, Finney returned to journalism first as a weekly newspaper editor and later as a reporter and editor for the *Des Moines Register*. He said he has had a personal blog on his MySpace page since 2005 "without incident."[35]

After his column at the *Hartford Courant* was ended and he was reassigned as travel editor in 2003, Denis Horgan started a personal blog. Editor Brian Toolan saw a conflict of interest and ordered him to stop blogging. This set off a firestorm of protests on the Internet, leading Toolan to explain his action in a *Nieman Reports* article. Toolan's reasoning was that the public identified Horgan with the *Courant*, and therefore it was inappropriate when the ex-columnist "created a new journalistic platform for himself and began opining on issues, institutions and public officials that reporters and columnists at the paper must cover."[36] For his part,

Horgan argued that Toolan had infringed on his freedom of speech. "[T]he soldiers and police can't come into my house to tell me what to think and what to write on my own time but my editor can."[37]

While Bobby Caina Calvan was reporting for *The Sacramento Bee* and its parent McClatchy Newspapers from Iraq in 2007, he quarreled with an American soldier who questioned his identification at a Baghdad checkpoint. Calvan expressed his frustration about the incident – "in a snarky, arrogant way," as *The Bee*'s public editor characterized it – in a personal blog he was using to stay in touch with his family and friends. The blog wasn't private, of course; almost nothing on the Internet is. For his complaint about a soldier, Calvan and his employer were bombarded with hate email, and one blogger nominated the reporter for a "Jerk of the Year" award. His editors in McClatchy's Washington bureau, who hadn't known about his blog, promptly announced a new rule: "No personal blogs allowed."[38]

The Benefits of Interactivity – and the Pitfalls

Before the Internet, "Big Media" treated the news as a lecture, Dan Gillmor writes in *We the Media*. Now, what Gillmor calls "the former audience" can talk back, and the news has become a conversation.[39]

Eagerly embracing the idea of a conversation, news sites are inviting user comments. They want to take advantage of the web's interactivity to create a lively forum on current events, and they want to fulfill the expectations of site visitors who are accustomed to having their say on the web.

Jim Brady, former executive editor of *washingtonpost.com*, said it is "absolutely essential" to engage readers interactively. "It builds immense loyalty with readers, it allows communities to form around common interests, it makes readers feel like they're participating and not watching from the outside."[40]

Unfortunately, allowing reader comments makes news websites vulnerable to mean-spirited, profane, and uninformed postings like these:

- On the website of *The Indianapolis Star*, some users posted comments ridiculing an Army reservist from Indianapolis who had been killed in Iraq.[41]
- On the website of *The Orange County* (California) *Register*, the target was an obese woman who gave birth to a son she had not known she was carrying until two days before his arrival. The comments contained made-up "facts" about her: that her house was a mess because she was too lazy and fat to clean it, that she ate Krispy Kremes all day, and that the state was trying to take her baby away because she was an unfit mother.[42]
- On the website of *The Cincinnati Enquirer*, some users responded to a story about a woman killed by a drunken driver in a bar parking lot by demanding to know why she was out at 2 a.m. on a school night.[43]

"We haven't yet figured out how to filter conversation," said Kinsey Wilson, the former *USA Today* web chief.[44] "We're struggling to get a handle on this," said Geneva Overholser, director of the School of Journalism at the University of Southern California's Annenberg School for Communication.[45] "There's still a great need for filtering out the noise," said Ken Sands, *Congressional Quarterly*'s executive editor for innovation.[46]

Consider the difference in how reader commentary typically is handled in newspapers and online.

Before publishing a letter to the editor, the newspaper verifies that the letter actually was written by the person whose signature appears on it. Letters then are edited, and the writer is not permitted to use coarse language, make personal attacks, or misstate facts.

On the web, in contrast, many sites allow fictitious "screen names." Electronic filters block vulgarities but not personal attacks and factual misstatements. Few sites screen comments before they are posted; on most sites, it is up to users to flag questionable comments. Only then are they reviewed and, if found to be offensive, taken down. *The Orange County Register*'s website puts a "remove comment" button next to every user comment, and if two users click on it, the comment comes down automatically. (Until the case of the obese mother, three clicks were required to remove a comment.)[47]

David Zeeck of *The News Tribune* in Tacoma is not troubled that the standards for online comments are looser than those for letters to the editor. "Online, expectations are different. The conversation is more casual. The discussion is at a very different level." He offered this analogy: "At a town meeting, people meet together to decide issues, and there are clear rules of order. Later, when the same people gather at the local tavern, the discussion is more spirited and free-wheeling. That's what we are seeing in the online postings: a more robust exchange." The two kinds of conversations are depicted by Pulitzer Prize-winning cartoonist Tony Auth in Figure 18.1.

Like most news sites, Zeeck's *News Tribune* asks readers to flag inappropriate language, defamation, and inaccuracy. "Then we read it and may take it down. If someone is repeatedly abusive, we will delete the user's account."[48]

In Point of View: "It's the Ideas, Not the Names, That Count," editor Carole Tarrant of *The Roanoke Times* defends the practice of allowing people to post comments using screen names.

Kinsey Wilson said *USA Today* is seeking to connect readers with other readers whose insights can expand an understanding of the news.

For example, we've found that on health reporting, people are willing to share personal experiences that inform and resonate with other readers. That said, this is an area that's still messy. There are the predictable rants about politics, tirades on race. ... We can't pre-screen our more than 10,000 comments posted each day, but we act on the basis of complaints. We ban repeat offenders. They might try to get on with a different identity, which is possible, but people tend to go away when they have trouble getting on. We've tried to deal with this with vigilance, clear standards, and good technology.[49]

Figure 18.1   Two kinds of conversation
CARTOON COURTESY OF TONY AUTH

When *The New York Times* opened its website to reader comments about news coverage and editorials in late 2007, it hired a staff of editors to screen the comments before they went online. This was a substantial investment that most websites say they cannot afford. *The Times* wanted to avoid a lack of civility while engaging in a conversation with the readers.

It should come as no surprise that some readers objected to *The Times'* efforts to curb racism, name-calling, and other examples of rudeness. One objected to censoring of speech, "however derogatory, mean-spirited, or offending it is. We need an open dialogue." Another wrote, "Mandating tepid civility in blog comments has an ideological component. 'Politeness' bars sharply worded disagreement by dissenters against those who claim to be authority, but [doesn't] usually bar dismissive or patronizing arguments by authorities against the dissenters."[50]

In 2005, the *Los Angeles Times* experimented – for one day, as it turned out – with the idea of a "wikitorial," in which online readers were invited to rewrite the paper's editorial on the subject of the Iraq war. Instantly the site was flooded with vulgar messages. *The Times* announced that it was suspending the feature and expressed "thanks and apologies to the thousands of people who logged on in the right spirit."[51]

Deciding When to Link to Questionable Sites

One of online journalism's unique advantages is the ability to provide hyperlinks directing readers to pertinent material elsewhere on the web.

Linking contributes to transparent journalism by giving readers a chance to see source documents for themselves. Ken Sands of *Congressional Quarterly* urges journalists to inform readers what they know and how they know it. "They should publish transcripts of interviews. Audio clips are even better. You avoid accusations of 'taking something out of context' if you provide the raw information."[52]

Providing background information – for the old media, always a problem of broadcast time or newspaper space – is as easy as providing links to earlier stories. In his 2008 speech to journalism students, former editor John Carroll said: "[Y]ou can write accordion-like stories that can be expanded to match each reader's degree of interest. One person might give your story ten seconds; another might spend a rewarding half day with it."[53]

The ethical issue for online journalists is whether to link to graphic, hate-mongering, or otherwise offensive content. The concern is that the link will be interpreted as an endorsement. But search engines will enable users to find the site anyway, and these users may think the news site is being coy if it omits the link.

Here is a hypothetical example from the authors of the 2007 book *Advancing the Story*:

> Let's say you're doing a story on the increase in hate crimes in your community. One of the people included in your story is a member of the Creativity Movement, which believes Caucasians are meant to rule the world. Do you link to the organization's Web page to offer people more information about it? If so, do you need to link to a site that condemns such groups?

The best solution, these authors write, "is to make sure that you clearly identify each link for users to make sure they know where they are going when they click on it. At that point, the user can make an informed choice."[54]

"Today, more and more users are intensely familiar with the web and don't see a link as an endorsement," said Michael Arrieta-Walden of *The Oregonian*.[55]

Kinsey Wilson said *USA Today*'s site sometimes decides not to link to a story that its editors and reporters are skeptical about. One such example was a news account in the 2004 campaign – which proved to be false – that Democratic candidate John Kerry supposedly had been involved in an affair with an intern. "It could do harm, and our reporters were telling us that they doubted the report," Wilson said.[56]

The *Los Angeles Times* has a policy against linking to "external websites that include nudity, excessive obscenity, or other objectionable content."[57]

News sites have generally avoided linking to unspeakable violence, such as videos of terrorists beheading their hostages. In a paper for *poynteronline*, web expert Steve Outing wrote that by omitting such links, the news sites are "expressing their publishing standards" even though their users can find the videos quickly.

Outing wrote: "News organizations ... no longer are effective gatekeepers, shielding their audiences from material deemed too sensitive, controversial, or disgusting. All they can do on the internet – using whatever ethical guidelines they choose – is to regulate their own small slice of cyberspace."[58]

Maintaining Integrity (and Fairness) in the Archives

Before journalism went on the Internet, yesterday's newspaper and broadcast newscasts were quickly forgotten. In the digital age, nothing is forgotten. That infinite memory presents a problem for some people who once were in the news or who wrote comments for the news media that they now regret.

Clark Hoyt, public editor of *The New York Times*, wrote in 2008 that people were contacting his paper at the rate of about one a day to ask that the digital archives be erased or changed. They say "they are being embarrassed, are worried about losing or not getting jobs, or may be losing customers because of the sudden prominence of old news articles that contain errors or were never followed up."

The problem is exacerbated by a business decision of *The Times*, Hoyt wrote. To drive users to the paper's website, a program called search-engine optimization causes *Times* content, even when incorrect or incomplete, to appear at or near the top whenever a web user conducts a search.

If they had to re-report every story that is challenged as incorrect, *Times* editors told Hoyt, there would be no time to report that day's news.

Bob Steele of the Poynter Institute told Hoyt that he would be cautious about removing or altering content from the archive. "The public would have every reason to say: 'What else is missing? What else is altered?'"

Viktor Mayer-Schönberger, an associate professor of public policy at Harvard's John F. Kennedy School of Government, had a different answer for Hoyt: Newspapers should program their archives to "forget" some information, allowing low-profile content like news briefs to vanish from public access after a certain period. Significant stories could be kept longer, even indefinitely. The professor said computers should be like humans, who remember the important and forget the trivial.

Although a perfect solution is elusive, *The Times* has decided as a first step to correct errors when a person can offer proof. This solved the problem raised by a woman who worried that prospective employers would think she was guilty of resumé inflation because her *Times* wedding announcement, published 20 years earlier, incorrectly listed the university where she got her degree.[59]

The Daily Collegian, the independent student newspaper at Pennsylvania State University, was asked about three times a week in 2007–08 to remove or alter content in its archives. Devon Lash, editor in chief of *The Collegian*, wrote a policy declaring: "Our online archives act as a history of the events at Penn State and the surrounding community, and removing any content would go against our mission to inform and practice ethical journalism."

Lash's solution was similar to the one reached by editors at *The Times*. She wrote that content could be corrected or amended – and the original item flagged to indicate the alteration – if the person making the complaint submitted proof of an error.

The policy worked in favor of a man who had been charged with possession of child pornography while a Penn State student. He persuaded *The Collegian* to note in its archives that his record as a first-offender was expunged after he completed an accelerated rehabilitation program.

But *The Collegian* refused the request of one of its former staff members to delete certain opinions he expressed in his *Collegian* columns. He said he had changed his mind about those issues, and the years-old opinions were now embarrassing him in his job with the State Department.[60]

Journalists and the Citizen Bloggers

Journalists share cyberspace with the blogosphere, as the realm of citizen bloggers is called. To put it mildly, their relationship often has been contentious. But each of the two groups unquestionably has a strong influence on the other, and they share a need for gaining the trust of the audience.

In *The Weblog Handbook*, Rebecca Blood calls weblogs "the mavericks of the online world." From a "position outside the mainstream of mass media," she writes, blogs have an ability to "filter and disseminate information to a widely dispersed audience."

Alex S. Jones, a Pulitzer Prize-winning reporter who now is director of the Joan Shorenstein Center on the Press, Politics and Public Policy at Harvard University, sizes up the blogosphere:

> Bloggers, with few exceptions, don't add reporting to the personal views they post online, and they see journalism as bound by norms and standards that they reject. That encourages those common attributes of the blogosphere: vulgarity, scorching insults, bitter denunciations, one-sided arguments, erroneous assertions and the array of qualities that might be expected from a blustering know-it-all in a bar.[61]

There was a defining moment in 2004 in which the worlds of journalists and bloggers converged. It was at a "bloggers' breakfast" that the Democratic National Convention gave for bloggers who had received credentials to cover the proceedings. Bill Mitchell and Bob Steele of the Poynter Institute described it:

> As much as some of the bloggers *looked* sufficiently scruffy and sleep-deprived to pass as reporters, they *acted* quite differently. It wasn't so much their applause for Barack Obama and Howard Dean that set the bloggers apart from the no-hands-clapping journalists lurking in the back of the room. It was the style and tone of the bloggers' questions: more conversational, less prepared, less *polished* than what you'd expect from journalists.

Except for two quite pointed questions that blogger David Weinberger put to retired AP correspondent Walter Mears [whom AP had called out of retirement to blog from the convention]. Their exchange crystallized, for just a few moments, two of the worlds on display in the room. ...

Weinberger: "So, who are you supporting for president?"

Mears shook his head and refused to say. "How could you trust what I write?"

Weinberger followed up: "Then how can we trust what you write in your blog?" Later that evening, Weinberger described Mears' response in a post to a blog he was keeping for *The Boston Globe*: "Mears gave an articulate defense of the canon of journalistic professionalism, and the craft and value of objectivity."

"Of course I respect that," Weinberger added. "How can you not? We need professional journalists. But for most blogs, we want to know what the writer's starting point is. That's not because we're subjective journalists. It's because a blog is a conversation among friends, and when you're arguing politics with your pals, it'd just be weird to refuse to say where you stand.[62]

Mitchell and Steele observe that most journalists would resist revealing their political preferences in public, as Mears did. "Traditionally in journalism, credibility means a story rings true. It's accurate. It's in context. The reporting and presentation are fair. In the blogosphere, credibility may borrow from those values but is likely also shaped by what the individual blogger – or group of bloggers – stands for."[63]

Although journalists are not a monolithic group, they have reached a consensus on most of the ethical issues discussed in this text. As journalists confront ethical issues, Mitchell and Steele write, it is "a matter of measuring up to existing, generally accepted standards. For bloggers who have not yet addressed the issue, it's first a matter of figuring out what their standards might be – and then measuring up."[64]

Several blogging experts have urged citizen bloggers to accept voluntary standards. "The weblog's greatest strength – its uncensored, unmediated, uncontrolled voice – is also its greatest weakness," Rebecca Blood writes in *The Weblog Handbook*.[65] Like other leaders in the blogosphere, she emphasizes transparency. "It is unrealistic to expect every weblogger to present an even-handed picture of the world, but it is very reasonable to expect them to be forthcoming about their sources, biases, and behavior."[66]

Blood advocates six standards:

1 Publish as fact only what you believe to be true. ("If your statement is speculation, say so.")
2 If material exists online, link to it when you reference it.
3 Publicly correct any misinformation.
4 Write each entry as if it could not be changed; add to, but do not rewrite or delete, any entry. ("Changing or deleting entries destroys the integrity of the network.")
5 Disclose any conflict of interest.
6 Note questionable and biased sources.[67]

The philosophical differences between traditional journalism and the blogosphere are illustrated in Blood's first and fifth standards. The standards of the profession demand that a journalist report as fact only what he or she *knows* to be true, not *believes* to be true. These standards also require that a journalist *avoid* a conflict of interest, not merely *disclose* it, unless the conflict is unavoidable or insignificant.

Bloggers take delight in catching mistakes in the "MSM" or mainstream media. Kelly McBride of the Poynter Institute calls bloggers "the watchdog guarding the watchdog." Bloggers, she writes, "question and criticize the professional media, who question and criticize the powerful."[68] The bloggers themselves are less delicate, informing the MSM: "We can fact-check your ass."[69]

As noted in Chapter 12, fact-checking bloggers pounced on CBS's "60 Minutes Wednesday" program of September 8, 2004. Dan Rather cited four memos, purportedly written by George W. Bush's commanding officer, as evidence that the future president received preferential treatment while a Vietnam-era pilot in the Texas Air National Guard. Bloggers said the memos were forged. CBS ultimately conceded that it could not prove they were authentic.[70]

Bloggers also have discovered news that the traditional media have overlooked. A prime example is the birthday party on December 5, 2002, that led to Mississippi Republican Trent Lott's departure as Senate majority leader. In remarks on the occasion of Strom Thurmond's 100th birthday, Lott said the country would not have "all these problems" if Thurmond had been elected president in 1948, when he ran on a segregationist platform.

Reporters present at the party failed to recognize the significance of Lott's statement. But it was not lost on bloggers watching on C-SPAN. They wrote about it on the Internet until the traditional media started paying attention. A few weeks later, Lott stepped down.[71]

Point of View

It's the Ideas, Not the Names, That Count

Carole Tarrant (Editor of *The Roanoke Times*)

Let me introduce you to the members of a hidden community.

Meet Roenoke, Ziranthia, TripleAction-Jones, Justafan and Georgia Boy.

These colorfully named people regularly inhabit the message boards of our Web site, *roanoke.com.*

After we post our stories on the site, these folks and many others step up and begin the conversations about the news.

They question a city council's vote. They speculate on a coach's decision. They wonder about the effect of a round of local layoffs. They tell us, very quickly, if our reporting fell short.

Continued

All in all, they rarely agree, but they mostly respect one another.

And amid this robust discussion sometimes emerges a moment of poignant humanity. Our reports on tragic deaths will often produce messages of comfort – strangers reaching out to strangers, offering condolences or expressing the outrage that we often want to in public but can't.

This is what community is all about, whether it's real or virtual.

So who are these people who so expressively pound their keyboards?

I've never met a one of them. I can't tell you their hometowns, their genders or their occupations – or, for that matter, their real names.

I don't need to know. What's important to me are their real-time, unfiltered ideas. To me, the anonymous comments on message boards represent a truly democratic snapshot of ourselves, one stripped of any status or "Well, you know who he is" sniping.

I learn from them and am alternately moved and disturbed by them.

But not every newspaper editor shares my comfort with the anonymity of these postings. Many are struggling with the ugliness that occasionally erupts in the form of racist tirades or personal attacks.

They have shuttered their message boards entirely or attempted to require identification (such as you can on the Internet, where there's practically no reliable means of verification).

We've experienced our own ugly flare-ups at *roanoke.com*. Online editor John Jackson has banned some users outright and tossed yellow flags at others.

He and his team regularly review posts after they go up on the site. They vigorously debate which to delete and where to draw the line.

The easy calls are the outright offensive posts, those full of bigotry and poison. But harder are those that attack individuals, typically those in positions of authority in government and our schools.

Our online team sometimes wishes those writing the posts would pause before hitting the "send" button. "They forget there are people behind this," says multimedia producer Meghan Martin.

Yet our message boards do a service by giving a voice to those who can't risk speaking out publicly – to those who can't, for very good reasons, write signed letters to our editorial page.

Where, for example, can teachers turn when they are seriously unhappy with a school superintendent? *Roanoke.com*'s message boards captured the boiling resentment that preceded the superintendent's recent departure.

In the best cases, our anonymous message boards allow people to speak from their hearts, without fear of judgment. We give them the freedom to speak the unspeakable.

I'm reminded of an old saying when I read some of the postings: I may not agree with what you say but I'll defend your right to say it.

It's a foundation of freedom of the press and should extend online – though it may tax us and prompt us to reexamine our ethics in a new technological era.

From these anonymous postings we can learn, we can be moved, we can be disturbed.

And what is wrong with that?

Carole Tarrant wrote this column for the May 18, 2008, issue of *The Roanoke Times*. It has been excerpted for publication in this text.

Case Study No. 21

For a Reporter-Blogger, Two Personalities

On his day job, John L. Micek reports on politics in the Pennsylvania State Capitol while scrupulously striving to avoid any a hint of bias.

But this reporter for *The Morning Call* in Allentown likes to have a little fun, too. Most days, before he starts work on stories for the newspaper, Micek discards his objective-reporter mode and becomes – in his words – a "snarky smartass." In this persona he writes a "devious" political blog skewering the very politicians he will report on that day. "It's bizarre," Micek said. "It's almost like I'm two different people."

The blog is called "Capitol Ideas," http://blogs.mcall.com/capitol_ideas/ (see Figure 18.2), and its readership consistently ranks in the top three of the website's 17 blogs.

Like many newspaper reporters, Micek took up blogging as a side job. Except that it's no longer a side job; blogging has become part of his duties.

And Micek loves it.

The content and style of the blogs are foreign to the decades-old conventions of journalism – be fair, be objective, and verify, verify, verify. Online, there is wide acceptance of the notion that the rules are not the same as they are in print and broadcast.

Micek said his blogging approach is to spice his notebook leftovers with what he calls a "tabloidy attitude," a knowing voice he picked up from being a fan of *The New York Post*. The Capitol in Harrisburg has "news breaking out all over the place," Micek said. Before the blog, he said, 90 percent of material he gathered stayed in his notebook. Then there wasn't a place for it in the paper. Now there is: on the website.

Micek posts his blog directly onto the web. His editor, Peter Leffler, said he asks Micek and the other staff bloggers to give him a sense of what they plan to do in their blogs, and he goes online a couple of times a day to check their postings. He said that when the blogs were started, the intention was to edit them before posting. That soon proved "unworkable" because of the volume of copy and the time pre-editing would require.

The two personalities of Micek were on display in his coverage of Vice President Dick Cheney's speech to Republican activists at Harrisburg on September 8, 2007.

Micek's blog report began:

Figure 18.2
John L. Micek's home page
REPRINTED BY PERMISSION OF *THE MORNING CALL*

We're just back from VP Dick Cheney's utterly news-free speech at the Harrisburg Hilton. With just a year left to go dictating the affairs of the universe, Cheney con-

Continued

tented himself with taking a valedictory lap in front of the 140 or so party faithful who had, depending on their degree of faithfulness, paid $250 to $2,500 for the pleasure of hearing him speak and/or having their picture taken with him.

By the time the next morning's paper was printed, Micek had shed the irreverent tone and found enough substance in Cheney's remarks to lead his *Morning Call* story with: "Vice President Dick Cheney called Friday for extension of the Bush administration's tax cuts, warning of 'one of the largest money grabs in American history' if congressional leaders allow them to expire."

Micek said he treats blogging responsibly. "But I think you can do online journalism with snark and humor. That makes things interesting."

Micek said most subjects of news coverage don't hold his blog against him when he's reporting for the paper, and he attributed that to his practice of "fair abuse; I try to smack everybody equally." Micek said it helps that he has been on the beat for nearly a decade and has established a reputation for fairness. "I think my sources are sophisticated enough to know that a mild spanking on the blog does not equate to unfair treatment and/or bias in the dead-tree product."

Not that he lacks critics. Micek said that when he poked fun at Republican gubernatorial candidate Lynn Swann's campaign in 2006, the ex-football star's staffers bristled. "It took them some time to figure out I was messing with them in the blog but would give them a fair shake during the day," he said.

A byproduct of the blog, Micek said, is that he gets tips that lead to news stories for the print edition, as well as "back-channel discussions that have enriched my knowledge and added new dimensions to my understanding of my beat."

Micek also said his blog had broken down the wall between him and his readers. If he gets something wrong, people will tell him quickly. "I don't have to wait until next day's paper to fix it."

His goal is to get readers to go from the blog to the paper and then back to the blog. Reeling people in, he said, is what the business is about.

Ardith Hilliard, former editor of *The Morning Call*, sees the web as an entirely different medium, one that "invites a chatty, personality-laden form of communication" and "involves instant interaction with the audience." She said Micek and his editors had agreed that he should not take "editorial-like stances on issues but instead focus on the funny, the absurd, the atmospheric material about the state capitol" that rarely appears in newspapers.

To illustrate how Micek can assume an edgy tone on his blog without taking an editorial position, Hilliard mentioned his handling of Philadelphia Senator Vince Fumo's parliamentary maneuver in a Senate committee. Fumo, trying to head off a constitutional amendment banning same-sex marriages and civil unions, made a tongue-in-cheek proposal to outlaw divorce. His point was that if the amendment's backers really wanted to protect the institution of marriage, the best way would be to make it impossible for couples to dissolve their unions.

"This is why we so totally love this place," Micek blogged. "Just when you think the General Assembly has run out of ways to surprise you, someone comes along and introduces a measure so nuts that the affairs of state get turned on their head and the

Continued

political process becomes a piece of perfor-mance art."

Hilliard said Micek was being irreverent but without taking an editorial position on the effort to ban same-sex unions.

"It is true that infusing one's writing with personality and attitude can come dangerously close at times to expressing opinion," Hilliard said. "Blogging by a reporter, therefore, is not without risk, and some surely stray over the line. I believe that John and our other bloggers have avoided that mistake."

Bob Steele of the Poynter Institute said reporters' revealing their opinions was a problem before the Internet, and it "can be problematic for the readers who may question the independence and fairness of the reporter." Tensions are exacerbated with blogs, he

said, because of an expectation that they will be edgy and because they are edited with less rigor than content of the print newspaper.

Tom Rosenstiel, director of the Project for Excellence in Journalism, said a reporter who adopts a different personality online is comparable to one who goes on a television talk show and spouts opinion. "You can't go on ranting and raving about the president and your opinion of him; then you've become something other than a reporter," Rosenstiel said. "You can't go back and say, 'Now I'm covering you, Mr. President, and I'm objective.'"

Rosenstiel said that same reporter could go on television and maintain credibility by behaving within journalistic standards. The same goes for blogs, he said.

This case is adapted from a report that Sara Ganim wrote for the December 2007 issue of *The Lion's Roar*, a publication of Pennsylvania State University's College of Communications. Ganim graduated in 2008 and now is a staff reporter for the *Centre Daily Times* in State College, Pennsylvania.

Questions for Class Discussion

- If you were a reader of *The Morning Call*, would you suspect bias in Micek's reporting in the newspaper based on what he writes for his blog?
- If you were a subject of John Micek's reporting, would it affect your relationship if he expressed a negative opinion about you in his blog? Would you be satisfied

with his statement that he tries to "smack everybody equally"?
- Do you think the verification standards for journalist-written blogs are different from those for print and broadcast reporting?
- Do you think blogs should be edited before they are posted?

Notes

1 "13 Seconds in August," http://www.startribune.com/local/12166286.html
2 Nancy Barnes, "Bridge project shows the power of interactive media," *Star Tribune*, Dec. 2, 2007.
3 "13 Seconds in August."
4 Sara Quinn, "A year later, '13 Seconds in August' commemorates bridge collapse,"

http://www.poynter.org/content/content_view.asp?id=147779, July 31, 2008.
5 John Carroll, "The future (we hope) of journalism," Creason Lecture at the University of Kentucky, April 1, 2008. The text of the lecture is at: http://www.poynter.org/content/content_view.asp?id=142379

6   Bill Kovach and Tom Rosenstiel, *The Elements of Journalism: What Newspeople Should Know and the Public Should Expect* (New York: Crown Publishers, 2001), 21–2. Kovach and Rosenstiel trace the origin of "modern journalism" to English coffeehouses and American "publick houses" that gathered information from travelers in the early seventeenth century.

7   David Shedden, "Why the new media isn't: a personal journey," http://www.poynter.org/content/content_view.asp?id=125651

8   Jeffrey Cole et al., *The UCLA Internet Report: Surveying the Digital Future* (Los Angeles: UCLA Center for Communication Policy, 2000), 5.

9   J. D. Lasica, "The Starr investigation," in Tom Rosenstiel and Amy Mitchell (eds.), *Thinking Clearly: Cases in Journalistic Decision-Making* (New York: Columbia University Press, 2003), 36–40.

10 Cecilia Friend and Jane B. Singer, *Online Journalism Ethics: Traditions and Transitions* (Armonk, NY: M. E. Sharpe, 2007), 31.

11 Shedden, "Why the new media isn't: a personal journey."

12 Fred Mann, "'New media' bring a new set of problems," http://www.poynter.org/content/content_view.asp?id=4298, May 1, 1998.

13 Dan Gillmor, *We the Media: Grassroots Journalism by the People, For the People* (Sebastopol, CA: O'Reilly Media, 2004), 134.

14 Author's telephone interview with Bob Steele, Sept. 7, 2007.

15 Author's telephone interview with Robert H. Giles, Sept. 10, 2007.

16 Author's telephone interview with Joann Byrd, Sept. 25, 2007.

17 Author's telephone interview with Kinsey Wilson, Sept. 26, 2007.

18 Author's telephone interview with David Zeeck, Oct. 26, 2007.

19 Author's telephone interview with Michael Arietta-Walden, Sept. 25, 2007.

20 *Examining Our Credibility* (Washington, DC: American Society of Newspaper Editors, 1999), 7.

21 John McIntyre, "Editing is not a frill," http://weblogs.baltimoresun.com/news/mcintyre/blog/2008/02/editing_is_not_a_frill.html, Feb. 20, 2008.

22 Bill Mitchell and Bob Steele, "Earn your own trust, roll your own ethics: transparency and beyond," http://www.poynter.org/content/content_view.asp?id=78158, Jan. 15, 2005.

23 Dana Hull, "Blogging between the lines," *American Journalism Review*, December 2006/January 2007, 64–5.

24 Jill Rosen (ed.), "Bloggin' in the newsroom," *American Journalism Review*, December 2003/January 2004, 10.

25 "*Washington Post* reveals 10 web principles," *Editor & Publisher*, July 5, 2007.

26 Author's telephone interview with Robert H. Giles, Sept. 10, 2007.

27 Author's telephone interview with Michael Arietta-Walden, Sept. 25, 2007.

28 Howard Goodman, email to the author, Sept. 5, 2008.

29 Mike Gangloff, *The Roanoke* (VA) *Times*, mike.gangloff@roanoke.com, Oct. 5, 2007.

30 *The Dallas Morning News*, "Newsroom guidelines," June 2007.

31 Memo from *Washington Times* editor-in-chief Wesley Pruden, "Newsroom policy on electronic publishing," Jan. 4, 2006.

32 Steve Olafson, "A reporter is fired for writing a weblog," *Nieman Reports*, Fall 2003, 91.

33 Joe Strupp, "*Houston Chronicle* links to ex-reporter's blog that got him fired," *Editor & Publisher*, Feb. 24, 2006.

34 Ben Westhoff, "Blogger's remorse," *Riverfront Times*, Dec. 29, 2004.

35 Daniel P. Finney, email to Shannon Kahle, Aug. 12, 2008.

36 Brian Toolan, "An editor acts to limit a staffer's weblog," *Nieman Reports*, Fall 2003, 92 3.

37 Mark Glaser, "Will Denis Horgan blog again?", http://www.ojr.org/ojr/wiki/, May 9, 2003.

38 Armando Acuna, "Green reporter, Green Zone dispute, red-hot rhetoric," *The Sacramento Bee*, Nov. 11, 2007.

39 Gillmor, *We The Media*, xxiv, xxv.

40 Quoted in Pat Walters, "Dealing with comments: a few interesting approaches," http://

www.poynter.org/content/content_view.asp?id=
123155, May 31, 2007.

41 Dennis Ryerson, "We don't want a few to spoil
community conversation," *The Indianapolis Star*,
March 17, 2008.

42 Kelly McBride, "Dialogue or diatribe: one woman's
story," http://www.poynter.org/content/content_
view.asp?id=123269, May 18, 2007.

43 Bob Steele, "Baggy pants, drunken driving
and day care: Cincy's challenges with user
comments," http://www.poynter.org/content/
content_view.asp?id=123629, May 24, 2007.

44 Author's telephone interview with Kinsey
Wilson, Sept. 26, 2007.

45 Author's telephone interview with Geneva
Overholser, Oct. 12, 2007

46 Ken Sands' email to author, May 30, 2008.

47 McBride, "Dialogue or diatribe: one woman's
story."

48 Author's telephone interview with David Zeeck,
Oct. 26, 2007.

49 Author's telephone interview with Kinsey
Wilson, Sept. 26, 2007.

50 Clark Hoyt, "Civil discourse, meet the internet,"
The New York Times, Nov. 4, 2007.

51 Friend and Singer, *Online Journalism Ethics*,
137–8

52 Ken Sands' email to author, May 30, 2008.

53 Carroll, "The future (we hope) of journalism."

54 Debora Halpern Wenger and Deborah Potter,
*Advancing the Story: Broadcast Journalism in a
Multimedia World* (Washington, DC: CQ Press,
2007), 278.

55 Author's telephone interview with Michael
Arietta-Walden, Sept. 25, 2007.

56 Author's telephone interview with Kinsey
Wilson, Sept. 26, 2007.

57 *Los Angeles Times* Standards and Practices
Committee, "The *Times*' guidelines on obscenity
and taste issues," accessed at: http://www.latimes.
com/news/local/la-times-taste-guidelines,0,
1543340.story

58 Steve Outing, "The thorny question of linking,"
http://www.poynter.org/content/content_view.
asp?id=73151, Oct. 21, 2004.

59 Clark Hoyt, "When bad news follows you," *The
New York Times*, Aug. 26, 2007.

60 Devon Lash, email to the author, Sept. 4, 2008.

61 Alex S. Jones, "Bloggers are the sizzle, not the
steak," *Los Angeles Times*, July 18, 2004.

62 Mitchell and Steele, "Earn your own trust."

63 Ibid.

64 Ibid.

65 Rebecca Blood, *The Weblog Handbook: Practical
Advice on Creating and Maintaining Your Blog*
(Cambridge, MA: Perseus Publishing, 2002), 115.

66 Ibid., 116.

67 Ibid., 117–21. Blood credits Dave Winer, *Scripting
News*, for his ideas on points 1 and 5.

68 Kelly McBride, "Journalism in the age of blogs,"
http://www.poynter.org/content/content_view.
asp?id=71447, Sept. 16, 2004.

69 Jeff Jarvis, "My *New York Post* op-ed on
Rathergate," http://www.buzzmachine.com/
archives/2004_09_19.html, Sept. 19, 2004. Jarvis
credits blogger Ken Layne for creating the slogan
in 2001.

70 Friend and Singer, *Online Journalism Ethics*, 18.

71 Ibid, 136. Also, Thomas B. Edsall, "Lott decried
for part of salute to Thurmond," *The Washington
Post*, Dec. 7, 2002.

Learning Goals

This chapter will help you understand:

- why it is essential that the public be able to trust the truthfulness of the news media's photographs and video;
- how a news photograph can be distorted either by stage-managing the scene or by manipulating the image;
- the standards that photojournalists have adopted to assure the integrity of their images;
- how photojournalists make decisions about using photographs whose content may be offensive to the audience; and
- the psychological harm that can be caused merely by taking photographs, even if they are not disseminated to the public.

Brian Walski was sunburned, hungry, and sleep-deprived on April 1, 2003, as he sat down with his laptop computer to send the *Los Angeles Times* photographs he had taken on the battlefield in Iraq.

The *Times* photojournalist selected two images of a British soldier standing in front of a group of Iraqi civilians, most of whom were seated. The soldier was instructing the civilians to take cover from Iraqi gunfire. In one image, the soldier gestured with an outstretched left arm while holding his weapon in his right. In the other, the soldier was not pointing, but among the civilians there was action that the other image lacked: a man holding a child seemed to be approaching the soldier.

On his computer screen, Walski combined the image of the gesturing soldier with the one in which the man and child were prominent in the center of the frame. It appeared that the soldier and the man were interacting, making the composite a more powerful news image than either of the originals. Walski transmitted the composite without telling his editors in Los Angeles what he had done.

The *Times* published the photo three columns wide on its front page and shared it with other Tribune Company newspapers.

At the *Hartford Courant*, Walski's photo impressed assistant managing editor Thom McGuire so much that he ran the photo the full six columns across the *Courant*'s front page.

Later, a *Courant* employee was searching for some images in a computer and came across the Walski photo. He noticed that some of the seated civilians seemed to appear twice. When McGuire was notified, he magnified the image 600 percent. What he saw made him "sick to my stomach." He phoned his counterpart at the *Times*, Colin Crawford, with the grim news that the photo was a fake.

Crawford was shocked. "I said out loud, 'No way! There must be a technical, digital ... satellite glitch explanation,'" he later told Kenny Irby of the Poynter Institute.

It took a day for Crawford to track down Walski, who was still shooting and transmitting photographs from southern Iraq. Walski confessed that he had combined the images – an act that violated both *Times* policy and the profession's widely accepted standard of zero tolerance of altered images. In a satellite-phone conversation, he was fired.

The *Times* ran an editor's note the next day along with the two original images and the composite. The *Courant* did the same. The *Chicago Tribune*, which had published the composite on an inside page, also notified its readers.[1]

Photojournalists generally empathized with Walski's drive to produce excellent photography while enduring gunfire, desert heat, and a shortage of food, water, and sleep. But they did not condone what he did. "The only thing we have to offer the public is our credibility," said a former president of the National Press Photographers Association, John Long of the *Courant*. "We can say that it is awful once, but if happens again and again we'll destroy ourselves. ... We have to have accurate information."[2]

Walski, a veteran of 25 years as a photojournalist and a staff member of the *Times* for nearly 5 years, sent his colleagues an email apology. "This was after an extremely long, hot and stressful day, but I offer no excuses here," he wrote. "I deeply regret that I have tarnished the reputation of the *Los Angeles Times*. ... I have always maintained the highest ethical standards throughout my career and cannot truly explain my complete breakdown in judgment this time. That will only come in the many sleepless nights that are ahead."[3]

Reporting, and Distorting, Through Images

Photography dates from two inventions announced in 1839–40 after years of experimentation: Louis-Jacques-Mandé Daguerre's daguerreotype and William Henry Fox Talbot's calotype. In France in 1839, Daguerre announced that he had discovered how to create a permanent image using a box camera and a highly polished, silver-plated sheet of copper on which the image was "fixed," or stabilized, with salt water.[4]

In England the following year, Talbot reported his discovery of a negative/positive process that shortened exposure times and allowed multiple prints to be made from a single negative.[5] The inventions created a technology with great potential for science, art, and journalism.

Professor Louis W. Hodges of Washington and Lee University describes photography's essential role in modern journalism:

> Though their messages overlap, pictures and words communicate different things. In conveying feeling and eliciting emotions (sympathy, anger, horror), pictures are usually superior to words. ... On the other hand, words are inherently superior to pictures in communicating concepts, propositions or ideas. Thus the right words coupled with the right pictures can communicate ideas as well as strong feelings about those ideas. A written statement about the concept of freedom, for example, can carry greater meaning when it is accompanied by a picture of newly released hostages.
>
> For these reasons news photographs are not mere adjuncts or appendages that just accompany stories. Pictures are integral to the larger journalistic function of telling people about their world. Pictures can grab attention in ways that a lead paragraph cannot, and that is part of their journalistic purpose. But their more important communicative function is to tell a story, to communicate meaning.[6]

However, the miraculous technology of photography can be abused to give journalism's audience an image depicting a scene that never happened. Photojournalists can deceive the audience by:

- stage-managing (posing or "setting up") the scene being photographed; or
- altering the content or context of an otherwise authentic photograph.

Tampering with reality "is a violation of everything journalism stands for," Professor Russell Frank of Pennsylvania State University wrote in an essay published in the *Los Angeles Times* a few days after Brian Walski's transgression in the desert. Frank explained why the stakes are so high:

> Whoever said the camera never lies was a liar. Photographers – including some news photographers – have always arranged scenes and posed subjects. They also have been known to cut and paste one image onto another for comic or dramatic effect. Computers have just made it easier.
>
> Photo editors have zipped up open flies (*Orange County Register*), grafted Oprah's head onto Ann-Margret's body (*TV Guide*), moved the Great Pyramids of Egypt (*National Geographic*), and covered immodest women (Louisville *Courier-Journal* and *The New York Times*).

Despite all this fakery, readers continue to believe that what they see in a news photo really happened. They almost have to. They need to feel as if they can get reliable information somewhere.

But journalists know very well that this trust is a fragile thing. Try to persuade people that fakes are real enough times and they'll start thinking that the real ones are fake. That is why the *Times* moved so quickly after Walski's fake was discovered.[7]

As Professor Frank mentioned, photographers have tampered with reality ever since the beginning of the craft. One of Daguerre's rivals, Hippolyte Bayard, was frustrated by the French government's failure to recognize his own considerable contributions to photography. To protest, he posed as a corpse for a fake photograph and, on the back, wrote that "the unhappy man threw himself into the water in despair." The ruse worked; two years later, the Société d'encouragement pour l'industrie nationale gave Bayard 3,000 francs.[8]

In the third decade of the age of photography, the American Civil War produced examples of fakery using both stage managing and image manipulation. Photographers posed the same soldiers for photographs showing them fighting the enemy or lying dead in the battle's aftermath. A popular full-length photograph of President Abraham Lincoln was created by placing Lincoln's portrait on the body of Senator John C. Calhoun of South Carolina.[9]

In the twenty-first century, Professor Hany Farid of Dartmouth College has developed electronic tools to detect tampering with photographs and images. He began his research after discovering that federal rules of court evidence gave digital images the same credence as those on film, even though digital photography is easier to manipulate in ways that are harder to detect. "While I was primarily motivated by the issue of photographic evidence in the courts," he said in an interview with author Ron Steinman, "my hope is that our work will also help the media, among others, contend with the issue of digital manipulation."[10] Farid's website, "Photo tampering throughout history," provides a valuable, illustrated history of photo manipulation, digital or otherwise.[11]

Professional Standards for Still Images

It can be argued that even though digital technology makes manipulation of photographs easier today, the integrity of journalistic images has never been greater. This is due mainly to the near-universal acceptance of the principle that *no* digital manipulation can be tolerated. Transgressions receive enormous publicity within the profession – thanks mainly to the Internet – because they are rare and thus noteworthy.

The zero-tolerance concept is based on two factors: First, because the public is well aware of computer software that can easily alter images, the only way to maintain trust is for journalists to ban any alterations, no matter how benign (such as zipping the fly of a boy's pants). And second, *zero* is an easily understood, inflexible number; once photographers and photo editors start making exceptions, these exceptions can only lead to a loss of perspective that results in more significant exceptions.

Ethics codes of the National Press Photographers Association, as well as the photo policies of many newsgathering organizations, explicitly prohibit tampering with what is known as documentary photography – that is, news photographs. The NPPA's code says: "Editing should maintain the integrity of the photographic images' content and context."[12] The Associated Press states in its policy that it will never alter the content of photographs, adding: "Our pictures must always tell the truth."[13] In prohibiting any alteration of a photo's content, *The Washington Post*'s policy explains: "This means that nothing is added or subtracted from the image such as a hand or tree limb in an inopportune position."[14] *The New York Times*' policy prohibits adding, rearranging, distorting, or removing people or objects.[15]

Most newsroom codes permit the computer equivalent of what was known in yesterday's chemical darkrooms as "burning and dodging." Parts of the image can be darkened or lightened to improve reproduction, so that what the audience sees is closer to what the photographer saw. (In the darkroom, a technician would focus the enlarger's beam on an area of the image that needed to be darkened by "burning," or shield an area that needed to be lightened by "dodging.") The technique of "toning," or improving contrast, is similarly allowed to compensate for detail lost in mass printing.

However, even burning, dodging, and toning are ethically wrong if they are used to change the context of a news photograph. When O. J. Simpson was arrested on murder charges in 1994, his police photo ran on the cover of *Time* after being deliberately darkened by the magazine's artists, who also added a five o'clock shadow. The alteration was readily apparent to the public because *Newsweek*'s cover used the same photo without retouching.

Another normally acceptable editing technique is "cropping" – removing extraneous parts of an image at its borders. This focuses the viewer's attention on the most important part of the picture, which can be printed larger because the cropping has saved space. Cropping is necessary because it is impractical for photographers to frame scenes precisely as they shoot; even with digital cameras, they must allow a margin of error.

Cropping can be used for questionable purposes. During Franklin Delano Roosevelt's tenure as president (1933–45), sympathetic photographers and photo editors never showed the public the wheelchair and leg braces he required for mobility as a result of having been stricken years earlier by polio. "In twelve years," historian Doris Kearns Goodwin wrote, "not a single picture was ever printed of the president in his wheelchair. No newsreel had ever captured him being lifted into or out of his car. When he was shown in public, he appeared either standing behind a podium, seated in an ordinary chair, or leaning on the arm of a colleague."[16] Contemporary photojournalists probably would not empha- size Roosevelt's disability, but they would not hide it, either.

Until the late decades of the twentieth-century, "flopping" portrait photos was routine in newspapers. Rather than have a person appear to gaze off the page, the editor producing the layout would order the engraver to reverse the photo. That resulted in the image that the subject sees in a mirror (but not the image that others see). No wonder that this technique came to be rejected as borderline fakery.

Most print photojournalists reject stage-managing of news photographs – that is, directing the people being photographed to do something for the benefit of the camera. These photojournalists argue that a posed photograph cannot ethically be presented as a "found moment." A noteworthy example of stage managing occurred in the *Los Angeles Times* in 1993. Covering a fire scene, *Times* photog- rapher Mike Meadows suggested that a firefighter go to a swimming pool and pour water over his head to cool off. The result was a stunning photograph, but when photo director Larry Armstrong discovered the circumstances, he suspended Meadows. "When you manipulate the situation," Armstrong said, "you manipulate the news."[17]

The very presence of cameras can change a scene, of course. "People change behavior when they know that their picture is being taken, and it is difficult to hide cameras, especially TV. That means that photographers' influence on the scene is unavoidable …, " Louis Hodges writes.

Hodges is not troubled by photographers' staging photo scenes or manipulating images if, in his opinion, they are done for the right reason. "[D]octoring of pictures – digitally or otherwise – is neither good nor bad in itself," Hodges writes; "alteration is good if the manipulations – no matter the technique used – succeed in depicting the world as forcefully and accurately as possible."[18] With due respect to Hodges, many in the profession would argue that if photojournalists can alter scenes and photographic images to achieve realism, then reporters can by the same logic invent quotations and create composite characters. This text takes the posi- tion that neither photojournalists nor reporters should deliberately distort the events they witness, no matter how benign their purpose.

Under the profession's standards, posing can be acceptable if the resulting image is not a documentary news photograph and the posing is obvious to the viewer. For example, a story about a new chief executive officer of an automobile company might be accompanied by a photograph of the executive wearing a hard hat and standing in front of an assembly line. No one will reasonably assume that the CEO actually works in the factory.

Right or wrong, magazine art directors grant themselves leeway in modifying photographs that news photo editors do not. "The general feeling," said Robert Newman, art director for *inside.com*, "is that the covers of magazines are commerce, they're selling tools, a commodity. … The image has become another graphic element, like type and color, to be altered at will to fit an editorial and graphic concept."[19]

A liberal interpretation of that rationale presumably led to such extreme examples as darkening the Simpson mug shot in *Time* on June 27, 1994; to straightening the teeth of Bobbi McCaughey, the Iowa mother of septuplets, in *Newsweek* on December 1, 1997; and to superimposing Martha Stewart's head on a model's body in *Newsweek* on March 7, 2005, when Stewart was released from prison, where she had lost weight.[20]

Lynn Staley of *Newsweek* said her magazine might retouch cover photos to remove blemishes or small wrinkles, "but after a bad experience with Mrs. McCaughey's teeth a few years ago, we won't do anything that will require surgery in real life."[21]

Newspapers and magazines alike use photo illustrations, which can either be a posed photograph (usually in a studio with no digital alteration) or a digitally altered photograph. Kenny Irby of the Poynter Institute says a photo illustration "is illustrative in nature and is clearly out of the realm of reality. Traditionally, it is an approach used for fashion, food, and product photographs."[22]

The Washington Post allows "a work of fictional imagery," but the fiction must be self-evident. "If a caption is necessary to explain that the content is not real, then we should not use the image," *The Post*'s policy says.[23]

To illustrate the story "How the Right Went Wrong" for its issue of March 15, 2007, *Time* magazine published a cover photo of President Ronald Reagan that had been altered to make it appear that he was crying. The alteration was subtly acknowledged inside the magazine, where David Hume Kennerly was credited for the photograph and Tim O'Brien for the "tear."[24] After its contrived cover photo of Martha Stewart, which was acknowledged in the table of contents, *Newsweek* changed its policy so that future photo illustrations would be labeled on the cover.[25]

The very term "photo illustration" is newsroom jargon that readers may not understand. Rather than using the term as a label, editors would be more transparent if they explained exactly what has been done to the photograph.

Even so, it is the image and not the accompanying text that makes the greatest impression on the audience. Deni Elliott and Paul Martin Lester wrote in a column for *News Photographer* magazine: "[I]t should come as no surprise that, for almost all viewers, when visual and textual messages are in conflict, readers will remember the visual. The visual message wins out."[26]

A 1994 incident illustrates the point made by Elliott and Lester. *New York Newsday* published a composite photo placing Olympic figure skater Nancy Kerrigan and her rival Tonya Harding together on the ice six weeks after Kerrigan had been clubbed on the right knee by an associate of Harding. The image overwhelms the caption's disclosures that the two "appear to skate together" and that the image is a "composite photo." Steven R. Knowlton writes in *Moral Reasoning for Journalists*, "The reader is angry for having been fooled, however briefly, and for being so gullible as to be taken in. And the newspaper now has a reader who will look at what it publishes hereafter with a new suspicion. Or, maybe, not look at it at all."[27]

Integrity Standards in Television News Video

While print journalists have reached a consensus against stage-managing their subjects, the line for television has been far less clear.

The late Travis Linn, a CBS bureau chief and then a professor at the University of Nevada/Reno, wrote in 1991 that "[i]n the minds of most television journalists, there is innocent staging and there is blatant and unethical staging." His article in *Journal of Mass Media Ethics* identified three "basic motivations" for staging: convenience of editing, convenience of time, and convenience of story. While writing that all three are dangerous ethically, Linn said they could be arranged "in a hierarchy of ethical transgression."

- *Convenience of editing*: "It is ordinary practice when shooting a feature, for example, for a videographer to ask a subject to walk into a building twice, allowing the camera to capture the action from both outside and inside the building." This practice generally draws few objections among the videographers. "[T]he argument goes – What does it matter? The person was walking in anyway!"
- *Convenience of time*: "[T]he subject of a news story is asked to repeat an action that occurred before the camera arrived or to carry out an action that is expected to occur later, because the reporter does not have time to wait for the real action." For example, if the camera is not present at a news conference when a person announces his or her candidacy for mayor, the candidate usually will agree to reread the announcement. "Television journalists discuss this kind of staging at length," Linn wrote, "and the discussions usually end with a division between the purists and those who ask, if it has already happened or clearly is going to happen, what is wrong with making it happen while the camera is there?"
- *Convenience of story*: The journalist gives "instructions or directions to the subject of a news story to cause the story to develop in a certain way, when there is no reason to believe it would develop in that way otherwise." This practice, Linn wrote, is unacceptable. While at CBS, he spotted a video from the Rio Grande that seemed too good to be true, and was. "Just as a border patrol truck pulled to a stop and the officers got out, a border patrol plane swooped low overhead, momentarily blotting out the image of the rising sun." Linn called for the raw tape, which showed the scene being enacted three times. "On the soundtrack I could hear a voice cuing the patrolmen in the truck just as the plane was swooping down, 'Okay now! Walk to the gate!' If the labor movement had been stronger in Texas, the border patrolmen would have been entitled to the Screen Actors Guild minimum for their performance." Linn rejected the staged scene.[28]

In their 2008 online book *Photojournalism, Technology and Ethics*, Scott Baradell and Anh D. Stack write that the difference in standards between print and video takes on new importance in today's converged media environment. Newspaper photographers increasingly are shooting news video for their papers' websites. "[I]n the minds of many print photojournalists, TV's justifications for setting up shots represent a slippery slope," Baradell and Stack write.[29]

Al Tompkins of the Poynter Institute said that "still photographers, generally, have a harder line than TV folks have had." Rather than softening the line, Tompkins said, "I would strengthen it. As more people learn to shoot and edit video using their phone, iMovie and other home edit programs, they will understand the deception more and will be less and less tolerant of it." Tompkins also noted that the National Press Photographers Association's code of ethics "forbids staging – period. It applies to video and still equally."[30]

Editing video and sound for television presents another set of ethical hazards. The Radio Television News Directors Association's ethics code states that an electronic journalist should not "manipulate images or sounds in any way that is misleading." The code also counsels the journalist to "use technological tools with skill and thoughtfulness, avoiding techniques that skew facts, distort reality or sensationalize events."[31] The National Press Photographers Association's code says: "Do not manipulate images or add or alter sound in any way that can mislead viewers or misrepresent subjects."[32]

Case Study No. 23, "Just How Fast Do Ice Boats Go?", illustrates how a well-intentioned effort to improve a video can result in distortion.

In its publication *Newsroom Ethics: Decision-Making for Quality Coverage*, RTNDA's educational foundation lists guidelines created by Poynter's Al Tompkins. Among the guidelines are these: "Don't add sounds that did not exist unless it is clear to the audience that they have been added in the edit room. Don't add sounds that you obtained at another scene or from another time or place if adding the sounds might mislead the audience."[33]

Elaborating in *The Elements of Journalism*, Bill Kovach and Tom Rosenstiel lay down a principle of "do not add" in any kind of reporting. This principle would bar rearranging events in time or place, or creating composite characters. As for sound manipulation, the authors write: "If a siren rang out during the taping of a TV story, and for dramatic effect it is moved from one scene to another, it has been added to the second place. What was once a fact becomes a fiction."[34]

RTNDF's *Newsroom Ethics* cautions electronic journalists to be judicious in adding music to video. Music "has the ability to send complex and profound editorial messages," and journalists contemplating whether to add music "must ask themselves whether the music adds an editorial tone to the story that would not be present without the music."[35]

Restraint in adding special effects also is urged by *Newsroom Ethics*. "Slow motion, slow dissolves, tight cropping and framing, dramatic lighting, and unusual angles can all send subtle or even overt messages to the viewer about a person's perceived guilt, power or authority."[36]

Brooke Barnett and Maria Elizabeth Grabe of Indiana University conducted an experiment in which audiences watched videos of news events in both standard speed and slow motion. All the events shown were of disturbing content: a flood in a small town, a house fire, a protest at an abortion clinic, and a gang-related shooting. The research yielded three major findings: First, viewers are more likely to blame suspects shown in slow motion than those shown in standard speed. Second, slow motion makes news stories "seem less fair and informative and more sensational." Third, slow motion magnifies the negative nature of certain news stories, "making viewer experiences of bad news feel worse." Barnett and Grabe regard slow-motion video as a distinctive feature of "tabloid news packaging," along with "obtrusive voice inflection, excessive use of zoom movements, and sound."[37]

When news events are reenacted to show how they happened, the reenactments should be clearly labeled to avoid any possibility that viewers will think they are seeing authentic video.

Making Decisions about Offensive Content

Photojournalists regularly confront questions of how to report the news with authenticity while avoiding giving offense to the audience. This subject was discussed in Chapter 15, and is elaborated on here.

The public can be expected to react negatively to images depicting graphic violence, gore, dead bodies, nudity, indecent behavior, perceived invasion of privacy, and juveniles doing things that might endanger them.

Decisions on this kind of content have to be on a case-by-case basis. These decisions weigh the degree of offense and the news value of the specific photograph or video.

Sherman Williams, assistant managing editor/visual journalism of the *Milwaukee Journal Sentinel*, says he considers the following factors in deciding whether to use a graphic image:

- *The scale of the event.* The bigger the news – think 9/11, Hurricane Katrina – the more likely Williams will run it. There were few reader complaints, for instance, about the photograph of the firefighter holding a dead child in the aftermath of the bombing of the Oklahoma City federal building on April 19, 1995, in which 168 people were killed. "The event was huge," Williams said, "and the photo summed it up."
- *Who is involved.* If the image is graphic and the people involved are ordinary people involuntarily thrust into the news, Williams is less likely to run it. In addition, the audience may be tolerant of a graphic image if the subject survives, but decidedly offended by the image if the subject dies.
- *Whether the event is close to home.* There are two competing considerations. The first is that proximity argues for running the image. The other is that the photo is more likely to hurt someone in the audience, and readers will identify with the photo subject.

- *Whether the image will appear in print or online.* "I don't know why," Williams said, "but people react more to what they see in the print newspaper than what they see online. When we have run the same photo in print and online, we have gotten many more complaints from the print readers."[38]

Case Study No. 22, "Would You Run This Photograph?", is an opportunity to examine the pros and cons of using a photograph that is likely to offend a significant number in the audience.

When journalists conclude that the news value of a sensitive photograph obliges them to use it, they may also consider ways of minimizing the likely offense. In print, these considerations are running the photo on an inside page rather than on the front page, running it small rather than large, and running it in black and white rather than in color. Depending on the photo's composition, it might also be possible to crop out an offensive detail while preserving the newsworthy elements of the image. Online, an editor could run a cautionary note suggesting user discretion and then require the user to click on a link in order to see the photograph. On television, an announcer could warn viewers of the nature of the image and give them time to turn away.

Newspapers sometimes have sought to explain in a caption or an editor's note why they used a photograph that they expect many readers to find offensive. Those who favor this technique say that explaining the decision is a matter of accountability to the audience. One of these is Kenny Irby of the Poynter Institute, who writes: "[W]e should be willing to disclose why we make a decision. ... We should share a certain level of reflective thinking and even our vulnerability."[39] Ethicist Michael Josephson, who favors explanations, suggests wryly that the practice makes journalists appear "a little less arrogant."[40] Vin Alabiso, former Associated Press vice president and executive photo editor, would run the explanation because readers tend to assume that journalists do not consider readers' sensibilities. "We shouldn't think that what we do is so complicated and mysterious that we can't give them our thinking," Alabiso said. "I'm influenced by my experience of appearing on panels with readers to examine photos. The readers are often won over by the arguments of the professionals."[41]

On the other side of the issue are journalists who ask questions like these: Shouldn't readers expect that *all* editorial decisions have been carefully thought out? If we don't offer an explanation on every sensitive photograph, would readers assume that the other photographs have *not* been carefully considered? If we do explain every time, would readers think we are protesting too much about how hard our jobs are?

The *San Jose Mercury News* offered an explanation on June 19, 1996, when it published a photograph of Richard Allen Davis holding up both of his middle fingers seconds after being convicted of murdering twelve-year-old Polly Klaas. Below the photograph, which took up more than a third of the front page, *Mercury*

News editor Jerry Ceppos placed a note to readers that said Davis was showing "contempt for the system that convicted him." He wrote that "ever since Davis' arrest, I've wanted to know about the character of a man who could kill Polly Klaas." He invited readers to tell him what they thought about his decision to publish the photograph, and 1,246 readers did by fax, phone, and mail. They approved running the picture, 815 to 431.

Five other newspapers in the San Francisco Bay area published the photo of the obscene gesture on their front pages. The *Sacramento Bee* mentioned the gesture prominently in its coverage but did not publish a photo. "We didn't run it to show that Davis is a despicable, disgusting, contemptible human being," *Bee* editor Gregory Favre said. "What he did spells that out thousands of times more than any picture could ever do."[42]

Photo editors should be wary of images that show people doing something that appears dangerous, because parents fear that their children will mimic what they see. The *St. Paul Pioneer Press* learned that lesson on January 24, 2000, when readers protested a photograph of a 16-year-old boy peering into the barrel of a pistol. "It shocked me. The first rule is that every gun is loaded," one reader said. "What were you thinking?" another demanded to know.

The photograph illustrated a feature about a police officer's demonstration of fake and real guns. The officer tries to make the teenagers aware of how powerful guns are and of how easy it is to confuse fake and real guns. The pistol that the boy was examining in the photograph had been modified to make it inoperable, a fact that the caption failed to mention. However, as Bob Steele of the Poynter Institute noted, the photograph should not have been used even with a complete explanation. "It still would be about a young man pointing a weapon in his face, which is not what the story is about," Steele said.[43]

Another category of sensitive images is known in the profession as "public grief." These photos – showing ordinary people in public under horrifying circumstances, such as the distressed mother in Case Study No. 3, "The Death of a Boy" – are usually scorned by the audience as callous intrusions into privacy. These photos, often quite poignant, are a source of controversy in the profession because of the competing emotions they evoke – empathy for the subjects, anger with the news media for the perceived intrusion.

Full-frontal nudity, whether of adults or children, rarely appears in the mainstream news media, probably because editors and news directors sense that such images will provoke anger in the audience. To borrow a phrase often used by people complaining about the news, journalists could ask themselves whether they would want members of their families to be depicted in such an embarrassing manner (almost certainly not).

An exception was made by many editors in 1972 when photographer Huynh Cong "Nick" Ut photographed terrified children who had endured a napalm bombing in Vietnam; one of the children was nine-year-old Phan Thi Kim Phuc, who was burned, crying, and completely nude. Decades later, Ut's photograph is regarded as one of the iconic images of the Vietnam War and a powerful statement about the ravages of war.

When a story is about nudity – as, for example, the fad of "streaking" at public events in the 1970s – print photo editors generally take care in selecting or cropping images to avoid showing genitals or female breasts. Television discreetly blurs part of the video. KXTV of Sacramento, California, used that editing technique in June 2000 when an 18-year-old female celebrated receiving her diploma by taking off her graduation robe, while wearing nothing underneath.[44]

Intrusion by Photojournalists

Photojournalists often make the compelling argument that if they take a picture, there is time later to make a calculated decision about whether to use it; but if they do not take the picture, any discussion back at the newsroom will be pointless. However, the act of taking a photograph can cause harm, whether or not the image is disseminated to the public.

In *Photojournalism: An Ethical Approach*, Paul Martin Lester described the photographer's ethical quandary:

> During a controversial news event, when a father grieves visibly over the loss of a drowned child, a writer can stay behind the scenes with pen and paper hidden. A photographer is tied to a machine that must be out in the open and obvious to all who are present. ...
>
> Long lenses or hidden-camera techniques can be used, but the results are usually unsatisfactory. Focus, exposure, and composition problems are increased with the use of telephoto lenses or hiding a camera. ...
>
> The photographer, unlike the hidden writer, can be the target of policemen, family members, and onlookers who vent their anger and grief on the one with the camera. ...
>
> Because photographers must be out in the open to take pictures, the photographer's ethical orientation must be more clearly defined than with writers who can report over the telephone. A photographer must have a clear reason why an image of a grieving parent is necessary.[45]

The authors of *Doing Ethics in Journalism* suggest that photojournalists ask themselves questions like these: "Is this a private moment of pain and suffering that needs to be seen by our readers or viewers?" "Am I shooting at a distance that is not obtrusive or potentially revictimizing individuals?" "Am I acting with compassion and sensitivity?"[46]

After teacher Christa McAuliffe was killed along with six other crew members when the space shuttle Challenger exploded shortly after launch on January 28, 1986, her church in Concord, New Hampshire, scheduled a memorial service that evening. Journalists crowded into St. Peter's Roman Catholic Church to cover the service.

Quoting eyewitnesses, editor Mike Pride of the *Concord Monitor* described what happened: "Reporters, photographers, and television camera people commandeered the first ten rows. They shot back at the few mourners. TV cameras moved down the aisles filming weeping people. A reporter tried to question a praying mourner."

Pride was present the next night when his own church, St. John's Roman Catholic, held a memorial service. He wrote: "[T]he Rev. Dan Messier, a young priest, descended from the sanctuary to comfort a young boy in the front pew. It was as though a single duck had flown into a blind occupied by 50 hunters. Rapid-fire clicks and flashes zeroed in on the scene as the boy buried his head in Messier's shoulder."

Pride wrote that he had to separate his personal feelings from his professional feelings. His paper used the photograph of the priest hugging the child. "I'm not sure it was worth a thousand clicks of the shutter, but it told a touching story. The mourner in me felt abused by the media in the church, but the editor in me had to run the picture."[47]

Case Study No. 22
Would You Run This Photograph?

Photojournalists and their editors often must decide whether to publish, broadcast or post online a photograph that is likely to offend a significant number in the audience. These decisions have to be made on a case-by-case basis, weighing the news value of the image against the degree of offense. As you make your own decision about each of these iconic images, give concrete reasons for voting yes or no.

Fire-Escape Collapse, 1975

Stanley Forman, a photographer for the *Boston Herald*, had finished his work and was about to leave the newsroom on July 22 when he got a report of a fire in a neighborhood of Victorian rowhouses on Marlborough Street. Forman rushed to the scene, following one of the fire engines. He immediately ran to the back of an apartment building, where the fire had trapped a woman and a girl on a fifth-floor fire escape.

While firefighter Bob O'Neil lowered himself from the roof and a truck crew raised a 50-foot ladder, Forman found a position to shoot pictures of what he thought would be a routine rescue.

As O'Neil reached the fire escape, he told 19-year-old Diana Bryant that he was going to step onto the ladder and she should hand

Continued

the child to him. He was reaching for the ladder when the fire escape gave way.

Forman took pictures as Bryant and two-year-old Taire Jones fell. Then he turned away because he didn't want to see them hit the ground. "I can still remember turning around shaking," he told BBC News 30 years later.

Bryant sustained multiple head and body injuries and died hours later. Her body broke the fall of the child, who survived.

With one arm, O'Neil was able to hang onto the broken fire escape and hoist himself to safety.

Back at the *Herald*, Forman developed his negatives and was surprised when he saw the photo of the woman and child plunging from the broken fire escape. Until then, he said on BBC, "I didn't realize how dramatic it was."

The photo (see Figure 19.1) appeared on the *Herald*'s front, taking up nearly the entire tabloid page. Forman made prints for The Associated Press, which distributed them worldwide. At least 128 American newspapers used the picture. The next spring, it was awarded a Pulitzer Prize.

"There was much debate over using such a horrific picture," Forman said. "I was never bothered by the controversy. … My photograph prompted people to go out and check their fire escapes and ushered in a law that meant that the owner of the property is responsible for fire-escape safety."

Figure 19.1 July 22, 1975: A two-year-old child and her babysitter, a 19-year-old woman, plunge from a fifth-story fire escape in Boston. The woman was killed; the child, who landed on her body, survived
PHOTO BY STANLEY FORMAN. REPRINTED BY PERMISSION OF STANLEY FORMAN

Continued

Vin Alabiso, who directed The Associated Press' photo operations from 1990 to 2003, praised Forman for taking a picture that led to reforms. "Absolutely I would run the photo. It's compelling and it captures a moment that explains an issue with far greater impact than anyone can write. On a personal level, it makes a reader ask: 'If we had a fire, would my children know the way out?'"

Drowning and Grief, 1985

As the body of five-year-old Edward Romero was brought out of a lake and laid on a grassy embankment, his grieving family gathered around his lifeless form. Sheriff's deputies kept a television crew from filming the scene, but John Harte of *The Bakersfield*

Californian ducked under a deputy's outstretched arms and shot eight frames from five feet away.

The next morning, July 29, accompanied by the headline "A family's anguish," a photo of the Romeros appeared on the front page of *The Californian*. The dead boy's face, in a half-open body bag, is clearly visible (see Figure 19.2). The child's father kneels over the body. Standing at left, a rescue worker reaches out to comfort members of the distraught family.

Readers were outraged at what they saw as an intrusion into the family's moment of horror. The paper received 500 letters, 400 phone calls, 80 subscription cancellations, and a bomb threat that emptied its building for an hour and a half.

Figure 19.2 July 28, 1985: The family of Edward Romero gathers around the five-year-old drowning victim's body. Edward's father kneels in anguish over the body, while a rescue worker tries to comfort other family members
PHOTO BY JOHN HARTE. REPRINTED BY PERMISSION OF *THE BAKERSFIELD CALIFORNIAN*

Continued

Harte had sped to the scene that Sunday after a police scanner reported a drowning at a lake 25 miles northeast of Bakersfield. Fifteen minutes after he arrived on the scene, divers found Edward's body. Harte got his pictures and drove back to town to develop his film and make the prints. Managing editor Bob Bentley, reached by phone, came in to view images and discuss them with the Sunday staff. He decided to publish.

The Californian had a policy against publishing photos of dead bodies except in rare circumstances, but Bentley decided that the picture was too powerful not to run. He knew there had been other drownings in the same area that summer, and he thought the photo would make an impression on parents.

The Associated Press sent Harte's photo around the country. A number of papers published it, and they too received reader complaints.

Bentley soon reconsidered his decision. He apologized to *Californian* readers in his Sunday column and told *Chicago Tribune* columnist Bob Greene, a critic of the photo: "By running that picture we alienated the hell out of our readers, and if we don't respond to that, we're stupid."

The reader protest did not dissuade Harte from his conviction that his photograph was both news and a public service. "We're not a sensationalistic newspaper, and our usual policy is not to run this kind of picture," he told *Washington Journalism Review* (the predecessor name of *American Journalism Review*). "It's just a question of whether or not it's news. And it was. It just so happens that the news is often unpleasant and has to be reported."

Deni Elliott and Paul Martin Lester discussed the Harte photo in their ethics column in *News Photographer* magazine. They said the definition of news in a given situation is a complex mix of factors, but they listed two elements that they said *should not* be definitive factors:

- "The fact that something makes for a 'hell-of-a-good picture' does not make it news."
- "The publication of news through pictures or text cannot be justified by claiming that the publication will prevent further harm. … Empirically, the argument does not hold up. There is no good evidence that a picture of one drowned child has saved another."

Elliott and Lester wrote that in the two months prior to Edward Romero's death, 14 people had drowned near the same location on the Kern River. In the month after the controversy, only two drowned. "Cause-and-effect or coincidence?" the ethicists wrote. "There is no way to know for sure."

The authors of *Media Ethics: Cases and Moral Reasoning* also rejected the idea that the photo would make other parents more safety-conscious. These authors said Harte acted as "an undaunted professional" to get the picture but concluded:

> Perhaps in the name of reporting news, the photojournalist in this case was actually caught in those opportunistic professional values that build circulation by playing on the human penchant for morbidity. … No overarching purpose emerges that can ameliorate the direct invasion of privacy and insensitivity for these innocent victims of tragedy.

More than two decades after the Romero drowning, the Associated Press' Vin Alabiso said a photo like Harte's might get the same

Continued

reaction locally, "but in the larger world, the response would be different. A photograph like this has a transcendent quality. This is incredibly powerful."

World Trade Center, 2001

On the morning of September 11, Associated Press photographer Richard Drew was taking pictures at a fashion show when his cell phone rang with an urgent call from his office. Instructed to hurry to the World Trade Center, Drew took a chance and caught a subway train, which he found to be eerily deserted.

Drew walked to a spot where ambulances were gathering. He heard people gasping in horror because people in the towers were jumping to escape the flames and smoke. With a 200-millimeter lens, he started photographing the falling bodies in sequences of ten to twelve frames each. "It's what I do," he explained later to *CBC Newsworld*. "It's like a carpenter, he has a hammer, and he builds a house. I have a camera and I take pictures."

After taking his pictures, Drew walked north to the Associated Press headquarters, then in Rockefeller Plaza. Inserting the disc of his digital camera into his laptop, he zeroed in on the picture you see in Figure 19.3. "You learn in photo editing to look for the frame," he told *Esquire* magazine. "You have to recognize it. That picture just jumped off

Figure 19.3   September 11, 2001: A victim falls from the World Trade Center
PHOTO BY RICHARD DREW. REPRINTED BY PERMISSION OF THE ASSOCIATED PRESS

Continued

the screen because of its verticality and symmetry. It just had that look."

AP sent the photo around the world. Many American newspapers used it, drawing complaints from their readers about the horror of the image and the disrespect that they thought journalists were showing by recording a man's death plunge.

The New York Times devoted nearly a full inside page to the photograph. The paper's then executive editor, Howell Raines, said the image of the one man "showed the magnitude of the situation and the loneliness." Although another editor expressed concern that "perhaps it's too close – close enough that people might be able to tell who it is," Raines ordered the photograph into the paper. He told the authors of *Running Toward Danger: Stories Behind the Breaking News of 9/11*: "The picture was about human suffering. In a tragic moment, you cannot be dishonest or evasive. ... I thought the picture told a story our readers needed to see. To suppress that picture would be wrong."

The Morning Call in Allentown, Pennsylvania, published the photo on the back page of the front section. Photo editor Naomi Halperin told her colleagues, "You know going into this that you're going to get reader response and it's going to be heavy and it's going to be angry." The outraged response was the largest *The Call* has ever received over a photo. Managing editor David Erdman told *CBC Newsworld* that he thought the photo forced anybody who looked at it to "think about what would I do ... what choice would I make and the absolute horror of making that choice."

Brian Storm, multimedia director at *msnbc.com*, said he and his team decided that the jumpers were an "essential part of the story," although they worried that a loved one could recognize a jumper. *Quill* magazine said Storm decided to create a site for the photos so that they could be accessed by users who, by linking to the site, had made a conscious decision to look at them.

Estimates of the number of people who jumped from the towers range from 50 (*The New York Times*) to 200 (*USA Today*). "How do you portray such a horrific event, in which thousands are killed?" asked AP's then-photo chief, Vin Alabiso. "Graphic images are often integral to visually reporting a graphic story. Otherwise, photographically, the severity of the news is misrepresented."

Reflecting on his experience in an interview with Peter Howe of *The Digital Journalist*, Drew said: "It wasn't just a building falling down; there were people involved in this. This is how it affected people's lives. ... I didn't capture this person's death. I captured part of his life."

Fury in Fallujah, 2004

After a year of war in Iraq, four Americans working for a security company were ambushed and killed on March 31 as they drove into the town of Fallujah. Their two sport utility vehicles were blasted with assault rifles, and then about 300 people gathered and set the vehicles and their passengers afire. The mob dragged at least two charred corpses through the town and hung them from the girders of a bridge over the Euphrates River.

Video and a variety of still images were obtained by the American news media. Editors and news directors sought to balance the news significance of the photos – a stunning expression of anti-American fury in Iraq

Continued

– against the likelihood that many in the audience would be offended by their grisly nature.

CNN, ABC, and CBS ran portions of the video along with warnings about its graphic content. Some of the gory images were deliberately blurred.

Editor & Publisher magazine reported that 7 of the 20 largest newspapers ran a photo of bodies on their front pages. The bridge photo shown in Figure 19.4 appeared on the front pages of the *Chicago Tribune*, *The New York Post*, *The New York Times*, *The Philadelphia Inquirer*, and the *San Francisco Chronicle*.

Some of the other papers ran photos of bodies inside. Chris Peck, editor of the *Memphis Commercial Appeal*, said he considered his region's community standards in deciding not to publish the most graphic photos on the front. The *Commercial Appeal* ran one photo on the front along with a warning about the graphic nature of an inside photo. Peck said, "I felt the truth of the photos needed to be shown to our readers. At the same time, I believe strongly that newspapers need to both explain their decisions and give readers some options about content."

Bob Mong, editor of *The Dallas Morning News*, was quoted in his own paper as saying that running a photo of bodies on the front page is "an unnecessary trauma for readers." He said, "I think you can convey the power of major events without explicitly showing bodies on the cover."

Figure 19.4   March 31, 2004: Iraqis chant anti-American slogans as charred bodies hang from a bridge over the Euphrates River in Fallujah, west of Baghdad
PHOTO BY KHALID MOHAMMED. REPRINTED BY PERMISSION OF THE ASSOCIATED PRESS

Continued

The same photo that appeared on *The New York Times'* front page also appeared on its website's home page. "We would not run a photograph [on the website] that would absolutely be a no to the newspaper," said Dan Bigman, the website's associate editor for news. "We're the same entity. We're not in the business of 'doing' one thing that's a little nastier online or a little grosser online, and the paper does something a little different for public consumption."

The Associated Press Managing Editors conducted an email survey of 13,642 readers of 29 member newspapers, asking whether they approved the publication of the bodies hanging from the bridge. The survey elicited 2,009 responses, of whom 58 percent approved. One reader who favored running the photo said, "We need to see the reality of war to make an informed choice about why we are at war and whether we should continue." According to a reader who opposed, "If this were my loved one, I would be anguished to see such photos used so casually and callously."

Ken Sands, then of *The Spokesman-Review* in Spokane, Washington, who designed the survey, said he was surprised that so many citizens approved running the photo. "Knowing that ahead of time, while we were still having an internal discussion, would have been helpful," he said.

Case Study No. 23

Just How Fast Do Ice Boats Go?

"Ice boat sailing is a rite of winter in Minnesota," explains news director Tom Lindner of KARE-TV in Minneapolis–St. Paul. "The boats are basically small sailboats with rudders attached. Instead of sailing on the water, they sail across the frozen lakes in winter."

On New Year's Eve 2004, the ice boat sailors were out on White Bear Lake, northeast of St. Paul. KARE-TV was there to try to capture a beautiful feature story that would include shots from the station's helicopters.

Reporter Ken Speake, who is legendary for his skillful storytelling about the people and traditions of Minnesota, wrote a script and recorded an audio track. However, he did not see the edited story before it aired.

When the story aired, the newsroom was abuzz over the deft editing and marvelous video.

A few days later, Lindner was at his dentist's office. The dentist, an ice boat sailor, told him he appreciated the coverage but added, "You know, those boats don't go as fast as you showed on TV."

When he heard that, Lindner said later, he knew he had better take another look at the video.

"I watched the story the next day with the photographer who also edited the story," the

Continued

news director said. "As I looked at the story, in my eyes, I knew what had happened. I asked the photographer, 'Did you speed up some of the shots?' He told me he had.

"The photographer said he changed the speed of the video because 'what I saw out there was not recorded by the camera.'"

What the photographer was saying is that the boats, viewed in person, appear to be moving much faster than they seemed to move on video. So the photographer used the station's editing system to speed up the video of the boats gliding across the ice.

"I met with our chief photographer to be sure that this was not a practice that was going on with great regularity, that this was an anomaly," Lindner said. "I think if we are going to manipulate the video, we should tell the viewers. Let them not guess; let us not represent what the reality was to the camera.

"The fact that my dentist looked at the picture and knew it was not real – we misrepresented reality to him. People should be able to trust our pictures."

The ice boat story, while beautifully told, misleads the viewer in a way that presents ethical concerns. The entire story turns on the notion of speed. The station did not alert the viewer to the idea that some images were altered. And the viewer had no way to know it because, unlike obviously slo-mo'ed video that can be visually compared to normal-speed images, the average viewer may not know how fast the boats sail in real life.

If video speed is changed, journalists should ask themselves: "What would the viewer say if he or she knew the truth about how this story was gathered and edited? Would the viewer feel tricked?"

Adapted from "*Newsroom Ethics: Decision-Making for Quality Coverage*, 4th edn. (Washington, DC: Radio Television News Directors Foundation, 2006), 33–5.

Questions for Class Discussion

- What guiding principle of the SPJ code is most involved in this case?
- Should KARE-TV have sped up the video of the ice boats?
- If the video speed is not changed, would the story work if the reporter explains to viewers that the boats actually move faster than they appear on TV?
- If the video is sped up, how could the station make this clear to the viewer? Could the reporter, for example, write a line saying, "On television, the boats seem to be barely moving across the ice, but we sped up the video to give you an idea of what it feels like when you are riding one of the boats across the lake"?
- What policy should television news staffs have about changing video speed or adding sound effects? Should the news director's approval be required? Should the editing technique be disclosed to the viewers?

Notes

1   This account of the Walski incident is based on Kenny Irby, "*L.A. Times* photographer fired over altered image," http://www.poynter.org/content/content_view.asp?i d=28082, April 2, 2003.

2   Jill Rosen, "Digital deception," *American Journalism Review*, May 2003, 10–11.

3   Irby, "*L.A. Times* photographer fired over altered image."

4   Department of Photographs, "Daguerre (1787–1851) and the Invention of Photography," in *Timeline of Art History* (New York: The Metropolitan Museum of Art, 2000–), http://www.metmuseum.org/toah/hd/dagu/hd_dagu.htm, October 2004.

5   The Getty Museum, http://www.getty.edu/art/gettyguide/artMakerDetails?maker=2005

6   Louis W. Hodges, "The distorting mirror: Ethics and the camera," unpublished manuscript.

7   Russell Frank, "Altered photos break public's trust in media," *Los Angeles Times*, April 7, 2003.

8   Paul Martin Lester, *Photojournalism: An Ethical Approach* (Hillsdale, NJ: Lawrence Erlbaum Publishers, 1991), 92.

9   Ibid., 95–7.

10 Ron Steinman, "An interview with Dr. Hany Farid, February 2008," http://www.digitaljournalist.org/issue0802/digital-forensics-an-interview-with-dr-hany-farid.html

11 Hany Farid, "Photo tampering through out history," http://www.cs.dartmouth.edu/farid/research/digitaltampering/

12 Ethics code of the National Press Photographers Association: http://www.nppa.org/professional_development/business_practices/ethics.html

13 Vin Alabiso, The Associated Press letter on photo policy, http://www.poynter.org/content/content_view.asp?id=46967

14 *The Washington Post* policy on manipulation of photographic images, http://www.poynter.org/content/content_view.asp?id=46964

15 *The New York Times, Guidelines on Our Integrity*, http://www.poynter.org/content/content_view.asp?id=46973

16 Doris Kearns Goodwin, *No Ordinary Time: Franklin and Eleanor Roosevelt: The Home Front in World War II* (New York: Simon and Schuster, 1994), 586.

17 Howard Kurtz, "L.A. Times gets burned by disaster photograph," *The Washington Post*, Feb. 2, 1994.

18 Hodges, "The distorting mirror."

19 Kenny Irby, "Magazine covers: Photojour nalism or illustration?", http://www.poynter.org/content/content_view.asp?id=15422, Dec. 30, 2002.

20 Sherry Ricchiardi, "Distorted picture, *American Journalism Review*, August/September 2007, 40.

21 Irby, "Magazine covers."

22 Irby, "The art and language of photography: A photojournalism glossary," http://www.poynter.org/content/content_view.asp?id=5657, Feb. 1, 1996.

23 *The Washington Post* policy on manipulation of photographic images.

24 Ricchiardi, "Distorted picture," 41.

25 Jay DeFoore, "*Newsweek* changes crediting policy following cover flap," *Photo District News*, March 8, 2005.

26 Deni Elliott and Paul Martin Lester, "Manipulation: The word we love to hate (Part 3)," *News Photographer*, October 2003.

27 Steven R. Knowlton, *Moral Reasoning for Journalists: Cases and Commentary* (Westport, CT: Praeger, 1997), 189.

28 Travis Linn, "Staging in TV news," *Journal of Mass Media Ethics*, vol. 6, no. 1, (1991), 47–54.

29 Scott Baradell and Anh D. Stack, *Photojournalism, Technology and Ethics: What's Right and Wrong Today?* (New York: Black Star, 2008) This ebook can be downloaded in PDF format: http://rising.blackstar.com/photojournalism-technology-and-ethics-whats-right-and-wrong-today

30 Al Tompkins, email to author, Nov. 18, 2008.

31 Ethics code of the Radio Television News Directors Association, http://www.rtnda.org/pages/media_items/code-of-ethics-and-professional-conduct48.php?id=48

32 NPPA code, http://www.nppa.org/professional_development/business_practices/ethics.html

33 *Newsroom Ethics: Decision-Making for Quality Coverage*, 4th edn. (Washington: Radio Television News Directors Foundation, 2006), 81.

34 Bill Kovach and Tom Rosenstiel, *The Elements of Journalism: What Newspeople Should Know and the Public Should Expect* (New York: Crown Publishers, 2001), 79.

35 *Newsroom Ethics*, 82.

36 Ibid.

37 Brooke Barnett and Maria Elizabeth Grabe, "The impact of slow motion video on viewer evaluations of television news stories," *Visual Communication Quarterly*, Summer 2000, 4–7.

38 Author's telephone interview with Sherman Williams, Oct. 12, 2007.

39 Irby was quoted in Bill Marvel and Manuel Mendoza, "Gruesome images: Does taste trump newsworthiness?", *The Dallas Morning News*, April 1, 2004.

40 Josephson's comment to the author.

41 Author's telephone interview with Vin Alabiso, Sept. 21, 2007.

42 Jay Black, Bob Steele, and Ralph Barney, *Doing Ethics in Journalism: A Handbook With Case Studies*, 3rd edn. (Boston: Allyn & Bacon, 1999), 218–20.

43 Michele McLellan, *The Newspaper Credibility Handbook: Better Ways to Build Reader Trust* (Washington: American Society of Newspaper Editors, 2001), 155–8.

44 *Newsroom Ethics: Decision-Making for Quality Coverage*, 4th edn. (Washington, DC: Radio Television News Directors Foundation, 2006), 23–4.

45 Lester, *Photojournalism: An Ethical Approach*, 4.

46 Black, Steele, and Barney, *Doing Ethics in Journalism*, 207.

47 Mike Pride, "A grieving Concord repelled by media misbehavior," *presstime*, March 1986.

20 Ethics in the Changing Media Environment

A review of the challenges faced by contemporary journalists

Learning Goals

This chapter will help you understand that:

- "infotainment" – focusing on the sensational – is a problem because it siphons resources from important news stories the public needs;
- the future of journalism may depend on finding a business plan that makes Internet news sites profitable enough to support larger staffs of journalists;
- although aspiring journalists should learn multimedia skills, performance standards could be lowered if everyone is expected to report every story in all media;
- news websites, the dominant news platform of the future, face lingering ethics issues;
- the traditional definition of journalism takes on new importance in the changing media environment; and
- journalists, though no longer the gatekeepers, still have the responsibility of making sense of the news.

When Anna Nicole Smith died in a Florida hotel-casino on February 8, 2007, the cable networks devoted 50 percent of their news coverage for two days to the saga of the *Playboy* centerfold model who had become a rich widow and then a star on reality TV. For all the news media measured by the Project for Excellence in Journalism (PEJ) – newspapers, network and cable television, websites, and radio – her story was the third-biggest of that week. The Smith story was surpassed only by events in Iraq and the debate over Iraq policy.[1]

Mark Jurkowitz, who analyzed the coverage for PEJ, pronounced the Smith coverage "one of those stories the media feel compelled to both cover and apologize for." NBC anchor Brian Williams observed on his February 8 evening newscast, "This may say a lot about our current culture of celebrity and media these days, when all the major cable networks switched over to nonstop live coverage this afternoon."[2]

Carl Hiaasen was blunt in his *Miami Herald* column: "[T]his is the *new* New Journalism, which is steered by a core belief that people would rather be smothered by seedy gossip about dead ex-Playmate junkies than be bothered with the details of North Korea's nuclear program."[3]

The Smith story – "what killed her, who fathered her infant, where her money would go" – dominated cable television for nearly a month, absorbing nearly one-fourth of the available news time. The network morning shows also covered the story intensively. Although many other news outlets "treated Smith's death as a blip on the radar screen," Jurkowitz concluded that the episode "speaks to cable's ability to magnify an event until it feels like the only story on the entire media agenda."[4]

The news media have historically been susceptible to what the authors of *The Elements of Journalism* call "the news as revealed truth, as sex, or as celebrity scandal." Gossip flourished in the "yellow press" of the late nineteenth century, the tabloid newspapers of the twentieth century, and gossipy radio shows like Walter Winchell's of the 1930s, 1940s, and 1950s.[5]

Now, in the twenty-first century, some news outlets fixate on a single big story in a desperate attempt to reassemble the audience that has been fragmented by the emergence of diverse sources of information.

The phenomenon illustrated by the Smith coverage is a blending of entertainment and information to yield "infotainment," a label that applies despite the morbid nature of this particular story. "Everybody wants to be entertained by the news," said Todd Gitlin, a professor in the Graduate School of Journalism at Columbia University. "Most people want no-problem news, goes-down-easy news, … news that evokes feelings, even if those feelings are feelings of fear."[6]

Michael Schudson and Susan Tifft, in an essay in the 2005 book *The Press*, see an uninformed citizenry and fix at least part of the blame on the trend toward infotainment. "Today, Americans are saturated with images, interviews, facts, and analysis, yet have a surprisingly superficial knowledge of the machinery of democracy or the rest of the world," Schudson and Tifft write. "Paradoxically, there is more quality news available than ever before, but it is often overwhelmed by the sheer volume of entertainment, consumer features, crime, and sensation."[7]

Infotainment has ethical implications for journalism, whose primary purpose is to give citizens the information they need to be free and self-governing.[8] If lighter fare gets more of the news media's resources, important civic topics get less.

Hence columnist Hiassen's rueful comment about the theory held by some in contemporary journalism that the public is more interested in the Smith gossip than in the prospect of a nuclear-armed North Korea.

The theory is also evidenced in a finding by Thomas Patterson of Harvard University that the percentage of news stories containing a moderate to high degree of sensationalism rose from 25 percent in 1980 to 40 percent in 2000. Patterson analyzed 5,331 news stories in newspapers and newsmagazines and on television in the 1980–99 period. Each story was coded high, moderate, or low for "sensationalism," which Patterson characterized as "breathlessness" or a "hyped" way of telling the story.[9]

There are indications, however, that the public may not be enthusiastic about this kind of news. The Pew Research Center for the People & the Press reported in August 2007 that Americans profess little interest in sensationalistic fare. In a Pew survey, 87 percent said they think celebrity scandals get more media attention than they deserve.[10] Parsing these figures, columnist Eric Alterman asked rhetorically in *The Nation* magazine: "[W]hat can possibly be the argument for giving people junk they don't even desire?"[11]

Bill Kovach and Tom Rosenstiel argue in *The Elements of Journalism* that an infotainment strategy is not good business any more than it is good journalism. "[W]hen you turn your news into entertainment, you are playing to the strengths of other media than your own. How can the news ever compete with entertainment on entertainment's terms? Why would it want to?"[12]

Kovach and Rosenstiel say news and entertainment have different values, with the news "based on relevance." News dressed up as entertainment, "though it may attract an audience in the short run and may be cheap to produce, will build a shallow audience because it is built on form, not substance."[13]

When people want to be entertained, they turn to comedy, drama, music, and the like. Not surprisingly, when people want to find out what is happening in their community and the world, they turn to the news media.

The challenge for journalists, Kovach and Rosenstiel say, is to tell important stories (for example, the threat of a nuclear-armed North Korea) in ways that will engage the audience. "Journalism is storytelling with a purpose," they write. Journalists need to find the information that people need to understand the world, and then make it meaningful and relevant.[14]

Case Study No. 24, "NBC's Controversial 'To Catch a Predator,'" offers an opportunity to debate that premise. Are the producers of this series using reality-television techniques, mixed with investigative journalism techniques, to illuminate a significant social problem? Or are they blurring the line between news and entertainment in a way that diminishes the network's credibility as a source of news?

The infotainment trend is one of the troubling features of the changing media environment. This closing chapter reviews other ethical challenges in contemporary journalism and offers commentary.

Who Will Pay For Journalism?

In the changing media environment, ethical duty is also involved in the question of how the cost of good journalism will be paid in the future. Without sound financial underpinning, news organizations will not be able to fulfill their social responsibility of delivering the information that citizens need.

For example, in an era in which Americans need more, not less, information about the global community, newspaper editors have responded to their diminished financial resources by focusing on local coverage. That decision is not without logic because, even after repeated cutbacks, newspapers still have more journalists to cover their regions than the broadcast and online outlets they compete against. Local news is a coverage category in which newspapers can dominate. However, with fewer correspondents abroad, American newspapers' coverage of international affairs has precipitously declined. The news industry is making a sobering statement when leading newspapers in cities the size of Boston, Philadelphia, and Baltimore deem themselves unable to afford foreign staffs.

As this text has noted, while the Internet has vast potential for reporting, websites are not yet profitable enough to support large news staffs on their own. Most of the content is provided by journalists working for the older media – newspapers and, to a lesser extent, broadcast.

As mentioned in Chapter 11, the Internet is fast and efficient for customers looking for used merchandise, for real estate, for jobs, or for used cars. But these customers are not interested in news when they perform these searches; news actually would get in their way. For that reason, web news probably requires a different business model than newspapers and broadcast stations, whose news or entertainment offerings attract an audience that is then rented to advertisers.

The new business model does not appear to be in sight. If online users cannot be persuaded to pay for access to news on the web, the burden falls on advertisers. So far, advertising revenue has fallen far short.

Some industry experts argue that newspapers and broadcast stations made a strategic error by not charging for access when they first started putting news on the web. The media entrepreneur Steven Brill is one of these critics; he says newspapers are "committing suicide by giving journalism away for free."[15]

Can the industry reverse course and start charging for its web news? Tom Rosenstiel, director of the Project for Excellence in Journalism, sees potential in the cable TV model, in which the fees of individual channels are included in a monthly access fee charged by the cable company. Under this model, Internet service providers would collect access fees for news websites as part of their monthly charge to the customers.[16] Journalist and author Walter Isaacson proposes micropayments – "a one-click system with a really simple interface that will permit impulse purchases of a newspaper, magazine, article, blog or video for a penny, nickel, dime or whatever the creator chooses to charge." Some surfers would balk, Isaacson wrote in a *Time* magazine article, "but I suspect most would merrily click through if it were cheap and easy enough."[17]

Other experts think charging for content would result in a net loss by depressing web traffic and, consequently, web advertising. Rick Edmonds of the Poynter Institute observes that charging for content had been tried unsuccessfully by many newspapers – notably Times Select, in which certain *New York Times* features were available only to subscribers. Edmonds also writes, "User registration, a halfway step to monetizing the audience, has largely been abandoned for the same reason – potential readers opted to go elsewhere rather than waste time on even a short registration form."[18]

The philanthropy model may save a few news organizations or create alternatives. Already there are several nonprofits dedicated to investigative reporting, the largest of which is Pro Publica, whose staff is headed by retired *Wall Street Journal* managing editor Paul Steiger. ProPublica intends to publish articles on its own website and offer those articles free for publication in other news organizations.[19] Joel Kramer, former publisher of the *Star Tribune* in Minneapolis, has launched *MinnPost.com*, a nonprofit enterprise covering Minneapolis, St. Paul, and the state of Minnesota. Its website states, "Our goal is to create a sustainable business model for ... journalism, supported by corporate sponsors, advertisers, and members who make annual donations."[20]

Whatever form it takes, a way must be found to underwrite a journalism that covers local communities and the world with precision and depth. Otherwise, the wondrous technology of the twenty-first century may have the side-effect of producing a less-informed citizenry.

Quality Implications of "Media Convergence"

One of the buzzwords of recent years has been "convergence," or producing journalism simultaneously on the platforms of print, broadcast, and the web. The platforms could be owned by the same company, or they could be owned by partnering companies that exchange reporting with each other.

In either form, cross-platform journalism requires its practitioners to possess multimedia skills in some degree.

Reporters might be called on to take photographs – either still or video – and photojournalists might be called on to write stories. Print journalists might do "talkbacks" on television in which they discuss the stories they have covered. Television reporters might write stories for print. And, importantly, all of these print and broadcast journalists would be expected to provide multimedia reports throughout the day for the affiliated website.

The goal is to serve an audience that has already "converged," drawing its news from diverse media sources.

In the 2007 book *Online Journalism Ethics: Traditions and Transitions*, Jane B. Singer raises the ethical question of whether convergence is in the public interest, since the different outlets will collaborate rather than compete. "Is the public better served by converged or partnered news organizations, which can provide more comprehensive and multifaceted coverage of important stories, or do such arrangements mainly curtail the number of voices a community hears?"[21]

A more fundamental ethics issue is whether it makes sense to assume that every journalist can perform every multimedia task equally well. The success of a good news organization has been built by journalists who specialize. If a news organization expects every journalist to do everything, the risk is that the acceptable level of performance will no longer be "excellence" but "good enough." That has

profound implications for the ability of journalism to provide the reliable information that the public needs.

A world-class reporter may be an incompetent photographer, and vice versa.
"Newsrooms aren't little Lake Wobegons, where everyone is above average and
can do everything well," Deborah Potter wrote in *American Journalism Review*.[22]

To be sure, the concept of combining skills is not new. At weekly newspapers
and small dailies, reporters have long been given cameras and instructed to shoot
pictures while they report. However, this historical precedent does not involve as
many different skills as are demanded in today's media environment.

A reluctant multimedia journalist in the 1950s was Gene Roberts, the future
metropolitan newspaper editor and Pulitzer Prize-winning author. Roberts had to
carry the Speed Graphic camera on his reporting assignments for the *Goldsboro*
(North Carolina) *News-Argus*. One of his assignments was to cover a court appearance of a police chief who had found himself in legal trouble. As the chief
approached in the courthouse corridor, Roberts raised his bulky camera and
blinded him with the flash. Roberts realized that he had not taken the picture, so
he raised the camera again. As the flash went off a second time, the chief started
pounding on Roberts' camera and then on the reporter/photographer himself.

"I got the picture," Roberts said, summing up the episode. "But I didn't get
the story."[23]

Another problem with the concept of multimedia journalism is that there often
isn't time for one person to do everything.

The *Los Angeles Times* sent two stellar journalists to Iraq in 2006 to report on
how the military was providing emergency medical treatment to those wounded
in combat. Reporter David Zucchino and photojournalist Rick Loomis collabo-
rated on a three-part series in the newspaper and a multimedia report on its
website.

Zucchino said that he had taken acceptable photographs for publication in the
past, but he could never have matched Loomis' stunning images, which were the
first in an American newspaper to show wounded soldiers on the battlefield in
Iraq. "If I had tried to report the articles *and* take the photos, the reporting would
have suffered as well," Zucchino said. "Reporting a complicated story under stressful circumstances takes a certain single-mindedness and attention to detail."

Even so, the two journalists shared the duty of recording interviews and ambient
sound for the website. "Between us, I think we got some very dramatic audio
that enriched the project," Zucchino said. "But holding out a tape recorder while
interviewing someone or while observing a situation is far less distracting than
trying to shoot photos."[24]

Today's journalists may — and tomorrow's almost surely will — need to be
conversant with the latest technology of reporting for the web. Convergence is
evolving into multimedia presentations on the web. That method of storytelling
holds great promise, as Chapter 18 explained, using as an example the *startribune.
com* report on how the 2007 Minneapolis bridge collapse changed the lives of the
people who were on the bridge. However, the success of multimedia journalism

depends on whether journalists will be allowed to play to their strengths and whether they will be given the time to do the job right.

A compromise might be to continue to assign reporters to reporting and photojournalists to photography, but to expect either to function in the other's specialty in rare cases when it is impractical to send both. In addition, an ability to use a video camera – far smaller and easier to operate than Gene Roberts' 1950s Speed Graphic – could help reporters do their basic tasks. The video could remind them of physical details of the news scene, give a better sense of the person interviewed, and capture the audio for accuracy in quotations.[25]

One traditional journalist, James M. Naughton, has advocated development of an electronic version of the Reporter's Notebooks. In his lifetime, reporters have progressed from taking notes on folded newsprint, to using the slimmed-down spiral notepads that could be carried easily in a suit coat pocket or purse, to deploying a hand-held audio recorder. It is, Naughton says, a natural evolution to imagine a device about the same dimensions as a Reporter's Notebook but with all the capability of an Apple iPhone – and more – to take still and video images, record audio and notes, and send all of it instantly to the reporter's computer or to an electronic news desk on a different continent. "I'm opposed to convergence, which is business speak for reducing journalism jobs," Naughton says, "but in favor of technology that makes news coverage more authoritative."[26]

Mark Deuze, a Dutch journalist now teaching at Indiana University, told the authors of *Online Journalism Ethics* that the quality of converged news will suffer if journalists "are overworked, frustrated, underpaid, stressed out and still expected to do more without additional rewards or benefits." If that happens, he said, "the public will look somewhere else for its news."[27] Deuze makes a telling point, but the lingering question is where the public will find its news if the entire industry takes the approach he describes.

The Internet's Unresolved Issues

As Internet news grows in popularity, it is essential that the profession resolve the ethical questions that have emerged in the transition from the older news media. These issues were identified in Chapter 18, and they are briefly addressed again here because they are among the serious ethical challenges of the new media environment.

Will journalism's standards of verification be maintained?

A variety of factors combine to pose a threat to the tradition of checking and rechecking that quality journalism requires. The Internet is a medium geared for speed. News sites have been thinly staffed. It is easy to update and correct Internet reporting. So the temptation is to get ahead of the competition by posting something and correcting it on the fly. In his Point of View "Decision-Making in the Digital Era," Jim Naughton argues for deliberation.

The question of verification becomes even more important if, as seems likely, the Internet becomes the dominant news medium. When the website is the mother ship, will its bosses suddenly allocate the resources to provide the kind of editing that is needed? Contemporary news-media history suggests the opposite. If a website has somehow succeeded without spending extra dollars on editing, there is no financial impetus to change.

Thus the decisions about editing standards for the web often are being made by default in this transition phase. If economics dictate skimpy staffing, it follows that the editing will be skimpy. The long-term veracity of Internet reporting is being shaped in the decisions being made (or not made) in today's environment.

In a medium built on interactivity, can civility be protected?

For many news consumers, one of the attractions of reading news on the web is that they can instantly (and usually anonymously) post comments reacting to what they have read. The problem is that the conversation abounds with vulgarity, misinformation, and defamatory allegations, not to mention downright meanness.

The profession should attach a high priority to figuring out how to moderate the Internet conversation. Some news organizations are experimenting with possible solutions.

Ken Sands of *Congressional Quarterly* noted that social networking sites have succeeded in keeping the conversation on a higher plane. These sites, Sands said, are accepted as "communal places," encouraging respect from the users. They also require registration, they have strict rules of conduct, and they have volunteer moderators who patrol the sites round the clock.

Sands suggested that news sites can learn from the social-networking example. He said that instead of using "a heavy hand" to filter the conversation – a tactic that leads to resentment – they could give their sites "a communal feel" and enlist volunteer moderators.[28] *USA Today* and *The Washington Post* are among outlets that have adopted elements of social networking on their websites. Kinsey Wilson, in a separate interview, reported that *USA Today*'s staff bloggers "have a direct daily relationship" with their audience, and that this is reflected in the tone of the posted comments. "There is a level of civility and respect for the group," Wilson said.[29] In an article in *Columbia Journalism Review*, Adam Rose reported that web editors at *usatoday.com* recognize reader contributions by posting a list of the best comments each day. At *washingtonpost.com*, Rose wrote, "readers can create profiles, send private messages to other readers, add others as friends, and track their posts over time."[30]

How can mainstream journalists take advantage of blogging's strengths while preserving their hard-earned reputation of fairness?

Encouraged by their bosses, journalists of mainstream organizations have been flocking to cyberspace to write online journals that expand their reporting and invite a conversation with the audience. Emulating the success of the best citizen bloggers, these journalists adopt a more relaxed – some would say snarky – style of writing. Unlike the citizen bloggers, journalist bloggers should resist expressing opinions about the people and events they cover – opinions that could color the way their audience perceives them, and thus reduce credibility.

It doesn't help that, as these journalists produce blogs testing the limits of neutral reporting, they often post their work without a critical review. No matter how good and how experienced a journalist may be, the journalist is taking a risk by venturing onto the high wire without the safety net of an editor's scrutiny.

This text takes the position that blogging by mainstream journalists is a good idea, as long as the journalists do not neglect their primary reporting duties, and as long as they maintain their neutrality and the appearance of neutrality on all media platforms. The best way to assure those goals is to edit blogs to the exacting standards of traditional journalism.

A Question With New Significance: What Is Journalism?

The practice of journalism requires an obligation to the truth, a loyalty to the citizens, a discipline of verification, and an independence from the people and institutions being covered.

That definition from *The Elements of Journalism*[31] serves as a job description for anybody who aspires to be a journalist. The definition applies to a staff member of a mainstream print, broadcast, or online organization. It applies as well to a citizen blogger or anyone else who purports to report and comment on the news, even as a hobby.

This text has sought to identify and discuss the ethics standards that journalists live by. Those standards help journalists gain the trust of the citizens who are seeking reliable information they need to be self-governing in a democracy. Ethical journalists, regardless of their platform, are *credible*.

In this era of transition, some mainstream news organizations are trying to engage their audience in the newsgathering process.

One technique is "crowdsourcing," in which news organizations publish, broadcast, or post invitations asking their audience for help when they begin working on a project. In 2007, *Florida Today*, based on the east coast of central Florida, invited readers to help the paper assess the truth of a tip that homeowners were being overcharged for storm-insurance premiums. Assistant managing editor Matt Reed said verification of the tip would be difficult because insurance policies are not a part of the public record. On his blog, Reed invited homeowners to show reporters their policies and allow reporters to bring appraisers into their homes. Hundreds of homeowners responded, and appraisers visited at least two dozen homes. Their findings enabled the paper to publish a front-page story reporting that "companies were methodically overstating" the premiums by as much as $600.[32]

Reed said the appraisers hired by the paper determined that companies inflated premiums by overstating the replacement value of the homes. "In a few cases," Reed said, "we found that insurers had coded the homes as luxury houses with expensive fixtures and finishes, when they were actually basic middle-class places with builder-grade fixtures."[33]

It is important to note that what *Florida Today* got from crowdsourcing were tips that the paper and its experts then checked out. The Knight Citizen News Network, which offers training on its website (http://www.kcnn.org), cautions that "crowdsourcing can be risky." KCNN quotes Skip Hidlay, executive editor of the *Asbury Park* (New Jersey) *Press*: "We never use anything given to us by crowdsourcing raw. Verify. Verify. Verify." Hidlay told KCNN that in an investigation of a major homebuilder, reporters checking out readers' tips found that only one in three was accurate.[34]

Some news organizations have enlisted unpaid volunteers to do community news reporting. Their contributions are properly called *user-generated content*. The term sometimes applied to this kind of information, *citizen journalism*, is a misnomer if the citizen fails to meet journalism's standards of precision and neutrality.

For example, a story about a Rotary Club charity event under the byline of the club's publicity chair is not likely to cause problems, but even such an innocuous news release must be authenticated. In contrast, there is a likelihood of inaccuracy and unfairness if a newspaper depends on citizen contributors – even dueling contributors – to report on a combative debate over where to locate the town's new middle school.

Before news organizations disseminate user-generated content, verification by a professional journalist is essential.

Kelly McBride of the Poynter Institute emphasizes the difference between professional journalism and so-called citizen journalism. In an essay in 2006 about a newspaper's website that invited contributors to "write stories," McBride wrote:

It's great that newspapers host these sites. It's a wonderful service for community. They are often interesting, vibrant, and exciting. But it's not journalism. So don't call it that. Journalism is an independent act of gathering and assembling information by an organization. The work is completed in service of the audience. The journalists' loyalties are with the reader and viewer. ... [Y]ou expect those values to guide the process of gathering news. You wouldn't expect that from a candidate's PR woman writing a press release.[35]

In her Point of View, "A Difference in Reporting on Rumors," McBride analyzed in 2008 how the blogosphere and professional journalism approach the delicate matter of reporting on the personal lives of politicians and their families. It is, she wrote, "the difference between speculation and verification."

Ethical Journalists' New Gatekeeper Role

Today's news consumer can draw on a dazzling array of information sources. The day is long past when editors in a distant newsroom decided what information was worthy of passing along to the public, and what was not. "Journalists can no longer be information gatekeepers in a world in which gates on information no longer exist," Cecilia Friend and Jane B. Singer write in *Online Journalism Ethics*.[36]

Twenty-first-century journalism requires a different interpretation of the gatekeeper role. A democratic society now depends on journalists to be its surrogates in sifting the huge volume of information available, testing it for accuracy, and helping citizens understand it.

"Gatekeeping in this world is not about keeping an item out of circulation," Friend and Singer write. "[I]t is about vetting items for their veracity and placing them within the broader context that is easily lost under the daily tidal wave of 'new' information."[37]

In *The Elements of Journalism*, Bill Kovach and Tom Rosenstiel call this "the concept of applying judgment to the news." The new journalist does not decide *what* the people should know, but helps the audience *make sense* of it. The task of the new journalist/sense maker is to verify information and put it in a form that people can grasp it efficiently.[38]

Although the technology for delivering the news is changing radically, the public's need for reliable information is the same. Confronting a daily deluge of information, citizens will look for sources they can trust to be accurate, to be fair, to be independent.

More than ever, they will depend on ethical journalists.

Point of View

Decision-Making in the Digital Age

James M. Naughton

We tend in newsroom discussions to separate news judgment from other aspects of the craft, as if it were something only a few people can master and for which they should be paid extra.

But making sound judgments is a responsibility of every journalist at every level in broadcast, print, or new media. We constantly exercise news judgment in choosing what to report, whom to interview, whom to trust, how to illustrate, what to amplify, what to omit, how to make the story interesting, when to quote or paraphrase, when and where – or whether – to run the article, what the headline should be, when to follow up, and how to correct inevitable errors.

The problem nowadays is that we're expected to make the right calls on the run. We used to spend some of our time working to double- or triple-check information, to verify, to research context, to scour complementary and contradictory data, to think and then to craft an accurate and coherent account. Many journalists now spend valuable time scanning the web and surfing cable channels to be sure they're not belated in disclosing what someone else just reported, breathlessly, using sources whose identity we'll never know.

The digital age does not respect contemplation. The deliberative news process is being sucked into a constant swirl of charge and countercharge followed by rebuttal and rebuttal succeeded by spin and counterspin leading to new charges and countercharges.

Now there are no cycles, only *Now*. A journalist today is apt to be wedging someone else's information into a story nanoseconds before air time or press run, without the debate about tone and propriety we Watergate geezers could have with our editors.

When it's all-news-all-over, the demand is too often for the *new*, not necessarily for *news*. We need to elevate, not debase, news judgment. Sound judgment pays homage to speed but reveres accuracy. News judgment can abet courage or invoke caution. News judgment is conscious and conscientious. It is authoritative but not judgmental. It relates the new to the known.

And it must not go out of fashion, no matter how difficult the circumstances now. Ignore "Hard Copy." Read Matt Drudge for entertainment, not sourcing. Muster courage to pursue your own story, one that can be vouched for. Tell the viewer or reader what we don't know, can't prove, didn't have time to figure out.

Excerpted from an essay that James M. Naughton, then the president of the Poynter Institute, wrote for *The New York Times* on February 16, 1998.

Point of View

A Difference in How Rumors Are Reported

Kelly McBride

On Friday, Aug. 29, 2008, Republican presidential candidate John McCain selected Alaska Governor Sarah Palin as his running mate. That weekend, the Internet went wild with a rumor that Palin's youngest son was really her grandson.

On Saturday, a YouTube user named AmpersandPilcrow posted a nine-minute video asking the question and offering up some old family photos as evidence that Bristol Palin was really Trig Palin's mother. On Sunday, a Daily Kos user named cityzenjane linked to the video, provoking many in the DailyKos family to criticize.

By Monday, Governor Palin rebutted the rumor by telling folks that her son Trig is really her son, but that her daughter Bristol, 17, was pregnant, was planning to keep the baby, and would be getting married.

This prompted a lot of soul-searching among traditional journalists. When do we investigate rumors involving politicians? How should we address stories involving the minor children of politicians? Is the blogosphere dragging the news media into the mud?

The answer to that last question is: Not really. Chances are, even without the Internet, reporters would have addressed the pregnant teenage daughter of a vice presidential candidate. But the Internet does speed things up. And savvy professional journalists found this story an opportunity to distinguish their work from the chatter of masses.

It used to be that journalists had the luxury of more time and little competition when it came to rumors about politicians and their families. We spent weeks, even years, asking ourselves if rumors really mattered to a politician's ability to lead. Starting with Gary Hart and running through Clinton–Lewinsky, former New Jersey Governor Jim McGreevy, Idaho Senator Larry Craig, and presidential hopeful John Edwards, I think I can say that rumors do matter. It's not whether we professional journalists report them, but how.

That takes us back to the object lesson of Bristol Palin's pregnancy. If you had watched the YouTube video and then read any news story on that rumor, you would have seen the difference between speculation and verification. The difference between anonymity and accountability. And the difference between uncertain sourcing and certain sourcing.

There's a good chance that the average Joe out there in the audience is picking up on these differences, too. And yes, I know, there are times when old-school media are guilty of all the failings of the blogosphere and more.

Yet, what it comes down to is this: Our values are different and we serve a different purpose.

Continued

I'm not suggesting that bloggers become more like professional journalists or that we become more like bloggers. Instead, it seems that we are destined to closely coexist in the information ecosystem. The blogosphere is transforming the mainstream media, not replacing it – and certainly not dragging it into the mud.

Adapted from an essay that Kelly McBride, ethics group leader at the Poynter Institute, wrote for *poynteronline* on Sept. 3, 2008. The original essay is at http://www.poynter.org/column.asp?id=67&aid=149822

Case Study No. 24

NBC's Controversial "To Catch a Predator"

"To Catch a Predator," a series of hidden-camera investigations in which *Dateline NBC* publicly shames men who have been lured by the prospect of sex with a teenager, has been widely praised for focusing attention on predators who lurk in the Internet's chat rooms. The program has resulted in the arrest (as of August 2008) of at least 263 of the program's targets.

In 2005, the National Academy of Television Arts and Sciences nominated "To Catch a Predator" (then called "Dangerous Web") for outstanding investigative journalism in a newsmagazine; in 2006, American Women in Radio and Television gave the series an award for outstanding documentary (midlength format).

Chris Hansen, the NBC correspondent who is the series' star, has been honored by law enforcement and child advocacy groups. He has testified before a congressional committee investigating the problem of sexual predators. He has written a book, *To Catch a Predator: Protecting Your Kids from Online Enemies Already in Your Home*. And he has been popular on the speaking circuit; for example, after his one-hour lecture at Kansas State University, a capacity crowd gave Hansen a standing ovation.

Along with the praise, Hansen and the network have drawn criticism for this program, which combines information and entertainment in classic "infotainment" style.

What most concerns the journalism critics is the program's format: NBC journalists conduct their investigation simultaneously with investigations by the local police and the nonprofit watchdog group Perverted Justice. NBC pays a six-figure consultant fee to Perverted Justice.

These critics are troubled by the NBC team's interaction with the police and Perverted Justice. Dismissing the suggestion that NBC has given up its journalistic independence, Hansen describes the format as "parallel investigations" that are independent of each other.

"To Catch a Predator" began in 2004. NBC enlisted the expertise of Perverted Justice, which had been working with local stations to engage targets in Internet chats and lure them into a videotaped sting. In the first

Continued

two *Dateline NBC* segments, the police were not involved. After the broadcast of the second of those segments, taped in Fairfax County, Virginia, outraged citizens complained to police because the predators had not been arrested. After that, *Dateline NBC* got local police involved.

"The typical episode works something like this," Luke Dittrich wrote in *Esquire* magazine.

> *Dateline* leases a house in a small town somewhere in America and wires it for sound and video. Members of Perverted Justice ... pose in online chat rooms as underage teens living in that small town. If an adult man starts hitting on one of these fake kids, the Perverted Justice decoys save the transcripts of his chats. Eventually, the man is invited over to the wired house for a liaison. When he arrives, Chris Hansen confronts him with a printout of Perverted Justice's chat transcripts and attempts to interview him. As soon as he leaves the house, local cops (the Takedown Team) arrest him and charge him with online solicitation of a minor. Each episode focuses on a decoy house in a single city and documents the catching of six or seven men.

On a Sunday in November 2006, about two dozen people gathered in the Terrell, Texas, neighborhood of Louis Conradt Jr, a 56-year-old lawyer who was chief felony assistant district attorney in Rockwall County. A police SWAT team was there, and so were Hansen, his camera crews, and representatives of Perverted Justice. Conradt had never gone to the house in nearby Murphy, Texas, that *Dateline NBC* had wired, but police said he had engaged in explicitly sexual exchanges on the Internet with a Perverted Justice volunteer posing as a 13-year-old boy. "Online

solicitation of a minor" is a violation of Texas law, and the police outside his house had an arrest warrant and a search warrant. When Conradt did not answer the door, the police forced their way inside. In a hallway they confronted the prosecutor, who was holding a handgun. "I'm not going to hurt anybody," they quoted him as saying; then, they said, he shot himself in the head. He died shortly after an emergency helicopter took him to a Dallas hospital.

Hansen filed a report for NBC's *Today* show the next morning. Two weeks later, in an interview with Douglas McCollam for an article in *Columbia Journalism Review*, Hansen said that on a human level he felt bad about Conradt's death. McCollam quoted him as continuing: "If you're asking, do I feel responsible, no. I sleep well at night."

Hansen and David Corvo, *Dateline*'s executive producer, both told McCollam that there was no evidence to suggest that Conradt was aware of *Dateline*'s presence when he shot himself.

McCollam questioned Hansen about the consulting fee NBC is paying to Perverted Justice. He said Hansen responded that there was nothing wrong with the fee, comparing it to the networks' practice of keeping retired generals or FBI agents on retainer. He quoted Hansen as saying: "In the end I get paid, the producers get paid, the camera guy, why shouldn't they?"

In his article, McCollam rejected Hansen's analogy, writing: "Perverted Justice is a participant in the story, the kind of outfit that would traditionally be covered, not be on a news outlet's payroll." He quoted Bob Steele of the Poynter Institute, who said hiring an advocacy group intensely involved in a story was "different from hiring a retired general who is no longer involved in a policy-making

Continued

role." McCollam also wrote that the money NBC is paying Perverted Justice provides investigative resources that local police forces cannot afford. "But for NBC's deep pockets," McCollam wrote, "no 'parallel' police actions would take place."

Twenty-three men were arrested in the Texas sting, after they had been lured to a "decoy house" in the town of Murphy. Seven months later, the Collin County district attorney's office decided not to pursue any indictments. Luke Dittrich wrote in *Esquire* that the arrests had been found to be illegal. "Under Texas law, there are only certain circumstances under which a police officer can make an arrest without a prior warrant," Dittrich wrote. "But in all of these 'To Catch a Predator' decoy-house arrests, it will come to light that not only was there no warrant but the police had done literally no prior investigation. Instead, they simply camped outside the decoy house and arrested the men who emerged after receiving a prior signal from the *Dateline* crew inside."

Kelly McBride of the Poynter Institute is one of the journalism ethicists troubled by "To Catch a Predator." In practice, she wrote for *poynteronline*, "parallel investigations are messy." As she saw it, the three investigations

are motivated by different goals and values: "The journalists, in theory, want to inform the public about a threat to children. The Perverted Justice folk want to shame and expose potential pedophiles. And the cops want to arrest those who break the law."

She said Dittrich's *Esquire* article, detailing the Texas sting that ended in a suicide,

> makes it appear almost impossible for the journalists, the citizens and the cops to stay true to their own goals and not to assume the work of the other. That's because they need each other. *Dateline* needs the cops to draw their guns and chase down the bad guys in order to get dramatic video. Perverted Justice needs *Dateline* to promote its cause. And the cops want to look competent and tough.

Hansen defended the parallel-investigation format in an interview with Dittrich, saying that the arrangement is fully disclosed on the air. "We disclose all the methods in this story, in terms of paying Perverted Justice as consultants [and] Perverted Justice's relationship to the law enforcement investigation."

"Disclosure is not the answer here," McBride wrote in her critique. "Independence is."

Questions for Class Discussion

- Should *Dateline NBC* have retained Perverted Justice as consultants for its "To Catch a Predator" series?
- Should the local police be involved in the stings conducted by *Dateline NBC* and Perverted Justice?

- Do you think the three "parallel" investigations are independent of each other? If they are not, does that pose an ethical problem?

Notes

1 Mark Jurkowitz, "Anna and the astronaut trigger a week of tabloid news," Project for Excellence in Journalism, http://www.journalism.org/node/4096, Feb. 12, 2007; "Anna Nicole Smith – anatomy of a feeding frenzy," Project for Excellence in Journalism, http://www.journalism.org/node/4872, April 4, 2007. For its weekly content index, including the Feb. 12 report, PEJ analyzes content from 48 news outlets representing 5 media sectors: newspapers, network television, cable television, websites, and radio.

2 Jurkowitz, "Anna and the astronaut trigger a week of tabloid news."

3 Carl Hiaasen, "We have seen the future, and it's not pretty," *Miami Herald*, March 4, 2007.

4 Jurkowitz, "Anna and the astronaut trigger a week of tabloid news."

5 Bill Kovach and Tom Rosenstiel, *The Elements of Journalism: What Newspeople Should Know and the Public Should Expect* (New York: Crown, 2001), 152–3.

6 Gitlin is quoted by David Shaw, "News as entertainment is sadly becoming the norm," *Los Angeles Times*, July 11, 2004.

7 Michael Schudson and Susan E. Tifft, "American journalism in historical perspective," in Geneva Overholser and Kathleen Hall Jamieson (eds.), *The Press* (Oxford: Oxford University Press, 2005), 40.

8 Kovach and Rosenstiel, *The Elements of Journalism*, 12, 17.

9 Thomas E. Patterson, "Doing well and doing good: How soft news and critical journalism are shrinking the news audience and weakening democracy – and what news outlets can do about it," Joan Shorenstein Center for Press, Politics and Public Policy, Harvard University's John F. Kennedy School of Government, 2000, 4. The report was accessed at http://www.hks.harvard.edu/presspol/research_publications/reports/softnews.pdf

10 Pew Research Center for the People & the Press, "Public blames media for too much celebrity coverage," Aug. 2, 2007. The survey was based on a nationally representative sample of 1,027 adults conducted July 27–30, 2007. Accessed at people-press.org/report/346/public-blames-media-for-too-much-celebrity-coverage

11 Eric Alterman, "It ain't necessarily so," *The Nation*, Sept. 10, 2007.

12 Kovach and Rosenstiel, *The Elements of Journalism*, 154.

13 Ibid., 154–5.

14 Ibid,, 149.

15 Lee Thornton, "Can the press fix itself?" *American Journalism Review*, February/March 2009.

16 Bob Garfield interview with Tom Rosenstiel, "Extra! Extra! We still want news," National Public Radio, http://www.onthemedia.org/transcripts/2008/03/28/05, March 28, 2008.

17 Walter Isaacson, "How to save your newspaper," *Time*, Feb. 5, 2009.

18 Rick Edmonds, "Is paid online content a solution or an impossible dream?" http://www.poynter.org/column.asp?id=123&aid=158663, Feb. 20, 2009.

19 "Pro Publica completes initial staffing," news release on http://www.propublica.org/about/pr-new-team-sept2-2008, Sept. 2, 2008.

20 "About us," http://www.minnpost.com/about/

21 Cecilia Friend and Jane B. Singer, *Online Journalism Ethics: Traditions and Transitions* (Armonk, NY: M. E. Sharpe, 2007), 198.

22 Deborah Potter, "Doing it all: Having the same person report and shoot the stories may save money, but at what cost?", *American Journalism Review*, October/November 2006, 94.

23 Gene Roberts related this anecdote to students at Pennsylvania State University, Oct. 31, 2007.

24 David Zucchino's email to author, May 30, 2008.

25 This point of view was expressed both in Dan Gillmor, *We the Media: Grassroots Journalism By the People, For the People* (Sebastopol, CA: O'Reilly Media, 2004), 130; and by Bill Mitchell of the Poynter Institute in an interview with the author, June 4, 2008.

26 James M. Naughton's email to author, Sept. 9, 2008.

27   Mark Deuze, "Conversing about convergence," in Friend and Singer, *Online Journalism Ethics*, 207.

28   Ken Sands' email to author, May 30, 2008.

29   Author's telephone interview with Kinsey Wilson, Sept. 26, 2007.

30   Adam Rose, "Louts out," *Columbia Journalism Review*, September/October 2008, 10–11.

31   Kovach and Rosenstiel, *The Elements of Journalism*, 12.

32   Knight Citizen News Network, "A guide to 'crowdsourcing': Reader-supplied information and documents help nail down stories," http://www.kcnn.org/tools/crowdsourcing

33   Matt Reed, email exchange with the author, Aug. 18, 2008.

34   Knight Citizen News Network, "A guide to 'crowdsourcing.'"

35   Kelly McBride, "The problem with citizen journalism," http://www.poynter.org/column.asp?id=67&aid=97418, Sept. 24, 2006.

36   Friend and Singer, *Online Journalism Ethics*, 218.

37   Ibid.

38   Kovach and Rosenstiel, *The Elements of Journalism*, 24.

Conclusion: Some Thoughts to Take With You

Capsules of advice for aspiring journalists

As you complete this study of news media ethics, reflect on what you have learned – and what you should take with you as you enter the journalism workplace, where your decisions will affect the lives of others.

The most important lesson is to think through your decisions when you are confronted with an ethical question. Identify the values involved in possible courses of action, analyze them dispassionately, and reach a decision that you can defend.

Some journalists will say that in a deadline environment, there is no time for a process of critical thinking. The reality is that only rarely must a decision be made in an instant. Even if you do have to decide in an instant, your practice in this course can guide you to a sound decision – and often, the ethical question can be anticipated, when there is time to consider your options.

As you enter the journalism profession, please remember the lessons that this textbook has sought to impart:

- In any decision, practice critical thinking – a systematic, logical approach. This does not mean you should dismiss your emotional response to a situation; if it *feels* wrong, it may well *be* wrong. But go beyond your reflexes to rationally consider arguments for or against a proposed course of action.
- The Golden Rule remains the best rule there is. Even though it will not solve every problem, putting yourself in the place of the person affected is a good way to assess the rightness of your decision.
- You owe your first allegiance to your audience – the readers, the viewers, the listeners, the online users. This allegiance must be a vital factor in any decision you make.
- Your mission is to give your audience the truth as best you can determine it. This requires more than simply getting the facts right. Provide the context that gives meaning to the facts.
- Although you may not be able to report the story *completely* in a single day, be sure that *everything* you do report is true and in context. Acknowledge any key questions that you have not been able to answer.
- You owe your audience respect. However, practicing journalism is not like running a store; the customer is *not* always right. When your reporting or decisions are challenged, carefully review them. If the complaint is right,

correct your mistake and reform your procedures if necessary. If you think the complaint is wrong, explain your decision.

- In the newsroom, people have to trust each other. Plagiarism, fabrication, and manipulation of images could – and should – be a death sentence for your career.

- Be fair to your sources. Identify yourself as a journalist and make it clear that your purpose is to obtain information to be disseminated to the public. *You* are responsible for making sure your sources understand any ground rules about how information will be attributed.

- Deceiving a source should be done only in extremely rare cases. Deception can only be justified when it is the only way to obtain information that is vital to the public – in terms of human lives, not dollars and cents. That is the kind of information that cannot be obtained through conventional reporting techniques. Furthermore, you must be willing to disclose your methods to the audience.

- Do not manipulate the people you report on, treating them as the means to achieve your own ends. Likewise, as the surrogate for the audience, do not allow yourself to be manipulated by your sources and diverted from the truth.

- Your journalism must be free of bias. Although you may hold opinions about the people and events you cover, it is a test of your professionalism that you filter these biases from your news accounts.

- Do not take public positions on political candidates and controversial issues. To tell others of your opinions is to invite them to find those opinions in your reporting. Remember that people see you as a journalist 24/7; in their eyes, you are never "off duty."

- Be independent of those you cover. A journalist is an observer, not a participant. Generally, it is only in a crisis – when you are *the only person* or *the best person* to save a life or avoid an injury – that you should you put down your notebook and become a participant.

- Avoid the appearance of a conflict, and disclose any unavoidable appearance of conflict. Turn down gifts or perquisites offered because of your occupation. Ask yourself: Would the average person be offered this gift or perk? If the answer is no, turn it down.

- Be compassionate. Recognize that people may be hurt when you report the truth. In those cases, minimize harm. Never use your power as a journalist to inflict harm gratuitously.

- When your reporting would expose private information that would embarrass the subjects of the news coverage, weigh the value of the information to the public against the degree of harm that the subject might suffer. Consider what zone of privacy the subject can reasonably expect. A public official doing public business deserves the least privacy, an ordinary person involuntarily thrust into the news deserves the most.

- It is not acceptable for you to publish, broadcast, or post something just because someone else will. Do not lower yourself to the standards of your least ethical competitor.

- Practice the scientific method in your reporting: Start with a thesis, then conduct research to see if that thesis is valid. Falling in love with your story could blind you to evidence that your thesis is not true. Your goal is to find the truth, not necessarily to validate your thesis.
- The burden is on you, the journalist, to prove the truth of what you report – not for an adversary to prove that your reporting is false.

Now, this final piece of advice: Your education in journalism ethics will help you determine the morally correct course to take in a given situation. Defining what is right and wrong is, however, only half the battle. You can expect powerful pressures to follow a different course of action. It will require courage to resist these pressures and to do what is right. Be ready to stand on principle.

Case Study Sources

1: The Journalist as a Witness to Suffering

- Sonia Nazario, reporter, and Clarence Williams, photographer, "Orphans of addiction," *Los Angeles Times*, Nov. 16–17, 1997. Williams' photographs won the 1998 Pulitzer Prize for feature photography and may be viewed at: http://www.pulitzer.org/works/1998,Feature+Photography. The series also was one of three finalists for the Pulitzer Prize for public service.
- Susan Paterno, "The intervention dilemma," *American Journalism Review*, March 1998.
- Tran Ha, "A journey through the 'ethical minefield,'" http://www.poynter.org, A3608, April 14, 2000.
- Bob Steele, "Journey through the 'ethical minefield,' part 2," http://www.poynter.org, A 3611, April 17, 2000.
- Sonia Nazario, email to the author, July 17, 2008.
- Shannon Kahle's telephone interview with Clarence Williams, Aug. 15, 2008.

2: Roughed Up at Recess

This case is excerpted, with permission, from *Newsroom Ethics: Decision-Making for Quality Coverage*, 4th edn. (Washington, DC: Radio Television News Directors Foundation, 2006), 20–1. Additional reporting by the author included email exchanges with Bob Segall, May 28–29, 2008, and a telephone interview with Segall, May 30, 2008.

3: The Death of a Boy

This case is excerpted, with permission, from Michele McLellan, *The Newspaper Credibility Handbook* with a discussion guide by Bob Steele (Washington, DC: American Society of Newspaper Editors, 2001), 182–7.

4: Deciding Whether to Identify a CIA Agent

- Scott Shane, "Inside a 9/11 mastermind's interrogation," *The New York Times*, June 22, 2008.
- *The New York Times*, Editors' Note, June 22, 2008.
- Clark Hoyt, "Weighing the risk," *The New York Times*, July 6, 2008.

- Bob Steele, "When principles collide: The *NYT* and the CIA interrogator," http://www.poynter.org, A146501, July 5, 2008.

5: Covering Police, Wearing Their Uniform

This case is adapted, with permission, from a paper written by Lindsay Bosslett in 2003 while she was a student at Pennsylvania State University. The case was updated after Shannon Kahle's telephone interview with Caroline Lowe on April 10, 2008, and Lowe's email message to Kahle on April 15, 2008. Bosslett's sources in 2003 included:

- Interview with Caroline Lowe, Nov. 18, 2003.
- Interview with Rob Daves, Nov. 23, 2003.
- "About Caroline Lowe," biographical sketch posted on www.wcco.com
- Minnesota State Colleges and University performance newsletter, "Crime reporter shares 'cop school' training," Fall 2002.
- Joe Kimball, "Working as a cop, she'll keep a Lowe profile," *The Star Tribune*, July 18, 2003.
- Brian Lambert, "Reporter-turned-copy walks thin blue line," *The Pioneer Press*, July 22, 2003.
- Lambert, "Reporter conflict is in the eye of the beholder," *The Pioneer Press*, July 25, 2003.
- Caroline Lowe, "Covering the crime beat," The School of Law Enforcement, Criminal Justice and Public Safety newsletter, Spring 2001, Metropolitan State University.

6: Carrying the Torch, Stirring Controversy

This case is adapted, with permission, from a paper written by Jeff Rice in 2003 when he was a student at Pennsylvania State University. The case was updated after the author's Sept. 30, 2008, email exchange with Dick Rosetta. Rice's sources included:

- Lee Benson, "Torch run just isn't conflicting," *Deseret News*, Jan. 9, 2002.
- Catherine S. Lake, "Newspapers, TV struggle with ethics of reporters carrying Olympic torch," The Associated Press, Jan. 11, 2002.

7: On Lunch Break, Defending Reagan

This case is a slightly edited version of a column in *The Chicago Reader* on June 18, 2004. Copyright © 2004, *The Chicago Reader*. Reprinted by permission.

8: A Love Triangle on the Evening News

- KNBC.com, "Mayor acknowledges relationship with TV anchor," July 3, 2007.
- Duke Helfand and Steve Hymon, "Mayor reveals romantic link with TV newscaster," *Los Angeles Times*, July 4, 2007.
- Duke Helfand and Meg James, "Telemundo reassigns mayor's girlfriend," *Los Angeles Times*, Sept. 25, 2007.
- Shawn Hubler, "The mayor and his mistress," *Los Angeles Magazine*, May 2008.
- Charles Kaiser, "A.M. Rosenthal, 1922–2006," *The New York Observer*, May 21, 2006.
- *The New York Times, Ethics in Journalism*, Section 26.

9: Sharing Ad Profits, Creating a Crisis

- Felicity Barringer, "Newspaper magazine shares profits with a subject," *The New York Times*, Oct. 26, 1999.
- Michael A. Hiltzik and Sallie Hofmeister, "Remorseful, *Times* publisher promises changes," *Los Angeles Times*, Oct. 29, 1999.
- Barringer, "Ex-publisher assails paper in Los Angeles," *The New York Times*, Nov. 4, 1999.
- Narda Zacchino, "Staples incident rocks *Times*, inside and out, *Los Angeles Times*, Nov. 9, 1999.
- Scott Winokur, "L.A. *Times* ad deal labeled a 'fiasco,'" *San Francisco Examiner*, Nov. 28, 1999.
- David Shaw, "Crossing the line: A *Los Angeles Times* profit-sharing arrangement with Staples Center fuels a firestorm of protest in the newsroom – and a debate about journalistic ethics," *Los Angeles Times*, Dec. 20, 1999.
- James Risser, "Lessons from L.A.," *Columbia Journalism Review*, January/February 2000.
- Robert G. Magnuson, "How do we protect integrity in an increasingly complex world?", from "Embracing Journalism's real value: Building the business, protecting the principles," the Poynter Institute, January 2001.

10: Duke Lacrosse: One Newspaper's Journey

This case is excerpted, with permission, from Rachel Smolkin, "Justice delayed," *American Journalism Review*, August/September 2007. Additional source: WTVD and The Associated Press, "Duke lacrosse case timeline," http://abclocal.go.com/wtvd/story?section=news/lcal&id=4242164

11: On TV, a 4-Year-Old's Visit to Death Row

This case is adapted, with permission, from *Newsroom Ethics: Decision-Making for Quality Coverage*, 4th edn. (Washington, DC: Radio Television News Directors Foundation, 2006), 41–3. Additional source:

- David Carson, Texas Execution Information Center, "Richard Cartwright," May 20, 2005. http://www.txexecutions.org/reports/344.asp

12: *Newsweek* and the Flushing of the Koran

- Howard Kurtz, "*Newsweek* apologizes: Inaccurate report on Koran led to riots," *The Washington Post*, May 16, 2005.
- Jack Shafer, "Down the toilet at *Newsweek*," May 17, 2005, http://www.slate.com/id/2118826/
- CNN, "Reliable sources: A look at the *Newsweek* controversy," May 22, 2005, http://transcripts.cnn.com/TRANSCRIPTS/0505/22/rs.01.html
- Josh White and Dan Eggen, "Pentagon details abuse of Koran," *The Washington Post*, June 4, 2005.
- Eric Schmitt, "Military details Koran incidents at base in Cuba," *The New York Times*, June 4, 2005.
- The author's email exchange with Michael Isikoff, May 13, 2008.

13: Swimming in a Newsmaker's Backyard Pool

- Alita Guillen, "Reporter leaves NBC5 amid Stebic controversy," http://cbs2chicago.com/topstories/Lisa.Stebic.Craig.2.338140.html, July 10, 2007.
- Eric Zorn, "Amy Jacobson interview on WGN-AM: 'I can't apologize enough,'" http://blogs.chicagotribune.com/news_columnists_ezorn/2007/07/amy-jacobson-in.html, July 11, 2007.
- Bob Steele, "A different kind of 'pool video' makes waves in Chicago," http://poynter.org A126509, July 12, 2007.
- Eric Zorn, "Jacobson's job too high a price for doing her job," http://blogs.chicagotribune.com/news_columnists_ezorn/2007/07/jacobsons-job-t.html, July 12, 2007.
- "Origins of controversial Jacobson-Stebic video: CBS 2 answers questions of how controversial tape came to be," http://cbs2chicago.com/westsuburbanbureau/Amy.Jacobson.Craig.2.338229.html, July 12, 2007.
- Robert Feder, "The video that got Amy fired," *Chicago Sun-Times*, July 12, 2007.
- Zorn, "How many times did Amy Jacobson go to the Stebic house? Did she share information with police? Let's ask her!", http://blogs.chicagotribune.com/news_columnists_ezorn/2007/07/how-many-times-.html, July 13, 2007.

- Phil Rosenthal and David Greising, "Reporter briefed police on Stebic," *Chicago Tribune*, July 13, 2007.
- Steele, "Jacobson case: Collaborating with cops?", http://poynter.org A126635, July 13, 2007.
- Carol Marin, "Dogged reporter went too far," *Chicago Sun-Times*, July 15, 2007.
- Carol Fowler, email to Shannon Kahle, June 12, 2008.
- Zorn, "Amy Jacobson files suit in 'pool party' case," http://blogs. chicagotribune.com/news_columnists_ezorn/2008/07/amy-jacobson-fi.html. posted July 7, 2008. This posting contains the text of the lawsuit.
- Lucinda Hahn, "Tale of the tape," *Chicago* magazine, http://www. chicagotribune.com/news/chi-amy-jacobson-chicago-magazine,0,653477.story, Dec. 4, 2008.

14: Revealing Arthur Ashe's Secret

This case is adapted, with permission, from a paper written by Jaime Fettrow in 1999 while a student at Pennsylvania State University. Her sources included:

- Jay Black, Bob Steele and Ralph Barney, *Doing Ethics in Journalism: A Handbook With Case Studies*, 3rd edn. (Boston: Allyn & Bacon, 1999).
- Greg Boeck and Mike Dodd, "Life on the road: The game of sex," *USA Today*, Nov. 14, 1991, A1.
- Louis A. Day, *Ethics in Media Communications: Cases and Controversies*, 2nd edn. (Belmont, CA: Wadsworth, 1997).
- Frank Deford, "Arthur Ashe," http://premium.cnnsi.com/tennis/features/1997/ arthurashe/svcexcpt.html, March 20, 1999.
- "Earvin 'Magic' Johnson's HIV is at undetectable levels, doctors say," *Jet*, April 21, 1997, 53.
- "It was an AIDS 'outing,'" USA Today, April 10, 1992.
- Sal Maiorana, "CBS Sportsline History: Arthur Ashe," http://cgi2.sportsline. com/u/page/historian/ashe.htm, March 20, 1999.
- "Magic + Isiah," http://www.cyberramp.net/~batman/articles/magic.htm, March 20, 1999.
- Peter Prichard, "Arthur Ashe's pain is shared by public and press," *USA Today*, April 13, 1992, A11.
- Laura B. Randolph, "Cookie Johnson on: The Magic 'miracle,'" *Ebony*, April 1997, 72–6.
- "Readers: Diverse opinions on Johnson," *USA Today*, Nov. 19, 1991, C12.
- "Readers react to privacy issue, newspaper's role in Ashe story," *USA Today*, April 13, 1992, C2.
- Cindy Shmerler, "Friends kept secret 3 years," *USA Today*, April 9, 1992, C3.

- Rachel Shuster, "Arthur Ashe 1943–1993; Ashe legacy goes beyond sports, race," *USA Today*, Feb. 8, 1993, C1.
- Peter Vecsey, "Rumors fly about Magic, but the motives are selfish," *USA Today*, Nov. 12, 1991, C6.
- DeWayne Wickham, "Stop the Voyeurism and gossip-peddling," *USA Today*, April 13, 1992, A11.
- Gene Policinski, "The Arthur Ashe AIDS story is news: And like it or not, it is our job to pursue news stories," *The Bulletin* of the American Society of Newspaper Editors, July/August 1992, 17.

The case also draws on email exchanges in July 2008 – conducted by Shannon Kahle and Gene Foreman with Peter Prichard, former editor of *USA Today*, and with Gene Policinski, former managing editor/sports of *USA Today*.

15: Identifying a 13-Year-Old Rape Victim

This case is adapted, with permission, from Alissa Wisnouse's honors thesis at Pennsylvania State University in 2002. (Her married name is Alissa Barron Stranzl.) Her sources included:

- Alissa Wisnouse's telephone interviews with Tom Birdsong (March 11, 2002) and Johnna A. Pro (March 22, 2002).
- Wisnouse's email exchanges with Bill Mitchell (April 4, 2002) and Jill Geisler (April 5, 2002).
- Dan Gigler, "Crafton Heights girl, 13, missing," *Pittsburgh Post-Gazette*, Jan. 3, 2002.
- Johnna A. Pro, "Teen's parents fear Internet link in disappearance," *Pittsburgh Post-Gazette*, Jan. 4, 2002.
- Dennis B. Roddy and Jon Schmitz, "Suspect Scott Tyree: 'A classic long-haired computer guy,'" *Pittsburgh Post-Gazette*, Jan. 5, 2002.
- Eleanor Chute, "Girl reunited with grateful parents who 'feel blessed,'" *Pittsburgh Post-Gazette*, Jan. 6, 2002.
- Sally Kalson, "Alicia's web sites pose a very disturbing question," *Pittsburgh Post-Gazette*, Jan. 9, 2002.
- John G. Craig Jr, "To name or not to name: Sex-crime cases pose a privacy concern," *Pittsburgh Post-Gazette*, Jan. 20, 2002.
- Jill Geisler, "You can't unring a bell, but you can stop ringing it," http://www.poynter.org, A4934, March 16, 2000.
- *Pittsburgh Post-Gazette Stylebook*, 1997.

The case also draws on these sources:

- Shannon Kahle's telephone interview with Mary Kozakiewicz, Sept. 5, 2008.

- Gene Foreman's telephone interview with Mary Kozakiewicz on Dec. 10, 2008, and their email exchange Dec. 8–11, 2008
- Johnna A. Pro's email message to Shannon Kahle on June 20, 2008.
- Nicole Wisensee Egan, "Abducted, enslaved – and now talking about it," *People*, April 16, 2007.

16: Reporting on a Vulgar List in the News

- Mary Niederberger and Nikki Schwab, "'Top 25' list details students' looks, bodies," *Pittsburgh Post-Gazette*, April 26, 2006.
- Sarah Goldstein, "Top 25 reasons to hate high school," http://www.salon.com/mwt/broadsheet/2006/04/27/top25/, April 27, 2006.
- Eleanor Chute and Torsten Ove, "Discipline in Mt. Lebanon 'list' furor may be soon," *Pittsburgh Post-Gazette*, April 28, 2006.
- Sally Kalson, "Cake-eaters gone vile: The Mt. Lebanon High School 'Top 25' list is worse than you might think," Pittsburgh Post-Gazette, April 30, 2006.
- Page Rockwell, "Another look at top-25 lists: Turns out the Mt. Lebanon High School 'Top 25 of 2006' is grosser than we thought," http://www.salon.com/mwt/broadsheet/2006/05/05/mount_lebanon/, May 5, 2006.
- Niederberger and Laura Pace, "Harassment session result of sex list," *Pittsburgh Post-Gazette*, May 10, 2006.
- *Pittsburgh Post-Gazette*, "Editorial: Posting profanity/Schools have Internet lessons yet to teach," May 15, 2006.
- Chute, "DA says no charges over Mt. Lebanon 'Top 25' list," *Pittsburgh Post-Gazette*, May 25, 2006.
- Niederberger, "Family files suit over Mt. Lebanon High School 'Top 25' list," *Pittsburgh Post-Gazette*, June 24, 2006.
- Linda Wilson Fuoco, "Mt. Lebanon schools cleared in handling of explicit 'Top 25' list," *Pittsburgh Post Gazette*, July 8, 2006.
- The author's telephone interviews with Susan L. Smith and Mary Leonard on April 18, 2008.

17: Covering a Public Official's Public Suicide

- Patrick R. Parsons and William E. Smith, "R. Budd Dwyer: A case study in newsroom decision making," *Journal of Mass Media Ethics*, vol. 3, no. 1, 84–94.
- Robert L. Baker, "Portraits of a public suicide: Photo treatment by selected Pennsylvania dailies," *Newspaper Research Journal*, vol. 9, no. 4, Summer 1988, 11–23.
- Robert C. Kochersberger Jr., "Survey of suicide photos use by newspapers in three states," *Newspaper Research Journal*, vol. 9, no. 4, Summer 1988, 1–10.

- Robert Biance and Ken Guggenheim, "Use of suicide film debated at news, television desks," *The Pittsburgh Press*, Jan. 23, 1987.
- Gary A. Warner, "Invitation to suicide leaves newsmen wondering why," *The Pittsburgh Press*, Jan. 23, 1987.
- Paul Vathis, "Eyewitness account by the AP's photographer," *Editor & Publisher*, Jan. 31, 1987.
- http://www.liveleak.com/view?i=860c9b9f3b&p=1 (video of the suicide).

18: Rumsfeld's Q&A With the Troops

- "Chattanooga reporter's e-mail to colleagues," Romenesko's news media site, Dec. 9, 2004, http://poynter.org/forum/view_post.asp?id=8447
- CNN.com, "Reporter planted GI's question for Rumsfeld," Dec. 9, 2004, http://www.cnn.com/2004/WORLD/meast/12/09/rumsfeld.reporter/index.html
- Gail Gibson, "A guardsman's question has continuing effect," *The Sun*, Baltimore, Dec. 9, 2004.
- Joe Strupp, "Editor backs embed in Rumsfeld incident but criticizes aftermath," *Editor and Publisher*, Dec. 9, 2004.
- *USA Today*, "Publisher: Reporter needed to tell of Rumsfeld Q&A role," Dec. 10, 2004.
- Howard Kurtz and Thomas E. Ricks, "Reporter prompted query to Rumsfeld," *The Washington Post*, Dec. 10, 2004.
- James Bandler, "Reporter discloses his help to soldier on armor question," *The Wall Street Journal*, Dec. 10, 2004.
- Dan Fost, "Reporter helped orchestrate GI's query to Rumsfeld," *San Francisco Chronicle*, Dec. 10, 2004.
- Saul Hansell, "G.I.'s query to Rumsfeld prompted by reporter," *The New York Times*, Dec. 10, 2004.
- Tom Rutten, "Free to shoot from the hip," *Los Angeles Times*, Dec. 11, 2004.
- CNN "Reliable Sources," transcript for Dec. 12, 2004.
- Clarence Page, "Just answer the question, Mr. Rumsfeld," *Chicago Tribune*, Dec. 12, 2004.
- Eric Mink, "The question that saved lives," *St. Louis Post-Dispatch*, Dec. 15, 2004.

19: Spying on the Mayor in a Chat Room

- Bill Morlin, "West tied to sex abuse in '70s, using office to lure young men," *The Spokesman-Review*, May 5, 2005.
- "Spokesman-Review investigation of Jim West: Spokesman-Review editor Steven A. Smith addressed your questions about our series of stories on the

mayor," http://www.spokesmanreview.com/, May 9, 2005; May 17, 2005; June 23, 2005.
- "The outing of Mayor Jim West: A case study in ethics in journalism," http://restoringthetrust.org/casestudy/critiques.html, with critiques by David Zeeck of the *Tacoma News Tribune*, Dan Richman of the *Seattle Post-Intelligencer*, and John Temple of the *Rocky Mountain News*, Denver.
- Janet I. Tu, "Newspaper's ruse raises issue of journalism ethics," *The Seattle Times*, May 6, 2005.
- Joe Strupp, "Truth our mission: 'Spokesman-Review' deserves credit for its undercover work," *Editor and Publisher*, June 2005, 62.
- E. J. Graff, "The line on sex: When is a scandal merely voyeurism," *Columbia Journalism Review*, September/October 2005, 9.

20: When a Story Gets Its Subject Arrested

This case is excerpted, with permission, from Sharyn Vane, "Too much information?", *American Journalism Review*, June 1998.

21: For a Reporter-Blogger, Two Personalities

This case is based on a report that Sara Ganim, a senior at Pennsylvania State University, wrote for *The Lion's Roar*, a publication of Penn State's College of Communications in Fall 2007, and is used by permission of Ganim and the College. Ganim's report included interviews with John L. Micek, Tom Rosenstiel, and Bob Steele. Additional reporting by the author included telephone interviews and/or email exchanges with Micek; Ardith Hilliard, then editor of *The Morning Call*; and Peter Leffler, who supervises staff blogs at *The Call*.

22: Would You Run This Photograph?

Fire-escape collapse, 1975

- BBC News, "Picture power: Fire-escape drama," http://news.bbc.co.uk/1/hi/world/americas/4245138.stm, Sept. 30, 2005.
- Philip Patterson and Lee Wilkins, Media Ethics: Issues and Cases, 6th edn. (New York: McGraw-Hill, 2008), 114–16.
- The author's telephone interview with Vin Alabiso, Sept. 21, 2007.

Drowning and grief, 1985

- "Graphic excess," *Washington Journalism Review*, January 1986, 10–11.
- Deni Elliott and Paul Martin Lester, "What is news? The answer is not blowing on a whim," *News Photographer*, February 2003.

- Clifford Christians, Kim B. Rotzoll, Mark Fackler, Kathy Brittain McKee and Robert H. Woods Jr, *Media Ethics: Cases and Moral Reasoning*, 7th edn. (Boston: Allyn and Bacon, 2005), 116–19.
- The author's telephone interview with Vin Alabiso, Sept. 21, 2007.

World Trade Center, 2001

- CBC Newsworld, "Passionate Eye Showcase: The falling man," http://www.cbc.ca/passionateeyemonday/fallingman/
- Peter Howe, "Richard Drew," *The Digital Journalist*, http://www.digitaljournalist.org/issue0110/drew.htm
- Tom Junod, "The falling man," *Esquire*, September 2003.
- Cathy Trost and Alicia C. Shepard, *Running Toward Danger: Stories Behind the Breaking News of 9/11* (Lanham, MD: Rowman and Littlefield, 2002), 44, 210.
- Connie Kim, "A single day, a thousand images," *Quill*, November 2001, 22–3.
- The author's telephone interview with Vin Alabiso, Sept. 21, 2007.

Fury in Fallujah, 2004

- Jeffrey Gettleman, "Enraged mob in Falluja kills 4 American contractors," *The New York Times*, March 31, 2004.
- Julia Angwin and Matthew Rose, "When news is gruesome, what's too graphic?", *The Wall Street Journal*, April 1, 2004, B1.
- Matt Thompson, "Discussion is the policy," http://www.poynter.org, A63419, April 1, 2004.
- *Editor & Publisher*, Survey of newspaper use of Fallujah photos, April 2, 2004.
- Bill Marvel and Manuel Mendoza, "Gruesome images: Does taste trump news-worthiness?", *The Dallas Morning News*, April 1, 2004.
- Phil H. Shook, "Readers respond to Fallujah photos," http://www.poynter.org, A63968, April 13, 2004.

23: Just How Fast Do Ice Boats Go?

This case is excerpted, with permission, from *Newsroom Ethics: Decision-Making for Quality Coverage*, 4th edn (Washington, DC: Radio Television News Directors Foundation, 2006), 33–5.

24: NBC's Controversial "To Catch a Predator"

- Paul Farhi, "'Dateline' pedophile sting: One more point," *The Washington Post*, April 9, 2006.

- Tim Eaton, "Prosecutor kills himself in Texas raid over child sex," *The New York Times*, Nov. 7, 2006.
- Douglas McCollam, "The shame game," *Columbia Journalism Review*, January/February 2007.
- Luke Dittrich, "Tonight on *Dateline* this man will die," *Esquire*, August 2007.
- Dittrich, "Interview with Chris Hansen: the transcript," http://www.esquire.com, July 10, 2007.
- Kelly McBride, "What's wrong with 'To Catch a Predator'?", http://www.poynter.org, A128057, Aug. 9, 2007.
- Brian Ross and Vic Walter, "'To Catch a Predator': A sting gone bad," *ABC News: The Blotter*, Sept. 7, 2007.
- Eric Davis, "'Predator' host speaks about show, journalism career," *The Kansas State Collegian*, April 17, 2008.
- Jenny Tartikoff, NBC Universal, email message to Shannon Kahle, Aug. 12, 2008.

Index